Dramatic Form in Shakespeare
and the Jacobeans

Dramatic Form in Shakespeare and the Jacobeans

ESSAYS BY

LEO SALINGAR

The right of the
University of Cambridge
to print and sell
all manner of books
was granted by
Henry VIII in 1534.
The University has printed
and published continuously
since 1584.

CAMBRIDGE UNIVERSITY PRESS

Cambridge

London   New York   New Rochelle

Melbourne   Sydney

Published by the Press Syndicate of the University of Cambridge
The Pitt Building, Trumpington Street, Cambridge CB2 1RP
32 East 57th Street, New York, NY 10022, USA
10 Stamford Road, Oakleigh, Melbourne 3166, Australia

First published 1986

Printed in Great Britain at
the University Press, Cambridge

British Library cataloguing in publication data
Salingar, Leo
Dramatic form in Shakespeare and the Jacobeans:
essays.
1. English drama – Early modern and Elizabethan –
1500–1600 – History and criticism   2. English
drama – 17th century – History and criticism
I. Title
822'.3'09   PR651

Library of Congress cataloguing in publication data
Salingar, Leo.
Dramatic form in Shakespeare and the Jacobeans.
Bibliography: p.
Includes index.
1. Shakespeare, William, 1564–1616 – Criticism and
interpretation – Addresses, essays, lectures.   2. English
drama – 17th century – History and criticism – Addresses,
essays, lectures.   I. Title.
PR2976.S25   1986   822.3'3   85–18969

ISBN 0 521 30856 9

FP

Contents

To the memory of my parents,
Samuel and Tessie Salingar

Preface

All the essays assembled here have been published before, in a variety of books or journals, some of which are out of the way for the general student; I am grateful to the editors and publishers concerned for permission to reprint them. Several of the essays began life as special lectures or conference papers for university audiences. Most of them have been written in recent years but I have included a few which are much older. I cannot pretend that they add up to an inclusive or a progressive argument. But they all spring from the same long-continuing interest and I think they have enough in common, without much repetition, to gain something from appearing together within a single collection.

The essays are attempts at critical interpretation. My main topic has been one aspect or another of dramatic form, such as plot construction or a dramatist's way of presenting his characters. But the long-continuing interest could be more ambitiously described as the problem of the relations between Elizabethan drama and its setting: what were the conditions that favoured that exceptionally creative outburst? It might be more to the point to speak of 'Jacobean' drama, since the most crowded achievement came early in the reign of James I; for instance, *King Lear*, *Volpone* and *The Revenger's Tragedy* were all first produced by the same actors, in the same theatre, within little more than twelve months in the years 1605–6. That implies that imagination was working most intensively in the theatre at the moment when Shakespeare was discovering or revealing his full powers, and presumably it was stimulated by imitation of Shakespeare or in response to his challenge. However, not even the most zealous bardolater could claim that Shakespeare invented the new drama of his age or that he shaped it single-handed. In substance, then, the question remains: what social or technical conditions, what factors in cultural history, what conjunction of circumstances account for the emergence,

vii

across half a century, of English works of art constituting at once a public entertainment and the medium for highly organised, vigorous and subtle poetry? If that question could be met and answered convincingly we should understand the present better as well as the past.

I must quickly explain that none of these essays attempts to tackle that vast and intricate master-question extensively or head-on; they are all much more limited in scope. But I have tried to keep that question in view by connecting the study of particular Shakespearean or Jacobean plays with some part of the literary or theatrical or social history of the time. 'All art', as Synge wrote, 'is a collaboration' – a maxim applying with special force to the performing arts. And all plays, especially those with some capacity for survival, represent not only a collaboration between the writer, his actors and his original public but a compound of the immediate experience, hopes or fears shared by the writer and his public and of his or their memories or knowledge from the past, including knowledge of previous literature and of previous plays. The basis of dramatic criticism is the critic's response to the acted play, or the play read as if acted. But for the purpose of interpretation it is often useful (and certainly if the object of interpretation is to recapture as much as possible of the full reality of the play in its historical setting, it is indispensable) to bring to bear in the analysis appropriate comparative material from outside the text.

In discussing Jacobean plays I have touched repeatedly on the social or economic history of the time, though I have tried to keep speculation in check. Some digression into social conditions seems to follow from the nature of the plays themselves, since Jonson and Shakespeare's other younger contemporaries were much concerned with satire and dramatic situations 'near, and familiarly allied to the time'. They were commercial playwrights against the grain of their education, commercial playwrights criticising the effects of commercialism; their plays take shape from their perception of social change. In principle, the same or similar considerations apply to Shakespeare, yet Shakespeare's plays hold out very much less, or less direct, invitation to that sort of commentary. I do not think that means that Shakespeare was less realistic about money than Jonson and the rest. Or, necessarily, that he was more benevolent – even though he was described as 'gentle', and was evidently much less aggressive than Marlowe. But he seems much less irritated by the world than his contemporaries. At one level, that state of mind may reflect his satisfaction with success. At another level, it seems to reflect his exceptional responsiveness to the sympathies that hold men and women together in society and also link the present with the past (as evidenced by his English histories) and with hopes about the future (as evidenced by his romances). And possibly this deep responsiveness accounts for his enduring success as a stage writer more than anything else. He was working in a culture that set great store by public celebration. And he tends to celebrate rather than dissect society, even when portraying destructive impulses. The heroes isolated in his tragedies embody qualities that society needs or admires.

In a number of these essays I have brought in discussion of literary or dramatic sources, or of the possible influence of literary or dramatic genres, such as romance, the Morality plays or farce. Source-study has a part in tracing the history of ideas; and comparison between a later work and an antecedent (whether a direct source or merely an analogue) may throw light on particular facets of the later work or help us to see the assumptions or structural conventions the writer is building on. At the same time, source-study can and, I think, should have the contrary effect of bringing out what in the construction or thought of the later work is new, unprecedented or unconventional.

In two essays I try to examine the implications in the drama of Shakespeare's time of the salient words *art* and *wit*. In two others, I discuss Shakespearean characters. This is not with the intention of returning to bygone critical principles; but, precisely because Shakespeare's characters have become more familiar on the stage than any others, I think we need to remind ourselves of their distinctiveness and originality.

Among the essays here I have included the first one I published, that on *The Revenger's Tragedy*. Perhaps I should have revised it, but that would have meant changing or expanding it in several directions, partly to take account of the scholarly debates over authorship and partly to take account of the criticisms, direct or implied, of my own point of view. Those amount to saying both that I took the play too seriously and that I did not take it seriously enough. As to the latter, I cannot see that anything is gained for the play by maintaining that Tourneur, or whoever wrote it, was expressing his belief in orthodox Calvinist Christianity. Possibly that was his belief; but the momentary action of grace he includes in the mother's role is equivocal, and the general tenor of his play sardonic rather than affirmative. No doubt, on the other side, I was too much inclined to see Vindice as at first a potential hero, or champion of values; I should have given more weight to his obsession and could have pointed out how he partly resembles the Vice in Morality plays; and I should have noted how, owing to the pushful ironies in the plot, his enemies are all set to be destroyed or destroy one another even without his intervention. However, I should still want to say that *The Revenger's Tragedy* contains some of the most powerful stage poetry outside Shakespeare, that in construction it owes a lot to the Moralities, and that the author felt bitterly about an opposition between Court and Country. So I have left the article unchanged; I assume that anyone wanting to compare differing critical opinions would prefer to see it in its original form.

From the list of contents, the sagacious reader will have observed that I have roped in the author of *Don Quixote* as a sort of honorary Jacobean. I trust this needs no apology beyond recalling that the novel was promptly welcomed in England. In any case, *Don Quixote* is a supreme example of a theme I have been considering with regard to drama in other essays; I have tried to examine how Cervantes transforms a literary genre through his engagement with previous literature and Renaissance literary theories.

Quotations from Shakespeare's texts in this book are keyed to *The Riverside Shakespeare*, ed. G. Blakemore Evans (Boston, 1974), which has been followed with occasional modifications in punctuation and spelling. In chapter 7, '*King Lear*, Montaigne and Harsnett', however, lines from *King Lear* are numbered according to Kenneth Muir's revised Arden edition (1972), because of the frequent use I have made of Muir's footnotes.

Cambridge   L.G.S.
December 1984

1. Shakespeare and the Italian concept of 'art'

According to Drummond of Hawthornden, Ben Jonson in private talk said that 'Shakespeare wanted Art.' His later, public tribute was, of course, more generous:

> Yet must I not give Nature all: Thy Art,
> My gentle *Shakespeare*, must enjoy a part.
> For though the *Poets* matter, Nature be,
> His Art doth give the fashion.

One statement apparently contradicts the other; what factors, then, did Jonson mean by 'Art' within the totality of Shakespeare's work? Possibly in the private statement it refers to that deliberate care for verisimilitude and actuality that Jonson claims for himself in the Induction to *Bartholomew Fair*, as one 'loth to make nature afraid in his plays', by contrast to the unnamed author of *The Winter's Tale* and *The Tempest*. In the published tribute, 'Art' refers rather, as the following lines show, to a capacity for strenuous afterthoughts that Jonson was willing to attribute to his great rival, whatever his inward reservations about him; it bespeaks an intensely self-critical labour to reshape and refine a poet's first thoughts, partly as an assertion of learning, in defiance of 'Ignorance', but chiefly for the self-appointed ambition 'to write a living line', which seems to imply both enduring fame and the justification for it in perfected workmanship. Here and elsewhere, Jonson points back to the ancients, to Horace for instance, and forward to neo-classicism. And in the way he uses the word *art*, not simply as a neutral descriptive term, but as a reified abstraction and mark of approval, he shares the tone and assumptions of the Italian Renaissance. Art here is on a footing with Nature; it reaches, if it does not enclose, some absolute value. But how far did Shakespeare also share such assumptions from the Italian Renaissance? What was his thinking on the subject of Art? Or, to frame the question behind this present paper more exactly, how did Shakespeare use the word?

I

A difficulty in discussing this question is that modern usage, while certainly overlapping with Elizabethan usage, differs from it sharply in range and emphasis. When we meet the word *art* in modern use without a qualifier it is most likely to mean either the products of painting, sculpture, architecture and related crafts (as in such a book title as *The Oxford Companion to Art*) or else the abstract, aesthetic qualities held to characterise the fine arts in general (as in such a title as Collingwood's *Principles of Art*). But in Elizabethan usage neither of those meanings would have been evident and clear, or intelligible at all without a supplied context. Painting, sculpture and architecture were not decisively grouped together with music and poetry and given the new, collective label of the Fine Arts until the mid eighteenth century; while, as Paul Kristeller shows in his magisterial survey of the rise of 'The Modern System of the Arts', the polar distinction between Art and Science, which has governed all subsequent theories about the arts, was not firmly stated before D'Alembert's *Discours préliminaire* to the French Encyclopedia in 1751. Only in that period was the theory of the fine arts distinguished as a separate branch of philosophy, acquiring the newly coined term, *aesthetics*, to mark off its province.[1] Even so, it appears that 'the most usual modern sense of *art*, when used without any qualification', meaning painting and the other arts of design, aiming at 'the skilful production of the beautiful in visible form' (as the Oxford dictionary defines it), was not recorded in any English dictionary before 1880.[2]

Medieval and, in general, Renaissance uses of the word stood much closer to classical Latin *ars* and Greek *techne*, meaning any acquired and purposeful knowledge or skill, without distinguishing between aesthetic and utilitarian applications, and without carrying any necessary approval signal.[3] A typical example from Shakespeare's time comes in a complaint of 1606 from the London artisan skinners, to the effect that the master and wardens of the Skinners' Company are now outsiders to the trade,

> whereby they have noe compassionate feeling of the abuses in the sayd Art or misterye, to the utter overthrowe of the sayd Art in verye short tyme.[4]

A major area of exception, where the word *art* could carry a charge of social dignity, was the liberal arts course in medieval schools and universities, which acknowledged poetry, in so far as it partook of grammar and rhetoric, and included music, as a form of mathematical theory.[5] But painting, sculpture and architecture (until the Renaissance) were mechanical, not liberal arts. And in any case, the evidence of book titles suggests that the academic sense of *art* was not the dominant reference of the word in English in the sixteenth century. Under the letters A to G, the *Short-Title Catalogue* mentions twenty-three books published in English between 1503 and 1639 with the word *art* in their titles; only four of them deal with one or another of the academic arts subjects, while the rest promise instruction in practices ranging from war, navigation, surgery or shorthand to the arts of pleasing at court, godly thriving, or godly dying. No book dealing with the art of painting was printed in England until 1598, when Richard Haydock published his translation of Lomazzo, although Hilliard was evidently writing his own manuscript treatise on *The Arte of Limning* at the same time,[6] and Henry Peacham's *Art of Drawing* was published soon afterwards, in 1606. In 1634, one John Bate, 'mechanician', published *The mysteryes of nature and art*, recommending proficiency in drawing and painting in the midst of miscellaneous tips about the properties of metals, medical cures, fireworks, water-works and other 'excellent experiments not unworthy the knowledge of any ingenious Artist whatsoever'; and such miscellaneousness had been typical of the sphere allotted to *art* across the preceding century. In his widely read *Vanitie and uncertaintie of Artes and Sciences*, Cornelius Agrippa had swept the liberal studies, including poetry and music, law, medicine and theology, into the same rag-bag as acting and alchemy, merchandise and heraldry, witchcraft and religious inquisition, whoredom and the art of begging.

Nevertheless, academic usage prevailed to the extent that any *art*, and notably any book so called, was presumed to consist of a set of precepts or rules, reduced to a system. For example, in his *Mathematicall Preface* of 1570 to *The Elements of ... Euclid*, John Dee defines 'An Arte', such as that of mathematics or any of its derivatives, as 'a Methodicall complete Doctrine' of the relevant knowledge needed.[7] Similarly, Puttenham defines the *art* in his *Arte of English Poesie* as 'a certaine order of rules prescribed by reason, and gathered by experience'.[8] The same emphasis on 'rules and maxims' gives the leading sense of *art* as late as 1755, in Johnson's *Dictionary* – where there is no specific reference to painting or sculpture under the heading of *art*, and where the terms *art* and *science* are still virtually interchangeable. Romantic theories about artistic creation were soon to reverse this leading implication within the word.

Agrippa's diatribe thrusts forward another secondary sense of *art*, latent throughout the sixteenth century, the sense of *art* as synonymous with cunning, guile or deceit.[9] Agrippa opposes the arts to Scripture. Later writers counterpose Nature with Art as a possible agency of falsification. In his famous essay on the cannibals, for example, Montaigne contrasts them favourably with Europeans in terms of the difference between wild and cultivated fruits: 'there is no reason', he says, to clinch his argument, 'art should gaine the point of honour of our great and puissant mother Nature'.[10] In Tasso and Spenser, a similar thought joins the theme of sexual temptation. In the enchanted garden of Armida, the 'art' at work in the meandering streams, the groves, caves and flowers was so concealed, and

> So with the rude the polished mingled was
> That natural seemèd all and every part,
> Nature would craft in counterfeiting pass,
> And imitate her imitator art;

and the 'art' was equally hidden in Spenser's Bower of Bliss:

> One would have thought, (so cunningly, the rude
> And scorned parts were mingled with the fine,)
> That nature had for wantonesse ensude
> Art, and that Art at nature did repine;
> So striving each th' other to undermine,
> Each did the others worke more beautifie.[11]

High civilisation and exoticism meet and mingle in these passages of pastoral, or rather, horticultural writing, and literary echoes blend with the fascination of technology – corresponding, it seems, to the century's enthusiasm over geographical and scientific discovery. Writers in the early Middle Ages had ridiculed the pretensions of art, painting in particular, to 'ape' the products of Nature; writers in Shakespeare's time see Art and Nature contending on equal, or seemingly equal, terms.[12]

This enhanced belief in the potency of art came chiefly from Italy, together with the bias that led on towards the modern classification of the fine arts and modern theories of aesthetics. The new ideology emerged in Florence in the fifteenth century, with the claim of sculptors, painters and architects to be esteemed as liberal, not mechanical, artists, endowed with theory as well as practice;[13] by the mid sixteenth century, it was consolidated in Vasari's *Lives*, which first gave currency to the belief in an artistic renaissance. Theoretically-minded artists, from Uccello to Alberti, Piero della Francesca, Dürer and Leonardo, advanced the thought of the visual arts as vantage-points for the understanding, or even the mastery, of nature; and something like a nineteenth-century idea of progress informs the historical arrangement of Vasari's *Lives*, culminating with the 'divine' Michelangelo.

The production of works of sculpture or painting as demonstrations of skill and the willingness of Renaissance patrons to commission or seek out works as examples of an individual artist's style – in other words, the appearance of connoisseurs – fostered the conception of art as an independent province of human effort, to be judged and admired for standards of its own, representing an abstract cultural value.[14] Vasari generalises such conceptions, especially in the theoretical prefaces to the three periods into which his *Lives* are grouped. Reviewing his own notion of progress in the Preface to Part II (the fifteenth century), for example, he concludes 'that it is inherent in the very nature of these arts [of painting, sculpture and architecture] to progress step by step from modest beginnings' towards 'perfection'. This sounds like Aristotle's account of the natural growth of tragedy, but Vasari goes on to give a different turn to the idea by adding that he has 'seen almost the same progression in other branches of learning', and 'the fact that the liberal arts are all related to each other in some way is a persuasive argument' on his side.[15] All the arts, then, belong to a family, and the factors common to them are motive powers in general culture.

The arts constituted a family for Renaissance critics because they all shared the common purpose of imitating nature. Secondly, there was the reciprocal influence of literary humanism and the visual arts, in the pageantry of courts, for example, and the strong influence of classical rhetoric and poetics on the criticism of painting, as summed up in the Renaissance commonplace, *ut pictura poesis*.[16] And the assumption that that similitude implied an underlying unity of values was self-confirming, since modern art for the Renaissance was, precisely, a rebirth of the methods and standards of the antique. Hence the term, *art*, could take on a new authority in literary criticism as well as the criticism of painting. In his *Arte poetica* of 1564, Minturno, criticising the episodic structure of modern romances, could maintain that Art should always keep to 'one law' like Nature herself, which Art imitates; and, without yet quite defining the later boundaries of the fine arts, he demands,

what art, what science, what discipline can be found (not architecture, not music, not painting, not sculpture, not military affairs, not medicine) in which anyone works without endeavouring to follow the steps of the ancients...?[17]

And, castigating the loose structure of English popular plays in the same spirit, Sir Philip Sidney declares,

which how absurd it is in sence even sence may imagine, and Arte hath taught, and all auncient examples justified, and, at this day, the ordinary Players in Italie will not erre in.[18]

The sense of rules, of teaching, is still prominent in the way both critics want to use the word 'Art' (with a capital A), but at the same time the word has come to carry the weight of a universal law or an independent entity.

Probably this more elevated conception of Art, as well as the first historical steps towards identifying the word with the visual arts, was due to the Italians whose immense achievements were celebrated in Vasari's *Lives*. Vasari urges that the greatest moderns transcend rules, and surpass their predecessors by virtue of spontaneity, inventiveness and grace. But he was also the founder of the first Academy of Design, and his book repeatedly suggests analogies between the visual arts and engineering or geometry. He is keenly interested in the resolution of technical problems – of perspective and foreshortening, for instance – and in exhibitions of technical difficulties overcome.[19] He attributes general value to qualities such as order and harmony; proportion is even a 'universal law' governing the three visual arts.[20] Above all, Vasari gives primacy within the three arts to 'design', which at the outset he derives from the mind of God, and to which he gives an aura of objectivity by describing it as 'the animating principle of all creative processes'.[21] In keeping with this keynote, he cites Michelangelo saying of Titian that he would have been a supreme painter, had he been 'assisted by art and design as much as he was by nature';[22] which comes near to the terms in which Ben Jonson discussed Shakespeare.

Two themes of approval very frequent with Vasari and other Italian art critics were evidently familiar to the Elizabethans as well: the theme of illusion of life in an imitation, and the theme of transcendence in art. For Vasari, the progress of painting and sculpture, from Giotto onwards, meant above all progressive lifelikeness and animation in the rendering of the human figure. Among the quattrocento masters, Ghiberti ('the first to imitate the works of the ancient Romans') made his statue of St John the Baptist 'like living flesh'; 'life itself seems to be stirring vigorously within the stone' of Donatello's St George, and Vasari tells how the sculptor addressed his favourite statue, Il Zuccone, with '"Speak, damn you, speak!"', while similarly he remarks of Masaccio's painting of St Paul 'that the figure needs only speech to be alive'. And the masters of Vasari's own century surpass their predecessors not only in variety of figurations but also in 'truth': the figures of Raphael

are truth itself: for . . . the flesh seems to be moving, they breathe, their pulses beat, and they are utterly true to life;

likewise, he repeats that Giulio Romano was snatched to heaven because he made 'sculptured and painted bodies breathe'.[23] Secondly, Italian theorists, including Vasari, emphasise the theme of rivalry in the arts: competitions between artists, comparisons between ancients and moderns, comparisons between separate arts, as in Leonardo's *paragone* between poetry and painting and, finally, contests between Art and Nature – somewhat as in the passages I have quoted already from Montaigne, Tasso and Spenser. Thus, Vasari quotes Poliziano's epitaphs, saying that the art of Giotto and of Fra Filippo Lippi could match the arts of Nature, and Bembo's hyperbolical epitaph for Raphael, 'by whom in life / Our mighty mother Nature feared defeat'; and he gives as his own opinion that if only Michelangelo could have completed his statues for the Medici chapel in San Lorenzo, 'then art would have demonstrated that it surpassed nature in every way'. In the same vein, an epitaph by Ortelius says that Nature may have called Bruegel to death because she 'feared that his genius for dexterous imitation would bring her into contempt'; and Titian took as his motto, '*Natura potentior ars*', 'Art mightier than Nature'.[24] The common thread in these two themes of illusion and transcendence is the thought of painting or sculpture appearing to overcome its material limitations.

Although there is no evidence that Shakespeare had read Vasari, he was clearly familiar with and even, at times, fascinated by these outstanding themes of humanistic art-criticism.[25] On the other hand, unlike Ben Jonson, he does not appear to have shared the Italian conception of Art in the abstract. To a large extent, he uses the word *art* in the common and miscellaneous Elizabethan way. When he refers to the fine arts (to use the later term), as he often does, he detaches himself from any belief in a regulative law, or in any unique power within the visual arts to triumph over Nature; and the arts he gives dramatic emphasis to are those of medicine and magic, arts involving wonder and illusion, but concerned with changing, not merely imitating, life.

Shakespeare uses the word *art* and some derivatives, like *artificial*, rather more than a hundred times in all. In many uses, his reference is either indefinite or ambiguous. But in perhaps a fifth of his instances he refers to specific forms of skill, such as love-making or swordsmanship, and in another quarter to arts, notably medicine and magic, involving knowledge of mysterious secrets of nature; in *Macbeth*, for example, he names the 'arts' of swimming, physiognomy, witchcraft and medicine. But, in addition to the witchcraft references, *art* in a handful of passages means falsity or deception (as when Angelo in *Measure for Measure* (II.ii.182) speaks of 'the strumpet, / With all her double vigour, art and nature', or Pisanio in *Cymbeline* (III.iv.120) denounces 'Some villain, / Ay, and singular in his art'). On the other side, in about a quarter of the examples, *art* or *arts* refer to academic learning, as notably in *Love's Labour's Lost* – where the subject is treated with irony, however – or else to eloquence or rhetoric, as when Gertrude asks Polonius for 'More matter with less art' or when Claudio says Isabella 'hath prosperous art / . . . And well she can persuade'. And in perhaps another score of passages, the sense of *art* stretches out from book-learning to some more general sense of *savoir-faire* or trained wisdom applied in conduct, as when Mercutio teases Romeo with

Now art thou sociable, now art thou Romeo; now art thou what thou art, by art as well as by nature;   (II.iv.89)

or the Archbishop of Canterbury maintains that 'the art and practic part of life / Must be the mistress to this theoric' newly revealed by Henry V (I.i.51); or Viola discerns that the Clown's 'practice' is 'As full of labour as a wise man's art' (III.i.66). These are mostly positive usages, though not without ambiguity.

There are very many places where Shakespeare discusses or alludes to what we should call the arts, and about ten passages where he uses the word *art* to mean painting or one of the other arts of design – including Marina's needlework, which 'composes / Nature's own shape of bud, bird, branch or berry, / That even her art sisters the natural roses' (*Pericles*, V. Cho. 5). But it is striking that

Shakespeare very rarely speaks of *art*, in an aesthetic context, without a qualifier (the main exceptions coming as late as *The Winter's Tale*), and never gives to *art*, meaning aesthetic skill, the weight of authority the word carries in writers like Vasari, Minturno, Sidney and Ben Jonson. He obviously loved music, which he mentions and employs repeatedly, but he never speaks of the performer's or the composer's 'art' (when Hortensio, in *The Shrew* (III.i.66), tells Bianca that he 'must begin with rudiments of art', he means a method of learning to play the lute in a few easy lessons; and, whether written by Shakespeare or not, the song in *Henry VIII* (III.i.12) touches primarily on the power of soothing or healing with the lines, 'In sweet music is such art, / Killing care and grief of heart / Fall asleep, or hearing, die'). In the Sonnets, Shakespeare says he is 'Desiring this man's art, and that man's scope' (29); he deplores the spectacle of 'art made tongue-tied by authority' (66); and he tells the Friend, his 'Muse', in Sonnet 78 that 'thou art all my art'. But in the first two passages *art* seems to mean general accomplishment or learning, and only in the third is it used unmistakably for the poet's craft, as Puttenham or Ben Jonson might have used the word, and even then, with a hint of disclaiming superficial artifice. The Prologue to *Two Noble Kinsmen* praises Chaucer's 'art', but those lines were almost certainly by Fletcher, and Shakespeare's only specific reference to the 'art' of poetry on the stage comes in Timon's punning sarcasm to the Poet (V.i.83):

> for thy fiction,
> Why, thy verse swells with stuff so fine and smooth
> That thou art even natural in thine art.

Again, in *3 Henry VI* (III.ii.184) Richard of Gloucester declares that, in order to gain the crown, he can 'wet [his] cheeks with artificial tears', 'frame [his] face to all occasions', 'play the orator', 'deceive', 'change shapes', and 'set the murtherous Machevil to school'; but in spite of the dramatist's very many references, literal or figurative, to the practice of acting, he never names it as an *art*, even in Hamlet's studied advice to the Players.

Shakespeare was evidently alert to many aspects of the visual arts: tapestries and the 'painted cloth', emblematic pictures, miniatures, print shops, monumental statuary, the 'wanton' mythologies in the Lord's collection in *The Taming of the Shrew*, Imogen's carved chimney-piece, the 'singularities' in Paulina's 'gallery'. In 1613 he was commissioned to design the Earl of Rutland's *impresa*, which

Burbage painted. He uses the term *art* for painting or sculpture half-a-dozen times, as distinct from poetry and music; he is at home in the technical language of painting; and he dwells upon the themes of lifelike illusion and transcendence from humanistic art-criticism. All this suggests a strong Italian influence, direct or indirect. But at the same time, his many references to statuary and painting suggest detachment, reservations, even recoil or something like cultural resistance, together with vivid appreciation. In *1 Henry VI*, to take a very early play, the Countess of Auvergne uses the portrait of Talbot she possesses as a means of entrapment, with a suspicion of witchcraft about it (II.iii):

> Long time thy shadow hath been thrall to me,
> For in my gallery thy picture hangs;
> But now the substance shall endure the like.

Talbot undeceives her, with a Robin Hood-like winding of his horn; his 'substance' is his soldiers. And when, later, Talbot falls among 'these dead' on the battlefield, Sir William Lucy imagines how 'but his picture' could terrify the French (IV.vii.83); the picture is associated with a pathetic fallacy and with the fact of death. In the garden scene in the same play, showing the origin of the Wars of the Roses, Plantagenet challenges Somerset to 'proclaim [his] thoughts' in 'dumb significants', since he is 'tongue-tied and so loath to speak' (II.iv.25); Somerset picks a red rose as his emblem; Warwick puns on the word 'colours' (implying dishonesty); and Somerset taunts another of his opponents with a warning not to prick his finger on a thorn, 'Lest, bleeding, you do paint the white rose red'. Again in the same play, Alençon promises the French witch, Joan la Pucelle, 'We'll set thy statue in some holy place, / And have thee reverenc'd like a blessed saint' (III.iii.14); and in contrast, but ambiguous contrast, Suffolk, bringing Margaret to marry Henry VI but already infatuated with her himself, urges himself to 'Bethink thee on her virtues that surmount, / And natural graces that extinguish art' (V.iii.191). These verbal associations of pictures with death or dumbness, of painting with blood or falsity, and of works of art with idolatry or witchcraft are frequent, almost regular, in Shakespeare's subsequent plays. In *2 Henry VI*, Queen Margaret, jealous of her husband's mourning for Gloucester, conjoins the thought of idolatry with an antithesis between noble and plebeian icons: 'Erect his statuë and worship it, / And make my image but an alehouse sign' (III.ii.80); similarly, in *Two Gentlemen of Verona*, Julia, contemplating her rival's 'picture' or 'shadow', imagines how the disloyal Proteus will 'worship' this 'senseless form' – but, 'were there sense in his idolatry, / My substance should be statue in thy stead' (IV.iv.200). The association of painting with blood reappears, for example, when Troilus exclaims, 'Fools on both sides, Helen must needs be fair, / When with your blood you daily paint her thus' (I.i.90), or when Coriolanus calls his battle stains 'this painting' (I.vi.68); and the other extension of the idea of 'painting', to thoughts of cosmetics and falsity, comes out, for example, when in soliloquy Claudius compares his own 'painted word' to 'The harlot's cheek, beautied with plast'ring art' (III.i.50). And, to give one more example for the moment, Shakespeare's ambivalence towards the painter's art comes out in Lady Macbeth's speech to her husband (II.ii.50):

> The sleeping and the dead
> Are but as pictures; 'tis the eye of childhood
> That fears a painted devil. If he do bleed,
> I'll gild the faces of the grooms withal,
> For it must seem their guilt.

Thoughts of violence, motionlessness and delusiveness come together here; and Lady Macbeth's words suggest the speculative possibility that Shakespeare's language about painting harks back to some early experience of fascinated terror, conceivably before something like the wall painting of the Last Judgement in the Stratford-upon-Avon Guild Chapel.[26]

However that may be, some negative association qualifies nearly all of Shakespeare's glowing images based on the Renaissance trope of art outgoing nature.[27] The first impressive example comes from the Titianesque poem of *Venus and Adonis*, in the description of the horse (289 ff.):

> Look when a painter would surpass the life
> In limning out a well-proportioned steed,
> His art with nature's workmanship at strife,
> As if the dead the living should exceed;
>   So did this horse excel a common one,
>   In shape, in courage, colour, pace, and bone.

Here already Shakespeare manifests his inclination to take the art-critics' paradox or hyperbole and reverse it in favour of physical life:[28] this exceptional living horse at least equals the painted one, which is 'dead'. So, too, the long, detailed account of the imaginary picture of the siege of Troy that Lucrece turns to in her grief opens with a reference (1373) to artistry as a skill in depicting bloodshed: 'A thousand lamentable objects there, / In scorn of nature, art gave liveless life.' This hint of lifelessness is all the more striking because the long description of the picture demonstrates Shakespeare's keen responsiveness to pictorial images, through the way Lucrece reacts to it.[29]

In several plays after *1 Henry VI* – in *Two Gentlemen* and in *Hamlet*, for instance – a portrait makes part of the action or the dialogue. And in Bassanio's casket scene in *The Merchant of Venice* Shakespeare repeats the trope of nature excelling a superlative work of art, 'Fair Portia's counterfeit' (III.ii.115), where the animated eyes suggest some miniature by Hilliard. But for a long time he has no other developed conceit about art's rivalry with nature in his plays, in spite of the prominence he had given to the theme in *Venus and Adonis* and *The Rape of Lucrece*; as if he considered it appropriate to a poem for aristocratic connoisseurs like Southampton, but less to his purpose on the stage.

Then, however, in close sequence, come four late plays – or five, if we count *Pericles*, with its *imprese* and the lines about Marina's needlework – where passages about pictorial art stand out: *Antony*, *Timon*, *Cymbeline* and *The Winter's Tale*. The tone varies, but in all of these plays Shakespeare juxtaposes pictorial art with living nature, but also with the life in poetry and drama. Since there are no counterparts in Shakespeare's source for the Poet and the Painter who speak first in *Timon*, and since he has no similar professional debate in any previous plays, it looks as if their subject of a *paragone* between the arts has acquired a special interest for him. Moreover, the art themes in all four plays overlap, with a common reference to the classical background of the Renaissance. Possibly Shakespeare's interest here was provoked largely by the return of Inigo Jones to England in 1604, and the beginning of his collaboration with Ben Jonson in 1605, a couple of years before the writing of *Antony*. Scholars have often considered whether their court masques influenced the dramatic construction of Shakespeare's last plays. But there may also have been a wider intellectual challenge or stimulus from the talk or the ideas of Inigo Jones, with the proficiency he was being praised for in 'the elegant arts of the ancients'[30] and his unique familiarity with modern Italian art.

Antony and Cleopatra sets the stage presence of the lovers over against the creation of their legend. It opens with what is virtually a

pictorial gesture, from a spectator within the canvas, as if in a scene
by Veronese: 'Look, where they come! / Take but good note ...
Behold and see.'[31] When Shakespeare reaches the narration of
Cleopatra's first meeting with Antony, he makes Enobarbus improve
upon Plutarch's description of her costume – 'like the goddesse
Venus, commonly drawn in picture' – and pick up, only to
embellish, Pliny's account of the famous Venus of Apelles
(II.ii.197):[32]

> For her own person,
> It beggar'd all description: she did lie
> In her pavilion – cloth of gold, of tissue –
> O'er-picturing that Venus where we see
> The fancy outwork nature.

Later on, Antony's elegy for himself – 'Sometime we see a cloud
that's dragonish' (IV.xiv.2) – is likewise conceived in pictorial terms.
Literary antecedents have been noted for his comparisons between
changing cloud shapes and the shapes of a bear, or lion, or horse; but
the central lines in his speech compose a contemporary landscape:

> A tower'd citadel, a pendant rock,
> A forked mountain, or blue promontory
> With trees upon't that nod unto the world,
> And mock our eyes with air.

And Antony confirms the link with the visual arts when he adds,
coining a new verb, 'even with a thought / The rack dislimns'. The
unusual noun, *rack*, had just appeared in Ben Jonson's account of the
Masque of Hymen of 1606, for which Inigo Jones had prepared an
Italianate machinery of moving clouds for the first time in an English
court show.[33] But then Cleopatra's speech – independent of Plutarch
– commenting on her own mental image of Antony after his death
(V.ii.97) makes a kind of riposte to these tributes to painting:

> Nature wants stuff
> To vie strange forms with fancy; yet t' imagine
> An Antony were nature's piece 'gainst fancy,
> Condemning shadows quite.

Fancy had been Enobarbus's word for painting, which the words
piece and *shadow* also imply; but to *imagine* a demigod, to 'dream'
of him in voice and action, is the prerogative of poetry.

This implicit criticism of the claims made for the pictorial arts
becomes more trenchant in *Timon* and *Cymbeline*. In the dialogue

between Poet and Painter that introduces *Timon*, the latent dramatic issue is the effect of patronage, which actuates insincerity in both of them, but the surface question is the representation of truth to life. 'Let's see your piece', says the Poet (I.i.28), and, admiring a figure, 'To th' dumbness of the gesture / One might interpret.' 'It is a pretty mocking of the life', the Painter replies, with affected modesty, and (proffering what was presumably a new studio term),[34] 'Here is a touch; is't good?' To which the Poet replies, like a critic on his mettle, 'I will say of it, / It tutors nature. Artificial strife / Lives in these touches, livelier than life.' Not content with awarding the credit due to merely aping nature, he follows the high line of mannerists like Lomazzo, to the effect that 'the precepts of Arte' call for idealisation or heightened decorum in portraiture, 'supplying the defects of nature, by the helpe of arte'; but his compliment is intended to elicit the Painter's flattery in return. Iachimo, in *Cymbeline*, is a more discriminating connoisseur. He, too, admires a 'strife' for transcendence, as between 'workmanship' and material in the tapestry showing Cleopatra meeting 'her Roman' that hangs in Imogen's bedchamber (II.iv.74); but when he comes to describe the 'chimney-piece' of 'Chaste Dian bathing' to her agonised husband, he adopts a reservation:

> Never saw I figures
> So likely to report themselves. The cutter
> Was as another Nature, dumb; outwent her,
> Motion and breath left out.

Iachimo's judiciousness is a refinement of torture. But his object is to sound convincing. And his reservation about the work of art is in keeping with his own soliloquy earlier, in the bedchamber scene, when he had called Imogen's sleep the 'ape of death' (II.ii.31) and compared it with a 'monument' lying in 'a chapel'. Those lines echo Lady Macbeth's, 'The sleeping and the dead / Are but as pictures'; and there is a further thread of association between the bedchamber scene in *Cymbeline* and the sinister pictorial episode in *The Rape of Lucrece*, since Iachimo compares himself to 'Our Tarquin' (II.ii.12), like Macbeth, with his 'ravishing strides' (II.i.55) towards the murder of Duncan. Shakespeare repeatedly inverts the art-critics' view of the tension between art and life.

Perhaps that particular thread of association was unconscious. But Shakespeare was evidently interested in the rivalry between painting and acting. In *An Apology for Actors*, written about the same time as *Cymbeline*, Thomas Heywood repeats the commonplace that 'oratory is a kind of speaking picture', in order to claim that acting can do more than either, by 'action, passion, motion', to stir 'the spirits of the beholder'.[35] Shakespeare executes a sophisticated variation on the same argument in *Cymbeline*, when he makes Imogen, on the way to Milford Haven, urge and re-urge her unhappily mute companion, Pisanio, to tell her what is on his mind. 'One but painted thus', she says (III.iv.6), 'Would be interpreted a thing perplex'd / Beyond self-explication.' Obviously, Shakespeare counts on the actor playing Pisanio to match, by his dumb show, which Imogen describes in detail, the vaunted expressiveness of painting. But what Imogen wants, and drama alone can give, is the living communication of speech.

Shakespeare's final and supreme demonstration of the superiority of drama over the pictorial arts comes in the last scene of *The Winter's Tale*. We have just heard (V.ii.97) that the statue of Hermione is supposed to be the work of

that rare Italian master, Julio Romano, who, had he himself eternity and could put breath into his work, would beguile Nature of her custom, so perfectly he is her ape. He so near to Hermione hath done Hermione that they say one would speak to her and stand in hope of answer.

'Could [he] put breath into his work': the reservation has become familiar by now. Renaissance writers were attracted by the thought of automata and moving statues,[36] and this play is about to demonstrate such a marvel, a moment or so after Leontes has said, 'The fixure of her eye has motion in't, / As we are mock'd with art' (V.iii.67). Moreover, unlike the court ladies appearing as mythological images of themselves in Inigo Jones's masques, the stage Hermione shows the wrinkles due to the passage of time. Possibly Shakespeare made his choice of a 'rare Italian master' because of his reputation for *trompe-l'oeil* effects; in any case, his genuine but generic-sounding name, Julius the Roman, contributes to that sleight-of-hand or flickering ambiguity between actuality and impossibility characteristic of this romance where Sicilians have been wrecked on the sea-coast of Bohemia and the Delphic Oracle has been consulted about a Russian princess.[37] This is precisely the sort of Shakespearean defiance of realism that Ben Jonson pokes fun at in the Induction to *Bartholomew Fair*.

In *The Winter's Tale*, however, the statue scene has been preceded by the dialogue between Perdita and Polixenes (IV.iv.79–97), the most deliberate of Shakespeare's discussions touching on the theory

of the arts. Without realising it Polixenes there has justified the
extraordinary transformations at the end of the play when he says,
'This is an art / Which does mend Nature – change it rather; but / The
art itself is Nature'; it is 'an art / That Nature makes'. Only, the *art*
Polixenes is defending is not painting or sculpture, but the skill of
grafting, of the gardener; a craft closer to science than to *art* in the
dominant modern use of the word. In effect Perdita has been siding
with Montaigne's essay 'Of the Cannibals'; but the nearest analogue
that has been noted to Polixenes' views comes from the closing pages
of *The Arte of English Poesie*, where Puttenham tries to distinguish
between poetic artifice and courtly dissembling.[38] Art, says Puttenham, is sometimes an 'ayde' to nature or even an 'alterer' and
'surmounter' of nature's 'skill', both functions illustrated by the
Physician and the Gardener, who can 'embellish' fruits and flowers,
including the 'gillifloure' and 'carnation' that Perdita is wary of. In
contrast, the function of the painter or carver is 'onely' that of 'a bare
immitatour of natures works, following and counterfeyting' them,
like a 'Marmesot'. Then there is an art 'as it were ... contrary to
nature', such as carpentry or dancing, though – with a phrase
Shakespeare may have utilised for Cleopatra – 'nature alwaies
supplying stuffe'. And finally, the poet's art, 'holpen by a cleare and
bright phantasie and imagination', includes and surpasses all of these
functions, 'even as nature her selfe working by her owne peculiar
vertue and proper instinct'. Or, as Polixenes restates it, 'over that art
/ Which you say adds to Nature, is an art / That Nature makes'.
Dramatic spectacle belongs to this kind of art, assuming that it
follows a true path of human emotion, expectation and experience.

The pictorial arts fare disappointingly, then, on Shakespeare's stage,
or rather, below the highest pitch of their admirers. On the other
side, the 'arts' which contribute frequently to the unfolding of his
plays are those of medicine and magic exploring and applying nature's secrets, as with the 'secret art' of 'physic' practised by Cerimon
in *Pericles* (III.ii.32). Again and again, either medicine or magic is
necessary to his plots.

Shakespeare is exceptionally respectful towards doctors.[39] While,
in words at least, he associates painting with death, he shows the
physician's art restoring to life. The French court in *All's Well*
marvels at Helena's medical 'art'. Cerimon recovers Thaisa from
seeming death, and in *Romeo and Juliet* and *Cymbeline* medical
cunning goes even further, by inducing a semblance of death which is

only temporary. This restorative capacity belongs to a central motif in Shakespearean romance, the return of a character from supposed or apparent death.

However, medicine is not always successful; Lady Macbeth's doctor cannot cure her. Magic may be sinister as Leontes fears when Hermione's statue finally comes to life – 'If this be magic let it be an art / Lawful as eating' (V.iii.110); but it may also be harmless or beneficent, like that of Rosalind's pretended helper in *As You Like It* (V.ii.60), 'a magician, most profound in his art, and yet not damnable'. Either way, good or evil, genuine or pretended, magic on Shakespeare's stage is always efficacious; it can always be said to perform what it promises. It may be wrongly adduced to explain a surprising but natural course of feeling, as in Brabantio's accusation of 'arts inhibited' against Othello (I.ii.79). But Shakespeare regularly associates magic, whether real or supposed, with stage illusion as such, from *Henry VI* and *The Comedy of Errors* onwards; or more precisely, he associates it with the illusions his characters are involved in. For instance, the 'art' of the Weird Sisters produces the supernatural show that irrevocably deludes Macbeth (IV.i.101), the ultimate 'equivocation of the fiend / That lies like truth' (V.v.42).

In *The Tempest*, Shakespeare uses and emphasises the word *art* more than in any other play; it refers once to Prospero's 'liberal' studies (I.ii.73) and no less than ten times to his magic. We first hear it, from Miranda (I.ii.1), to account for the storm scene, with its unprecedented naturalism; and from then on it explains Prospero's extensive control over the other characters' movements and his capacity to project illusions, notably the illusions of death and return from the dead. So close is the link between Prospero's magic and the business of stagecraft that we, modern commentators, are often tempted to identify the two, speaking of Prospero's 'art' as another name for Shakespeare's and of Prospero the character as a mask of the dramatist. But although Shakespeare certainly prompts this association of ideas, it seems to me that he uses Prospero's *art* as a metaphor for his own procedure, not a literal and complete synonym. Even when Prospero refers to the masque he is going to 'Bestow upon the eyes of this young couple' as 'Some vanity of mine art' (IV.i.41), he is speaking about his magical power (corresponding to the 'art' of the Weird Sisters, or that of Glendower in *1 Henry IV*, who can summon musicians 'a thousand leagues from hence' (III.i.47, 224)); it would be irrelevant for him to be claiming credit here as a playwright. Similarly when in the Epilogue the actor playing Prospero confesses that now he lacks 'Spirits to enforce, art to enchant', he means primarily the compulsive force of magic. In Shakespeare's vocabulary, the word *art* stands for something important, but limited. It does not cover the poet's imagination, or the excitement of sound and movement on the stage, or that insight into feeling and that capacity to anticipate an audience's reactions that govern the general movement of a play. Nevertheless, it may point to something vital within Shakespeare's plays, the power to conjure up illusion and, by means of illusion, to 'mend Nature', as Polixenes says, or 'change it rather'. Yet in important ways that operative power comes nearer to Francis Bacon's view of scientific endeavour than to the notion of art in critics like Vasari. Possibly modern aesthetic preconceptions interfere with our understanding of this side of Shakespeare.

2. Is *The Merchant of Venice* a problem play?

In response to the question I am using as title and opening to this paper – is *The Merchant of Venice* a problem play? – the short answer, I presume, must be, no. W. H. Auden could, indeed, assert that '*The Merchant of Venice* is, among other things, as much a "problem" play as one by Ibsen or Shaw', and he could point out that debates over the traditional condemnation of usury in the highly mercantile society of the sixteenth century affect the character conflict in the play.[1] But that is not the same as saying that an exposition of some theme of social tension, whether usury or anti-semitism, for instance, follows from the working-out of a large part of the plot – as we might say of modern plays in the wake of *Ghosts* or *An Enemy of the People*. Nor is Shakespeare here intent, like Shaw, upon examining the reasoning that supports a controversial opinion or protects a prejudice. Nor does *The Merchant* contain that compound of intense questioning and bitter humour over sex that marks *All's Well*, *Measure for Measure* and *Troilus and Cressida* and led F. S. Boas in 1896 to borrow the term 'problem play' for Shakespeare criticism from the Ibsenites.[2] On the contrary, the prevailing tone in *The Merchant* is a tone of romance. In his often quoted study of the play, Harley Granville-Barker could describe it, in effect, as 'a fairy tale' that Shakespeare humanised with realistic characters, even as 'the simplest of plays, so long as we do not bedevil it with sophistries'.[3] Granville-Barker had no patience with the acting tradition that made a grand climax of pathos out of Shylock's final exit. Nevertheless some shade of uncertainty remains which is not due purely, I think, to modern history, but to the composition of the play. Many recent critics, without wishing to see a return to the sentimentalised Shylock of Henry Irving's day, concur in finding emotional loose ends within *The Merchant of Venice*, hints of moral tension that go beyond the functional requirements of presenting a conflict on the stage, or discrepancies between the emotional undercurrents and the surface of judgement established by the plot, such as we find, on a larger scale, in *All's Well that Ends Well* and *Measure for Measure*, later in Shakespeare's career. It seems to me that what may be called the realistic qualities in *The Merchant* and what may be called its problematic qualities are intimately connected; that is to say that both together belong to and represent a new phase in Shakespeare's development as a writer of comedies.

Of course the question of how to categorise *The Merchant of Venice* is not a modern or a Victorian discovery, but dates back at least to the eighteenth century. Nicholas Rowe said, in 1709, that although it was 'Receiv'd and Acted as a Comedy', he '[could not] but think it was design'd Tragically by the Author', because it contained 'such a deadly Spirit of Revenge' and cruelty as '[could not] agree either with the Stile or Characters of Comedy'.[4] Samuel Johnson, on the other hand, found unity within the play, in a summary assessment that matches Granville-Barker's: 'The comick part raises laughter, and the serious fixes expectation.' But in his superb *Preface to Shakespeare* of 1765, he emphasised a *general* difference between Shakespeare's plays and the categories of criticism, or, at least, of the category-conscious neo-classical criticism of his time. Johnson held that Shakespeare's real genius lay in comedy rather than tragedy. All the same, he argued that[5]

Shakespeare's plays are not in the rigorous and critical sense either tragedies or comedies but compositions of a distinct kind; exhibiting the real state of sublunary nature, which partakes of good and evil, joy and sorrow, mingled with endless variety of proportion and innumerable modes of combination; and expressing the course of the world, in which the loss of one is the gain of another; in which, at the same time, the reveller is hasting to his wine, and the mourner burying his friend; in which the malignity of one is sometimes defeated by the frolick of another; and many mischiefs and many benefits are done and hindered without design.

Now, there is much in this paragraph that expresses the writer's bias towards drama as a mirror of universal moral principles rather than a text for theatrical performance; and much in the sense of life's unregulated variety that speaks for the author of *Rasselas* and *The Vanity of Human Wishes* rather than the author of *The Taming of the Shrew* or *Macbeth*. Yet surely Johnson was also pointing objectively to a distinctive and constant turn of mind in Shakespeare, which comes out, from the beginning of his work, in the prominence of characters with a comic potential in his tragedies (think of Richard III or Mercutio, for instance) and in hints of tragic possibilities on the margins of comedy. From the outset, from his adaptation of Plautus in *The Comedy of Errors*, Shakespeare was more lastingly influenced by the models of classical New Comedy than Samuel Johnson perceived. Even so, *The Comedy of Errors* opens with a framing plot from romance, suggesting pathos rather than humour; and early in the first scene of the main plot, Antipholus of Syracuse describes his servant, Dromio, as

> A trusty villain, sir, that very oft,
> When I am dull with care and melancholy,
> Lightens my humour with his merry jests.

A moment later, he reacts to an incomprehensible message from, as he thinks, the same Dromio — actually, his servant's twin — with

> I am not in a sportive humour now . . .
> Come, Dromio, come, these jests are out of season;
> Reserve them till a merrier hour than this —

and the farcical misunderstandings of the main plot are released. But there is an edge of 'care and melancholy' in the leading actors that sharpens all the outlines of the farce; and the sense that there is a time and 'season', and hence a limit, for jesting governs Shakespeare's treatment of the festive elements in comedy down to *Twelfth Night* and beyond. Part of his nearly consistent comic strategy is precisely to approach the limit. For example, in the opening dialogue of *Much Ado* (written not long after *The Merchant*) there is a brief but significant digression about a character we do not hear of again, on whom Leonato comments, 'How much better is it to weep at joy than to joy at weeping!'; and in the scene in *All's Well* (IV.iii.) where the French Lords, young Bertram's friends, come to think of him as a scoundrel indirectly responsible for the death of his wife, one of them observes, more sententiously and perplexingly:

How mightily sometimes we make us comforts of our losses! . . . The web of our life is of a mingled yarn, good and ill together: our virtues would be proud, if our faults whipt them not, and our crimes would despair, if they were not cherish'd by our virtues.

These speeches from Leonato and the French Lord sound like variations on what Johnson considered to be Shakespeare's governing theme. Shakespeare was hardly intent, as Johnson perhaps implied, upon shaping each of his plays into a kind of map, 'expressing the course of the world'. He was not a realistic playwright quite as Johnson made out, or not consistently so. But he was clearly interested in the intertexture of experience and in the strange borderland where 'good and evil, joy and sorrow' encroach upon their opposites.

The Merchant of Venice is the earliest of his comedies, and perhaps the earliest of his plays, where this kind of interest declares itself strongly. It shares with three subsequent Shakespearean comedies – Much Ado and the two so-called problem plays of All's Well and Measure for Measure – the external characteristic that all four of the main plots of these plays, comprising a separate group among his comedies, were derived from Italian novelle. And it shares a distinctive structural feature with the other three novella comedies. Most of Shakespeare's comedies end with a scene of recognition leading to wedding celebrations. But in the four novellistic plays a marriage takes place early or in the middle of the plot and yet celebration or consummation is delayed because the heroine must confront an ordeal; in The Merchant, and again in All's Well and Measure for Measure, the ordeal takes the form of a dilemma or puzzle that the heroine or her friends have to resolve. This seems to be the feature that drew Shakespeare's interest to novella material for his comedies.[6] At the same time Shakespeare gives the characters in these plays an extra degree of sententiousness, an inclination towards general reflection about life, that they had not shown in his comedies before. 'In sooth I know not why I am so sad': the first line in The Merchant of Venice strikes a new note of psychological questioning.

A plot involving a problem with serious consequences and a reflective style of dialogue seem to bring The Merchant close to the territory of modern realistic discussion plays. Certainly the opening scene seems to turn in that direction. Through the easy-flowing, occasionally colourful verse Shakespeare sketches the background of Venice's international trade and establishes an atmosphere of patrician sociability. How can the speakers account for Antonio's melancholy? Is a 'sad' or a 'merry' disposition determined by a freak of 'Nature', who

> hath fram'd strange fellows in her time:
> Some that will evermore peep through their eyes,
> And laugh like parrots at a bagpiper;
> And other of such vinegar aspect
> That they'll not show their teeth in way of smile
> Though Nestor swear the jest be laughable?

Or is a depressed mood the fault of a voluntary error, the mistaken attitude of one of those who 'have too much respect upon the world./They lose it that do buy it with much care'? The topic of the servant's jesting from *The Comedy of Errors* resurfaces as a theme for amateur psychiatry, in a style much closer to relaxed conversation than any sustained passage that Shakespeare had written previously, without any evident contrivance for the sake of the plot and without any distinct effort for verbal display; even Gratiano's set speech in favour of a life of jesting becomes a sign of his personal temperament. Similarly, Bassanio's glowing description of Portia, which raises the whole poetic pitch of the first scene, is kept within a frame of psychological probabilities. Bassanio has no knowledge yet of the extraordinary provisions surrounding Portia's marriage; he broaches his project to Antonio with realistic embarrassment and his romantic enthusiasm is tempered realistically with acknowledgement of the financial 'hazard' involved in courting a rich heiress. Bassanio's 'hazard' is due to provide the main thrust of the plot, rather than the discussion of Antonio's 'sadness'. Nevertheless, contrasts between 'sad' and 'merry', grim and festive dispositions continue through the first half of the play; and the closing scene, with its emphasis on an idealised harmony of music by moonlight, picks up again and transposes the topics of the opening conversation as well as rounding off the plot. Jessica says she is 'never merry when [she hears] sweet music', and Lorenzo explains why; Portia restates the value of a certain regard for 'the world', while both Lorenzo and Nerissa praise a 'stillness' and 'silence' (in due 'season') that Gratiano had decried; and Antonio is not only restored to his wealth but restored, as he puts it, to 'life and living', even though he remains alone while the other characters move off in couples. The end responds to the beginning in poetic, if not intellectual, terms.

On the other hand, Shakespeare is far from aiming at dissolving improbabilities all the way through, and his two main creative drives in the play, the invention of Shylock and the development of Portia, exhibit opposing and ultimately (I think) unreconciled impulses, towards what may be called realism and towards romance. Shakespeare has altered the story of the Lady of Belmont, but not for greater verisimilitude. Bassanio's description of Portia with her 'golden fleece' suggests some parallel with Medea, but when we see her she seems, for all her lively wit, more like the reverse of a Medea – a fairy-tale princess imprisoned by a spell. Here the dramatist has changed his sources twice over. In the *novella* by Ser Giovanni that Shakespeare was using, the Lady of Belmont is a widow who reflects both sides of the medieval image of woman, first as temptress and then as mediatrix. She frees the hero's godfather from the moneylender's cruel bond after the hero, Giannetto, has finally been helped to win her. But at first her law has been that gentlemen visiting her country must make love to her in bed, marrying her if they succeed but, if they fail, forfeiting all their possessions; by drugging their bedtime glass of wine, she has taken good care that they should fail. In Portia's case, Shakespeare not only replaces this seduction motif with the legend of the choice of caskets but changes the legend too by altering the wording on the leaden casket, from the pious inscription, 'Who so chooseth me, shall find that [that] God hath disposed for him', to 'Who chooseth me must give and hazard all he hath.' As Geoffrey Bullough points out in his study of Shakespeare's sources, 'This is what Giannetto did each time he went to Belmont, and by choosing lead Bassanio is doing for love of Portia what Antonio in his different way has done for him.'[7] Moreover, Shakespeare's treatment of the caskets legend means in effect that Bassanio delivers Portia from bondage to her father's will before Portia delivers Antonio in return. This change from the *novella* entails more than censoring the bedroom episodes. Unlike the Lady in the *novella*, Portia is symbolically contrasted with the power of fatherhood. And while Portia obeys her own father – unlike Shakespeare's previous heroines, Juliet, and Hermia in *A Midsummer Night's Dream* – the playwright transfers an act of defiance to Jessica, a character new to the Venetian story (and incidentally provides ridicule of Old Gobbo in Launcelot's part). When Portia confronts Shylock in the trial scene she faces an outraged father as well as a vindictive usurer. As imaginative creations therefore Portia and Shylock are interdependent, although they stand for opposing values and are depicted in contrasted styles. The oxymoron or displaced associations of Shylock's 'merry bond' expresses much of the underlying artistry in the play.

Portia is the first of Shakespeare's mature, wise and lovable heroines. Mainly, of course, she is created for us through her own speeches, with their transition from mischievous wit to gracious eloquence, but her role is also prepared for and sustained through the admiration of the other characters. Shylock enters without any such preparation, but the clipped wording of his introductory speech – 'Three thousand ducats, well' – at once establishes a strong, unanticipated personality with startling dramatic economy. His words seem to bite into lived experience much more sharply than the sociable talk in the opening scene; as he angles with Bassanio, we feel the pressure of hidden calculations and repressed feelings, where the sheltered young aristocrat is out of his depth; and when Shylock lets himself go, as in 'my meaning in saying he is a good man' (or again, later, in 'Hath not a Jew eyes?'), his comparative volubility gives a sense of the release of pent-up emotion, rather than idle rhetorical repetition. He is one of the first characters for whom Shakespeare has invented a background of personal motivation over and beyond what is needed for the mechanism of the plot, as appears (after the aside leaving no doubt about his hatred) through his indirect reaction to Antonio's cold demand for a loan and then in his sudden shift from muttered hesitation to explicit challenge (I.iii.103–29):

> – Three thousand ducats – 'tis a good round sum.
> Three months from twelve; then let me see, the rate –
> – Well, Shylock, shall we be beholding to you?
> – Signior Antonio, many a time and oft
> In the Rialto you have rated me
> About my moneys and my usances . . .

And, as he goes on:

> Well then, it now appears you need my help . . .
> You, that did void your rheum upon my beard,
> And foot me as you spurn a stranger cur
> Over your threshold; moneys is your suit.
> What should I say to you? Should I not say,
> 'Hath a dog money? Is it possible
> A cur can lend three thousand ducats?' Or
> Shall I bend low and in a bondman's key,
> With bated breath and whisp'ring humbleness,
> Say this:
> 'Fair sir, you spet on me on Wednesday last,
> You spurn'd me such a day, another time
> You call'd me dog; and for these courtesies
> I'll lend you thus much moneys'?

This is fully dramatic verse, acting out the subject rather than talking about it – as for instance with the curled lip and forced expulsion of breath required by the phrase, 'spurn a stranger cur', or in the whine of 'a bondman's key, / With bated breath'; Shylock cannot resist seeing and hearing another self performing in an imagined dialogue that gives vent to his throbbing resentment. He puns on the words 'rate', 'rated' and 'cur', 'courtesies', not wittily but almost compulsively, as if he cannot evade certain repetitions of ideas. In his resentment as a Jew, he speaks momentarily for the bottom layer in Venetian society, the 'bondman' – whom he will recall again during his speeches in the trial scene. At this point, Shylock is far removed from a comic villain like Barabas or a stage miser like Euclio (the Roman ancestor of Harpagon); he exposes a raw nerve in the wealth- and pleasure-loving society of Venice.

At the same time, he exposes a gap in the portrayal of Antonio, whose insults to him contradict the grave courtesy of the rest of his behaviour – a contradiction Shakespeare does not try to explain. For the moment, Shylock, in spite of his resentment, seems to wish, or half-wish, for a contact with Antonio that at least acknowledges his human dignity. By repelling this advance and preferring to borrow as an 'enemy', Antonio seems to share some responsibility for the next move, as Shylock changes from 'a bondman's key' to the sinister proposition of his 'merry bond'.

In the theatre, we naturally presume that the bond will not remain a fantasy or 'merry sport', as Shylock calls it; but the stagecraft by which Shakespeare brings it close to a grim reality is masterly. Between the agreement about the bond, in Act I, Scene iii, and the central episode where at Belmont (in Act III, Scene ii) Bassanio both wins Portia and learns of Antonio's peril, ten short scenes intervene, occupying nearly a third of the play's acting time. The first and two more of those ten scenes, set at Belmont, point towards Bassanio's success by showing Morocco and then Arragon choosing the wrong caskets. Between the first scene for Morocco and the second, while time at Belmont appears to stand still, five scenes at Venice show the bustle before Bassanio's departure, interlarded with Gobbo's clowning and Jessica's elopement; Shylock only appears once, at home with his daughter. Then, in more staccato rhythm, come the scenes of Morocco's choice, news at Venice, Arragon's choice, and more news at Venice, with the reappearance of Shylock. Antonio only speaks a few insignificant lines in the whole course of this sequence. There is no proportion between acting time and fictional time, or between acting time and the magnitude of the events from the main plot directly shown on the stage. But the pacing serves wonderfully to 'fix expectation', as Dr Johnson says, and the whole sequence could be taken to justify his claim that Shakespeare's stage exhibits the 'mingled ... course of the world', in which 'the loss of one is the gain of another', and in which, 'at the same time, the reveller is hasting to his wine, and the mourner burying his friend'. Thus the first of what I have called scenes of news (II.viii) is given over to those indistinguishable but indispensable Venetians, Salerio and Solanio. Three lines refer us to the movements of Bassanio, Gratiano and Lorenzo; and, as we learn that Bassanio is at last 'under sail', we think of Belmont, where we have just witnessed Morocco's disappointment; but the speakers are thinking of 'the villain Jew' and his 'outcries' over ducats and daughter – and then of Antonio, with an uneasiness quickened by a report of the wreck of a Venetian ship and yet sweetened by their admiration for his tender parting from Bassanio. Although we guess the worst from the report about the ship, on stage it is still a guarded, indefinite rumour; but on the other hand, Shylock has become more menacing, all the more because he has called in the help of 'the duke'. The menace to Antonio is still indirect, but it is charged with a fresh emotion because Shylock has lost his daughter. To 'all the boys in Venice' he has become a figure of fun, but it is noticeable that to Solanio he is neither comic nor tragic but 'strange': 'I never heard a passion so confus'd, / So strange, outrageous, and so variable.' The 'mingled . . . course of the world' is concentrated into a 'confus'd' and 'variable' passion.

The second scene of reports at Venice (III.i) opens with definite news of Antonio's loss at 'the Goodwins' (Solanio and Salerio still wishing it were only a rumour) and continues with Shylock's vehement threat of 'revenge' and then his serio-comic subjection to reports from Tubal. Possibly improving upon hints from *The Jew of Malta*, Shakespeare makes Shylock justify his revenge 'by Christian example'; and he only makes Shylock refer to Antonio – 'There I have another bad match. A bankrupt, a prodigal, who dare scarce show his head on the Rialto' – in reply to Salerio and Solanio, and after they have been taunting him over Jessica. In his illuminating chapter about *The Merchant of Venice*, C. L. Barber has argued that the last part of this scene is 'dry' comedy in keeping with Bergson's analysis, with Tubal twitching Shylock like a puppet, and that, though 'there *is* pathos' in the dialogue when Shylock mentions Leah's ring, it only 'makes the laughter all the more hilarious'.[8] Much here depends upon our reaction to Jessica. Adding theft to elopement and extravagance to theft, has she been, as one modern critic holds, 'a callous little bitch', or can we hold, with another critic, that her 'prodigality', though a 'fault', is 'generous' and 'understandable'?[9] If *The Merchant of Venice* were a modern problem play, we should expect to find this question debated or examined, but Shakespeare leaves it in the air. He seems to bank on sympathy with a romantic elopement but on the other hand he keeps Shylock human in his scene with Jessica, an austere parent but by no means a harsh comic ogre. The effect of Shylock's disputed speech to Tubal when he recalls his wife's gift seems to me not 'hilarious' because mechanical, but 'strange' once again, with a disturbing shift of perspective. He has begun the dialogue with a self-pitying lamentation, bordering on the comic-grotesque: 'The curse never fell upon our nation till now, I never felt it till now . . . I would my daughter were dead at my foot, and the jewels in her ear! . . . no satisfaction, no revenge . . . no tears but a' my shedding' (III.i.83–96). 'Yes', says Tubal, almost the comic stooge:

> other men have ill luck too. Antonio, as I heard in Genoa –
> – What, what, what? ill luck, ill luck?
> – Hath an argosy cast away, coming from Tripolis.
> – I thank God, I thank God. Is it true, is it true?
> – I spoke with some of the sailors that escap'd the wrack.

This item brings Antonio's misfortunes a step closer than before:

> – I thank thee, good Tubal, good news, good news! Ha, ha! Heard in Genoa?
> – Your daughter spent in Genoa, as I heard, one night fourscore ducats.
> – Thou stick'st a dagger in me. I shall never see my gold again. Fourscore ducats at a sitting, fourscore ducats!
> – There came divers of Antonio's creditors in my company to Venice that swear he cannot choose but break.

This of course will mean a much bigger loss than fourscore ducats; but Shylock says:

> – I am very glad of it. I'll plague him, I'll torture him. I am glad of it.
> – One of them show'd me a ring that he had of your daughter for a monkey.
> – Out upon her! Thou torturest me, Tubal. It was my turkis, I had it of Leah when I was a bachelor. I would not have given it for a wilderness of monkeys.
> – But Antonio is certainly undone.
> – Nay, that's true, that's very true . . . I will have the heart of him if he forfeit . . .

Here, surely, Shakespeare is exploring the same indecorum or disproportionateness of human emotions that he makes Leonato reflect upon, in *Much Ado*, by saying 'How much better is it to weep at joy than to joy at weeping!' The decisive impulse towards Shylock's revenge comes, irrelevantly, from his outraged feeling as a father. But meanwhile the transaction with the ring has its own circularity, since what had been Shylock's love-token has become a commodity through his daughter's love-affair, going, by a deft stroke of dramatic accounting, in payment to one of Antonio's creditors.[10] A ring symbolises another kind of bond, as we are to witness in the following scene between Portia and Bassanio. There, Portia is to say to *her* bachelor, 'Since you are dear bought, I will love you dear.' But Shylock has no language to relate love and money.

If *The Merchant of Venice* were truly a problem play we should expect to find the culminating treatment of the problem in the trial scene. Certainly that contains a problem, in the narrow sense of an urgent puzzle that only the heroine knows how to solve. And of course it makes exciting theatre, with a resounding demonstration of a contrast between legalism and humanity. But whether it can be taken as an allegory of Justice and Mercy, the Old Law and the New, as some critics have claimed, is very doubtful.[11] Portia's famous speech on mercy, which has no counterpart in the original *novella*, contributes nothing to the result of the trial; and the whole clash of arguments in the courtroom seems to belong to the fashion in Renaissance literature, deriving from Roman schools of oratory, of constructing debating exercises upon imaginary points of law.[12] The excitement of the lawsuit moves on a different plane of interest from the moral questions that have been aroused concerning Shylock. Nothing is said, for instance, about the general place of usury in Venetian (or Elizabethan) society. Portia catches Shylock, with superb timing, in his own psychological trap. But the tension of sympathies aroused in Shylock's first meeting with Antonio, and again by Jessica's flight, is left unresolved, and yet returns to complicate the close of the trial. In Ser Giovanni, the annulment of the bond ends in laughter: 'Everyone present rejoiced greatly . . . and jeered at the Jew, saying, "He who thought to ensnare others, is caught himself." Then the Jew, seeing he could not do what he had wished, took the bond and tore it in pieces in a fury'[13] – thus disappearing from the story. Shakespeare, instead, at this point brings in another provision of Venetian law, that no one appears to have thought of except Portia, enabling the court to crush Shylock completely. Now, we can argue that Antonio shows mercy by persuading the court to remit the extreme penalty and that an Elizabethan audience would be simply gratified by Shylock's enforced conversion. But the former argument results from a contrivance added to the plot and the latter sounds like special pleading. Above all, there is no connection with a sense of justice in penalising Shylock for the benefit of 'his son Lorenzo and his daughter', whom he is far from having wronged in any perceivable way. This item is a piece of opportunism on the dramatist's part. For the sake of a romantic conclusion, and in keeping with the way he has modified Portia's story, Shakespeare crushes Shylock in his role as a father.

In his speeches at the trial, Shylock tellingly invokes the impersonal force of law and tellingly restates the contrasting theme of irrational or non-rational choice in life, canvassed by Antonio's friends at the beginning of the play. But the more powerful his presence has been, the more there seem to be elements of contrivance in his dismissal. Only a supreme playwright could get round this self-imposed obstacle successfully, and Shakespeare accomplishes it with dazzling skill. He gives Shylock a broken dignity in his parting speeches (how solemn Shylock's exit is depends, of course, upon the actor), before closing the courtroom scene in a comic *diminuendo*. Then, for the last scene, comes the formalised duet between Lorenzo and Jessica about remote tragic lovers, a lyrical exorcism dispelling the ugly possibilities latent in their part of the story, which leads on to sustained reflections, helped by music, on the idea of harmony, and finally to the passage of the lovers' recognition over the rings, potentially serious but prosaically light-hearted in tone. But the discords surrounding Shylock – a 'quasi-tragic' figure, as he has been called[14] – have been conjured away rather than resolved. As recent critics have pointed out, there is no factor of recognition or comic removal of error in the process of Shylock's defeat, and, on the other side, the final recognition scene is distanced from the main community in the play, unlike those in Shakespeare's other comedies. The invocation of harmony depends upon abstraction from Venetian affairs for its beautiful effect.

In some ways, then, *The Merchant of Venice* corresponds to the contemporary tendency in Italy towards serious comedy, or to the tendency towards tragi-comedy. Externally, it corresponds to tragi-comedy as Fletcher was to define it, in that it draws towards the danger, but not the death. Yet it has only very little in common with the strained nobility of sentiment characteristic of the tragi-comedy of the period. Shakespeare seems much more interested in the contradictions between irrational emotional impulses and social rationality as expressed (for example) by law – contradictions which need not result in theatrical realism but fit awkwardly, none the less, into the framework of traditional romance on the stage. That further incompatibility between moral theme and conventional dramatic form may justify critics in inventing the category of problem plays for *All's Well* and *Measure for Measure*. And although Shakespeare has stayed on the side of romance in *The Merchant of Venice*, he has also turned in the direction of those future problem plays.

3. Falstaff and the life of shadows

Theseus: The best in this kind are but shadows; and the worst are no worse,
   if imagination amend them.
Hippolyta: It must be your imagination then, and not theirs.

A Midsummer Night's Dream

What is it that makes us laugh about Falstaff? This is perhaps a
naïve, unanswerable question. In his magisterial lecture on 'The
rejection of Falstaff', Bradley set a part of it, the query why we laugh
at the fat knight, judiciously aside. Nevertheless, it is still tempting to
assail the indefinable and, throwing caution to the winds, to try to
sprinkle salt on the tail of that particularly large but paradoxically
lively bird, even at the risk of losing, along with the caution, the salt.
It is particularly tempting if we want to examine the general nature of
comedy and – a related but distinct set of questions – the place
Falstaff occupies in the two parts of *Henry I V*.

Some of the unavoidable niggles that beset this sort of inquiry are
that we do not all, as readers, laugh at the same things or even twice
at the same place; that we are much more prone to laugh in company
than alone; and that, even in the theatre, our laughter depends to
some extent on accidents of the occasion. Further, the impulse to
laugh, when studying Shakespeare, is to some extent lumbered with
the ponderous gear of annotations. And, more generally, a perfect,
utopian theory of laughter would take care of the difference between
the occasions when we laugh outright and the occasions when we
merely feel an inclination to laugh. But the present essay – caution
having been disregarded – cannot pause over such niceties (just as it
will only be concerned with the canonical or *echt* Falstaff, as the two
historical plays body him forth).

Perhaps the best starting-place is Bergson's theory of laughter,
insufficient though it is. According to Bergson, then, we laugh when
we perceive 'something mechanical encrusted on something living',
the physical encroaching upon the sphere of mental freedom, a
human being behaving like a physical object; at bottom, our laughter

is prompted by *raideur* rather than *laideur*, by 'the unsprightly' rather than 'the unsightly'.[1] In comedy, it is directed against the personage who has sunk his individuality in the routines of a social or professional or temperamental type, who has forfeited his waking spontaneity to some automatism of behaviour resembling absentmindedness. And, since mechanical thought or behaviour, though necessary within limits, is ultimately hostile to social evolution, or the *élan vital*, the underlying function of comedy is to marshal our collective and corrective laughter against such obstacles to freedom. This theory applies well to a great deal in Molière, and to Labiche, Bergson's second choice for purposes of illustration; equally, it could apply almost intact to the superbly intricate contraptions for laughter devised by Bergson's contemporary, Georges Feydeau.

However, Bergson's purview is limited by assumptions traditional with criticism, especially in France, such as the assumption that comedy and laughter are very nearly the same thing. Even within those limits, he pays no attention to those characters who make us laugh *with* them and not at them. And, as Albert Thibaudet noted in his study of Bergson, the philosopher's analysis of stage comedy, even in Molière, omits the indispensable factor of mobility: 'a comedy is a movement, I don't mean necessarily an action'.[2] For Thibaudet, this is a correlative to the subliminal movement we experience inwardly when responding to any work of art. However, by the same token, it is also an expression of Bergsonian *élan*. And perhaps one can carry this observation a step further and save the appearances for Bergson's theory of the comic by supposing that those stage characters who make us laugh intentionally, and not inadvertently, have become, at least for the time being, delegates for the author by anticipating some threatened incursion of the mechanical upon the vital and triumphantly reversing the flow. If so, they represent the upsurge of spontaneity over automatism, a process more fundamental to comedy than any enforcement of social correction. This line of reasoning may account also for those stimuli to laughter that other theorists have emphasised, though they are only marginal from Bergson's point of view, such as the laughter due to surprise or incongruity or to release from the breaking of a taboo. Although in cases like those our laughter may not have been prompted by 'something mechanical encrusted on something living', it could still be argued that the cause of it was the mental jolt of expecting to see a logical or a moral rule at work but finding instead that the mechanism of the rule had been overcome. This still has less to do with social solidarity than with the subconscious pleasure of release. But in the theatre there is surely also a further level of interplay on some such lines between the mechanical and the vital. Once the train of laughter has been set going, we seem to store up a reserve for extra additional laughter precisely in our alerted uncertainty as to when next and which way the cat is going to jump.

Falstaff is surely the grand example of such multiplicity, or deep duplicity, in the causes of laughter. 'The brain of this foolish-compounded clay, man', he can fairly claim, 'is not able to invent any thing that intends to laughter more than I invent or is invented on me: I am not only witty in myself, but the cause that wit is in other men' (2 *Henry IV*, I.ii.7–10). When Bradley and like-minded critics gloss over the causes why others laugh *at* Falstaff, it must be because they seem so obvious – 'gross as a mountain' – and not because they are unfathomable. First, of course, his fatness, a classic instance of what Aristotle would call the ludicrous arising from a defect that is not destructive or what Bergson would call the physical encroaching upon the mental (since it is represented as a consequence of his chosen way of life). Then his drinking, his cowardice (or, if you prefer, his 'instinct' not to be heroic), his apparently compulsive lying. Poins and the Prince foresee very well what mechanisms they will spring in him when they plan their 'jest' at Gad's Hill. And Shakespeare has made him a perpetual comic butt, because, as Harry Levin has pointed out, he has staged him as a walking paradox, a Renaissance knight without a horse; 'uncolted' (*1 Henry IV*, II.ii.39) by the Prince, and commissioned with nothing better for the war than 'a charge of foot'.[3]

On the other hand, when Poins anticipates 'the incomprehensible' (the illimitable) 'lies that this same fat rogue will tell', he hints at just the opposite side of Falstaff, his inventiveness, his inexhaustible resilience, his predictable unpredictability. These have to do with the reasons why we laugh *with* him. He is always quick at changing an awkward subject. And his lies are foxy evasions, not empty fantasies like the boasts of Baron Munchausen or the daydreams of Walter Mitty. They match the positive resourcefulness of his wit, his ability to play with words and, beyond that, to disconnect and recombine the accepted rules of moral judgement. In thought as in act, he is the arch-opponent of regularity: 'Give you a reason on compulsion? if reasons were as plentiful as blackberries, I would give no man a reason upon compulsion, I.' We laugh, one may suggest, at sallies like this both because he is cornered and knows he is cornered and because he can nevertheless trump up something almost indistinguishable from a valid reply, unexpected and, in the fullest sense, diverting. We laugh because he is caught out, because just the same he has been too quick for us, and further (I believe) because we are not sure which of these thoughts is uppermost. This kind of uncertainty is fundamental in comic tradition.

Falstaff's puns form one of his ways of circumventing mechanisms of thought, by taking advantage of what are possibly no more than accidental associations of ideas in language. He can treat 'reasons' like 'blackberries', for instance because the word was pronounced *raisins*; thereby evading an awkward truth. Or he can pun spontaneously, from high spirits, as when, later in the same tavern scene, he enjoins his companions to 'clap to the doors! Watch to-night, pray to-morrow' (*1 Henry IV*, II.iv.276–7) – out of sheer relief on learning that the stolen money he thought he had been filched of could be used for his benefit after all. His Biblical 'Watch and pray' not merely pretends to sanctify their proposed drinking-bout (or *watch*), but also recalls his fellow-thieves to their predatory highway code, thus covertly reinstating his own manliness at the same time.[4]

He is similarly inventive in the vocabulary of aggression, protestation, belittlement and abuse. If the others will not credit his valour on Gad's Hill, he is 'a shotten herring' or 'a bunch of radish'. Hal, disbelieving him, becomes 'you starveling ... you dried neat's tongue, you bull's pizzle, you stock-fish'. All this Carnival, or Billingsgate, raillery is, of course, part of the game that he shares with the Prince. In their first scene together, when Hal has disobligingly knocked down his attempts to find expressions for his alleged 'melancholy', Falstaff retorts, 'Thou hast the most unsavoury similes and art indeed the most comparative, rascalliest, sweet young prince.' Set point to the 'fat-witted' knight; but it seems clear enough why the Prince should enjoy his company.

The game they play calls for stylistic agility (for the copiousness in words the Elizabethans admired and for skill in calculated breaches of literary decorum) besides licensing a free-for-all of mock aggression. It was fashionable in the 1590s and was related to the new literary conception of wit that was then emerging. Nashe, for example, relishes what he calls the 'sport' of railing; after a two-page effusion over a literary enemy, he characteristically adds,

Redeo ad vos, mei auditores [back to you, listeners]: have I not an indifferent pretty vein in spur-galling an ass? If you knew how extemporal it were at this instant, and with what haste it is writ, you would say so. But I would not have you think that all this that is set down here is in good earnest, for then you go by St Giles the wrong way to Westminster; but only to show how for a need I could rail if I were thoroughly fired.[5]

Shakespeare's courtly wits, as in *Love's Labour's Lost*, indulge themselves in a similar vein. But it is especially appropriate to a Bohemian or adventurer of the pen like Nashe; indeed, it becomes Nashe's principal stock-in-trade, as he bawls his academically certified wares in the market-place. And it is peculiarly appropriate to Falstaff's position as a gently-bred adventurer who compensates through language for deficiencies in the more solid advantages due to his rank. In language, Falstaff is a lord. He commands a ruffianly composure of speech, a leisured pace permitting lightning thrusts, and a compendious range of tone including masterful coarseness. It is the coarseness that Hotspur wants to hear from Lady Percy when she swears (*1 Henry IV*, III.i.247–56). It distinguishes Falstaff completely from a mere 'swaggerer' of the day and ranter of playhouse tags like Pistol; style is his real, and his only real, ground of equality with the Prince. Yet his speech is repeatedly ambiguous in tone, corresponding to the indeterminateness of his social position. As William Empson has put it, 'Falstaff is the first major joke by the English against their class system; he is a picture of how badly you can behave, and still get away with it, if you are a gentleman – a mere common rogue would not have been nearly so funny.'[6]

Whether his tone for the moment is aggressive or not, Falstaff habitually asserts himself by defeating expectation. His very first appearance must have come as a surprise to the Elizabethans; they could have anticipated a wild gallant or a rumbustious clown to accompany Hal on to the stage, but not a corpulent, benevolent, apparently deliberative greyhead. On his opening words, noncommittal in tone ('Now, Hal, what time of day is it, lad?'), the Prince pounces with the imputation that his proper qualities are gluttony and sloth, which are much what stage tradition, if not historical legend, would attach to such a personage:

Thou art so fat-witted with drinking of old sack, and unbuttoning thee after supper, and sleeping upon benches after noon, that thou hast forgotten to demand that truly which thou wouldest truly know. What a devil hast thou to do with the time of the day?

But Falstaff at once shows that he has, on the contrary, a concern of
sorts with the passage of time, by asking a series of questions about
the future, in the course of which, far from admitting to sloth or
gluttony, he fleetingly adopts the voices of manly 'resolution',
'melancholy' solicitation, and even sorrowful 'amendment of life'
(I.ii.102). He may resemble Gluttony or Sloth – or alternatively, Riot
– but in himself, his manner implies, he is not to be identified with
any of them (any more than Jaques's melancholy is the scholar's or
the musician's or the courtier's, 'but it is a melancholy of mine own,
compounded of many simples, extracted from many objects').

And Falstaff's personality seems always in movement, going
against the stream of opinion. He repeatedly advances the idea of his
own worth, not simply by bragging when occasion favours, but by
jocular assertion and, especially in his early scenes, by insinuating
that the standards he could be criticised by, the yardsticks that
society commonly applies to worthiness, are habitually
misconceived or misplaced. He does not expect his assertions to be
taken 'in good earnest' any more (or any less) than Nashe; and, at
least before the battle scenes, he does not single out any one of
society's values for direct criticism (which might seem to fix him in
the vulnerable position of a malcontent or satirist). Instead, he works
through parody and calculated irrelevance, or the dissociation of
received ideas. His counter-attack on public values is mobile and
indirect, as, in the opening dialogue, when he responds to the
Prince's sarcasm by dignifying (or affecting to dignify?) his
occupation as a thief:

Indeed you come near me now, Hal, for we that take purses go by the moon
and the seven stars, and not by Phoebus, he, 'that wand'ring knight so fair'
[which disposes of Hal's question about 'the time of the day']. And I prithee,
sweet wag, when thou art a king . . . let not us that are squires of the night's
body be call'd thieves of the day's beauty. Let us be Diana's foresters,
gentlemen of the shade, minions of the moon, and let men say we be men of
good government, being govern'd, as the sea is, by our noble and chaste
mistress the moon, under whose countenance we steal.

Hearing this, an Elizabethan audience must have been so
sidetracked, or delighted, by the pell-mell parodies of euphuism,
balladry, popular romance, and even of the worship of Cynthia,
mistress of the sea, herself, that they could not muster any of their
proper indignation at the naked proposal Falstaff is putting forward
or at his hint that it is only fancy names, arbitrary titles, that
distinguish the honest citizen from the thief (as Gadshill supportively

observes a few scenes later, ' "homo" is a common name to all men'
(II.i.95)).

Whatever else Falstaff may be set to do in *Henry I V*, he has begun
with the ancient comic operation of turning the world upside-down.
And soon he returns to this even more insidiously. After the Prince
has rebuffed him with reminders about the gallows and has teased
him with the promise of a hangman's job, instead of the momentarily
hoped-for office of a judge, Falstaff shifts his key to the Biblical:

> But, Hal, I prithee trouble me no more with vanity; I would to God thou and
> I knew where a commodity of good names were to be bought;

and, as if mounting the pulpit:

> An old lord of the Council rated me the other day in the street about you, sir,
> but I mark'd him not, and yet he talk'd very wisely, but I regarded him not,
> and yet he talk'd wisely, and in the street too.
>
> (*1 Henry I V*, I.ii.81–7)

Part of Falstaff's ploy here is to pretend, in all generosity, that he has
been receiving blame because of Hal and not the other way about.
And in the midst of his sermonising he can suddenly swerve into a
good, downright tavernly oath: 'I'll be damn'd for never a king's son
in Christendom' (I.ii.97). But as soon as Hal, taking his cue from
this, taunts him with a reminder about taking purses, Falstaff reverts
to his Biblical strain: 'Why, Hal, 'tis my vocation, Hal, 'tis no sin for
a man to labour in his vocation' (I.ii.104–5). Critics, noting
Falstaff's very frequent allusions to the Bible (particularly the book
of Proverbs and the parable of the Prodigal Son), are fond of
explaining that he is ridiculing the language of Puritanism; but it was
equally the language of the Book of Homilies and the established
Church.[7] As far as parody goes, his subversiveness is comprehensive.

Yet he is not simply a stage jester any more than he is simply a
rogue. None of the roles that critics or other characters on the stage
attribute to him defines him adequately as a character or as a figure
in the play. He is not, for instance, a Morality-play Vice, however he
may be compared to such. Apart from anything else, it makes
nonsense of his relations with Hal to think of him as a
personification of the Prince's human proneness to sin, or to speak as
if he ever tempts the Prince successfully in the course of the play or
gains any ascendancy over his will. He is not a traditional braggart
soldier, if only because he is far too intelligent. He is not exactly a
Lord of Misrule; if he can be said to preside over revels in Eastcheap,

it is more in our imagination than in the view of his company as a whole. Nor is he exactly a trickster, or ironic buffoon, in the line of classical comedy, in spite of his aptitude for turning the world upside-down. He neither pursues any ingenious intrigue in the manner of New Comedy (though he swindles Mistress Quickly and Shallow) nor consistently entertains any world-changing fantasy like a hero from Aristophanes. He is too deeply enmeshed in common reality to imagine that he can change the world, and he takes his adventures as they come. He is constantly improvising, assuming a role. In the extemporised play scene that marks the highest point of his concord with Hal, he revels in parodying an actor; but through all his assumed voices we can hear a voice of his own, coming out most clearly perhaps in soliloquies – of which he has more than any other speaker in the play. It seems no accident that he became, in his own name, a legendary figure, as quickly and as lastingly as Hamlet. We seem to be in the presence of a richly complex personality, with a reserve of self-awareness underneath all his clowning.

In Maurice Morgann's apologia for Falstaff, there is a striking footnote where Morgann outlines the principles that, in his view, require a critic of Shakespeare to explain the characters of Shakespeare's people 'from those parts of the composition which are *inferred* only, and not distinctly shewn', and 'to account for their conduct from the *whole* of character, from general principles, from latent motives, and from policies not avowed'.[8] The 'historic' or biographical method of interpretation that Morgann erected upon this insight has been thoroughly, perhaps too thoroughly, exploded. And in Falstaff's case, such apparently solid biographical facts as we are given – that as a boy he had been 'page to Thomas Mowbray, Duke of Norfolk' and had known John of Gaunt – are not disclosed until the second half of the second play (2 *Henry IV*, III.ii.25–6, 324). Nevertheless, one can hardly deny that Morgann brought out something vital about the *impression* (to use his own term) that Shakespeare gives us about Falstaff and gives us from the outset. Only, Shakespeare's methods were not biographical in anything like the way that (for example) Ibsen's methods could be so described. One of the means that Shakespeare uses is to suggest through the dialogue that a particular role will fit Falstaff or that he will display a particular disposition of mind, and then almost at once to make the character belie it. As Falstaff speaks, we perceive that the characteristics we have been led to expect of him are incorrect or incomplete or shadowy approximations at best. It quickly turns out that Hal's first

description of him as Sloth and Gluttony is no more than a caricature. When he has behaved like a braggart soldier, he can switch to
the ironic buffoon. When he is patently and professedly acting ('as
like one of these harlotry players as ever I see!', says the Hostess (*1
Henry IV*, II.iv.395–6)), it turns out that he is pleading his own
cause. He is reputed to be misleading the Prince, but Falstaff himself
says just the opposite, and in any case we never see him do it.

Watching or reading the play, of course, we do not sift such
conflicting bits of evidence and work out a decisive verdict that
would satisfy a jury in a court of law. There is nothing like the
question whether Hal is really the irresponsible his father and the
others suppose him to be, a question Shakespeare takes care to set at
rest very soon. But with Falstaff, allegations and half-truths are
allowed to remain at the back of our minds, without being clearly
dispelled. We neither confirm nor reject them completely but are
allowed and even prompted to imagine that they may be true, but
only to limited facets of his character, or true to something in his
unseen conduct off-stage. These half-defined approximations are
like shadows in a picture that throw the figure into relief. To defeat
our expectations, then, is part of Falstaff's comic tactics, and to keep
us uncertain about the essential Falstaff is part of Shakespeare's
strategy as a comic playwright. But further, Shakespeare has given
Falstaff hints of an inner consciousness, at variance with his outward
roles, that go some way towards justifying Morgann's search for
'latent motives' and 'policies not avowed'.

Critics have been reluctant to consider that Falstaff has anything
like a conscience or any doubts about himself. Hazlitt praises his
'absolute self-possession' and 'self-complacency',[9] and Bradley insists that we laugh *with* Falstaff precisely because he is so 'happy and
entirely at his ease' in 'his humorous superiority to everything serious, and the freedom of soul enjoyed in it'.[10] And in W. H. Auden's
view, 'time does not exist' for Falstaff (but then Auden holds that the
essential man belongs to *opera buffa*, and is out of place in *Henry
IV*).[11] However, Falstaff (a 'proud Jack' to the tavern-drawers,
according to Hal (*1 Henry IV*, II.iv.11)) is not remarkable for
bonhomie; and he never expresses himself as cheerful or satisfied for
long. On the contrary, his favourite terms of reference for his
favourite subject, himself, imply, if they are taken in earnest, a sense
of injury and regret for neglected valour, lost innocence, and either
material or spiritual insecurity. His first speeches are questions about

the future, which we are given no reason to think are totally flippant. If he can loudly contradict his years in the heat of the robbery scene ('What, ye knaves, young men must live' (II.ii.90–1)), his next scene shows him affectedly brooding over them: 'There lives not three good men unhang'd in England, and one of them is fat and grows old' (II.iv.30–2). This cadence swerves, of course, into ludicrous self-mockery – 'I would I were a weaver, I could sing psalms, or anything' – and this whole speech is a typical mock diatribe or mock complaint, in which Falstaff's claims of 'manhood' and self-righteousness are incongruous with one another and doubly incongruous in the light of his behaviour.

Still, these are his two most frequent themes, with particular emphasis on the theme of religion. 'Before I knew thee, Hal', he has affirmed, 'I knew nothing, and now am I, if a man should speak truly, little better than one of the wicked' (I.ii.92–5). And later, with no one more appreciative than Bardolph to hear him:

Well, I'll repent, and that suddenly, while I am in some liking... And I have not forgotten what the inside of a church is made of, I am a peppercorn, a brewer's horse. The inside of a church! Company, villainous company, hath been the spoil of me.[12]   (III.iii.4–10)

Naturally, each of these outbursts of elderly grumbling, sorrowful grievance, or rueful contrition on the part of 'Monsieur Remorse', as Poins calls him, strikes us as yet another of Falstaff's jokes. And whenever he alludes to repentance, he quickly veers away from it. Nevertheless, persistent jokes on the same topic tell us something about what weighs on a man's mind; it seems as if Falstaff were one of those fat men in whom a thin man is struggling to get out. Without probing into 'latent motives', Shakespeare has portrayed in him, not 'absolute self-possession', but the condition of mind of a man of intellectual power, wounded in his self-esteem and conscience, who cannot bring himself to do anything about it, but finds an escape from his self-image in joking. Far from expressing 'self-complacency' or complete 'freedom of soul', his 'humorous superiority to everything serious', if it exists, seems to be gained at the cost of self-mockery – which mocks the world as well, in order to redress the balance. But without the potential, camouflaged seriousness in his jokes (together with the background of seriousness in the political action in the play), many of them would lose their force and point.

To return to his first scene for an example:

But, Hal, I prithee trouble me no more with vanity; I would to God thou and
I knew where a commodity of good names were to be bought ...

(I.ii.81–3)

The word *vanity*, which initiates Falstaff's diversion to Biblical
parody, is not simply a pretended rebuke to Hal's 'unsavoury similes'
but also an oblique acknowledgement of the seriousness running
through their previous talk, particularly by way of Hal's references
to hanging. And the irony about 'good names' (loaded with the word
commodity, which usually has a smack of skulduggery about it in
Shakespeare)[13] would lose half its dramatic point if it were no more
than a capricious quip or satiric side-thrust against the established
order. There is the second irony that Falstaff is pretending to be in
earnest, while hinting to the Prince, without openly admitting, that
on another level he is seriously engaged as well. That the two ironies
should work against one another both contributes to the continuity
of Falstaff's part in the play and adds to the store of laughter from
uncertainty in the minds of the audience.

By way of contrast, consider the tone Shakespeare was to give to
an ironist of a different stamp, Iago:

> Good name in man and woman, dear my lord,
> Is the immediate jewel of their souls.
> Who steals my purse steals trash; 'tis something, nothing ...
>
> (*Othello*, III.iii.155–7)

These are the sententious accents of hypocrisy. Iago is quite
indifferent to the maxim he is manipulating, and must be felt to be
indifferent so that we can concentrate on the effect of his words upon
Othello; whereas Falstaff knows very well that he is not really
pulling the wool over the eyes of the Prince, but he is personally, if
covertly, involved in what he says.

Once or twice in *Part 1* this concern shows more directly. When
Falstaff has to hide from the sheriff, Hal tells the others, 'Now, my
masters, for a true face and good conscience' (IV.iv.501–2) while
Falstaff exits with an aside – 'Both which I have had, but their date is
out, and therefore I'll hide me.' And as he approaches the battlefield,
he is given his second soliloquy. Since he comes on here in the
contemporary guise of a fraudulent recruiting officer and since this is
the first time he has gained any profit in the course of the play, we
should expect to find him in a mood of malicious glee if he were

simply a conventional stage rogue or Morality Vice. But instead, he is unexpectedly 'ashamed':

If I be not asham'd of my soldiers, I am a sous'd gurnet. I have misus'd the King's press damnably ... No eye hath seen such scarecrows. I'll not march through Coventry with them, that's flat ...

(IV.ii.11–13, 38–9)

He shrugs off this mood almost at once:

There's not a shirt and a half in all my company ... But that's all one, they'll find linen enough on every hedge.

We are very nearly back to the atmosphere of Eastcheap and Gad's Hill. All the same, the tone of genuine surprise, a novel tone in Falstaff's voice, shows that there has been a progression in his part. The war becomes a testing experience for Falstaff as, on a very different scale, it becomes a testing experience for Hal. It imparts a continuous movement to Falstaff's share in the play, from his early, half-comic protest to Hal – 'I must give over this life, and I will give it over' (I.ii.95–6) – to the slyly conditional resolution or prediction in his last soliloquy, which is also his closing speech:

If I do grow great, I'll grow less, for I'll purge [*repent*] and leave sack, and live cleanly as a nobleman should do.

(V.iv.163–5)

From beginning to end in *Part 1*, Falstaff is engaged with the passage of time, with concern about the future.

The theme of time is crucial to Shakespeare's presentation of what Edward Hall had described as 'The Unquiet Time of King Henry IV'. The guiding thought in the overplot of *Part 1* is the thought of 'redeeming time', with implications at once religious,[14] financial, chivalric and political. In financial terms, it branches out by way of talk about ransom and theft, auditing, debt, and repayment, to return, as it were, to the main line of the action by way of Hal's determination to 'pay the debt I never promised, / ... Redeeming time when men think least I will' (I.ii.209, 217). In the opening scene, though he does not use the word, Henry IV dwells on the thought of the Redeemer. Shakespeare has antedated his project to lead a crusade, treating it as Henry's intended means of absolving England from civil war and, by inference, absolving himself from his guilt as an usurper.[15] Hotspur, eager to 'redeem' 'drowned honour' (I.iii.205), tells his father and uncle that 'yet time serves wherein you may redeem / Your banish'd honours' (I.iii.180–1) – by changing allegiance for a second time in rebellion.[16] On his side, Hal promises to 'redeem' his reputation 'on Percy's head' and his father confirms that he has 'redeem'd ... lost opinion' in the battle (III.ii.132, V.iv.48). For the leading political actors, 'time serves', not to achieve honour, like knights-errant, but to redeem the honour they have already lost, or appear to have lost.

With his ignoble ambition to find out 'where a commodity of good names were to be bought' Falstaff is a parody of this political world. In Hal's company he is like a grotesque father-substitute, and he echoes the King in his grumbles over time mis-spent. His lawlessness and braggartism throw light on Hotspur. Above all, Falstaff is a man in a false position, just as the King, Hotspur, and Hal are all, in their different ways, men in false positions. But Falstaff, of course, has the saving grace of humour. He has an inclusive, if usually ironic, self-awareness that men like Henry IV and Hotspur cannot afford, though some of it seems to have rubbed off on to Hal. This is the obverse of his comic 'remorse': not a 'superiority to everything serious' or simply an addiction to the pleasures of the flesh, but a warm belief in the immediacy and, in the end, authenticity, of his personal existence. 'Banish plump Jack, and banish all the world', he exclaims to Hal, as their improvised play-acting breaks down in a moment of truth; and then, as he prepares to hide from the sheriff, 'Dost thou hear, Hal? Never call a true piece of gold a counterfeit' (II.iv.491–2). This cryptic admonition takes on fuller significance later, in the battle scenes. Falstaff's development there, in close proximity to the political actors, is far from one-sided. His cynical betrayal of his troop of 'ragamuffins' (V.iii.36) matches Worcester's double dealing. His low-minded 'discretion' is pitched against Hotspur's high-minded but futile 'valour'. The conclusion to his famous 'catechism', that 'Honour is a mere scutcheon' (V.i.140), cannot efface the resplendent heroism that Shakespeare gives the Prince, though it still leaves the purely chivalric motives in war and politics open to question.

But at the same time, as at the beginning of the play, the dramatist sets Falstaff in relation to the King, by his arrangement of the kaleidoscopic battle episodes. Taking a hint from Holinshed's statement that at Shrewsbury there were several knights 'apparelled in the king's suit and clothing' (but reducing the chronicler's emphasis on the King's 'high manhood'),[17] Shakespeare shows two episodes in which Douglas is engaged with the 'likeness' or the 'shadows' or the 'counterfeit' of the King. In the first (V.iii.1–29) Douglas kills Sir Walter Blunt, as he says he has already killed Lord Stafford, believing him to be the King himself, until Hotspur undeceives him ('The King hath many marching in his coats'). In the second (V.iv.25–38), meeting the King in person, he can hardly believe that Henry is not 'another counterfeit'. Hal drives Douglas off. Then, while Hal encounters Hotspur in resonantly epic style, in the action to which the whole course of the play has pointed, Douglas re-enters briefly and, in dumb show, apparently kills Falstaff.

But as soon as Falstaff has been left alone on the stage, he jumps up again, undercutting the lofty tones of the champions' verse in his savoury prose:

'Sblood, 'twas time to counterfeit, or that hot termagant Scot had paid me scot and lot too. Counterfeit? I lie, I am no counterfeit. To die is to be a counterfeit, for he is but the counterfeit of a man who hath not the life of a man; but to counterfeit dying, when a man thereby liveth, is to be no counterfeit, but the true and perfect image of life indeed...

(V.iv.113–19)

In this folk-play-style sham resurrection, and in his farcical sham killing of Hotspur immediately afterwards, Falstaff counteracts the high talk of politics and war. Courage in battle has been shown as a reality in the play, and the need for royal authority has been vindicated. But the political scenes have revealed expedience, double dealing, and even a kind of inward privation, not because Henry IV has been shown as a downright Machiavellian like Richard III, but because his rule has been established on false foundations and because the forward drives of conflicting political interests have generated their own ruthless momentum. Falstaff's counterfeiting here revives basic human impulses which the affairs of state would have thwarted or excluded.

At Shrewsbury, Henry has safeguarded his life by the employment of 'shadows'. In another sense also, Shakespeare has extensively used 'shadows' in both parts of the play to give life and imagined reality to the world in which Henry and Falstaff belong. History could be said to require that the action should shift across the country between north and south and that the main actors should refer to characters and events that are not shown on the stage. But in Henry IV Shakespeare has taken particular pains, more I think than in any other of his plays, to go beyond the strict requirements of dramatising history and conjure up the thought of England as a country and, even more strikingly, to conjure up images of individuals off-stage, known to the speakers in the play though unrecorded by the chroniclers.

What is at stake in the Percys' rebellion is the territory of England – 'this soil', as Henry calls it in his opening lines. Shakespeare imagines this, in its continuity and specific variety, as no other poet before him had done. In the first scene of *Part 1*, for instance, we hear of 'stronds' and 'fields' and 'acres', of Herefordshire and Windsor, and all 'the variation of each soil / Betwixt that Holmedon and this seat of ours'. Later, in the scene between Hotspur, Mortimer and Glendower, a map is an essential property. And when Hotspur falls, Hal reflects that

> When that this body did contain a spirit,
> A kingdom for it was too small a bound,
> But now two paces of the vilest earth
> Is room enough. This earth that bears thee dead
> Bears not alive so stout a gentleman.
>
> (V.iv.89–93)

Meanwhile, we have heard, for instance, of 'Severn's sedgy bank' and of Berkeley Castle (the name Hotspur cannot remember (I.iii.98, 242–9)), of Moorditch and the Wild of Kent and Falstaff's route through Coventry. And in *Part 2*, to say nothing of Falstaff's boasted acquaintance with 'all Europe' (II.ii.134), we hear of Northumberland's 'worm-eaten hold of ragged stone' at Warkworth (Induction, 35), of Oxford and Stamford fair, and particularly of localities in or near London – Eastcheap, the St Alban's road, Clement's Inn, Mile-End Green, Turnbull Street, Windsor, the Jerusalem chamber, the Fleet. Both parts are busy with the images of messengers, especially horsemen, hurrying with instructions or news or rushing to or from a battlefield. And each virtually begins with a striking image of this sort, of Sir Walter Blunt 'new lighted' (*1 Henry IV*, I.i.63) after his long ride from Holmedon or of the unnamed gentleman met by Northumberland's servant, Travers, 'spurring hard' and 'almost forespent with speed' on his 'bloodied horse', who had paused only to ask the road to Chester and then 'seem'd in running to devour the way' (*2 Henry IV*, I.i.36, 37, 38, 47) in his headlong flight from Shrewsbury. Amid all this evocation of England's place-names and roads and 'uneven ground' (*1 Henry IV*, II.ii.25) the earthy and earthbound figure of Falstaff seems solidly congenial; he 'lards the lean earth as he walks along' (II.ii.109).

Even closer to the sense of animated reality in both parts of the play are the allusive sketches of non-historical characters whom we hear of though never see. In *Part 1*, they range from the 'old lord of the Council' who (allegedly) had 'rated' Falstaff about Hal 'the other day in the street' (I.ii.83–4) by way of Hotspur's acid sketch of the 'popingay' who had 'so pest'red' him after the fighting at Holmedon (the 'certain lord' whose 'chin new reap'd / Show'd like a stubble-land at harvest-home' – men and country are thought of together (I.iii.33–5)), on to the 'mad fellow' by the wayside who had taunted Falstaff about his troop of 'totter'd prodigals', and to the prodigals' victim, 'the red-nose innkeeper of Daventry' (IV.ii.36, 34, 46–7). These marginal, off-stage figures, shadowlike but with separate lives of their own, intensify our sense of varied life in the stage characters themselves. They supply precisely what Morgann would call 'those parts of the composition which are *inferred* only, and not distinctly shewn'.

They are even more numerous in *Part 2*, especially in direct or indirect contact with Falstaff. Falstaff's first dialogue opens with a sarcasm reported from his doctor and with the knight's abuse of that 'yea-forsooth knave', his obdurate mercer, Master Dummelton (I.ii.36). (It is striking how, in *Part 2*, off-stage characters, as well as minor actors on the stage, are now given expressive, caricatural names.)[18] Through Mistress Quickly's chatter, we hear of her 'gossip', 'goodwife Keech, the butcher's wife' (II.i.93–4) and of 'Master Tisick, the debuty', who had admonished her while 'Master Dumbe, our minister' (II.iv.85, 88) was standing by. And in Shallow's scenes, at least (on my count) sixteen off-stage characters are identified, mostly by the ageing justice himself – from the three invisible Silences he asks after, and the four 'swingebucklers' and old Double (the bowman beloved of John of Gaunt), recalled from his 'Inns a' Court' days (III.ii.22), back to the 'arrant knave' William Visor of Woncote, whom nevertheless his servant Davy trusts he will 'countenance' in a lawsuit (V.i.38). With the help of names like Keech (butcher's fat), Simon Stockfish, Jane Nightwork and Silence's champion fat man, 'goodman Puff of Barson' (V.iii.89–90), as well as with drinking episodes and snatches of song, these Boar's Head and Cotswold scenes project a continuing, subdued impression as of a sort of scrimmage between representatives of Carnival and of Lent. From another point of view, it is a confused medley between everyday rascality and everyday law, complicating and enriching the historical theme of high justice, now central to the main plot. And with grimly sympathetic touches, sharp as engravings by Callot, these profusely inventive comic scenes bring home the rhythm of insignificant lives and insignificant deaths that shadow the high historical drama of war and statecraft. Moreover, they contribute something vital to the state of mind or quality of experience projected by *Part 2* as a whole, especially by way of Justice Shallow, that marvellous late-comer to *Henry IV*, with his trivial comforts and his senile reminiscences.

The predominant experience conveyed by *Part 2*, it seems to me, is the experience of uncertainty. It is the uncertainty, suspense, indecision that Northumberland expresses when he says:

> 'Tis with my mind
> As with the tide swell'd up unto his height,
> That makes a still-stand, running neither way.
>
> (II.iii.62–4)

Shakespeare makes the historical action unexciting, by contrast with *Part 1*, showing the rebellion suppressed, well before the end, by cold-blooded stratagem, not by fighting. He reduces even the death of Northumberland in battle to an incidental anticlimax, stripping it of the animation of circumstantial report (IV.iv.97–101). He treats the passage of history he is dealing with as an interim period, a period of waiting rather than doing, thus throwing new emphasis on the way the actors perceive themselves as 'time's subjects' (I.iii.110), peering into the future, reconsidering the past. One of his innovations in both parts of *Henry IV*, concurrent with the use of so many off-stage personalities, is the way Shakespeare now makes his characters recall past events at length, and this is particularly noticeable and effective in *Part 2*. The historical speakers think back to the battle of Shrewsbury and its antecedents – even, while Henry is dying, to the time before Richard II, as the anxious princes recall omens and popular beliefs preceding the death of Edward III:

> The river hath thrice flowed, no ebb between,
> And the old folk (time's doting chronicles)
> Say it did so a little time before
> That our great-grandsire, Edward, sick'd and died.
>
> (IV.iv.125–8)

This speech echoes both Northumberland's image about the tide and the theme introduced in the prologue by Rumour, the theme of 'surmises' and 'conjectures', of 'Conjecture, expectation and surmise' (Induction, 16; I.iii.23).

Throughout the play, remembrance of the past is set in tension against 'likelihoods and forms of hope' about the future (I.iii.35) or else 'forms imaginary' of apprehension (IV.iv.59), which run from the uncertainties agitating the rebel camp in the early scenes to the anxieties, even in victory, surrounding the deathbed of Henry IV. It is this form of mental tension, this general human experience, that Shakespeare is dramatising here (though it must have struck a specially contemporary chord at the moment when the play first appeared). About mid-way (in Act III, Scene i), there is a turning-point in the speeches rehearsing past events, when Henry has been questioning his whole troubled career and Warwick tries to explain that 'There is a history in all men's lives' (III.i.80) linking past and future in intelligible sequence. Whereupon the King exclaims, 'Are these things then necessities? / Then let us meet them like necessities.' But even here, what emerges is the expression of a frame of mind, not any decision affecting the plot. It is the characters' attitude towards current realities that Shakespeare is concerned with. As in *Part 1*, they are conscious of the pressures of 'time'. But in *Part 2*, it is more especially 'the condition of these *times*' that preoccupies them – 'The times are wild' ... 'these costermongers' times' ... 'the revolution of the times' – together with the signs they seem to hold about the 'times that you shall look upon' (IV.i.99, I.i.9, I.ii.168–9, III.i.46, IV.iv.60).

'Old folk' dominate the stage in *Part 2*, whereas youth is either dead and gone with Hotspur or subject to fears about the future with Hal (whose glory gained at Shrewsbury is kept, for good dramatic reasons, out of sight).[19] As L. C. Knights has pointed out, *Part 2* dwells on 'age, disappointment and decay'.[20] But this elegiac mood is countered in the comic scenes by the enjoyment of immediate, if trivial, pleasures, such as Mistress Quickly's appreciation of goodwife Keech's 'good dish of prawns' (I.i.96) or Shallow's enjoyment of 'any pretty little tiny kickshaws' to be produced by 'William cook' (V.i.27–8) and his anticipation of eating 'a last year's pippin of [his] own graffing, with a dish of caraways, and so forth' (V.iii.2–3). On the other side, Hal is obliged to regret that his princely appetite can still 'remember the poor creature, small beer. But indeed', he adds, 'these humble considerations make me out of love with my greatness' (II.ii.10–12). Such 'humble considerations' are made to seem relatively timeless; particularly where, towards the climax for Falstaff, Shakespeare cuts from the scene of preparations for dinner at Shallow's house (Act V, Scene 1) to the scene at London announcing Henry IV's death and showing Henry V's reconciliation with the Chief Justice, and then back to Shallow's house for the fruit (Act V, Scene iii) – as if, for the moment, the national crisis belonged not only to a different world but to a different order of time. Yet the distinction between the low world and the high is finely shaded. There is no more than a shaky grasp of reality in Mistress Quickly's muddled, rambling, suggestible mind, and in Shallow's gullible self-importance and his vanity about the past. Doll Tearsheet and Silence are complementary, if opposite, types. Altogether, since he is kept at a distance from the Prince, Falstaff's chosen company in *Part 2* is more easygoing, less sharp-witted, than his company in *Part 1*.

There are corresponding changes in Falstaff himself. In spite of the credit he has gained, with the help of Rumour, from Shrewsbury, he still depends ultimately on patronage from Hal. But he is thrown more upon his own resources, so that his capture of a prisoner of war seems like an accident; and the main line of his action, until the last moments of the play, is a spiralling progress from debt to debt. We see more of his social versatility than before, but we also hear more of his private reflection, as he sizes up himself and his world. He can inspire affection, at least the maudlin affection of Doll and Mrs Quickly. He is given less to outbursts of 'remorse' than before and more to exploiting the world as he finds it: 'A good wit will make use of anything. I will turn diseases to commodity' (something he can sell, this time, not something he wants to buy (I.ii.247–8)). He will fleece Justice Shallow if he can, on the strength of their old acquaintance, in sardonic complicity with 'the law of nature' (III.ii.331). He is as evasive and resourceful as before, but less impulsive, more detached and calculating. We hear more of the mellow, observant, leisured cadences in his prose. He is more of a philosopher and more of a rogue.

A recurrent subject of wryly amused reflection with Falstaff, in connection with the Page and then Prince John and finally Shallow, is the inequality between the Fat and the Lean. What occupies his mind is not so much thoughts of his own age and sickness, which he will evade if he can, as the contrast between his sense of implantation in life and the unsteadiness of his fortunes. His antipathy to Prince John inspires his most elaborate set speech (IV.iii.86–125), his soliloquy of mock-humanistic encomium in praise of drink and of wine-inspired wit, 'apprehensive, quick, forgetive, full of nimble, fiery and delectable shapes'. This is his most defiant plea for laughter and his own style of life. But his meeting with Shallow has begun to elicit another style from Falstaff, more objectively humorous but also more contemplative, as he measures the squire's history against his own. 'Lord, Lord, how subject we old men are to this vice of lying!' is a spontaneous (if ironic) reflection, not a set speech. And his first, richly grotesque, soliloquy about Shallow and how 'This same starv'd justice hath done nothing but prate to me of the wildness of his youth' is also Falstaff's first excursion of any length into his own past (III.ii.304–52); but – 'now has he land and beefs' (III.ii.327–8). His second soliloquy on the same topic (V.i.62–85) is more detached, with exactly balanced clauses of amused observation:

If I were saw'd into quantities, I should make four dozen of such bearded hermits' staves as Master Shallow. It is a wonderful thing to see the semblable coherence of his men's spirits and his. They, by observing him, do bear themselves like foolish justices; he, by conversing with them, is turn'd into a justice-like servingman ... It is certain that either wise bearing or ignorant carriage is caught, as men take diseases, one of another; therefore let men take heed of their company ...

This has the ring of shrewd, almost homely, unforced practical wisdom, so much that the dramatic irony in the last sentence is almost submerged. This speech marks the high point of Falstaff's role as an unruffled humorous critic of mechanical behaviour in other men. He goes on to anticipate how he will make 'Prince Harry' laugh over Shallow, though with a rueful glance at the gap between jester and patron – 'a fellow that never had the ache in his shoulders!' In his next scene (Act V, Scene iii), the news that Pistol (of all select companions) brings from court releases a mechanism in Falstaff himself, in the wild dream that 'the laws of England are at my commandement'.

It seems almost impossible for critics to agree about the rejection of Falstaff. Perhaps this shows a flaw in the writing of the play as a whole. Admittedly, there is a jarring note in Henry's rejection speech, though on the other hand the whole action ends on an unheroic note of subdued expectation, on the *diminuendo* of a half-line of verse. But perhaps also those who, like Bradley, deplore the dismissal of a comic spirit of freedom and those who, like Dover Wilson, justify the regal severity of Henry V, both minimise the comic side of Falstaff's downfall and his own share in bringing it about. A Falstaff temperate enough to approach the new king for favours privately or submissive enough to wait until sent for would be less funny than the Falstaff we see. A more amiable separation from Hal would be less in keeping with the character of Falstaff and less true to the logic of comedy, which does not require benevolence, still less indulgence, so much as what Shaw called disillusionment or, rather, a developed engagement between our sense of reality and fixed habits of human behaviour or else between realism and voluntary fantasy. But a realistic appraisal of the sustained business of government cannot be the province of comedy, as distinct from satire, at all.

The two Parts of *Henry IV* form an unprecedented study of statecraft and of the relations of statecraft to other sides of life. More than any other English plays, I think, they suggest the continuousness of the life of a whole people, through space and time and the mixture of typical human qualities. As such they must include more than comedy. On the other hand, the inclusive vision they contain of the ways men and women of different sorts confront social reality gives perspective and more salience than entirely comic surroundings could provide to the uniquely comic figure of Falstaff.

4. The design of *Twelfth Night*

Most readers of *Twelfth Night* would probably agree that this is the most delightful, harmonious and accomplished of Shakespeare's romantic comedies, in many ways his crowning achievement in one branch of his art. They would probably agree, too, that it has a prevailing atmosphere of happiness, or at least of 'tempests dissolved in music'. Yet there are striking differences of opinion over the design of *Twelfth Night*. Is it, for example, a vindication of romance, or a depreciation of romance?[1] Is it mainly a love-story or a comedy of humours; a 'poem of escape' or a realistic comment on economic security and prudential marriage?[2] And there are further variations. The principal character, according to choice, is Viola, Olivia, Malvolio or Feste.

To some extent, the play itself seems to invite such varying reactions: *Twelfth Night; or, What You Will*. Shakespeare here is both polishing his craftsmanship and exploring new facets of his experience,[3] so that the play has the buoyancy of a mind exhilarated by discovery, testing one human impulse against another, and satisfied with a momentary state of balance which seems all the more trustworthy because its limits have been felt and recognised. But in consequence, Shakespeare's attitude towards his people comes near to humorous detachment, to a kind of Socratic irony. He refrains from emphasising any one of his themes at the expense of the rest. He carefully plays down and transforms the crisis of sentiment in his main plot, while giving unusual prominence to his comic sub-plot. He distributes the interest more evenly among his characters than in *As You Like It* or the other comedies, providing more numerous (and more unexpected) points of contact between them, not only in the action but on the plane of psychology. And the whole manner of *Twelfth Night* is light and mercurial. The prose is full of ideas, but playful, not discursive. The poetry, for all its lyrical glow, gives a

53

sense of restraint and ease, of keenly perceptive and yet relaxed enjoyment, rather than of any compelling pressure of emotion.

Perhaps this attitude on Shakespeare's part is responsible for the inconsistency of his interpreters. Those who dwell on the romantic side of the play seem uncertain about its connection with the comic realism; while those who concentrate on the elements of realism have to meet the kind of objection gravely stated by Dr Johnson – that 'the marriage of Olivia, and the succeeding perplexity, though well enough contrived to divert on the stage, wants credibility, and fails to produce the proper instruction required in the drama, as it exhibits no just picture of life'. The question to be interpreted, then, is how Shakespeare is using the instrument of theatrical contrivance, which is present, of course, in all his comedies, but which he uses here with exceptional delicacy and freedom.

Briefly, Shakespeare has taken a familiar kind of love-story and transformed it so as to extend the interest from the heroine to a group of characters who reveal varying responses to the power of love. He has modified the main situation further, and brought home his comments on it, by using methods of construction he had mastered previously in his *Comedy of Errors*. And he has added a sub-plot based on the customary jokes and revels of a feast of misrule, when normal restraints and relationships were overthrown. As the main title implies, the idea of a time of misrule gives the underlying constructive principle of the whole play.

In *Twelfth Night*, as Miss Welsford puts it, Shakespeare 'transmutes into poetry the quintessence of the Saturnalia'. The sub-plot shows a prolonged season of misrule, or 'uncivil rule', in Olivia's household, with Sir Toby turning night into day; there are drinking, dancing, and singing, scenes of mock wooing, a mock sword-fight, and the gulling of an unpopular member of the household, with Feste mumming it as a priest and attempting a mock exorcism in the manner of the Feast of Fools. Sir Andrew and Malvolio resemble Ben Jonson's social pretender;[5] but Shakespeare goes beyond Jonson in ringing the changes on the theme of Folly and in making his speakers turn logic and courtesy on their heads. A girl and a coward are given out to be ferocious duellists; a steward imagines that he can marry his lady; and finally a fool pretends to assure a wise man that darkness is light. In Feste, Shakespeare creates his most finished portrait of a professional fool; he is superfluous to the plot, but affects the mood of the play more than any other of Shakespeare's clowns.

Moreover, this saturnalian spirit invades the whole play. In the main plot, sister is mistaken for brother, and brother for sister. Viola tells Olivia 'That you do think you are not what you are' – and admits that the same holds true of herself. The women take the initiative in wooing, both in appearance and in fact; the heroine performs love-service for the lover. The Duke makes his servant 'your master's mistress' and the lady who has withdrawn from the sight of men embraces a stranger. The four main actors all reverse their desires or break their vows before the comedy is over; while Antonio, the one single-minded representative of romantic devotion, is also the only character in the main plot who tries to establish a false identity and fails (III.iv.326–31); and he is left unrewarded and almost disregarded. Such reversals are, as Johnson says, devices peculiar to the stage, but Shakespeare makes them spring, or seem to spring, from the very nature of love. In *The Comedy of Errors* the confusions of identity are due to external circumstances; in *A Midsummer Night's Dream* Shakespeare begins to connect them with the capricious, illusory factor in subjective 'fancy' that is common to the madman, the lover and the creative poet. In *Twelfth Night*, he takes this similitude further. Love here will 'be clamorous, and leap all civil bounds', like a lord of misrule; 'love's night is noon', like Sir Toby's carousals. Love seems as powerful as the sea, tempestuous, indifferent and changeable as the sea. And fortune, or fate, reveals the same paradoxical benevolence in this imbroglio of mistakes and disguises: 'Tempests are kind and salt waves fresh in love.'

The analysis of love as a kind of folly was a common theme of Renaissance moralists, who delighted in contrasting it with the wisdom of the Stoic or the man of affairs. Shakespeare's treatment of the theme in *Twelfth Night* is a natural development from his own previous work, but he could have found strong hints of it in the possible sources of his Viola–Orsino story. Bandello remarks, for instance, that it arouses wonder to hear of a gentleman disguising himself as a servant, and still more in the case of a girl: but when you realise that love is the cause, 'the wonder ceases at once, because this passion of love is much too potent and causes actions much more amazing and excessive than that'; a person in love has 'lost his liberty, and ... no miracle if he commits a thousand errors'.[6] And Barnabe Riche tells his readers that in his story of *Apolonius and Silla*, 'you shall see Dame Error so play her part with a leash of lovers, a male and two females, as shall work a wonder to your wise judgement'.[7] In effect, then, what Shakespeare could take for granted in his audience was not simply a readiness to be interested in romance, but a sense of the opposition between romance and reason.

On this basis, Shakespeare can unite his main action with his sub-plot, bending a romantic story in the direction of farce. By the same contrivances, he can disclose the follies surrounding love and celebrate its life-giving power. And he can do this, without sacrificing emotional reality – which is not exactly the same as Dr Johnson's 'just picture of life' – because he takes his stage machinery from the traditions of a feast of misrule, where social custom has already begun to transform normal behaviour into the material of comic art.[8] The whole play is a festivity, where reality and play-acting meet. By presenting his main story on these lines, Shakespeare can develop his insight into the protean, contradictory nature of love with more economy and force than by keeping to the lines of an ordinary stage narrative. At the same time he can extend this theme through his realistic images of 'uncivil rule' in the sub-plot, disclosing the conflicting impulses of an aristocratic community in a period of social change, and touching on the potentially tragic problems of the place of time and order in human affairs.

Shakespeare's intentions may stand out more clearly when one compares his treatment of the Viola story with its possible or probable sources.[9] The ultimate source is held to be the anonymous Sienese comedy, Gl'Ingannati (The Deceived), first performed at a carnival of 1531 and frequently reprinted, translated or imitated in the course of the sixteenth century. Shakespeare may also have known Bandello's story, which follows the plot of Gl'Ingannati closely, omitting the subordinate comic parts; and he probably knew Riche's Apolonius and Silla (1581), derived indirectly and with variations from Bandello. Another source of the main plot must have been the Menaechmi of Plautus, which presumably had already contributed something to Gl'Ingannati, but affects the composition of Twelfth Night more directly by way of The Comedy of Errors. In any case, Shakespeare's situations were part of the common stock of classical and medieval romance, as Manningham saw at one of the first performances of Twelfth Night, when he noted in his diary that it was 'much like the Commedy of Errores, or Menechmi in Plautus, but most like and neere to that in Italian called Inganni' (one of the offshoots of Gl'Ingannati).

There are four essential characters common to Gl'Ingannati, Bandello, Riche and Shakespeare; namely, a lover, a heroine in his service disguised as a page, her twin brother (who at first has dis-appeared) and a second heroine. The basic elements common to all four plots are: the heroine's secret love for her master; her employ-ment as go-between, leading to the complication of a cross-wooing; and a final solution by means of the unforeseen arrival of the missing twin.

If Shakespeare knew Bandello or *Gl'Ingannati*, he altered their material radically. The Italians both take the romance motif of a heroine's constancy and love-service, set in a realistic bourgeois environment, and rationalise it with respectful irony. In Bandello, the irony is severely rational – because it is a tale of love, 'the wonder ceases at once'. In *Gl'Ingannati*, the tone is whimsical. 'Two lessons above all you will extract from this play', says the Prologue: 'how much chance and good fortune can do in matters of love; and how much long patience is worth in such cases, accompanied by good advice'.[10] Both Italian authors give the heroine a strong motive for assuming her disguise, in that the lover has previously returned her affection, but has now forgotten her and turned elsewhere. Both provide her with a formidable father in the background and a foster-mother like Juliet's Nurse, who admonishes and helps her; and both credit her with the intention of bilking her rival if she can. On the other side, they both respect the code of courtly love to the extent of stressing the lover's penitence at the end, and his recognition that he must repay the heroine for her devotion. 'I believe', he says in the play, 'that this is certainly the will of God, who must have taken pity on this virtuous maiden and on my soul, that it should not go to perdition ...'[11]

Riche keeps this framework of sentiment, vulgarises the narrative, and changes some of the material circumstances, generally in the direction of an Arcadian romance.

Shakespeare, for his part, changes the story fundamentally, broadening the interest and at the same time making the whole situation more romantically improbable, more melancholy at some points, more fantastic at others. He stiffens the heroine's loyalty, but deprives her of her original motive, her initiative and her family. In place of these, he gives her the background of a vague 'Messaline' and a romantic shipwreck, for which he may have taken a hint, but no more, from the episode of the shipwreck in Riche. Shakespeare's Viola, then, is a more romantic heroine than the rest, and the only one to fall in love *after* assuming her disguise. At the same time, however, Shakespeare enlarges the role of her twin brother and gives unprecedented weight to coincidence in the dénouement, which in both Italian stories is brought about more rationally, by the deliberate action of the heroine and her nurse; so that Shakespeare's Viola is also unique in that her happiness is due to 'good fortune' more than 'long patience', and to 'good advice' not at all.

In his exposition, therefore, Shakespeare sketches a situation from romance in place of a logical intrigue. But the purpose, or at any rate the effect, of his plan is to shift attention at the outset from the circumstances of the love-story to the sentiments as such, especially in their more mysterious and irrational aspects. Shakespeare may have taken hints, for Orsino and Olivia, from his predecessors' comments on the 'error' of 'following them that fly from us'. But however that may be, his comedy now consists in the triumph of natural love over affectation and melancholy. And, taken together, the leading characters in *Twelfth Night* form the most subtle portrayal of the psychology of love that Shakespeare had yet drawn.

Viola's love is fresh and direct, and gathers strength as the play advances. When she first appears, Viola mourns her brother, like Olivia, and by choice would join Olivia in her seclusion:

> O that I serv'd that lady,
> And might not be delivered to the world
> Till I had made mine own occasion mellow
> What my estate is.

(I.ii.41)

Shakespeare makes the most here of the vagueness surrounding Viola; she seems the child of the sea, and of time. But even when her feelings and her problem have become distinct she still commits herself to 'time' with a gentle air of detachment:

> What will become of this? As I am man,
> My state is desperate for my master's love;
> As I am woman (now alas the day!),
> What thriftless sighs shall poor Olivia breathe!
> O time, thou must untangle this, not I,
> It is too hard a knot for me t'untie.

(II.ii.36)

She has none of the vehement determination of the Italian heroines,[12] and, though nimble-witted, she is less resourceful and high-spirited than Rosalind. She foreshadows Perdita and Miranda in the romantically adolescent quality of her part.

There are stronger colours than this in Viola, admittedly. Before she appears on the stage, Orsino has spoken of the capacity for love inherent in a woman's devoted sorrow for her brother; and in two scenes in the middle of the play Viola herself speaks in more passionate terms. But in both cases her own feeling seems muffled or distorted, since she is acting a part, and in both cases her tone is distinctly theatrical. She tells Olivia how, if she were Orsino, she would

> Write loyal cantons of contemned love,
> And sing them loud even in the dead of night;
> Halloo your name to the reverberate hills,
> And make the babbling gossip of the air
> Cry out 'Olivia!'
>
> (I.v.270)

she tells Orsino, on the other hand, that her imaginary sister

> never told her love,
> But let concealment like a worm i'th' bud
> Feed on her damask cheek;
>
> (II.iv.110)

– in each case, with an overtone of romantic excess. She does not speak out in her own voice, therefore, until the later scenes, when the more vigorous (and more artificial) emotions of the older pair have had full play. Meanwhile, the hints of excess in her two fictitious declarations of love reflect on the others as well as herself: she speaks for Orsino in the spirit of his injunction to 'be clamorous, and leap all civil bounds'; while her image of repressed desire could apply to Olivia. Her own development in the comedy is closely attuned to the others'.

Shakespeare begins the play with Orsino. He follows Riche in making the lover in his comedy a duke (not, as with the Italians, a citizen), who has been a warrior but has now 'become a scholar in love's school'.[13] Orsino suffers from the melancholy proper to courtly and 'heroical' love; and Shakespeare fixes attention on his passion, which is more violent and 'fantastical' than in the other versions of the story, by keeping Orsino inactive in his court to dramatise his own feelings like Richard II. Unlike the Italian lovers, he has not been fickle, yet changefulness is the very essence of his condition. He twice calls for music in the play, but there is no harmony in himself. Within a few lines, he countermands the first order, to apostrophise the spirit of love:

> Enough, no more,
> 'Tis not so sweet now as it was before.
> O spirit of love, how quick and fresh art thou,
> That notwithstanding thy capacity
> Receiveth as the sea, nought enters there,
> Of what validity and pitch soe'er,
> But falls into abatement and low price
> Even in a minute. So full of shapes is fancy
> That it alone is high fantastical.

(I.i.7)

This apostrophe carries opposing meanings. 'Quick' and 'fresh', coming after 'sicken' a few lines before, imply the vigour of life, but they also prolong the grosser sense of 'appetite' and 'surfeiting'. The sea image glorifies Orsino's 'spirit of love' and, in relation to the drama as a whole, it prepares the way for the sea-change that comes to Viola and Sebastian; but it also leads on to the image of Sir Toby 'drown'd' in drink (I.v.131). And Orsino's most striking metaphors here, those of sinking and 'low price', suggest that what the speaker largely feels is chill and dismay. Nothing has any value by comparison with love; but also, nothing has any lasting, intrinsic value for a lover. Later, referring to the sea-fight, Orsino utters a similar paradox when he describes the 'fame and honour' Antonio had won in 'A baubling vessel ... / For shallow draught and bulk unprizable' (V.i.54). But there, the paradox enhances Antonio's courage; here, it is depressing.[14] For Orsino, the only constant feature of love is instability. He tells Viola (II.iv.18) that all true lovers are

> Unstaid and skittish in all motions else,
> Save in the constant image of the creature
> That is belov'd;

a moment later, it is the 'image' that changes –

> For, boy, however we do praise ourselves,
> Our fancies are more giddy and unfirm,
> More longing, wavering, sooner lost and worn,
> Than women's are;

and then, as he thinks of Olivia, it is the woman's 'appetite', not the man's, that can 'suffer surfeit, cloyment and revolt' (II.iv.99). Feste sketches the life of such a lover with fitting ambiguity: 'I would have men of such constancy put to sea, that their business might be every thing and their intent every where, for that's it that always makes a good voyage of nothing' (II.iv.75); they dissipate their advantages and can be satisfied with illusions. By its very nature, then, Orsino's love for Olivia is self-destructive, subject to time and change. Although, or rather because, it is 'all as hungry as the sea', it is impossible to satisfy. And it seems almost without an object, or incommensurate with any object, a 'monstrosity' in the same sense as Troilus's love for Cressida, in its grasping after the infinite.

Moreover, Orsino's 'spirit of love' seems something outside the rest of his personality, a tyrant from whom he longs to escape. His desires pursue him 'like fell and cruel hounds'. He wants music to diminish his passion, to relieve it with the thought of death. And when at last he confronts Olivia, something like hatred bursts through his conventional phrases of love-homage: 'yond same sovereign cruelty' (II.iv) is now (V.i) a 'perverse', 'uncivil lady', 'ingrate and unauspicious', 'the marble-breasted tyrant'. In his jealous rage he feels himself 'at point of death':

> Why should I not (had I the heart to do it),
> Like to th'Egyptian thief at point of death,
> Kill what I love? (a savage jealousy
> That sometime savours nobly).

> (V.i.117)

In all this, however, there is as much injured vanity as anything else. His 'fancy' is at the point of dying, not his heart; and it is fully consistent with his character that he can swerve almost at once to Viola, gratified and relieved by the surprise of her identity and the full disclosure of her devotion to himself. His emotions, then, give a powerful upsurge to the play, but they are kept within the bounds of comedy. His real 'error', in Shakespeare, is that he only imagines himself to be pursuing love. Olivia's, correspondingly, is that she only imagines herself to be flying from it.

With Olivia, even more than with Orsino, Shakespeare diverges from his possible sources, making her a much more prominent and interesting character than her prototypes. In the Italian stories, the second heroine is heiress to a wealthy old dotard, is kept out of sight most of the time, and is treated with ribald irony for her amorous forwardness. In *Apolonius and Silla*, she is a wealthy widow. In all three, she is considered only as rival and pendant to the Viola-heroine. Shakespeare, however, makes her a virgin, psychologically an elder sister to Viola, and better able to sustain the comedy of awakening desire. At the same time, she is the mistress of a noble household, and hence the focus of the sub-plot as well as the main plot.[15] When she first appears, she can rebuke Malvolio with aristocratic courtesy (I.v.91): 'To be generous, guiltless, and of free disposition, is to take those things for bird-bolts that you deem cannon-bullets.' But Olivia, like Orsino – like Malvolio, even – suffers from ignorance of herself, and must be cured of affectation; as Sebastian says (V.i.260), 'Nature to her bias drew in that.'

Her vow of mourning has a tinge of the same aristocratic extravagance as Orsino's 'spirit of love'. Orsino compares her to an angry Diana; but then there follows at once the account of her vow, which already begins to disclose the comic, unseasonable side of her assumed coldness:

> The element itself, till seven years' heat,
> Shall not behold her face at ample view;
> But like a cloistress she will veiled walk,
> And water once a day her chamber round
> With eye-offending brine; all this to season
> A brother's dead love, which she would keep fresh
> And lasting in her sad remembrance.
>
> (I.i.25)

Olivia is to be rescued from her cloister (like Diana's priestess in *The Comedy of Errors* or Hermia in *A Midsummer Night's Dream*)[16] and exposed to the sunshine. Feste warns her, in gentle mockery, that she is a 'fool'; the hood does not make the monk, and 'As there is no true cuckold but calamity, so beauty's a flower' (I.v.51). She is obliged to unveil her beauty, and has natural vanity enough to claim that ''twill endure wind and weather' (I.v.237); and Viola's speech, which stirs her heart, is also a form of comic retribution, hallooing her name to 'the reverberate hills' and 'the babbling gossip of the air' –

> O, you should not rest
> Between the elements of air and earth
> But you should pity me!
>
> (I.v.274)

'Element' is made one of the comic catchwords of the play.[17]

The comic reversal of Olivia's attitude culminates in her declaration of love to Viola, the most delicate and yet impressive speech in the play (III.i.149). It is now Olivia's turn to plead against 'scorn', to 'unclasp the book of her secret soul' to Viola[18] – and, equally, to herself. After two lines, she turns to the same verse form of impersonal, or extra-personal, 'sentences' in rhyme that Shakespeare gives to other heroines at their moment of truth:

> O, what a deal of scorn looks beautiful
> In the contempt and anger of his lip!
> A murd'rous guilt shows not itself more soon
> Than love that would seem hid: love's night is noon. –
> Cesario, by the roses of the spring,
> By maidhood, honour, truth, and every thing,
> I love thee so, that maugre all thy pride,
> Nor wit nor reason can my passion hide.
> Do not extort thy reasons from this clause,
> For that I woo, thou therefore hast no cause;
> But rather reason thus with reason fetter:
> Love sought is good, but given unsought is better.

Having already thrown off her original veil, Olivia now breaks through the concealments of her pride, her modesty and her feminine 'wit'. Her speech is mainly a vehement persuasion to love, urged 'by the roses of the spring'.[19] Yet she keeps her dignity, and keeps it all the more in view of the secondary meaning latent in her words, her timid fear that Cesario's scorn is not the disdain of rejection at all but the scorn of conquest. Logically, indeed, her first rhyming couplet implies just this, implies that his cruel looks are the signs of a guilty lust rising to the surface; and this implication is carried on as she speaks of his 'pride' (with its hint of sexual desire),[20] and into her last lines, with their covert pleading not to 'extort' a callous advantage from her confession. But in either case – whatever Cesario's intentions – love now appears to Olivia as a startling paradox: guilty, even murderous, an irruption of misrule; and at the same time irrepressible, fettering reason and creating its own light out of darkness. And, in either case, the conclusion to her perplexities is a plain one – 'Love sought is good, but given unsought is better.' This is Shakespeare's departure from the moral argument of his predecessors,[21] and it marks the turning-point of *Twelfth Night*.

There is still a trace of irony attaching to Olivia, in that her wooing is addressed to another woman and has been parodied beforehand in Maria's forged love-letter (II.v.). And this irony pursues her to the end, even in her marriage, when once again she tries, and fails, 'To keep in darkness what occasion now / Reveals before 'tis ripe' (V.i.153). But from the point of her declaration to Viola, the way is clear for the resolution of the whole comedy on the plane of sentiment. In terms of sentiment, she has justified her gift of love to a stranger. She is soon completely sure of herself, and in the later scenes she handles Sir Toby, Orsino and Cesario-Sebastian with brusque decision; while her demon of austerity is cast out through

Malvolio. The main action of *Twelfth Night*, then, is planned with a suggestive likeness to a revel, in which Olivia is masked, Orsino's part is 'giddy' and 'fantastical', Viola-Sebastian is the mysterious stranger – less of a character and more of a poetic symbol than the others – and in the end, as Feste says of his own 'interlude' with Malvolio, 'the whirligig of time brings in his revenges'.

Although Olivia's declaration forms the crisis of the main action, the resolution of the plot has still to be worked out. And here Shakespeare departs in a new way from his predecessors. Shakespeare's Sebastian, by character and adventures, has little in common with the brother in *Gl'Ingannati*, and still less with Silla's brother in Riche; but nearly everything in common – as Manningham presumably noticed – with the visiting brother in Plautus, Menaechmus of Syracuse. And Antonio's part in the plot (though not his character) is largely that of Menaechmus's slave in Plautus, while his emotional role stems from the Aegeon story that Shakespeare himself had already added to *Menaechmi* in *The Comedy of Errors*. These Plautine elements in the brother's story have been altered in *Gl'Ingannati* and dropped from, or camouflaged in, *Apolonius and Silla*. Whichever of the latter Shakespeare used for Viola, therefore, he deliberately reverted to Plautus for Sebastian, sometimes drawing on his own elaborations in *The Comedy of Errors*, but mainly going back directly to the original.[22]

Hence the second half of *Twelfth Night* is largely more farcical than its predecessors, whereas the first half had been, in a sense, more romantic. Shakespeare thus provides a telling finale, proper, as Dr Johnson observes, to the stage. But he does much more than this. His farcical dénouement gives tangible shape to the notion of misrule inherent in his romantic exposition. Faults of judgement in the first part of *Twelfth Night* are answered with mistakes of identity in the second, while the action swirls to a joyful ending through a crescendo of errors. And by the same manoeuvre, Shakespeare charges his romance with a new emotional significance, bringing it nearer to tragedy.

How are Viola and Olivia to be freed? In *Apolonius and Silla*, the widow, pregnant after her welcome to Silla's brother, demands justice of the disguised heroine, thus forcing her to reveal herself and clearing the way for her marriage to the Duke. Only when the rumour of this wedding has spread abroad does the wandering brother return to the scene and espouse the widow. In the Italian stories, the heroine reaches an understanding with her master by her own devices and the aid of her nurse, without any kind of help from the arrival of her brother; and this is a logical solution, since the heroine's love-service is the clear centre of interest. But Shakespeare has been more broadly concerned with love as a force in life as a whole. He has shifted the emphasis to the two older lovers, keeping Viola's share of passion in reserve. And even after the crisis, he continues to withhold the initiative the Italians had given her. Shakespeare is alone in making the heroine reveal herself *after* her brother's marriage with the second heroine, as a consequence of it. And the whole Plautine sequence in *Twelfth Night* is designed to lead to this conclusion. Hence, while the first half of Shakespeare's comedy dwells on self-deception in love, the second half stresses the benevolent irony of fate.

In the early scenes, fate appears to the speakers as an overriding power which is nevertheless obscurely rooted in their own desires (the obverse, that is, to Orsino's 'spirit of love', which springs from himself, yet seems to dominate him from without).[23] Thus, Viola trusts herself to 'time'; Olivia, falling in love, cries, 'Fate, show thy force: ourselves we do not owe'; and the letter forged in her name yields an echo to her words: 'Thy Fates open their hands, let thy blood and spirit embrace them.'[24] Antonio and Sebastian strengthen this motif and clarify it.

Antonio stands for an absolute devotion that is ultimately grounded on fate; he is the embodiment of Olivia's discovery, and his speeches on this theme are interwoven with hers. Shortly after her first lines about fate – and chiming with them – comes his declaration to Sebastian (II.i.47):

> But come what may, I do adore thee so
> That danger shall seem sport, and I will go;

and after her cry that love should be a gift, he tells Sebastian in more positive terms:

> I could not stay behind you. My desire
> (More sharp than filed steel) did spur me forth.
>
> (III.iii.4)

In the last scene, again, he proclaims to Orsino –

> A witchcraft drew me hither:
> That most ingrateful boy there by your side
> From the rude sea's enrag'd and foamy mouth
> Did I redeem.   (V.i.76)

The resonant sea-image of destiny here dominates the bewildered tone still appropriate, at this point, to a comedy of errors.[25]

Sebastian's part runs parallel with this. When he first appears (II.i), he feels the same melancholy as his sister, and shows a similar vague self-abandonment in his aims: 'my determinate voyage is mere extravagancy'. But a stronger impression of him has been given already by the Captain, in the outstanding speech of Viola's first scene:

> I saw your brother,
> Most provident in peril, bind himself
> (Courage and hope both teaching him the practice)
> To a strong mast that liv'd upon the sea;
> Where like Arion on the dolphin's back,
> I saw him hold acquaintance with the waves
> So long as I could see.

The Captain has told Viola to 'comfort [herself] with chance'; Sebastian is 'provident in peril', on friendly terms with destiny. When he bobs up resurrected at the end, accordingly, he does precisely what Malvolio had been advised to do, grasps the hands of the Fates and lets himself float with 'the stream', with 'this accident and flood of fortune' (IV.i.60, IV.iii.11).[26] By the same turn of mind, moreover, he imparts to the dénouement a tone as of clarity following illusion, of an awakening like the end of *A Midsummer Night's Dream*:

> Or I am mad, or else this is a dream . . .
>
> (IV.i.61)

> This is the air, that is the glorious sun,
> This pearl she gave me, I do feel't and see't,
> And though 'tis wonder that enwraps me thus,
> Yet 'tis not madness . . .
>
> (IV.iii.1)

'Mad' the lady may appear; but Sebastian – like Olivia before him, except that he does it in all coolness – is ready to 'wrangle with [his] reason' and welcome the gift of love. The comedy of errors in which he figures is thus both counterpart and solution to the initial comedy of sentiment. Riche had called his love-story the work of 'Dame Error'; Shakespeare, in effect, takes the hint, and goes back to Plautus.

Having planned his dénouement on these lines, moreover, Shakespeare goes further, adding a superb variation on his Plautine theme in the farcical scene leading up to Viola's meeting with Antonio (III.iv). This scene as a whole, with its rapid changes of mood and action, from Olivia to the sub-plot and back towards Sebastian, braces together the whole comic design. It brings to a climax the misrule, farcical humours and simulated emotions of the play – with Olivia confessing 'madness', Sir Toby triumphant, Malvolio *in excelsis* ('Jove, not I, is the doer of this . . .'), Sir Andrew allegedly 'bloody as the hunter',[27] and Viola, after her unavoidable coldness to Olivia, submitted for the first time to the laughable consequences of her change of sex. And the duel with its sequel perfects this comic catharsis. This duel, or what Sir Toby and Fabian make of it, bears a strong affinity to the sword-dances and Mummers' play combats of a season of misrule; it becomes another encounter between St George and Captain Slasher, the Turkish Knight. One champion is 'a devil in private brawl. Souls and bodies hath he divorc'd three'; the other is 'a very devil, . . . a firago . . . he gives me the stuck in with such a mortal motion that it is inevitable' – and 'They say he has been fencer to the Sophy.' Now in one sense the duel and what follows are superfluous to the main action, since it is not strictly necessary for Viola to meet Antonio, or to meet him in this way. But in effect this episode of misrule[28] contains the principal conflict between the serious and the ludicrous forces in the play; it prepares emotionally for the resurrection of Sebastian; and, by a further swerve of constructive irony, the additional, gratuitous comedy of errors involving Antonio gives new force to the main theme of the romance.

As it concerns Viola, the dialogue here restores the balance in favour of her character, in that her generosity and her lines against 'ingratitude' prepare the audience for her culminating gesture of self-sacrifice in the last act. But, more than this, Antonio's speeches stress the paradox of love that has been gathering force through the play:

> Antonio: Let me speak a little. This youth that you see here
> I snatch'd one half out of the jaws of death,
> Reliev'd him with such sanctity of love,
> And to his image, which methought did promise
> Most venerable worth, did I devotion.
>
> Officer: What's that to us? The time goes by; away!
>
> Antonio: But O, how vild an idol proves this god!
> Thou hast, Sebastian, done good feature shame.
> In nature there's no blemish but the mind;
> None can be call'd deform'd but the unkind.

> Virtue is beauty, but the beauteous evil
> Are empty trunks o'erflourish'd by the devil.
> *Officer:* The man grows mad, away with him! . . .
>
> (III.iv.359)

It is in keeping with the comedy of errors that Antonio here has mistaken his man, to the point of seeming 'mad', that Viola, happy to hear of her brother again, promptly forgets him – as Sir Toby notices (III.iv.386) – and that Antonio, as it turns out, should help Sebastian most effectively by so being forgotten. But this same quirk of fate brings the mood of the play dangerously near the confines of tragedy. The comedy has no answer to his problem of sincere devotion given to a false idol.[29]

Antonio stands outside the main sphere of the comedy. He belongs to the world of merchants, law and sea-battles, not the world of courtly love. His love for Sebastian is irrational, or beyond reason, and his danger in Orsino's domains is due, similarly, to irrational persistence in an old dispute (III.iii.30–7). But he gives himself completely to his principles, more seriously than anyone else in the play, and tries to live them out as rationally as he can. In contrast to the lovers (except possibly Viola), he is not satisfied with truth of feeling, but demands some more objective standard of values; in his world, law and 'time' mean something external, and harder than the unfolding of natural instinct. His problems are appropriate to *Troilus* or *Hamlet*. In one way, therefore, he marks a limit to festivity. Nevertheless, precisely because he takes himself so seriously, he helps to keep the comic balance of the play.

The comedy of errors in the main plot, the element of mummery and misrule, implies a comment on the serious follies of love, and bring a corrective to them. In the sub-plot (or -plots) – his addition to the Viola story – Shakespeare makes this corrective explicit and prepares for the festive atmosphere at the end. 'What a plague means my niece to take the death of her brother thus? I am sure care's an enemy to life . . .' 'Does not our lives consist of the four elements? – Faith, so they say, but I think it rather consists of eating and drinking.' Sir Toby, Maria, Feste, Fabian stand for conviviality and the enjoyment of life, as opposed to the melancholy of romance.

At the same time, however, the sub-plot action reproduces the main action like a comic mirror-image, and the two of them are joined to form a single symmetrical pattern of errors in criss-cross. Shakespeare had attempted a similar pattern before, in *The Comedy of Errors*, *A Midsummer Night's Dream*, and *Much Ado*, for example, but nowhere else does he bring it off so lightly and ingeniously.

In the main plot there is a lover who pursues love and a lady who tries to hide from it. In the sub-plot there is Malvolio, who pursues love, and Sir Toby, who prefers drinking. Olivia and Sir Toby are 'consanguineous' but of opposite tempers; the other two disturb both of them. On their side, Orsino and Malvolio are both self-centred, but one neglects 'state' and the other affects it; however, one is a lover who likes solitude, the other a solitary who turns to love. Both imagine they are in love with Olivia, while one is really fired by a forged letter, and the other is blind to the wife in front of his eyes. In the upshot, Orsino unwittingly helps to find a husband for Olivia, and Malvolio, a wife for Sir Toby. At the beginning of the comedy, Olivia had mourned a brother, while Orsino resented it; at the end, she finds a brother again, in Orsino himself.

Between Orsino and Olivia come the twins, Viola-Sebastian, opposite and indistinguishable. Between Malvolio and Sir Toby comes Maria, the 'Penthesilia' who forges a false identity. The twins are heirs to fortune, unsuspecting and unambitious; Maria is an intriguer, who signs herself 'The Fortunate-Unhappy'. In their first scene together, Sir Andrew 'accosts', 'woos' and 'assails' Maria, who drops his hand; Antonio likewise accosts, woos and assails Viola and Sebastian, who lose or ignore him. The symmetrical pattern is completed at the mid-point of the play, when Sir Andrew and Antonio confront each other with drawn swords. This encounter between the romantic and the comic figures is twice repeated, and on the last occasion it seems to be Viola's double who is the aggressor (V.i.175–80). Hence, although Sir Andrew and Antonio do not know each other or why they are quarrelling, they co-operate to bring about an unexpected result; Sir Andrew, to provide a wife for Sebastian, and Antonio, to provide a husband for Maria.

This dance of changed partners and reversed fortunes is much more complicated than anything in *Gl'Ingannati*. Shakespeare devises it partly by carrying the Plautine themes of twinship and of the lost being found again, or brought back to life, much farther than the Italian had gone; and partly by pursuing his own allied and festive theme of a Twelfth Night mask of misrule. By this means, he laces sub-plot and main plot together in a single intricate design.

The interest of the sub-plot is more varied, moreover, and its links with the main plot are more complex, than a bare summary of the action can indicate. In relation to the main plot, the comic figures are somewhat like scapegoats; they reflect the humours of Orsino and Olivia in caricature and through them these humours are purged away. Secondly, the sub-plot is a Feast of Fools,[30] containing its own satire of humours in Malvolio and Sir Andrew. And, from another point of view, Sir Toby's 'uncivil rule' is complementary to the problem of 'time' in the main plot.

Besides Malvolio, Sir Toby and Sir Andrew are to some extent parodies of Orsino. One will drink Olivia's health till he is 'drown'd' or 'his brains turn o' th' toe like a parish-top'; the other is a model of gentlemanly indecision, hopes to woo Olivia without speaking to her, and attacks Viola from jealousy. The strains of unconscious parody in the sub-plot help to amplify the general theme of delusion and error.

On Olivia's side, moreover, the disorder in her household is a direct reaction to her attitude at the beginning of the play.[31] Malvolio affects a grave austerity to please her, but the instincts are in revolt. Sir Toby redoubles the clamour of love for her and personifies her neglect of time and the reproach of the clock (III.i.130). Sir Andrew, a fool, helps to find her a husband. In Malvolio's 'madness' she comes to see a reflection of her own (III.iv.14), and at the end he takes her place in cloistered darkness.

In addition, the comic dialogue echoes the thought of the serious characters and twists it into fantastic shapes. To the serious actors, life is a sea-voyage: the comic actors deal with journeys more specific, bizarre and adventurous than theirs, ranging in time from when 'Noah was a sailor' to the publishing of 'the new map, with the augmentation of the Indies', and from the Barents Sea to the gates of Tartar or the equinoctial of Queubus. The serious actors scrutinise a fate which might be pagan in its religious colouring: the comic speakers, for their part, are orthodox Christians, and their dialogue is peppered with Biblical and ecclesiastical references. Sir Toby, for instance, 'defies lechery' and counts on 'faith'; Sir Andrew plumes himself on having 'no more wit than a Christian or an ordinary man has', and would beat Malvolio for no 'exquisite reason' save that of thinking him a Puritan;[32] the duel scene and the madness scenes are full of 'devils'. In part, these ecclesiastical jokes reinforce the suggestion of Twelfth Night foolery and of mock sermons like Erasmus's sermon of Folly; from this aspect, they lead up to Feste's interlude of Sir Topas. But in part, too, their tone of moral security to the degree of smugness gives a counterweight to the emotions of the serious actors.

Moreover, Sir Andrew and Sir Toby are both alike in feeling very sure of their ideal place in the scheme of things. They are contrasted as shrewd and fatuous, parasite and gull, Carnival and Lent; but they are both, in their differing ways, 'sots', and both gentlemen.[33] Their conversation is a handbook to courtesy. And while Sir Andrew is an oafish squire, who will 'have but a year in all these ducats', Sir Toby is a degenerate knight, who will not 'confine himself within the modest limits of order' and, possessed of the rudiments of good breeding, delights in turning them upside-down. He is repeatedly called 'uncivil' (II.iii.123, III.iv.253, IV.i.53), and his merry-making is out of time and season. He tells Malvolio, 'We did keep time, sir, in our catches'; but when at the end he leaves the stage with a broken head, driving Sir Andrew off before him, he is abusing the surgeon, on the lines of the same pun, for 'a drunken rogue' whose eyes are 'set at eight'. Despite his resemblance to Falstaff, Sir Toby has a smaller mind, and this shows itself in his complacency with his position in Olivia's household.

Malvolio is a more complex and formidable character. Evidently Maria's 'good practise' on this overweening steward was the distinctive attraction of *Twelfth Night* to Stuart audiences; but that does not mean (as some critics would have it, reacting against Lamb)[34] that Malvolio is presented as a contemptible butt. An audience is more likely to enjoy and remember the humiliation of someone who in real life would be feared than the humiliation of a mere impostor like Parolles. Malvolio is neither a Puritan nor an upstart, though he has qualities in common with both. Olivia and Viola call him a 'gentleman' (V.i.277, 280), as the steward of a countess's household no doubt would be, and in seeking to repress disorders he is simply carrying out the duties of his office:

Have you no wit, manners, nor honesty, but to gabble like tinkers at this time of night? Do ye make an alehouse of my lady's house, that ye squeak out your coziers' catches without any mitigation or remorse of voice? Is there no respect of place, persons, nor time in you?

(II.iii.87)

These early speeches to Sir Toby have a firm ring about them that explains Olivia's confidence in Malvolio, without as yet disclosing the 'politic' affectation that Maria sees in him. On the other hand, his principle of degree and order is simply a mask for his pride. He is 'sick of self-love', unable to live spontaneously as one of a community, as is hinted from the outset by his recoil from the sociable side of the jester's art – an office that also requires the

understanding of place, persons and time. And even before finding
Maria's letter, he shows the self-ignorance of a divided personality in
the daydream he weaves about himself and Olivia, indulging his
'humour of state'. Nevertheless, when his humour has been mocked
to the full, Shakespeare still makes him protest that he 'thinks nobly
of the soul', and he remains a force to be reckoned with right to the
end. With his unconscious hypocrisy in the exercise of power and his
rankling sense of injustice, he comes mid-way between Shylock and
the Angelo of *Measure for Measure*.

Sir Toby, Sir Andrew and Malvolio – all three – are striving to be
something false, whether novel or antiquated, which is out of place
in a healthy community; they are a would-be retainer, a would-be
gallant, a would-be 'politician'. But the conflict over revelry between
Malvolio and Sir Toby is a conflict of two opposed reactions towards
changing social and economic conditions. In Malvolio's eyes, Sir
Toby 'wastes the treasure of his time'. So he does; and so, in their
ways, do Olivia and Orsino. A natural way of living, Shakespeare
seems to imply, must observe impersonal factors such as time as well
as the healthy gratification of instinct – and in the last resort, the two
may be incompatible with each other. Hence, Malvolio in the end is
neither crushed nor pacified. He belongs, like Antonio, to the world
of law and business, outside the festive circle of the play. Both are
imprisoned for a while by the others. They stand for two extremes of
self-sacrifice and self-love, but they share a rigid belief in principle.
And neither can be fully assimilated into the comedy.

There are discordant strains, then, in the harmony of *Twelfth
Night* – strains of melancholy and of something harsher. As far as
any one actor can resolve them, this tasks falls to Feste.

Feste is not only the most fully portrayed of Shakespeare's clowns,
he is also the most agile-minded of them. He has fewer set pieces than
Touchstone and fewer proverbs than the Fool in *Lear*. He is proud of
his professional skill – 'better a witty fool than a foolish wit' – but he
wields it lightly, in darting paradoxes; he is a 'corrupter of words'.
Yet, besides being exceptionally imaginative and sophisticated, he is
exceptionally given to scrounging for tips. This trait is consistent
with the traditional aspect of his role, especially as the fool in a feast
of misrule, but it helps to make him more like a real character and
less like a stage type.

This money-sense of Feste and his awareness of his social status
bring him within the conflict of ideas affecting the other actors.
Although he depends for his living on other people's pleasure, and

can sing to any tune – 'a love-song, or a song of good life' – Feste is neither a servile entertainer nor an advocate of go-as-you-please. On the contrary, he is a moralist with a strong bent towards scepticism. 'As there is no true cuckold but calamity, so beauty's a flower ... Truly, sir, and pleasure will be paid, one time or another ... The whirligig of time brings in his revenges': one factor will always cancel another. As against Malvolio, he belittles the soul; but he shows hardly any more confidence in the survival-value of folly, and marriage is the only form of it he recommends. For Feste himself could very easily belong to the ship of fools he designates for Orsino, having his business and intent everywhere and making 'a good voyage of nothing'. (The same thought is present when he tells Viola that foolery 'does walk about the orb like the sun; it shines every where'.) There is a persistent hint, then, that his enigmas glance at himself as well as others, and that he feels his own position to be insecure. And it is consistent with this that he should be the only character in Shakespeare to take pleasure, or refuge, in fantasies of pure nonsense: 'as the old hermit of Prague, that never saw pen and ink, very wittily said to a niece of King Gorboduc, "That that is is."' It is impossible to go further than a non-existent hermit of Prague.

Feste is not the ringleader in *Twelfth Night*, nor is he exactly the play's philosopher. He is cut off from an independent life of his own by his traditional role in reality and on the stage, and what he sees at the bottom of the well is 'nothing'. He knows that without festivity he is nothing; and he knows, in his epilogue, that misrule does not last, and that men shut their gates against toss-pots, lechers, knaves and fools. A play is only a play, and no more. Yet it is precisely on this finely-poised balance of his that the whole play comes to rest. Orsino, Olivia, Viola, Sebastian, Sir Toby, Maria, Malvolio, Feste himself – nearly everyone in *Twelfth Night* acts a part in some sense, but Feste is the only one who takes this aspect of life for granted. The others commit errors and have divided emotions; but Feste can have no real emotions of his own, and may only live in his quibbles. Yet by virtue of this very disability, he sees the element of misrule in life more clearly than the rest, appreciating its value because he knows its limitations. A play to Feste may be only a play, but it is also the breath of life.

Feste is the principal link between the other characters in *Twelfth Night*. Unless Puck is counted, he is the only clown for whom Shakespeare provides an epilogue. And as it happens, his is the epilogue to the whole group of Shakespeare's romantic comedies.

A note on Shakespeare and Plautus

The Plautine motif of confused identities is present in *Gl'Ingannati*, and possibly in Riche. But a comparison of *Twelfth Night* with *Menaechmi* and *The Comedy of Errors* on one side, and with *Gl'Ingannati*, Bandello and Riche on the other, makes it seem certain that Shakespeare was consciously borrowing from Plautus in planning Sebastian's role, at the same time, however, enlarging this borrowed material on the lines of *The Comedy of Errors*:

(a) *Background*. In *Menaechmi*, there are twin brothers, long separated and unknown to each other; their father is dead. In *The Comedy of Errors*, they have been separated by a tempest; their father is alive. In both, one of the 'lost' brothers hopes to find the other in the course of his travels. In *Gl'Ingannati* and Bandello, the twin brother has been lost since the sack of Rome in 1527; he comes expecting to find his father, still alive, and his sister. In Riche, the brother sets off in pursuit of his sister, who has followed the Duke and has suffered shipwreck; their father is still alive. So far, *Twelfth Night* might be a compound of all the others.

(b) *Sebastian*. In *Menaechmi*, Menaechmus of Syracuse, searching for his brother, lands at Epidamnus with his slave. He is hot-tempered (Loeb edn, II.i:269) – a trait only emphasised here and in *Twelfth Night*. Leaving his slave, he meets in turn a cook, a courtesan and a parasite, who mistake him for his twin. He thinks them mad, or drunk, or dreaming (II.iii:373, 395), but sleeps with the courtesan, accepts her gifts – a mantle and a bracelet – and makes off 'while time and circumstance permit', thanking the gods for his unexpected luck (III.iii:551–3). He misses his slave, and gets involved in a squabble with his sister-in-law and her father, feigning madness to frighten them off. His doings react on his brother. Finally, the brothers meet, compare notes about their father, and recognise each other with the help of the slave.

Sebastian's actions follow exactly the same pattern. He appears in Illyria with a companion, then leaves him; he is going to the court, but has no definite goal since his twin sister has apparently died (II.i). Meeting his companion again, he says he wants to view 'the reliques of this town'; they separate a second time, after making an appointment (III.iii). He then meets in turn a clown, a parasite (Sir Toby) and his friend, and a lady, who mistake him for his twin. He thinks they are mad, or that he is mad or else dreaming, fights the parasite and his friend, but accepts the lady's invitation to accompany her (IV.i). He has missed his companion, but accepts the lady's gift of a pearl, welcomes 'this accident and flood of fortune', and agrees to marry her (IV.iii). Off-stage, he fights the parasite a second time (V.i.175–80). Meanwhile, his doings have reacted on his twin, partly through the agency of his companion. Finally, the twins meet, compare notes about their father, and recognise each other.

In *Gl'Ingannati*, the brother comes to Modena with a servant and a tutor, a pedant who describes the sights of the town in detail (III.i). He leaves them to go sight-seeing, meets the second heroine's maid, and agrees to visit the mistress, supposing her to be some courtesan (III.v). Then he meets her father and his own father, who take him to be his twin sister, dressed as a man; he calls them mad, and they lock him up with the second heroine (III.vii), whereupon he seduces her. He does not meet his twin sister until she is married.

In Bandello the only characters the brother meets at first are the second heroine and her maid; in Riche, only the second heroine.

With Sebastian, then, Shakespeare ignores *Gl'Ingannati* (except conceivably for the sight-seeing), and follows Plautus in detail. He had used much of this material before, in *The Comedy of Errors*. But there he had introduced variations (for example, the 'lost' brother's business affairs and the character of Luciana); here he goes back directly to his source.

(c) *Messaline*. Apparently no editor of *Twelfth Night* has explained satisfactorily why Shakespeare makes Sebastian come from 'Messaline', 'a town unknown to geography'. Perhaps this is because they have concentrated unduly on the Italian background of *Twelfth Night*; (compare Draper, who suggests Manzolino, or 'Mensoline', near Modena, *Audience*, pp. 262–3). But reference to Plautus offers a very likely solution. In *Menaechmi*, II.i the slave asks Menaechmus of Syracuse how long he means to go on searching for his twin: 'Istrians, Spaniards, *Massilians, Illyrians* (*Massiliensis, Hilurios*), the entire Adriatic, and foreign Greece and the whole coast of Italy – every section the sea washes – we've visited in our travels. . .' (Loeb edn, pp. 235–8). This scene corresponds to *Twelfth Night*, II.i, where Sebastian mentions 'Messaline', telling Antonio that his 'determinate voyage is mere extravagancy' because his sister is drowned. Hence it seems almost certain that Shakespeare invented the name 'Messaline', in connection with Illyria, from a reminiscence of these lines of Plautus (where, in addition, the speaker's name is Messenio); (compare *Times Literary Supplement*, 3 June 1955). This suggests that the parallel between Sebastian and Menaechmus was clearly present to Shakespeare's mind from the beginning.

(d) *Antonio*. In *Menaechmi*, the slave is a purse-bearer, warns Menaechmus against the dangers of Epidamnus, intervenes to save his master's twin from danger, is promised his liberty, has the promise withdrawn, and then has it renewed. Antonio's part corresponds to this closely. There is nothing like this in *Gl'Ingannati*, nor much in the Dromio of *The Comedy of Errors*. On the other hand, Shakespeare seems to have taken some traits in Antonio from Aegeon in *The Comedy of Errors* (compare n. 28, p. 264 below).

(e) The *Captain* who comes on with Viola in *Twelfth Night*, I.ii has only a minimal part as her confidant. In this, his only scene, his main speech concerns Sebastian; while the later news of his arrest at Malvolio's suit (V.i.275–7) recalls the legal business in *The Comedy of Errors*, like the arrest of Antonio. He therefore belongs to Sebastian's part in the composition of *Twelfth Night*, rather than Viola's. (There is a captain in *Apolonius and Silla*, but he tries to rape the heroine, and then disappears.)

(f) *Illyria*. The assumption that Shakespeare's knowledge of *Menaechmi* played a large – and not merely an incidental – part in the composition of *Twelfth Night*, throws some further light on Shakespeare's methods of construction. In particular, it suggests why he set the play in 'Illyria'. On the face of it, there is no special reason for this choice of a setting, except perhaps Viola's pun on 'Elysium' when the place is first mentioned. Although the name has since acquired a romantic aura from the play itself, there is nothing specially Arcadian or Ruritanian about 'Illyria' in *Twelfth Night*, and no strong local colour, as there is for Modena in *Gl'Ingannati*, or for Venice in Shakespeare's other plays. What there is, moreover, is slightly inconsistent; for Antonio's warning to Sebastian about the dangers of 'these parts', which he says are 'rough and inhospitable' (III.iii.8–11), is not exactly borne out by the rest of the play, and is vague in any case, so that it seems to belong to Antonio, not to Illyria. This speech can be traced back, however, to the more specific warning of the slave in *Menaechmi*, II.i:258–64, to the effect that Epidamnus is a town of 'rakes, drinkers, sycophants and alluring harlots', owing its very name to the tricks it plays on strangers – and this (together with the way the warning is falsified) does correspond very closely to Illyria as Sebastian finds it. Further, Hotson points out that the real Illyria of Shakespeare's day was known for riotous behaviour, drinking and piracy (*First Night*, p. 151). These touches account for the sea-fighting in *Twelfth Night* (but not the tricks of fortune), and otherwise they match with Epidamnus; so that Epidamnus and the real country together furnish the sketchy local colour of 'Illyria' in *Twelfth Night*. It looks, therefore, as if Shakespeare, having planned to modify the Viola story with the aid of Plautus, looked for a place-name that would fit the attributes he wanted, and chose 'Illyria' accordingly. If so, his memory could have prompted him from the same line of *Menaechmi* that yields the source of 'Messaline'.

(g) *Olivia's household*. Assuming that Shakespeare founded Illyria from Epidamnus, he would have looked to the mother-town for some of the inhabitants and their customs. There is a good deal of banqueting in Epidamnus, and some talk of lawsuits. And there is one important character whom Shakespeare had not used already in *The Comedy of Errors*. This is the parasite, Peniculus or 'Brush', a greedy drinker and a schemer. He pushes himself on the courtesan's house, urges his patron to dance at one point (*Menaechmi*, I.iii:197 – compare *Twelfth Night*, I.iii.140), and elsewhere provokes Menaechmus of Syracuse. And he seems to be reincarnated in the person of Sir Toby.

Secondly, there are the episodes of feigned inspiration, or frenzy, in *Menaechmi*, V, with a comic doctor and a scuffle over the wrong twin. Shakespeare had used these already in *The Comedy of Errors*, IV.iv. (compare n. 28, p. 264 below), but there was no reason why he should not use them again. They could well have furnished hints for the duel scene with its 'devils' in *Twelfth Night* and the scene of Malvolio and Sir Topas.

Moreover, anyone approaching the Viola story by way of Plautus would be inclined to give more prominence to the second heroine (the supposed 'courtesan' of the Italian tales) and her companions. And in fact, Olivia and her household, in their actions towards Sebastian, reproduce very closely the actions of the courtesan, her servants and the parasite in *Menaechmi*, without any hint of indebtedness to *Gl'Ingannati*, Riche or the transformed Plautine incidents of *The Comedy of Errors*. These considerations need not imply that Shakespeare imagined Olivia and her household simply as afterthoughts to the Plautine twin; but they do seem to suggest how, once he had begun thinking about the material in Plautus, the whole of his composition could have fallen into shape.

Finally, (h) *Errors and misrule*. The circumstances of the performance of *The Comedy of Errors* at the Gray's Inn revels of 1594 could well have suggested to Shakespeare the plan of introducing a Plautine comedy of mistaken identity into a larger framework of misrule (compare n. 8, p. 260 below). He had done something like this already in *The Taming of the Shrew*, where the sub-plot is a comedy of changed identities borrowed from Ariosto, and the framework story of Sly as a lord is an episode of misrule.

To sum up, it is plausible to reconstruct the composition of *Twelfth Night* somewhat as follows. Reading the Viola story, in Riche or elsewhere, Shakespeare was struck by the notion of 'error' implicit in 'following them that fly from us', and this gave him the hint for Orsino and Olivia. Secondly, 'error' suggested the role of Sebastian, with its Plautine farce and its romantic overtones of sea-adventure prolonged from *The Comedy of Errors*. And the same notion of 'error' also suggested the stage devices of misrule, prominent in the sub-plot of *Twelfth Night* and latent in the whole play. Though it leaves much of the emotional content of *Twelfth Night* untouched, this conjecture does seem to account for the way the whole stage design of the play holds so beautifully together.

5. Shakespeare and the ventriloquists

Relatively early in Shakespeare's career the minor poet, John Weever, affirmed the devotion of 'thousands' of spectators or readers to Romeo, Richard and others of Shakespeare's characters, his 'children' as the heavy-handed eulogist dubs them.[1] In the movement of opinion that established Shakespeare as the supreme dramatic poet in the course of the eighteenth and early nineteenth centuries (progressively clearing him of reproach for offending against the neo-classical rules of construction), his gift of character-portrayal was the outstanding theme for praise and wonder and character-study became the leading occupation of criticism. And Weever's metaphor of fatherhood, biological creation, re-emerged as an accepted critical fiction, almost a critical doctrine. Pope had repeated that Shakespeare was an instrument of nature, not a mere copier, and had said that each of his people was as distinct as an individual in real life; Johnson added, with a different emphasis, that his lifelikeness was not the result of any searching after personal idiosyncrasies but of Shakespeare's truth to typical human nature; others, like Morgann, began to treat the plays like psychological case-books, probing the depths of separate characters as if they were independent human beings. What impressed the commentators so forcibly was not merely the wealth of observation revealed by Shakespeare's people but their air of spontaneity, of free-standing autonomy, uninhibited by theatrical contrivance. Hazlitt says, for example, enforcing what had become an approved commonplace, that in *Antony and Cleopatra* 'the characters breathe, move, and live'; Shakespeare, he goes on, 'does not stand reasoning on what his characters would do or say, but at once becomes them, and speaks and acts for them'; and again, in *Hamlet*, 'the characters think and speak and act just as they might do, if left entirely to themselves. There is no set purpose, no straining at a point. The observations are suggested by the passing scene – the gusts of passion come and go like sounds of music borne on the wind.'[2] That simile, with its suggestion of an Aeolian harp, is a reminder of the romantic bias of Hazlitt's period. We can no longer, as reflecting critics, attribute such spontaneity to Shakespeare's characters, and we are cautious about the illusion of their separate personalities. Indeed, when Hazlitt was lecturing, Schlegel and Coleridge were already sketching out a theory of organic unity in Shakespeare, which might have led interpreters to subordinate character-study to the latent governing idea within each play as a whole. On the other hand, it is possible that in large measure the enthusiasm of the Romantics for creative freedom and psychological intuition was caused by, and not simply transferred to, their admiration for Shakespeare. And the illusion that each of his characters is a separate being with thoughts and impulses of his own cannot simply be argued away; the actors in every performance are there to revive it.

Belief in the spontaneity of Shakespeare's characters, as separate centres of consciousness, is closely allied to an interest in their capacity for self-awareness and introspection, an interest which Coleridge did a great deal to encourage. In this paper I shall try to examine some aspects of Hamlet, the favourite subject for this interest of the Romantics. I shall not set out to reinvestigate the details of Coleridge's faded portrait of the melancholy Prince, but I think there are still important questions to consider in his general statements about Shakespeare's methods of characterisation.

'Shakespeare shaped his characters out of the nature within', says Coleridge; 'but we cannot so safely say, out of his own nature, as an individual person ...' And, to bring home this elusive concept, Coleridge points, as he often does, to a radical contrast between Shakespeare and other playwrights:[3]

There is no greater or more common vice in dramatic writers than to draw out of themselves. How I – alone and in the self-sufficiency of my study, as all men are apt to be proud in their dreams – should *like* to be talking king! . . . Shakespeare in composing had no *I* but the *I* representative.

Other stage poets, then, according to Coleridge, are not creators, endowing characters with an independent life; they are essentially 'ventriloquists', projecting themselves through the mouths of all their puppets. Coleridge repeats this criticism several times. For example, in a play by Beaumont and Fletcher, 'the scenes are mock dialogues in which the poet solo plays the ventriloquist, but cannot suppress his own way of expressing himself'. And even Ben Jonson, for all his 'erudition', is guilty in *Sejanus* of 'an absurd rant and ventriloquism' such as can be found 'in no genuine part of Shakespeare' – 'ventriloquism, because Sejanus is a puppet out of which the poet makes his own voice appear to come'.[4] The figures in other writers' plays are one-sided, uniform, subjected to the author's voice, overshadowed by his self-importance, whereas Shakespeare's are abundant, varied and free. Or, to use Hazlitt's wording again, Shakespeare 'becomes' his characters, whereas other playwrights 'stand reasoning' about them, are straining to make a point.

Now, if we apply this contrast to the Elizabethans in general, it is clear that there is a share of injustice in it. Coleridge simplifies stage history; he ignores, or takes for granted, the new impulse in that assertive rhetoric that brings their characters to life. The 'high astounding terms' of Marlowe's Tamburlaine are still recognisably akin to those of medieval stage figures, Herod in the Coventry *Slaughter of the Innocents*, for instance, but they carry a new dynamic force. Herod boasts to the audience of what he is, or believes himself to be – 'the myghttyst conquerowre that eyuer walkid on grownd!';[5] but although he is certainly 'talking king' (and comic villain as well), there is no personal inflection in his voice. He simply lists his magical attributes, as in a herald's proclamation:

> To recownt vnto you myn innevmerabull substance,
>   Thatt were to moche for any tong to tell!
> For all the whole Orent ys vnder myn obeydeance,
>   And Prynce am I of Purgatorre, and Cheff Capten of Hell!

Tamburlaine, by contrast, boasts not of what he is so much as of what he wills himself to become:

> I am a Lord, for so my deeds shall prove,
> And yet a shepherd by my Parentage.
>
> (*Part 1*, I.ii.34)

His will creates a role, which is at once a commanding stage presence and a programme for action.

Again, to glance at another innovative role, consider these typical lines from Hieronimo's soliloquy at a crisis in *The Spanish Tragedy*:

> Thus therefore will I rest me in unrest,
> Dissembling quiet in unquietness.
>
> (III.xiii.29)

No doubt the author's voice is audible here, imposing a heightened self-consciousness on the speaker; and further, they are keynote lines, summarising the conduct of every active personage in the play.

But without such inner tension, and such projection and magnification of tension, there would be no Elizabethan tragic drama, not simply at the level of *The Spanish Tragedy*, but at the level of *Richard III* or even *Macbeth*.

Nevertheless, there is strength in Coleridge's generalisation. The will-to-power in Marlowe's heroes is always much the same will-to-power, and very few expressions of feeling are allowed to his characters out of the range of its magnetic attraction. Ben Jonson is much more subtle and on the surface more varied; but when, for instance, Volpone says, 'I glory / More in the cunning purchase of my wealth, / Than in the glad possession', we recognise the note that is common to all his active characters, the note of intellectual self-congratulation which blends together their otherwise discordant humours and also motivates the plot. Although he is a profound critic of manners, Jonson is only at one remove from 'talking king' in his own person. Webster dwells on the subjective sensations and the mental quirks of his characters; but when, for example, Flamineo exclaims,

> We endure the strokes like anvils or hard steel,
> Till pain itself make us no pain to feel,
>
> (*The White Devil*, III.iii.1)

he conveys the essential experience of all of them. Angry, feigning or resigned, they all come to life principally as victims, and the tragedy is a parade of their sufferings. None of Shakespeare's contemporaries can confer on their actors that degree of self-consciousness, or that capacity for self-questioning, that makes us feel completely that the speaker is a living person in his own mind, and so, consequently, for us. A partial exception is Middleton (who may, of course, have learned from Shakespeare); and – to offer one more brief typifying extract – we seem to hear the tones of a natural self-consciousness in speeches like Livia's soliloquy in *Women Beware Women*, when she has made up her mind to engineer the liaison between her brother and their niece:

> I am the fondest where I once affect,
> The carefull'st of their healths, and of their ease, forsooth,
> That I look still but slenderly to mine own;
> I take a course to pity him so much now
> That I have none left for modesty and myself.
>
> (II.i.65)

She knows herself, and does not know herself, like a living individual; and this kind of confident self-deception, which reveals the inner mind of the characters, is the guiding thread in Middleton's main tragedies. However, all Middleton's tragic characters are subject to much the same form of self-deception and follow it along much the same course. And, although Middleton shows us that each of them has in mind an 'I', a separate identity, he does not develop that consciousness beyond the discovery of self-deception, and he invites us to respond to it mainly in a critical spirit, from the outside.

As Coleridge emphasises, Shakespeare writes from an altogether different level of understanding. He 'shaped his characters out of the nature within' – which implies that he could share the subjective, the experiencing side of their feelings; 'but we cannot so safely say, out of his own nature, as an individual person' – which implies his freedom from emotional self-interest. And 'Shakespeare in composing had no *I* but the *I* representative.' In effect, this reconciles Pope's view of the individuality of Shakespeare's characters with Samuel Johnson's sense of their common humanity. At the same time, Coleridge suggests a view of the impersonality of great writing more positive and inclusive than the definitions put forward by Joyce and the early T. S. Eliot. And it comes very close to the insight Leavis expresses, with regard to tragedy, when he says that tragedy 'undermines and supersedes' self-centred and 'self-boosting' emotional attitudes:[6]

[Tragedy] establishes below them a kind of profound impersonality in which experience matters, not because it is mine – because it is to me it belongs or happens, or because it subserves or issues in purpose or will, but because it is what it is, the 'mine' mattering only in so far as the individual sentience is the indispensable focus of experience.

Leavis's distinction between the possessive and the impersonal aspects of experience in tragedy supplements Coleridge's distinction between the personal 'I' of the poet and his '*I* representative'. But Leavis's statement also suggests that in genuine tragedy we are made aware of both sides of the distinction, personal and impersonal or representative, together, and that in the experience which 'matters' for us we cannot have one without the other. And this reflection in turn, I think, has a bearing on what Coleridge says about Shakespeare's characters. I mean that in his leading tragic characters Shakespeare makes us aware of a gap between a character's image of himself and an image of a more complete humanity that could be described as an '*I* representative'. No individual could embody such a representativeness, or even define it. But on the other hand it is not simply a poetic mirage. A sense of what such complete humanity might be, or might require, emerges in the course of Shakespeare's mature tragedies, partly in the speeches of the leading characters and partly through the interplay of the action as a whole. It is partly indicated by negatives. But Shakespeare is the only Elizabethan dramatist to convey a sense of what Coleridge calls 'the *I* representative', while at the same time and by the same token he distinguishes it from a character's personal 'I'. And the deep-lying interest within his mature tragedies springs somewhere within that distinction, or gap. At the centre, or point of origin, is the way Shakespeare brings about the hero's perception of a division within himself.

This is not the same as speaking of a 'tragic flaw', because that seems to imply that apart from the flaw in question the hero would approach perfection – which is not what Shakespeare intimates. Nor would it help to return to Coleridge's speculations about Shakespeare creating such a character as Hamlet by meditating upon some inner quality of his own carried to excess,[7] if only because those speculations lead away from the impact and movement of drama. The notion of a gap within the hero's image of himself gives a better pointer, I think, to Shakespeare's method – a notion well brought out by Peter Ure in his essay on 'Character and role from Richard III to Hamlet', where he argues that the central interest in the tragic plays is the 'gap', the lack of 'consonance', between 'the hero's inward self ' and his office or role, as king, for instance, or avenger. A role is both a social and a theatrical concept, and hence for the audience as well as the character a provisional guide to the line the action will follow. But, as Ure points out, 'it is the character faced with his role, forced to decide about it, the quality of his response, that Shakespeare shows us, not just his performance in the role'.[8] In brief, the effective guiding line within the psychological movement of the play is the hero's efforts to close the gap. In Shakespeare's mature tragedies, this brings the hero's inward self into question besides his attitude towards his role.

Hamlet is the first play in which Shakespeare develops this method of characterisation at length. Many of the outstanding characters in his early plays, the figures who hold the stage and seem typically Shakespearean, are not notable for self-questioning but rather for self-assertive, humorous energy, like Richard III and Faulconbridge, Petruchio and Falstaff. Richard III only doubts himself for a moment, under the belated blows of conscience. And although

Shakespeare makes dramatic use of introspection very early, he does not bring it to the centre of interest even with Richard II or Brutus, who question their roles more than themselves. Something new in Shakespeare seems to be afoot when *The Merchant of Venice* opens with Antonio's 'In sooth, I know not why I am so sad'; but this puzzlement is left undeveloped in the play. In contrast, Hamlet's part begins with his reference to the mystery of his own state of feeling, and this mystery complicates Hamlet's response to his imposed duty of revenge until very near the end. Hamlet is agitated by the problem of himself, not only as a son, a prince, a lover and a revenger, but as a human being, a man among men. This conception of the hero is closely linked with two other features of the play which, together with it, give considerable substance to Coleridge's thought about Shakespeare and the '*I* representative'. One is the explicit concern of the play with speech, style, speaking out, communication through words. The other is the frequency of attempts to describe what a complete or authentic man would be like. These features are principally related to Hamlet, but they also belong to the construction of the play as a whole.

The play begins, of course, with a challenge, a question about identity: 'Who's there?' The setting is supposed to be dark and cold, as we soon learn, and suggests the wearing of large cloaks, like military greatcoats. There is an additional touch of nervous excitement in this military formula, since it comes from the wrong soldier, as we gather from the reply of the other sentinel, Francisco: 'Nay, answer me. Stand and unfold yourself.' This tiny exchange sets going far-reaching currents. *Unfold* – reveal yourself, come out of concealment, declare your allegiance and who you are. In this play Shakespeare is going to use the stage with an approximation to unity of place, since all the actors will be seen at Elsinore or nearby. Again and again we shall witness newcomers to the stage, or hear of strangers approaching Elsinore – Horatio, the Ghost, young Fortinbras, Rosencrantz and Guildenstern, the Players, and then Laertes and finally Hamlet himself returning – whose reasons for coming there will be questioned somewhat as Francisco questions his comrade. This is one dramatic basis for the emphasis the dialogue gives to the theme of speaking out. The verb *to speak* is heard fifteen times in the six acting minutes or so of the opening scene, together with related terms such as *answer*, *inform* and *impart*, implying the sharing of a secret.

Nearly all the characters have something to hide or to explain, from the King to the Gravedigger; most conspicuously, Hamlet. But his first speeches, beginning with an aside, amount to a refusal to answer questions, to discard his 'inky cloak' and 'unfold' himself, and even to a hint that no explanation is possible. His first two lines – 'A little more than kin, and less than kind', and 'Not so, my lord, I am too much in the sun' – contain a riddle about family relationships which touches his own identity (of what 'kind' is he, if not Claudius's kinsman?) and a hint of clinging to the shade. His first reply of any length, pouncing on his mother's word, 'seems', not only contrasts his inward state with 'customary' demonstrations of grief, which he compares to play-acting, but implies that he cannot even clarify it to himself. 'I have that within which passes show' may mean that I have more grief than I wish to show here, or more grief than custom and external shows can express, but again it may mean that what I have within is beyond the reach of expression at all, like the peace of God which passeth understanding. And that inwardly Hamlet is wrestling with the inexplicable comes out very soon, in his first soliloquy, where it appears that he not only cannot bear his mother's remarriage but cannot understand how her incest, as he thinks of it, can have been humanly possible, and cannot bear, or understand, the insistence of his own reaction: 'Must I remember? ... Let me not think on't!' Unlike Shakespeare's other heroes, Hamlet is shown at once at the deepest point of despair, and a part of his despair is precisely the difficulty of stating clearly to himself what he is feeling. Neither Richard II nor Brutus has had to encounter a similar conceptual difficulty in their moments of introspection:

> I have been studying how I may compare
> This prison where I live unto the world,

or,

> Since Cassius first did whet me against Caesar,
> I have not slept –

these are apparently statements of fact, in the indicative mood; the speaker himself knows what has been happening. But Hamlet at first can only express wishes, and negative wishes, in the mood of the subjunctive:

> O that this too too sallied flesh would melt, ...
> Or that the Everlasting had not fix'd
> His canon 'gainst self-slaughter! ...

and the rest of his soliloquy, apart from one assertion that the world is 'an unweeded garden', moves forward through exclamations, elliptic sentences circling around his mother, broken up and overlaid with interjections, and then a noun clause with an infinitive verb ('to post / With such dexterity to incestious sheets'), before settling for a moment into a plain statement ('It is not, nor it cannot come to good'), but only to lurch into another subjunctive: 'But break my heart, for I must hold my tongue.' Holding his tongue, then, is for the moment the only determination Hamlet can arrive at, and he arrives at it against his will.

The only account Hamlet gives of himself in this soliloquy is an incidental and dismissive contrast with the typical hero ('... no more like my father / Than I to Hercules'). But he compares his father to a god; and even in his inclusive expression of disgust with life ('How weary, stale, flat and unprofitable / Seem to me all the uses of this world!') – which incidentally contradicts his recent statement to his mother that he '[knows] not "seems"' – there is still a corner of his mind from which the world could appear beautiful and his own reaction not conclusive but pitifully and puzzlingly abnormal. Similarly, later, in his outburst of guarded candour to Rosencrantz and Guildenstern – 'What a piece of work is a man' – he keeps his cool description of his own unexplainable listlessness separate and distinct from his praise of man in the abstract. Man's intellect and 'faculties' – the amazing co-ordination of the human 'machine' (to apply the term so strangely inserted by Hamlet in his letter to Ophelia)[9] – can still impress Hamlet vividly in spite of and by contrast with his private experience. And during the middle scenes he returns repeatedly to reflections on such human completeness, or symbolic tokens of it: in his wonder at the First Player's professional self-command and in his advice to the actors; in his praise for Horatio, whose 'blood and judgement are so well co-meddled' that he is not 'passion's slave'; in his effusion over his father's picture during the closet scene; and in his soliloquy on how 'rightly to be great' in action when he contemplates Fortinbras and his army.[10] These reflections pull against his 'wild' aberrations in his 'antic disposition', his fits of rant and fury when he could 'drink hot blood', and his acid reduction of mankind to 'this quintessence of dust'. They are sketches describing a state of health and human integrity, rather than reachings-out towards any remote ideal.

Other speakers supplement these sketches; for instance, Ophelia, in her lament for the 'noble mind' and harmonious accomplishments of Hamlet in the past. Even Claudius adds a significant touch, during the scene where he is hooking Laertes to his side, when, in a crafty digression within a digression, he alludes admiringly to the 'witchcraft' on horseback of the Norman visitor to Elsinore, who 'grew unto his seat, / . . . As had he been incorps'd and demi-natur'd / With the brave beast' (IV.vii.81–90): a fleeting but classically evocative glimpse of the unity between mind and instinct in a man. Altogether, these various speeches constitute a line of poetic thought that Shakespeare was to develop further, especially in *Macbeth*, culminating in Macbeth's soliloquy on 'To-morrow, and to-morrow'. In that soliloquy Macbeth, who has been driven deep into unreality, seems to be asking himself what reality in human experience would be like: something tangible and immediate, for example, not elusive; free and composed, unlike a bad actor; clear, authentic, lasting and coherent. Although it works through negatives, that soliloquy is a concentrated example of what, I take it, Leavis means by the experience in tragedy that matters because it is what it is and not because it is 'mine', and of what Coleridge means by speaking of the '*I* representative' in Shakespeare. There is nothing in the tragedy of *Hamlet* to equal it. But in the character of Hamlet Shakespeare has for the first time portrayed a mind that raises such questions about human authenticity, and raises them out of an inward need.

Hamlet's reflections on the nature of man do not lend themselves to sequential dramatic treatment, or at any rate Shakespeare does not treat them that way. But he makes an important guiding-thread out of Hamlet's preoccupation with the act of speech, which affects both his attitude towards his role and his conception of his innermost self. 'But break my heart, for I must hold my tongue' was the upshot of his initial monologue. And the trajectory of his part brings him back repeatedly to a similar place of deadlock between heart and tongue. Almost at once, he is rushed through a cycle of opposites. 'I'll speak to it though hell itself should gape', he exclaims when he hears of the coming of the Ghost, but only to enjoin 'silence' upon his informants – 'Give it an understanding but no tongue' (I.ii.244–9). And again, 'I will speak to thee', when he meets the Ghost (I.iv.44), followed swiftly by a renewed injunction to his friends to be silent, with an elaborate mimicry of the 'doubtful phrase' or 'ambiguous giving out' they might be tempted to lend themselves to but for his express prohibition (I.v.140–87). Act I is virtually rounded off with 'And still your fingers on your lips, I pray' – transposing the tension from Hamlet's soliloquy.

After these expository scenes Shakespeare carries Hamlet's

concern with speech through what may be described as three more waves or cycles. The first begins in his reported visit to Ophelia, when he appeared to her 'As if he had been loosed out of hell / To speak of horrors' (II.i.80), but did not utter a word. It rises through the relaxed moments of his exchange with Rosencrantz and Guildenstern – 'to speak to you like an honest man', he says at one point (II.ii.268) – and it advances to a peak in his praise for the 'speech' he asks the First Player to repeat and then his appreciation of the Player's delivery (II.ii.434–557). But here Hamlet reaches a limit. When he had boasted, 'I have that within which passes show', contrasting his own feelings with the play-acting of public grief, he had been caught unawares in a paradox, which only now rises to the surface of his mind. That is the paradox that a man who feels what he does not 'show' resembles an actor, no less than the man who shows what he does not feel; but that a professed actor can exhibit a passion in its integrity although or even because he does not share it. A gap yawns for Hamlet between sincerity and communication. So he finds the Player's unmotivated expressiveness 'monstrous' by reference to his own condition, and falls steeply back towards the deadlock of his first soliloquy, castigating himself for 'say[ing] nothing' in his 'cause' and yet for 'unpack[ing his] heart with words', 'like a whore' (II.ii.550–87). He hopes to break out of his deadlock by means of the actual play, which may provoke Claudius to 'proclaim' his guilt,

> For murther, though it have no tongue, will speak
> With most miraculous organ.
>
> (II.ii.593–4)

This sounds like a desperate remedy for Hamlet's inhibition, but it points a way forward (if only 'by indirections').

He is still close to deadlock in his next sequence, the 'To be' soliloquy and the 'nunnery' scene. Then what I may call the second wave (after the exposition) begins at a high point, in his instructions to the Players:

Speak the speech, I pray you, as I pronounc'd it to you, trippingly on the tongue, ... for in the very torrent, tempest, and, as I may say, whirlwind of your passion, you must acquire and beget a temperance that may give it smoothness ... [And] suit the action to the word, the word to the action, with this special observance, that you o'erstep not the modesty of nature ...

(III.ii.1–19)

This advice may very well convey the professional views of the actor–poet, William Shakespeare, but it is also dramatically appropriate to Hamlet's mind and present purpose. His desire for speaking out, making the truth known, unburdening his heart and achieving revenge, can only be fulfilled adequately with a concern for style, for full and apt expression and hence resolution of feeling, neither too little nor too much;[11] and this matters acutely for his intentions in staging *The Murder of Gonzago*. This statement about lucid, significant speech shows Hamlet at the height of his collected thought, but it is a lucidity at a distance from himself, projected in a work of art. As soon as the performance begins he breaks his own rules, and the excitement of triumph carries him far beyond the pitch of 'temperance'. 'I will speak daggers to her, but use none', he assures himself when preparing to meet his mother; 'My tongue and soul in this be hypocrites' (III.ii.396–7). He is back, therefore, to his initial self-contradiction; so that after the heated accusations in the closet scene he is obliged to urge his mother to put out of her mind the thought 'That not your trespass but my madness speaks' (III.iv.146). Satisfactory utterance, 'a temperance that may give it smoothness', is still beyond his reach.

His soliloquy on his way to England ('How all occasions do inform against me' (IV.iv.32)) shifts to doing rather than saying, and to the public reverberation of events; it is 'occasions' now that 'inform'. But this is Hamlet's last soliloquy and self-interrogation. In the closing cycle of the tragedy he is in an altered frame of mind after his actions at sea, and this shows itself in a change in his attitude towards speech. He is more free. 'I have words to speak in thine ear will make thee dumb,' he writes to Horatio (IV.vi.24), in pointed contrast to his injunction after meeting the Ghost. He is a sharp critic, varying in mood but objective, about the language spoken by the Gravedigger, Laertes and then Osric.[12] Before the fencing-match, he can 'proclaim' his wrongs done to Laertes (V.ii.232), in his first open statement at the Danish court, directed, ironically, against himself. And then, as he is dying, his thoughts are with public 'report' of his 'cause'. 'O, I could tell you', he begins, and only breaks off to entrust the duty 'to tell my story' to Horatio. But by now he has only enough energy left to give his 'dying voice' for the Danish throne on behalf of the newly-arrived Fortinbras, and beyond that, 'the rest is silence'. He has come back full circle to his first soliloquy, but with something like acceptance instead of frustration. At the same time, he has changed places with Horatio completely as regards silence and speaking. It will fall to Horatio to become his deputy, apologist and storyteller and 'speak' in his stead 'to th' yet unknowing world / How these things came about'.

There are strong temptations in Hamlet's plight and temperament for a student of the play to identify himself with the hero as Coleridge did, and I have been suggesting that the methods of character-presentation Shakespeare has adopted contain further temptations of the same sort. But there are contrary impulses throughout the play, towards a more detached view, coming to rest on something like Coleridge's representative 'I', and these continue to the very end. For instance, there is a fresh trace of the paradox about acting in Shakespeare's giving the office of Hamlet's ultimate spokesman to the devoted but unimpassioned Horatio. And there is a touch of subdued irony, but of something more constructive as well, in giving to the impulsive Fortinbras the delivery of Hamlet's epitaph and the utterance of the last line of all in the play, 'Go bid the soldiers shoot.' That is an order to give a command. This introspective tragedy ends, as it had begun, with a gesture of military ritual.

6. Romance in *King Lear*

At first sight, there is something paradoxical about emphasising romance in a discussion of *King Lear*. Romance implies prominently, especially in the theatre, a tale of trials and strange adventures, culminating in a happy ending for the sympathetic characters – so that we can be 'pleased', as Dr Johnson says in praise of Nahum Tate's adaptation of Shakespeare, by 'the final triumph of persecuted virtue'. But, by removing the shock of Cordelia's death and restoring a fortunate ending to the plot, Tate reverses Shakespeare's decision; whereas the latter, in Johnson's words, has 'suffered the virtue of Cordelia to perish in a just cause, contrary to the natural ideas of justice, to the hope of the reader, and, what is yet more strange, to the faith of chronicles'. He has taken a legend familiar to his first auditors from many previous versions, including the old play of about 1590, *The True Chronicle Historie of King Leir*, and altered the ending so as to show the deaths of Cordelia and Lear just at the point where all previous writers had reinstated them in happiness and prosperity.

Nor, of course, is the ending Shakespeare's only departure from the old spirit of the legend; far from it. From the King's first outburst of wrath, barely a hundred lines after the opening of the play, it becomes evident that we are to witness a tragedy at the pitch of *Hamlet*, full of 'danger' from the 'fell incensed points / Of mighty opposites', where the protagonists are to impress us by their will and power, not by a simple opposition of goodness and wickedness, and where the action is to stretch this power towards breaking-point. And not merely does Shakespeare conform to expectations about the pattern of action proper to a tragedy by dwelling on the King's downfall from high estate, but he intensifies that pattern, and drastically reshapes the legend, by recalling the sense of overwhelming guilt, the rage and fury, the death-wish, the violent blinding, and the contrasted motifs of fratricidal strife and a daughter's devotion, from two of the prime models of classical tragedy as the Elizabethans knew it, Seneca's two plays about Oedipus.[1] Sidney's tale of the Paphlagonian king and his sons, the source of Shakespeare's innovatory sub-plot, had already been derived from the Theban legend by way of Heliodorus, as the dramatist no doubt realised;[2] in any case, Gloucester's story, reduced as it is at first to the grade of a domestic intrigue, serves to universalise the terrible and the pitiful in Shakespeare's treatment of the King's story; it serves to make the destructiveness lurking in human beings seem inescapable, omnipresent. It is barely imaginable that Shakespeare himself could have devised an artistically congruent happy ending, even after writing his first four acts; but, had he been forced by circumstances to leave the final act to a collaborator, it is impossible to suppose that fidelity to the legend would have produced any effect other than anticlimax.

Nevertheless, Shakespeare was not tied to literary models, nor were his public. Previously, he had followed convention with his tragic plays to the extent of basing them on stories already stamped as tragic, in the sense of leading directly to the deaths of their protagonists, as in *Romeo and Juliet*, *Julius Caesar*, *Othello* and *Hamlet* (if we assume that his principal model for *Hamlet* was a play by Kyd on the lines of *The Spanish Tragedy*, rather than the saga of Saxo Grammaticus and Belleforest). But to turn Lear's story into a tragedy was to break from convention. It does not follow, however, that each and all of Shakespeare's innovations in the narrative would have struck his first public as unambiguously tragic, even within the loosely defined (or, as Sidney said, 'mungrell') category recognised by the Elizabethans. Indeed, the first records of his play describe it as a 'history'. Earlier dramatisations of British pseudo-history infused with Senecanism had been printed as *A Tragedie of Gorboduc*, or *The Lamentable Tragedie of Locrine*; and the antiquated, anonymous *True Chronicle Historie of King Leir*, revived for printing in the wake, presumably, of Shakespeare's new production,[3] had figured briefly in the Stationers' Register for 1605 (though not on the title-page) as a 'Tragedie' or a 'Tragecall historie'. But Shakespeare's play was entered in the Stationers' Register as 'Master William Shakespeare his historye of King Lear', and was published, in the Quarto of 1608, as *M. William Shak-speare: His True Chronicle Historie of the life and death of King Lear and his three daughters. With the unfortunate life of Edgar, sonne and heire to the Earle of Gloster, and his sullen and assumed humor of Tom of*

Bedlam. Apparently the classification of Shakespeare's contribution to the legend was less than self-evident, at least for the printers. If so, there is some excuse for their uncertainty, in view of the many episodes hailing from romance, or romanticised moral interludes, interwoven with the patently tragic new developments in the story. The author of the old play had made a romance out of a folk-tale. The substantial paradox in Shakespeare's treatment is that, having converted the old play into a tragedy, suppressing some of its romantic episodes, he not only kept others for his own use but added fresh details in the tradition of stage romance, unknown to previous versions of the legend and foreign to his previous methods in tragedy. As critics have often noted, the reconciliation between Lear and Cordelia points forward to the tone and central themes of Shakespeare's last plays,[4] but this is far from being the only moment in *King Lear* where the tragic burden is modified, or complicated, by association with romance.

A number of such associations have been pointed out by Maynard Mack, who seeks to analyse the exceptional resonance of the speeches in *King Lear*, the way the speakers project themselves as emblematic type-figures as well as individuals, by reference to the mixed tradition of allegory and romance which Shakespeare draws upon to amplify the essential *données* of his story. One 'archetypal theme' that Mack describes as the Abasement of the Proud King is contained in the romance-parables of Robert of Sicily, which are relevant – as Mack shows – to Shakespeare's play, though not to earlier forms of the Lear legend; in the Middle English version of the romance, for example, Robert finds himself degraded to a fool's costume, is forced to eat with the palace dogs, and is repudiated by his own kinsmen, while an angel assumes his appearance and his throne, until such time as the humbled monarch acknowledges himself 'a fool' before God[5] (it could be added that this romance theme was dramatised several times in the fifteenth and sixteenth centuries, on the Continent and in England).[6] More generally, Mack draws attention to the resemblances between incidents in *Lear* and 'exemplary and emblematic' features of the Tudor Moralities: for instance, the King's preparation for death recalls *Everyman*; changes of costume by Kent, Edgar and the King, connoting changes of status or moral condition, resemble changes of costume in such plays as *Magnificence* (which also dwells on the polarity between kingship and folly); and there are further echoes from the Morality tradition in Edmund's Vice-like role as deceiver, in the imprisonment of the virtuous Kent in the stocks and in Gloucester's temptation by despair.[7] The significance of these parallels is of course generic, not particular; they bring out a vein of latent or incipient commentary, a pattern of moral interpretation and expectancy which the language and unfolding actions of the play will either break or confirm. And in the play as a whole Mack finds an inclusive pattern, 'the shape of pastoral romance' – the shape, that is, of a plot resembling *As You Like It*, containing type-figures of loyalty and treachery, where, because of enmity between brothers, a ruler and his companions are exiled from 'the world of everyday', and its problems, and exposed to unprotected but natural surroundings, where they see the falsities of the society they have left and undergo 'something like a ritual death and rebirth'; on this reading, *King Lear* is a pastoral 'turned upside-down', or rather, 'the greatest anti-pastoral ever penned'.[8] I find Mack's reading here strongly suggestive, but possibly too limiting and clear-cut; and 'pastoral', in particular, carries some irrelevant associations. It seems to me that the aspects of *King Lear* Maynard Mack is concerned with can be better designated by reference to the popular tradition of narrative and stage romances like *Apollonius of Tyre*, which may be described as 'exemplary', in the sense that they illustrate the watchfulness of providence by showing families cruelly separated, exposed to danger and at last miraculously reunited. This tradition (older, more primitive but more inclusive than Renaissance pastoral) had attracted Shakespeare's interest from the beginning of his career (in the framing plot of *The Comedy of Errors*) and was to fascinate him at the end. Whereas pastoral focused on social conventions, 'exemplary' romance could appeal to hopes and fears about the enduringness of love and the directing destinies of a lifetime. With this scope of romance in view, it seems to me that *King Lear* can be described as very largely a romance inverted.

Certainly the old play of about 1590 had shaped the legend into an 'exemplary' romance, demonstrating the benevolence of providence through the trials, adventures and ultimate rewards of the virtuous characters. The playwright drenches the legend in domestic sentiment. Leir's love-test is not, as another contemporary has it, 'a fond needless question, as some use to dally with young children',[9] but the well-intentioned ruse of a doting, recently widowed father, who, although he is prudently warned against 'forc[ing] love, where fancy cannot dwell' (line 76),[10] hopes to trick his favourite daughter into consenting to marry. The playwright treats the rivalry between the sisters as a Cinderella story. And he insists on the Christian piety of his sympathetic characters: Leir in his sufferings is called 'the myrrour of mild patience' (755), and when threatened with murder – an innovation in the legend – he responds with, 'Let us submit us to the will of God' (1656); while his faithful counsellor, Perillus (whose presence is also an innovation), has been praying – with good effect, as the event shows – for the help of a 'just *Jehova*' (1649). For her part, Cordella is a diligent church-goer – a 'Puritan' (2577), according to the sarcastic Gonorill – who similarly prays (2540), with similar success, before the battle engaged on her father's behalf by her equally God-fearing husband.

As William Elton has shown at length,[11] Shakespeare obliterates this Christian piety, not only making Lear and his subjects consistently pagan but overturning the trust in divinity voiced by the old play. And instead of 'mild patience', Shakespeare's king lashes himself into 'noble anger'. The whole spirit of the play is transformed, and several episodes inserted by the earlier dramatist disappear completely.

On the other hand, this transformation lends added significance to those episodes, such as the storm, which Shakespeare takes over from the old play, and to those which he attaches to their common scenario. Instead of divesting his tragedy consistently of association with romance, he not merely borrows his supporting plot from the *Arcadia*, but introduces fresh incidents related to stage romance, without warrant either from the old play or from Sidney. Very possibly (as F. D. Hoeniger has argued, from the feeling for the primitive in *King Lear*), Shakespeare had heard the main story as a folk-tale, and had begun to turn it over in his imagination, long before seeing it in the old play or reading it in Holinshed.[12] Such a genesis might help to account, for example, for the startling incrementation of the scenes with Poor Tom and the Fool. In addition Shakespeare had been drawn for some time to the theme of authority within the family, or the clash between love and obedience, in settings as much romantic as tragic; during the ten years or so before writing *King Lear*, he had created a succession of outraged fathers, abusing, rejecting and even cursing their daughters, in quarrels over their daughters' marriages or wishes in marriage: old Capulet, Egeus, Shylock, Leonato in *Much Ado*, Polonius, Brabantio. In all six plays (except *Romeo*, where Shakespeare is following his source-story), the father is a widower like Lear; and in the last four, Shakespeare enlarges or alters the story he is working from so as to emphasise the possessive anger in the role. And, within a few years of depicting the reconciliation between Lear and Cordelia, Shakespeare was again to turn, in his sequence from *Pericles* to *The Tempest*, to plots revolving around father and daughter, but this time with a changed inflexion, showing the love and innocence of a daughter leading to the salvation of an exiled or a self-deceiving father. *King Lear* occupies a central place, a turning-point, in the total series of such stories and motifs in Shakespeare, most of them associated with the material of romance. Similarly, the variations of a romance type he added to the Lear legend appear to stem from his distinctive treatment of the salient theme of father and daughter.

Unlike the writer of the old play, Shakespeare builds up Lear's position as a king as well as a father; the authority of age, rule, fatherhood and his own commanding temper are bound together in Lear's mind by natural magic and the sanction of the gods. However, his authority is first challenged by Cordelia's response to the love-test, as in previous versions of the legend. In Holinshed, the youngest daughter's reply has the tang of an aphorism or a riddle: 'assertaine your selfe, that so much as you have, so much you are woorth, and so much I love you, and no more'.[13] In the old play (278) she is direct and dutiful:

> I hope my deeds shall make report for me:
> But looke what love the child doth owe the father,
> The same to you I beare, my gracious Lorde.

Shakespeare's Cordelia seems equally direct:

> I love your Majesty
> According to my bond, no more nor less;

but, precisely because she invokes the philosophically central conception of a 'bond', her words are charged with a fateful ambiguity. A bond had originally been a fetter of imprisonment (a denotation still active in *Cymbeline*, with Posthumus's 'cold bonds').[14] By conflation with a homonym, meaning peasant or serf, it conveyed the sense of subjection as well as constraint, as in *bondman* or *bondage*; this is the twist Edmund gives Cordelia's word in the forged letter where he makes out that Edgar has written: 'I begin to find an idle and fond bondage in the oppression of aged tyranny' (I.ii.49). On the other hand, *bond* had also come to signify an agreement or covenant; but even in this sense, which is the most frequent with Shakespeare, it could point in either of two directions, towards alliance or coercion. On one side, the allegedly innocent bond or 'band' between Aumerle and his associates 'For gay apparel' at Bolingbroke's 'triumph day' (*Richard II*, V.ii.65), or the 'everlasting bond of fellowship' in marriage between Theseus and Hippolyta (*Midsummer Night's Dream*, I.i.85), or 'love's bonds' in *The Merchant of Venice* (II.vi.6); on the other side, the specific legal sense (new in the 1590s, according to *O.E.D.*) of a document containing binding obligations. Such are the 'rotten parchment bonds' denounced by Gaunt in *Richard II* (II.i.64), and the 'merry bond' referred to more than thirty times in Shylock's play. In *Two Gentlemen of Verona* (II.vii.75), Julia fondly believes of Proteus's love that 'His words are bonds, his oaths are oracles'; but she evidently feels that *words* are less whole-hearted than *oaths*, and *bonds* less deserving of faith than *oracles*. *Bonds* in this usage imply a possible doubt, requiring a strong assertion to overcome it, as in the proverb, 'An honest man's word is as good as his bond'; *bonds* may be called sacred, as when Troilus bewails the breaking of 'the bonds of heaven',[15] but in themselves they are merely legal contracts, and to emphasise them in metaphors dealing with love and sincerity implies a secular tone of reasoning, with a glance towards scepticism. Feste, apparently, takes the prevalence of the new, legal sense of the term as a symptom of bad faith and of the disconcerting relativity or ambiguity of language: 'But indeed, words are very rascals since bonds disgrac'd them.'[16]

There is something cold and measured, then, in Cordelia's 'bond', and the touch of pique in her father's reproof is understandable:

> How, how, Cordelia? Mend your speech a little,
> Lest you may mar your fortunes.

At the same time, his tone arouses the suspicion that what he reacts to in her speech, though refusing to acknowledge it, is predominantly the implication of 'bondage'. From her side, Cordelia tries to press home the sense of covenant for mutual benefit, and reciprocal but not unlimited obligation:

> Good my lord,
> You have begot me, bred me, lov'd me: I
> Return those duties back as are right fit,
> Obey you, love you, and most honour you.

> Why have my sisters husbands, if they say
> They love you all?
>
> (I.i.95)

Cordelia strikes hard at the superstition of authority. She wants a rational definition of love, compatible with freedom. 'Begot', 'bred', 'lov'd': she details in turn the natural or biological ties with her father, the social or familial and the spontaneously personal. And, unlike her counterpart in the old play, she looks directly forward to spontaneous love in marriage, which will subtract 'half' the 'love', 'care and duty' demanded from her by her father.

At the equivalent point in the old play, the pious monarch has his single spurt of rage: 'Peace, bastard Impe, no issue of King *Leir*' (312). Shakespeare's king does not use the word here (though later he abuses Goneril as 'degenerate bastard' (I.iv.254)), but he storms against Cordelia with more terrible violence:

> Let it be so: thy truth then be thy dow'r!
> For by the sacred radiance of the sun,
> The mysteries of Hecat and the night;
> By all the operation of the orbs,
> From whom we do exist and cease to be;
> Here I disclaim all my paternal care,
> Propinquity and property of blood,
> And as a stranger to my heart and me
> Hold thee from this for ever.
>
> (I.i.108)

He strips his fatherhood of love and social obligation, reducing it to the one ineradicable tie of birth, which he would renounce if he could. He curses Cordelia as if he thought of her as a 'bastard'. He reduces his mental world to the mental world of Edmund, of whose illegitimacy the audience have already heard, by Shakespeare's interweaving of the two plots. The next scene opens with Edmund's invocation to Nature, the 'goddess' to whose 'law / My services are bound' (obligated, confined and directed). This is the first time that Nature is deified in the play, but Lear has already 'bound' himself, without knowing it, to the same 'law'.

Shakespeare's arrangement of these early scenes suggests that his reasons for taking his sub-plot from Sidney's tale of misplaced trust in a bastard son lay very close to his thoughts about the consequences of treating Cordelia as if she were a 'bastard'. In any event, the word *base* stands out as a repeated motif in the first half of *King Lear*, a key to Shakespeare's distinctive innovations on the legend; *base*, meaning illegitimate, ignoble, low, servile, worthless – the negation of all that Lear and his courtiers have believed in. Six times Edmund repeats 'base' or 'baseness' (as well as 'bastard') in his soliloquy, with scornful defiance for 'the plague of custom' and 'the curiosity of nations' – attributes, however contestable, of an organised society. And *base* is Kent's term of contempt for the social upstart, Oswald (I.iv.86, II.ii.16). But *baseness* recoils, as it were, against Kent, against the other legitimist, Edgar, and against Lear as well. When, after venting his spleen against Oswald, Kent is forced by Cornwall into the stocks, Gloucester protests on his behalf that this 'purpos'd low correction / Is such as basest and contemned'st wretches / For pilf'rings and most common trespasses / Are punish'd with' (II.ii.142); the Morality-play icon of virtue martyred in the stocks becomes an icon of social transposition, of the confusion of moral values. Kent's championship of the old order has brought him to what seems like the vilest degradation. But, three acting minutes later, Edgar, who is in part Gloucester's victim, will save his life by assuming voluntarily 'the basest and most poorest shape / That ever penury, in contempt of man, / Brought near to beast' (II.iii.7). Here again Shakespeare's departure from his narrative sources involves a movement towards 'baseness'. And 'baseness' takes on dynamic force in Lear's mind in his decisive quarrel with Goneril and Regan, when, after appealing in vain to the 'bond of childhood' and fuming over Kent's imprisonment in the stocks, he is compelled to listen to the cold logic of his daughters' refusal to harbour his unnecessary retinue:

> Return to her? and fifty men dismiss'd?
> No, rather I abjure all roofs, and choose
> To wage against the enmity o' th' air,
> To be a comrade with the wolf and owl –
> Necessity's sharp pinch. Return with her?
> Why, the hot-bloodied France, that dowerless took
> Our youngest born, I could as well be brought
> To knee his throne, and squire-like, pension beg
> To keep base life afoot.

> (II.iv.207)

Baseness here is the counterpart to his rejection of Cordelia; a few speeches later, Lear's thought of it recalls Edgar:

> O, reason not the need! our basest beggars
> Are in the poorest thing superfluous.
> Allow not nature more than nature needs,
> Man's life is cheap as beast's.

> (II.iv.264)

It is in this crucial speech, where Lear glimpses, as if for the first time, the possibility, and even the exemplariness, of total destitution, that he begins to echo the high-pitched tones of Seneca's Oedipus, passionate to visit his own guilt on the world around him. In the *Thebais*, when Oedipus is told of the war between his sons, he cries out (in language heightened further by the Elizabethan translator), not for peace, but for destruction:

> Your weapons and artillery for war bring out with speed,
> Consume with flame your native soil, and desolation breed
> In ev'ry house within the land; a hurly burly make
> Confusedly of every thing. Make all the realm to quake,
> And in exile their days let end; make level with the ground
> Each fenced fort and walled town: the Gods and all confound,
> And throw their Temples on their heads; their Images deface,
> And melt them all; turn upside-down each house in ev'ry place.
> Burn, spoil, make havoc, leave no jot of City free from fire,
> And let the flame begin his rage within my Chamber dire . . .
>
> This civil war is nothing like to that which I devise:
> These trifling broils for such a Sea of harms cannot suffice . . .
> Some heinous Fact, unheard-of yet, some detestable deed
> Must practised be; as is to me, and mine by Fate decreed . . .[17]

In Shakespeare's scene, the King contemplates for a moment the 'patience' that had been displayed by Leir in the old play, rejects it in favour of 'noble anger', and throws himself into the strains of Oedipus:

> No, you unnatural hags,
> I will have such revenges on you both
> That all the world shall – I will do such things –
> What they are yet I know not, but they shall be
> The terrors of the earth!
>
> (II.iv.278)

In the course of his next sentence, comes the first outburst of *Storm and tempest*; and Lear will soon be heard, on the heath, commanding the hurricane to 'spout / Till you have drench'd our steeples, drown'd the cocks', and ordering the thunderbolt to 'Strike flat the thick rotundity o' th' world', to 'Crack nature's moulds, all germains spill at once / That makes ingrateful man!' (III.ii.1–9). Whereas in the old play Leir had been tricked by Ragan into going from her court into the wilderness, the immediate cause of departure in Shakespeare's play is the King's angry choice; and by the same dramaturgical decision, Shakespeare turns from the precedent of the old play to that of Seneca. However, there is continuity in Lear's mind, from thoughts of *baseness* to annihilation.

Moreover, Shakespeare distances Lear's cursings from any Senecan parallel. 'You think I'll weep', Lear tells his daughters, immediately after uttering threats intended to be terrifying (II.iv.283);

> No, I'll not weep.
> I have full cause of weeping, but this heart
> *Storm and tempest.*
> Shall break into a hundred thousand flaws
> Or ere I'll weep. O Fool, I shall go mad!
> *Exeunt Lear, Gloucester, Gentleman and Fool.*

Lear's curses are hysterical, grotesque and pitiful as well as tragic according to any Senecan model. His tirades are qualified by an awareness of human weakness and folly, in the vein of folk-tales or moral interludes. At the same time, his helplessness, his pathetic exposure, belongs to circumstances of romance, to the pattern of contrast between castle or city and sea or wilderness that recurs again and again in romantic adventures. In Shakespeare's treatment of the story, exposure to the storm seems an answering consequence to Lear's reduction of his moral world to *baseness*, his exclusion of love and breeding from the 'bonds' contained in nature; it is a physically extreme and morally devastating exposure, not, as in the old play, merely an unhappy flight. And Shakespeare's thunder is wholly different from the thunder that is heard as a providential signal in the old play. Nevertheless, in all probability Shakespeare owed his first suggestion for the storm scenes to the anonymous earlier playwright, who had been the first among the narrators of the Lear legend to convert the King's journey to Cordelia for assistance into an episode from romance.

Shakespeare brings in reminiscences from romance, also, even where he alters the plot of the old play, or enlarges it. Although King Lear's world is predominantly pagan, for example, there are moments in the play that recall romances of chivalry. Shakespeare dismisses the absurd wooing scene from the old play where the French king and his companion, disguised as palmers, set out in quest of the famed princesses of Britain and, by a happy accident, meet the outcast Cordella; yet he keeps the tone of chivalry in Lear's reference to France and Burgundy, 'long in our court ... [making] their amorous sojourn' (I.i.47), and in France's resounding troth-plight to 'Fairest

Cordelia, . . . most rich being poor, / Most choice forsaken, and most lov'd despis'd' (I.i.250) – the counterpoint to her father's imputation of baseness. Possibly because of the magnetic influence of the first authority for the Lear legend, Geoffrey of Monmouth, there are passing references to the Arthurian world (through 'Camelot', 'Merlin' and 'Childe Rowland'). And the trial-at-arms between Edgar and Edmund, with Edgar as an unknown champion, is a chivalric episode independent of Sidney's story.

In the old play, Perillus (a new figure in the legend) accompanies his king, but not disguised, like Kent; in Sidney's tale, the legitimate son, cast off by his father, becomes a private soldier, not a disguised beggar, and goes to help his father intentionally, instead of meeting him unexpectedly. As well as recalling the symbolism of changes of dress in the Morality plays, the equivalent passages in Shakespeare's play recall the tradition of romances, with their mysterious encounters, concealed identities, hazardous journeys and unexpected meetings. (As a clumsy token of that tradition, there is the episode in the old play where Cordella and her husband, for no compelling reason, dress up as simple country-folk for an excursion to the French coast, where they fall in with and succour Leir and Perillus, after the old men have been robbed of their money and have been forced to pay for their Channel crossing by exchanging cloaks with the mariners.) With the doubtful exception of *Titus Andronicus*, Shakespeare had not used personal disguise in his previous tragedies (even Iago cloaks his purpose, but not his identity); the employment of disguises, so frequent in *King Lear*, is a signal of romance conventions.

Concurrently, however, these romance-like disguises contribute to Shakespeare's variation on the theme of the Abasement of the Proud King. In Moralities such as *Magnificence* and *The Cradle of Security*, changes of costume had served to show regal pride reduced to the status of folly; but there was an alternative theme, during Shakespeare's early career, in the shape of medleys of allegory, history and romance, showing a king mastering his own vices and searching out hidden crimes in his kingdom with the aid of disguise (somewhat like Henry V on the eve of Agincourt). One such play (which Shakespeare could well have known, since it was acted by his then company, Strange's men, in 1592–3) was *A Knack to Know a Knave*, which has two series of overlapping episodes; in one series, the king learns to govern his own desires magnanimously, while in the other he purges his kingdom of social abuses through the instrumentality of a new servant named Honesty, who has presented himself to the king, unsummoned, as a 'plain' fellow, 'A friend to your grace, but a foe to Flatterers',[18] and who exposes, among others, an upstart, sycophantic courtier. Honesty is both a personified quality from the moral interludes and the mysterious servant-helper from romance; and Kent's role follows the same general lines. In view of the prominence Shakespeare gives to Edgar, who has one of the few Saxon names in a cast otherwise British and Norman,[19] it is worth adding that the monarch in *A Knack* is another Edgar, the Saxon king.

The early Jacobean variant on plays of this type was a group showing the ruler himself as a detective in disguise – plays such as Marston's *Fawn* and *The Malcontent*, Middleton's *Phoenix* and, in particular, *Measure for Measure*. In his modifications of the Lear legend, Shakespeare recalls the plays using this motif, at the point where the King, after deciding to 'abjure all roofs', begins to equate himself with the 'poor naked wretches' of whom hitherto he has taken 'too little care'. Only here, the King's adviser is the Fool; it is the representative subjects, Kent and Poor Tom, who are disguised; and the King's pursuit of ideal justice becomes the fantasy of a madman. In traditional romance, the wandering hero may meet supernatural helpers; here, he meets Poor Tom, apparently possessed by devils. The central episodes in Shakespeare's play depend upon the use, and the inversion, of allegorical motifs from romance.

In the reconciliation between Lear and Cordelia, on the other hand, Shakespeare strikes the note of serious romance more purely and fully than in any of his plays before. The King's return, his rage exhausted, to a childlike contact with nature through his chaplet of flowers, plucked from 'our sustaining corn', even though they are no more than 'idle weeds' (IV.iv.5); Cordelia's invocation to the 'blest secrets' and 'unpublish'd virtues of the earth' to 'spring' as remedies with her tears; the King's awakening, to music, in the Doctor's care, and finding himself dressed in 'fresh garments' without his knowledge; the 'medicine' of Cordelia's kiss (IV.vii.26), and her outpouring of the pity, tenderness and forgiveness he has been craving; and Lear's response, unbelieving at first, but then so compelling that later, in defeat, he will prize the love of Cordelia, even in a prison, far above the signs of majesty he had formerly clung to so tenaciously: in this marvellous sequence Shakespeare is surely exerting his deepest powers to dramatise, at the edge of possibility, some of the hopes and wishes implicit in popular romance. And how important to the dramatist this sequence was, with its conjunction of flowers, music and healing, and its dream-like vision of unearthly serenity, is evident from the Marina episodes in *Pericles* and the variations on the same underlying themes in the plays that follow. One result of reversing the traditional outcome of the battle between Cordelia's forces and her sisters' – and presumably Shakespeare's reason for changing the legend at this notable point – is precisely that it throws the renewed love between Lear and Cordelia into high relief.

Yet it is also this sequence of tenderness in the tragedy that makes Cordelia's death such a painful shock. At the same time, the shock is not unprepared for. Even in the reconciliation scenes, Shakespeare marks a difference between dream-like vision and the pressures of tragedy. When Lear is wakened by Cordelia, he thinks of himself as 'bound' – 'bound / Upon a wheel of fire'; 'And to deal plainly, / I fear I am not in my perfect mind' (IV.vii.45, 61). It is mentally impossible for Lear to accept and confront all that he has lived through in the course of the play. And when, in defeat, he consoles himself, if not the sterner Cordelia, with 'We two alone will sing like birds i' th' cage; / ... And take upon's the mystery of things / As if we were God's spies' (V.iii.9–17), he is conjuring up a fantasy – an ironic reprise of the romantic stage-motif of the prince-detective, this time as hermit, scrutinising his kingdom.

On a broader view of the play, moreover, this clash at the end between idealising vision and harsh event follows the general pattern that Shakespeare has imparted to the action, a pattern or rhythm of successive waves of hope revived, in the manner of romances, only to be dashed again by waves of misery and anguish. It is a kind of dialectic between romance and tragedy. When, for example, Kent is in the stocks, he reads the letter from Cordelia, and calls upon Fortune to 'smile once more, turn thy wheel' (II.ii.173) – as, in romances, Fortune well might; but, with Kent still on the stage, at once Edgar enters as Poor Tom, in a 'shape' even 'baser' than Kent himself – believing, however, that his abject transformation will save his life: 'That's something yet: Edgar I nothing am' (II.iii.21). And Edgar persistently supposes that he has touched the bottom of misfortune, that 'The lamentable change is from the best, / The worst returns to laughter' (IV.i.5), only to discover that the world's 'strange mutations' are even more 'hateful' than he had imagined

(IV.i.11) – until, in the remarkably abrupt scene of the off-stage battle (V.ii), his assurance of 'comfort' to Gloucester is revoked within two lines of dialogue, and his only encouragement remaining is to affirm that 'Men must endure.' Equally, for the audience, there have been moments when horror was relieved or hope revived by seeing Cornwall's servant, or Gloucester's tenant, or Gloucester, or Albany react against heartless tyranny; from this point of view, it is sheer luck when Edgar meets Oswald and kills him, intercepting Goneril's letter, and a stroke of poetic justice when he overthrows Edmund and Edmund repents. But 'men / Are as the time is', as Edmund says, and in the 'time' pictured on the stage, the time of Edmund and Goneril, luck and poetic justice are unreliable – powerless against the force of things, the main drift of ruthless self-seeking, which Edmund himself cannot, in the end, control. What Dr Johnson calls 'persecuted virtue' is vindicated, even where its deficiencies have been most severely tested, on the plane of moral judgement, but it is too much to expect that it will 'triumph' with material trophies as well. Yet even in the closing scene Shakespeare keeps up the pressure of dramatic manoeuvres whereby hope is aroused only to be repressed. After it seems that Edgar has cured as well as rescued his father, it emerges from his 'brief tale' (V.iii.182) that he has made himself known to him too late. 'Mov'd' by this story, Edmund repents, and prepares to save his prisoners' lives; but he fails to send his message in time. And a part cause of this fatal delay is one of the very incidents in the plot that the audience have been led to expect and look forward to, Kent's return in his own name; his recognition scene with his master, when the moment at length comes for it, is balked. To the very last, Lear is allowed to imagine for the space of a few lines that Cordelia is still breathing; Albany, that he can restore the King to 'absolute power'; and Edgar, for an instant, that Lear has only fainted.

These oscillations between hope and dismay for the audience spring from Shakespeare's changes or extensions of his sources. And most of them are connected with the stage traditions of romance. This is not to say, of course, that all Shakespeare's innovations lead in one direction; much more than the sequence of the plot is involved, for instance, in the new motifs that can be described, by analogy at least, as the Abasement of the Proud King and 'a ritual death and rebirth', and, again, in the latent analogy with Seneca's Oedipus that Shakespeare has brought into the story. Still, most of the effect of suspense in the action goes with new characters, principally Kent and Edgar, whose roles are largely devoted to that result; and Shakespeare took the movements of these two from the stage tradition of mixed allegory and romance, giving them major if not quite leading importance. And a repeated consequence of Shakespeare's innovations in the plot is to set up a dialectic between expectations belonging to romance and those attached to tragedy, between inalienable hopes and the sternest moral realism. In this respect, moreover, Shakespeare's extensions to the Lear legend seem to follow from his reinterpretation of the core of it. Having taken over the legend as outlined by the old play, with its contribution of romantic adventures, Shakespeare turns these adventures into a myth of guilt and suffering, but also into a myth of loyalty and love. The second bears the stamp of tragedy no less than the first, because, it seems, only the deaths of Cordelia and Lear on the stage can communicate the full poignancy of the ideal values they have come to embody; and hence Shakespeare's most striking alteration of the legend, the change he has made at its end. But he has come to tragedy along a route prepared by romance, and has used allusions to romance, or romance inverted, so as to fortify his tragedy as well as extending it.

'Rebirth' is perhaps too positive and comforting a term for Lear's state of mind amid the agitation, pathos and bleakness of the closing scenes. If the last phase of the tragedy carries a distinguishable moral lesson at all, it is more like Edgar's message of 'ripeness' and endurance. Nevertheless, the scenes of Lear's reunion with Cordelia contain Shakespeare's most powerful evocation of a sense or vision of a new life. When he returns to a similar vision, in his later tragi-comedies, he is careful to distance it from association with the current of everyday reality and to emphasise that it belongs to the realm of theatrical art. But the elements of romance within *King Lear* are none the less central within his whole development as a dramatist.

7. *King Lear*, Montaigne and Harsnett

Is there any cause in nature that make these hard hearts?

King Lear can perhaps be regarded as the expression of a sense of crisis within the social thought or the general culture of the age. It evidently represented an important shift in Shakespeare's methods as a playwright, as if he felt a need to present a tragic conflict within a broader framework of ideas than before. In *Julius Caesar*, *Hamlet* and *Othello* the settings are comparatively realistic and the dramatic interest presses on the psychology of the leading characters and their close interaction. In *Lear*, by contrast, the leading characters are kept apart much of the time and, except at vital points, the portrayal and interplay of their personalities is, for Shakespeare, relatively sketchy; while their setting, the fictional world they inhabit, begins to take on the contours of fable or romance. In the scenes on the heath, which embody Shakespeare's most striking modification of the old legend, the close-meshed engagement of personalities which had been so notable in the central passages of *Othello* gives place to a form of drama in which the hero's personal travail is combined with quasi-choric fantasies belonging to folly and madness and with the generalised emotional impact of the storm. Similarly, *Lear* could be called more philosophical than Shakespeare's previous tragedies, in the sense that the speakers so often and so insistently raise general questions about the nature of man.

Macbeth sustains this kind of interest while also continuing that psychological probing that had been crucial in the earlier tragedies. But in the plays written after *Macbeth* Shakespeare seems to be returning from one side or another to trains of imagination he had been exploring more particularly in *Lear*. *King Lear* is largely a fable about alienation: an old king drives away not one but two people he should have loved and trusted, is himself forced morally into a kind of exile where he loses his sanity, but is succoured by those he had driven away. Shakespeare duplicates this pattern in his sub-plot; and he returns to variations on the theme of semi-wilful exile in a sense in

Antony, and plainly in *Coriolanus* and in *Timon* – *Timon* coming very close to *Lear* in the rhythm of the hero's excessive expectations of compliance from those around him, followed by a furious reaction against society in his exile. And in his late romances Shakespeare again returns to themes from *King Lear* both in giving a key position to relations between fathers and daughters and in making the motif of exclusion or exile central to each of the plots. As in *Lear*, the romances exhibit disjunctions and continuities between civilisation and nature and locate the breakdown of civilised concord in failures of love, trust or gratitude. And though it may be excessive to call each of the late romances a fable, they show the dramatist pushing further along the line foreshadowed in *Lear* of subordinating his powerful interest in personality to the general design of each play.

It can be argued that in the new directions Shakespeare took in *King Lear* a weighty factor was his reading of Florio's Montaigne. He also borrowed more localised matter from Samuel Harsnett's *Declaration of Egregious Popish Impostures*, published in the same year as Florio, 1603. With a work so rich as *Lear* in reflection and allusion it would be rash to single out any literary source as decisive. And we have no biographical hints to go by. But the evidence assembled by Kenneth Muir in his edition of *Lear*[1] and in *Shakespeare's Sources* makes it highly probable or even certain that Shakespeare was recalling one or other of these two books repeatedly. More than a hundred words from the vocabulary of the play have been attributed to Florio's Montaigne; Muir gives, with some 'caution', a list of 96 of them, of which 42 are peculiar to *Lear* in Shakespeare's writings and another 20 are used by him in *Lear* for the first time[2]. Obviously, some of these words could have reached the play from any of a multitude of other sources (including Harsnett)[3]. Collectively, however, they amount to very strong evidence for Shakespeare's interest in Montaigne, especially when some words common to both are considered in context, and above all when account is taken of the many passages containing similar ideas that Muir and others have adduced. Caution is very necessary again with regard to parallels or resemblances of thought, as Pierre Villey pointed out long ago in his study of Montaigne's influence on Bacon, since a modern reader is prone to exaggerate any coincidence of ideas between two major Renaissance authors, neglecting possible common sources and overlooking the contribution of the mass of forgotten minor literature of the time.[4] On the other hand, it would have been distinctly surprising if Shakespeare did not take a special interest in the most richly suggestive explorer of men and manners from the previous generation, whom Samuel Daniel was hailing, in his prefatory poem addressed to Florio, as a 'Prince' and 'great Potentate', who had 'adventur'd' more 'of himselfe' than any writer before him.[5]

Discussing Montaigne's influence, or possible influence, on Shakespeare, Robert Ellrodt has maintained that it had already passed its peak by the time of *King Lear*.[6] This may well be true with regard to Ellrodt's chosen theme of analytic self-consciousness, since Lear 'hath ever but slenderly known himself'. Nevertheless, his tragedy is allied to a major concern of the *Essays* through its emphasis on the meanings of 'nature', a word used more often there than in any other Shakespeare play. One can hold (with critics like John Danby or Rosalie Colie)[7] that what is at stake in the tragic conflict is Hooker's conception of a divinely ordained and graduated world-order, as against a Machiavellian conception of self-interest. But many of the actors' utterances about 'nature' do not refer directly to either of those concepts. They refer primarily instead to man's genetic make-up, his basic needs and resources, or the interconnection between body and mind; in short, to the subjects Montaigne had made his own. Again and again the characters turn to thoughts – about sexuality, sickness and health, old age, preparedness for death, or men's beliefs about and their ignorance of the human condition – which recall the frequent topics of the *Essays*, raising similar questions if not reaching the same answers. Most of the reasoning in the play seems to be coloured by Montaigne.

One essay peculiarly relevant in this connection is II, viii: 'Of the Affection of Fathers to their Children'. Notwithstanding the sudden twists and turns of exposition customary with Montaigne, this chapter is exceptionally single-minded, and it is packed with observations on contemporary life and with striking sketches of men the essayist knew, sketches offering, it has been said, 'a premonition of the world of Balzac';[8] as it happens, this chapter was also one of the few from which Bacon was to borrow substantially for an essay of his own, that 'Of Parents and Children' in his edition of 1612.[9] Montaigne's central discussion, dealing with the use and abuse of paternal authority, starts from a far-reaching proposition about nature:

If there be any truly-naturall law, that is to say, any instinct, universally and perpetually imprinted, both in beasts and us, (which is not without controversie) I may, according to mine opinion, say, that next to the care, which each living creature hath to his preservation, and to flie what doth hurt him, the affection which the engenderer beareth his offspring holds the second place in this ranke.

(Florio, 2.67)[10]

Attachment to our own creations belongs to the very 'frame' of nature, which direct us towards the future, whereas any reciprocal feeling from children, such as gratitude, cannot be so deeply entrenched (67); it is even a fallacy to suppose that filial recognition is based on 'a naturall instinct' at all (85). At the end of his chapter Montaigne draws from his leading principle a startling inference, which Bacon in turn paraphrases by remarking that 'the noblest works and foundations have proceeded from childless men, which have sought to express the images of their minds where those of their bodies have failed'. But meanwhile Montaigne dwells on how fathers can thwart or misconstrue 'the Law of Nature' (80), ruining their own and their children's lives by self-centredness. Most parents look for pets in their children, not rational beings; they may 'liberally' indulge them as infants, but 'miserably pinch it' for their 'necessaries' when adults. A main cause of this is a father's 'jelousie' of his grown children, as if 'supposing they solicite us to be gone hence'; but if we fear this effect of 'the order of things' then 'we should not meddle to be fathers' (68). Montaigne later adds the reservation that he is thinking of noblemen, not husbandmen, for whom children are a benefit (71). It is 'meere injustice' for 'an old, crazed, sinnow-shronken, and nigh dead father', one 'over-burthend with yeares', to cling to his surplus goods – the 'pompe and trash whereof hee hath no longer use or need' – instead of distributing them in time 'amongst those, to whom by naturall decree they ought to belong'; 'otherwise without doubt there is both envy and malice stirring'. With a father like this, who will 'suffer' his children 'to lose their best days and yeares, without thrusting them into publike service and knowledge of men', the children are 'often cast into dispaire'; and much of the blame for the crime, 'pilfering' and 'debauches' Montaigne has witnessed among gentlemen's sons attaches to their fathers' avarice (69–70, 72–3). In any case, profit is a 'very slipperie' motive for love (67), and a father is 'miserable' who retains his children's affection, 'if that may be termed affection', only by that means, or hoards his wealth in order to be 'honoured, respected and suingly sought unto' by his children (70).

Even more sharply, Montaigne condemns the use of 'violence' against children to exact 'servility in compulsion' (70). He hates the 'custome' of extorting excessive 'reverence' in forms of address – 'As if nature had not sufficiently provided for our authoritie. We call God-almighty by the name of father, and disdaine our children should call us so' (75). All such inflations of authority are 'tyrannicall' and 'ridiculous'. In contrast, Montaigne upholds the example of the Emperor Charles V, whose 'worthiest action' was to resign wealth and power to his heir when he realised that he was past his prime (73).

Among the character-sketches to support his argument, Montaigne includes the biting portrait of the nobleman 'whose youth had beene very imperious and rough' and who bullies his household incessantly in his fretful and 'tempestuous' old age. 'He is had in awe, he is feared, ... he is respected his belly-full.' Yet all the time that he 'flattereth himselfe' on his strict management, 'his masterie' and 'his absolutenesse', he is 'cleane falne from them like a childe'. His servants deceive him, 'soothingly' but systematically. Behind his back, his wealth is 'lavishly wasted ... in riotous spending'. If one of his servants is feeble-mindedly diligent, 'he is presently made to suspect him'; if he dismisses a servant, the latter disappears – 'but whither? onely out of his sight, not out of his house'. The master is too slow and confused to detect the fraud, and in due course he is persuaded by letters procured for the purpose to take the dismissed man back into his 'office'. By 'forging causes, and devising colourable excuses' the servants really manage the estate; even letters for the master are either concealed from him or else read to him by one of his men (who 'will presently devise what he thinketh good, whereby they often invent, that such a one seemeth to ask him forgivenesse, that wrongeth him by his Letter'). In short, the nobleman only 'lookes into his owne businesse' in the form of a 'designed and as much as may be pleasing image, so contrived by such as are about him, because they will not stirre up his choler, move his impatience, and exasperate his frowardnesse' (76–7). Montaigne adds that he has known 'many' comparable households. As a pendant to this picture of senile tyranny (which is said to represent the Marquis de Trans) he reports the passionate grief of Marshal Monluc, whose son had died in early manhood without ever glimpsing how much his father loved him, because of the father's 'austere humour' and 'severe-surly-countenance' (79).

Montaigne discusses the making of wills. There are old men who 'play' with their wills 'as with apples and rods'; they disregard long-standing 'merit' because of 'a word ill taken', so that 'not the best and most frequent offices' from their children but 'the freshest and present worke the deed'. Or they found a preference on 'divinations' about a young child's development, which are often wrong – as they would have been in Montaigne's case (82). It is far better to rely on law and custom than on such 'private humours and frivolous fantasies'. As to their widows, men leave them with too much power or else too little security.

'Moreover', where motherhood is concerned, 'experience doth manifestly shew unto us, that the same naturall affection, to which we ascribe so much authoritie, hath but a weake foundation.' Wealthy families give their infants to peasant wet-nurses to suckle – a 'custome' giving rise to a kind of 'bastard-affection' in the nurses, 'more vehement than the naturall' – while the peasant women are obliged to send their own babies away, often, in Montaigne's part of the country, to be suckled by goats, whose willingness in turn shows that *'Beasts as well as we doe soone alter, and easily bastardize their natural affection'* (84–5). Edmund's reflection in *Lear* on mankind's 'goatish disposition' sounds like a spin-off from Montaigne's anthropology.

Men, it seems, mistake the force of instinct. Since God has given us 'capacitie of discourse', 'we should not servily be subjected to common lawes' like beasts, but should utilise our 'reason'; 'we ought somewhat to yeeld unto the simple auctoritie of Nature: but not suffer her tyrannically to carry us away' (67–8). The ideal – much as in Terence (70) – is a 'well ordred affection' with 'loving friendship' between fathers and children. But just as a father should curb his 'natural power' over his children, so he should regulate his 'naturall inclination' towards them, showing love, 'if they deserve it', to the measure of 'reason' and in the light of his 'experience' of their characters (68, 74). For his own part, Montaigne would be willing in advanced age to share the management of his estate with his children and finally to give them possession of his manor-house, living nearby so as to enjoy their company; but not to live with them ('by reason of the peevish frowardnesse of my age'), and not to place his gift beyond his power to 'revoke' it: 'I would reserve what I pleased unto my selfe.' As they grew up, he would try to 'breede' in his children 'a true-harty-loving friendship, and unfained good will'. However,

if they prove, or be such surly-furious beasts, or given to churlish disobedience, as our age bringeth forth thousands, they must as beasts be hated, as churls neglected, and as degenerate avoided.

(74–5)

To go to law with one's family is to be trapped in 'civil bonds'. Montaigne would deliver himself from anxieties on that score (inward 'treasons'), 'not by an unquiet, and tumultuary curiosity', but by way of a mental detour or 'diversion' characteristic of him. He would compare others with himself; he would look within. 'If others deceive me, yet do I not deceive myself' (78–9).

On the whole this chapter brings forward the humanist idealism in Montaigne. Shakespeare in *King Lear* is much less confident about rationality. But in the chapter he could have found a study of the relations between age and youth, parents and children, immeasurably more searching, realistic and challenging than anything in the versions of the Lear legend or even in Sidney's tale about the Paphlagonian king. And the coincidence of verbal echoes and variations on identical moral themes is so strong between the essay and the first two acts in *King Lear* as to imply that Shakespeare was not merely recalling the essay here and there while he was penning the play but that he had been considering it in detail about the same time as he was planning the scenes of exposition and had altered his narrative source-material accordingly. For example, as W. B. D. Henderson has pointed out, the essay contains 'the abstract of Lear's abdication, and the philosophy of Edmund's forged letter'.[11]

Among the words from *Lear* which are new or rare in Shakespeare a number occur in this chapter of Florio's Montaigne, which are close to key subjects within the play: *curiosity, interested, bastardizing, pined away, bellyful, copulation*. Montaigne uses his title-word, which provoked considerable interest, to point out the distinctive content or method of his chapters ('Here is simply an Essay of my naturall faculties...'; 'my Judgement..., whereof these be the Essaies');[12] and Edmund employs the word in a similar way, for its one instance in Shakespeare's plays, when he tells his father, concerning the letter he has forged, that he hopes Edgar has intended it 'but as an essay or taste of my virtue' (I.ii.44). He adds the synonym *taste*, to make his meaning seem clear; but he is speaking, like Montaigne, about a literary composition.[13] What he wants his father to understand – though not believe – is that the document may be no more than a literary exercise to try out or disclose his (Edmund's) moral probity; while for himself there is the hidden joke that it is an experiment, a 'prentice-work, to try out his powers in intrigue. Not only has he borrowed the letter's 'philosophy' from Montaigne's chapters on fathers, but the circumstance of the forgery, the allegation of '*the oppression of aged tyranny, who sways, not as it hath power, but as it is suffer'd*', and the subsequent charade of hide-and-seek all recall the conditions in the household of the Marquis de Trans.

In Holinshed and the other chronicle versions of the Lear story Shakespeare is likely to have known the king proposes the love-test without any intention of abdicating. In the old play, King Leir resolves to 'resigne these earthly cares' as soon as he has married off his daughters, but there is no abdication scene.[14] Shakespeare gives weight to the abdication and presents it in terms closely resembling what Montaigne has to say about the abdication of Charles V. This applies particularly to the metaphor-translated-into-action of the old King's desire to 'unburthen' himself, to be followed by his response to Tom's nakedness, his need for sleep, and then his dying words, 'Pray you, undo this button.' Montaigne, leading up to the exemplary case of Charles V, quotes a saying common with fathers, ' "I will not put off my clothes before I be ready to goe to bed" '; and he praises the Emperor precisely because

he had the discretion to know, that reason commanded us, to strip or shift our selves when our cloathes trouble and are too heavy for us, and that it is time to goe to bed, when our legs faile us.

Conversely, 'this fault, for a man not to be able to know himselfe betimes, and not to feele the impuissance and extreme alteration, that age doth naturally bring', has undone most great men's reputations (72–3). In the decision of Shakespeare's king to resign his rule there are rational and irrational factors combined, and without the former the latter would lose their tragic force.[15] Montaigne's comments surrounding the precedent of Charles V bear on both sides of the question as Shakespeare presents it.

In *The Mirror for Magistrates*, as in Geoffrey of Monmouth and, by inference, in Holinshed, it is the daughters or the sons-in-law who give Lear a personal retinue, in a compromise settlement after they have rebelled and dethroned him from the half of the kingdom he had originally kept for himself.[16] In Shakespeare it is the King who decides upon the 'reservation of an hundred knights', to be 'sustain'd' at Goneril's and Regan's expense (I.i.131–4). We cannot be sure whether this reflects a premeditated plan or, as seems more likely, an impulse to salve his dignity in his raw disappointment over Cordelia. In any case, it bears an inverted resemblance to Montaigne's theoretical project to share his goods with his children in old age, leaving 'the use and fruition of all unto them, the rather because it were no longer fit for me to weald the same', but yielding nothing beyond his power to 'revoke', and intending to 'reserve what I pleased' in 'the disposing of all matters in grosse' (74). In the play, Montaigne's words re-echo through the debate that has already opened between Kent and the King: 'Reserve thy state; ... Revoke thy gift' – 'This shall not be revok'd' (I.i.148, 163, 178). Lear's retention of the knights (who are absent from the old play) amplifies the image of his self-will. And, with more economy than the chroniclers, Shakespeare goes on to make it a crucial instrument in his plot, since the retinue becomes the *casus belli* between the King and his daughters. 'I gave you all', he reminds Regan,

> Made you my guardians, my depositaries,
> But kept a reservation to be follow'd
> With such a number.[17]

(II.iv.248)

In the scene on the heath where the King imagines Poor Tom has been 'brought ... to this pass' of nakedness 'by his daughters', the Fool reverts sarcastically to the same thought: 'Nay, he reserv'd a blanket, else we had all been sham'd' (III.iv.64). By this point the motifs borrowed from Montaigne have spread from a rearrangement of the incidents in the opening scenes to affect the whole texture of ideas in the play.

Shakespeare may well have noted Montaigne's asides in this chapter about the 'unrulie appetite' of women and their lust to 'usurpe' authority in a household, 'either by wily craft or maine force' (78, 84); Goneril and Regan are more violent, as well as more calculating, than their counterparts in the chronicles or the old play. Like Montaigne, he makes explicit the relation between the old man's failure to understand his children and his failure to understand himself. In all probability, he took suggestions from the same chapter in depicting the tensions between motives of status and feeling, love and selfishness at work in Lear's break with Cordelia. He certainly drew upon Montaigne's comments on the oppositions between sons and fathers to develop Gloucester's story. Montaigne's essay may even have prompted the first suggestion of coupling Gloucester's story with Lear's. But it is noticeable that resemblances with this chapter fade out of the play by the end of the second act. It is as if Shakespeare concentrated upon this particular chapter with a particular purpose, the setting out of the exposition in his play.

On the other hand, there are echoes from other essays by Montaigne running through the play, to the end of the fourth act at least, notably from 'An Apologie of *Raymond Sebond*' (II, xii) and 'Upon Some Verses of *Virgil*' (III, v). W. B. D. Henderson has gone so far as to claim that Shakespeare took, mainly from the 'Apologie', his leading thought of Lear as 'a Renaissance God–King' who must be humiliated until he can find 'redemption', 'purged by such pains and benefits as Christianity, and the Christian humanists, had prescribed for the salvation of such a soul'. This is not only excessive but falsifies, puts a tendentious reading on, Shakespeare and Montaigne alike.[18] Nevertheless, Henderson is justified in emphasising the importance for *King Lear* of Montaigne's attack on man's intellectual pride: 'He must be stripped into his shirt' (II, xii; Florio, 2.188).

Lear's intense exasperation and the shock or bewilderment of his sympathisers soon reach beyond localised, personal questions to search for the human sources of evil and to set in doubt the whole scope of the natural order in human affairs. Shakespeare, as L. C. Knights has written, has 'submitted himself' to something like 'the famous Cartesian intellectual doubt':[19]

Some of the most fundamental questions concerning the nature of man are posed in a way that precludes all ready-made answers, that, in fact, so emphasizes the difficulty of the questions as to make any sort of answer seem all but impossible.

For the intellectual factors in the passionate upheaval at the centre of the play, the formulation of thoughts that provoke or grasp at general principles in the midst of emotional conflict, and even for the prevailing sense Knights alludes to of meeting questions that are fundamental but can hardly be answered, Shakespeare seems strongly indebted to that important precursor of Cartesian doubt, Montaigne. In the essay 'Of the Affection of Fathers to their Children', the significance of 'naturall affection' is repeatedly put in doubt; at the outset, it is even – though in passing – made a question 'not without controversie' whether there is any 'truly-naturall law', any instinct perpetual, universal and common to animals and men, at all (67). Elsewhere the essayist dwells again and again on two general principles bearing on the same doubts: first, that, whatever philosophers may have said, man is ignorant about his composition, his own nature; and, second, that Nature has been obscured or corrupted by civilisation. Both of these principles are active in *King Lear*.

Between these two propositions, considered in the abstract, there is the obvious contradiction that if nobody knows what 'nature' is it cannot be said that we pervert it.[20] But Montaigne is thinking now of one aspect and now of another of the wide range of meanings covered by 'nature' in Renaissance usage. His criticisms follow a consistent mental temper even though, by intention, they are not brought together in any consecutive, systematic treatise, even in the 'Apologie'.

Coming to terms with old age is one of his urgent preoccupations. When Regan taunts her father (II.iv.143),

> O, Sir! you are old;
> Nature in you stands on the very verge
> Of her confine,

and when Goneril follows her (II.iv.194) with

> All's not offence that indiscretion finds
> And dotage terms so,

in effect they are enforcing Montaigne's thoughts on the subject. Death from old age is not the only 'naturall' form of death, as people say (that is, it is not 'generall, common, and universall'); on the contrary, it is exceptional, a 'rare privilege' from nature: 'Indeed it is the limit, beyond which we shall not passe, and which the law of nature hath prescribed unto us, as that which should not be outgone by any' (I,lvii, 'Of Age'; Florio, 1.369). Cato the Younger had thought the age of forty-eight 'very ripe', 'considering how few men come unto it'; and, with a phrase Shakespeare may have remembered for Edgar, Montaigne later adds: 'It is the body, which sometimes yeeldeth unto age; and other times the mind' (1.371). In 'Upon Some Verses of *Virgil*' he writes:

both wisedome and folly shall have much a do, by enterchange of offices to support and succour me in this calamity of age ... Well may my judgement hinder me from spurning and repining at the inconveniences which nature allots me to indure; from feeling them it cannot;

and he comes back again to 'the doting and crazed condition of our age' (3.65, 124).

But age is no more than the last phase of that constant struggle or mutual interference between body and mind that Montaigne dwells upon at great length in the 'Apologie', using it as his main argument for scepticism. The senses deceive the mind and the mind the senses. 'Let a Philosopher', he says, be fastened securely in a wire cage to the 'steeple' of Notre Dame and, in spite of his 'reason', 'that exceeding height must needs dazzle his sight, and amaze or turne his senses'. Montaigne himself has experienced from the heights of the Alps how 'if but a tree, a shrub, or any out-butting crag of a Rock presented it selfe unto our eyes, ... it doth somewhat ease and assure us from feare' – and yet 'we cannot without some dread and giddiness in the head, so much as abide to looke upon one of those even and downe-right precipices ...: Which is an evident deception of the sight' (2.314–15). (Yet it was in vain that 'a worthy Philosopher pulled out his eyes', since sound no less than sight can fool the mind (2.315).) On the other side, 'what we see and hear, being passionately transported with anger, we neither see nor heare it as it is ... Our senses are not onely altered, but many times dulled, by the passions of the mind' (2.316–17); while conversely 'the accidents of sickenesse ... make things appeare other unto us, then they seeme unto the healthie ...' (2.321). Shakespeare must surely have been using these passages when he makes Lear check his anger against Cornwall with the reflection that 'we are not ourselves / When Nature, being oppress'd, commands the mind / To suffer with the body' (II.iv.104), or declare, in the midst of the storm, that 'when the mind's free / The body's delicate' (III.iv.11); and, above all, in the startling scene dramatising sense-deception at Dover Cliff.[21]

Philosophers have made an 'imaginarie' commonwealth out of the 'little world' of man (2.246); their endless speculations about the soul show that the mind's attempts to know itself result merely in words (2.251–68). No more can philosophers 'know their owne being', the reasons why the body instinctively moves or changes (2.247); *in the corporall part, man is no more instructed of himselfe, then in the spirituall* (2.270). How much, for example, can Aristotle or Galen teach us 'of what matter men are derived and produced one from another'? (2.269). Montaigne returns to the subject of our ignorance about human generation, in a mood this time of wonder rather than scepticism, in his essay 'Of the Resemblance betweene Children and Fathers' (II, xxxvii).[22]

Wee neede not goe to cull out miracles, and chuse strange difficulties: me seemeth, that amongst those things we ordinarily see, there are such incomprehensible rarities, as they exceed all difficulty of miracles. What monster is it, that this teare or drop of seed, whereof we are ingendred brings with it; and in it the impressions, not only of the corporall forme, but even of the very thoughts and inclinations of our fathers? Where doth this droppe of water containe or lodge this infinite number of formes?

(2.496–7)

This touches a question that throbs deep in *King Lear*.

The question is prepared for at the outset when Gloucester introduces Edmund – 'there was good sport at his making, and the whoreson must be acknowledged' (I.i.22). For Lear it is crucial; meeting it shapes his whole experience in the play. So closely has he bound up the moral expectations with the physical fact of paternity that disillusionment threatens to tear his mind apart. His first mention of 'nature' matches paternal instinct with moral virtue in his children:

> Which of you shall we say doth love us most?
> That we our largest bounty may extend
> Where nature doth with merit challenge.
>
> (I.i.50)

In his rage with Cordelia, he wishes at once to annul the biological as well as the personal ties between them:

> By all the operation of the orbs
> From whom we do exist and cease to be,
> Here I disclaim all my paternal care,
> Propinquity and property of blood,
> And as a stranger to my heart and me
> Hold thee from this for ever.
>
> (I.i.110)

Birth is one of the 'mysteries' governed by the stars; nevertheless, Lear is convinced that the fact of birth entails moral imperatives. He tells France that Cordelia is 'a wretch whom Nature is asham'd / Almost t'acknowledge hers' (I.i.211); by which he means, superficially, that it is abnormal and shocking for a daughter publicly to rebuff her father and, more powerfully, that such intransigence is contrary to the whole cosmic order. That, it seems, would be his rationalisation of the speech. But at a deeper level he seems convinced – in contradiction to Montaigne's view in the essay 'Of the Affection of Fathers' – that filial gratitude must be an instinct implanted by birth. So, in his first confrontation with Goneril, he calls 'ingratitude' in a child a 'marble-hearted fiend' (I.iv.257), and declares that Cordelia's 'fault', now 'small' by comparison, had 'like an engine, wrench'd my frame of nature / From the fix'd place' (I.iv.266). No doubt his *frame of nature* is his personality as a coherent whole; but at the heart of this, the suggestive phrase seems to imply, is that paternal love which Montaigne had described – in contradistinction from children's love for their fathers – as an instinct, derived from 'nature', 'ayming to . . . advance the successive parts or parcels of this her frame' (2.67). Certainly, in his next speech, his terrible curse, Lear calls upon 'Nature' as a 'Goddess' to

> Suspend thy purpose, if thou didst intend
> To make this creature fruitful!

The first and most fitting punishment he imagines for Goneril, as a 'thankless child', is to be a punishment in 'her womb'. It is probably indicative of Shakespeare's train of thought here that some of the most striking words in Lear's speeches, all of them new or unique in the plays, appear to have been taken from a reading of Florio: *marble-hearted, sterility, derogate, disnatur'd.*[23]

In his meeting with Regan Lear perhaps distinguishes between

> The offices of nature, bond of childhood,
> Effects of courtesy, dues of gratitude.
>
> (II.iv.176)

But the four terms in apposition clearly overlap; and, while *nature* is separated from, for example, *courtesy*, the distinction only serves to emphasise that the *offices* of nature are moral obligations, physically inherited. So too, as Lear meets Goneril again, he thinks of her as

> my flesh, my blood, my daughter;
> Or rather a disease that's in my flesh,
> Which I must needs call mine.
>
> (II.iv.219)

And in his next scene, his first in the storm, the identification in Lear's mind between sexual begetting and moral prerogatives has gained the strength of an obsession:

> Crack Nature's moulds, all germens spill at once
> That make ingrateful man!
>
> (III.ii.8)

The way he identifies his children's obligations with his own physical self comes out again in

> filial ingratitude!
> Is it not as this mouth should tear this hand
> For lifting food to't?
>
> (III.iv.14)

Within this rhetorical question is a shock of violent feeling more primitive than moral indignation. Only when he turns mad is Lear able to think of the identification between moral life and physical life no longer as an unshakeable axiom but as an agonising question:

Then let them anatomize Regan, see what breeds about her heart. Is there any cause in nature that make these hard hearts?

(III.vi.74)

Gloucester had said that 'the wisdom of Nature can reason it thus and thus, yet Nature finds itself scourg'd by the sequent effects' (I.ii.101). That comment on reason's limits had been comparatively trite. Lear's question goes much deeper. His tragedy, as he feels it during the storm scenes, is not only that his daughters have betrayed him, or that he fears he may have betrayed himself, but that nature, the very stuff of humanity, has betrayed him as well. It is that that goads him beyond rage to madness. But to put his question, unanswerable though it is, is a step for Lear towards release.

There is an echo of these thoughts in Kent's speech in a later scene:

> It is the stars,
> The stars above us, govern our conditions;
> Else one self mate and make could not beget
> Such different issues.

(IV.iii.32)

This scene was omitted from the Folio text of the play; possibly in part because Shakespeare came to think such choric repetition was not needed.

Nature for King Lear means the social order as well as the source of physical life. The course of the play will shatter the assumptions about society that he shares with his loyal subjects – and, in effect, with many, if not most, of the play's first spectators. Nothing in the narrative sources points directly to any such social implication of the legend. In those moments when Lear is driven to question or reject the whole constitution of civilised society, Shakespeare is again drawing largely from his reading in Montaigne.

The first explicit challenge comes from Edmund's first soliloquy:

> Thou, Nature, art my goddess; to thy law
> My services are bound. Wherefore should I
> Stand in the plague of custom, and permit
> The curiosity of nations to deprive me,
> For that I am some twelve or fourteen moonshines
> Lag of a brother? Why bastard? Wherefore base?

(I.ii.1)

These lines give a mocking twist to his submissive acknowledgement towards Kent in the previous scene – 'My services to your Lordship' (I.i.28). Edmund is plainly an outsider with a grievance, and a scoundrel. Since he could not expect to inherit Gloucester's estate in any case because he was the younger son, there is an impudent sophistry in his harping on his bastard origin. As Bradley remarks, 'it is hard to say' how far Edmund 'is serious in this attitude, and really indignant at the brand of bastardy'. But this is partly because of what Bradley calls 'a certain genuine gaiety' and even a 'cheery' tone in the soliloquy, which distinguishes Edmund from the coldly systematic machiavellism of Iago,[24] or the sardonic tone of the malcontent Don John, the bastard in *Much Ado*. In tone, he much more resembles the buoyant Faulconbridge in *King John*. On the other hand, the latter has and needs no doctrine, and is even prepared to forgo his advantage in law as an elder brother, relying on the natural advantages his bastard origin has given him as the son of Richard Coeur-de-lion. It is as if Edmund, lacking any trump card of this potency, has turned to a theory to strengthen him instead. Yet at the same time, his words threaten to undercut the position taken for granted by Lear, who will also (in all consistency) appeal to Nature as his 'Goddess'. If Nature is indeed a more-than-human arbiter of right and wrong, then Edmund's inferences from that premise may seem as logical as Lear's.

Edmund probably owes his word, *curiosity* – which he appears to use here in the sense of capricious refinement, with an overtone of officious meddling – to Florio,[25] and the attitude behind it to Montaigne, who insistently contrasts Nature and Custom. Custom is immensely variable, self-contradictory, arbitrary and compulsive. In his chapter 'Of Custome' (which leads, however, to a warning against innovation), Montaigne begins with the proposition that '*Custome is a violent and deceiving schoole-mistris*' (Florio, 1.105). In his final chapter, 'Of Experience', he writes,

It is in the hands of custome to give our life what forme it pleaseth: in that it can do all in all. It is the drinke of *Circes*, diversifieth our nature as she thinkes good;

(3.340)

and in his chapter 'Upon Some Verses of *Virgil*' he says of his own writings:

The wisedome and reach of my lesson, is all in truth, in liberty, in essence; disdaining in the catalogue of my true duties, these easie, faint, ordinary and provinciall rules; all naturall, constant and generall, whereof civilitie and ceremonie are daughters, but bastards ... For there is danger, that we devise new offices, to excuse our negligence toward naturall offices, and to confound them ... [And] we see ... that among nations, where lawes of seemelinesse are more rare and slack, the primitive lawes of common reason are better observed, the innumerable multitude of so manifold duties stifling, languishing and dispersing our care.

(3.117–18)[26]

Montaigne's first admirers took this 'lesson' particularly to heart (however differently from Edmund). In her Preface to her edition of the *Essais* in 1595, Montaigne's *fille d'alliance*, Marie de Gournay, summed up his teaching as first of all 'la connaissance de nous mêmes, celle du bien et du mal et surtout en face du tyrannique aveuglement de la coutume';[27] and in his dedicatory verses to Florio, Daniel saluted his author for having

> made such bold sallies out upon
> *Custome*, the mightie tyrant of the earth,
> In whose *Seraglio* of subjection
> We all seeme bred-up, from our tender birth.

As Edmund's speech on 'the plague of custom' unfolds, he takes in these suggestions of an alien, tyrannical and yet effeminate (or 'languishing') power, together with the paradox that the true 'bastards' are the codes of 'civilitie'. Ignoring the reservations and ambiguities in Montaigne's standpoint, his is already the language of D'Amville in *The Atheist's Tragedy* and the *libertins* of the next generation.[28]

In Edmund's mind, his own natural superiority comes directly from his bastardy – from what his father has already called the 'good sport at his making':

> Why brand they us
> With base? with baseness? bastardy? base, base?
> Who in the lusty stealth of nature take
> More composition and fierce quality
> Than doth, within a dull, stale, tired bed,
> Go to th'creating a whole tribe of fops,
> Got 'tween asleep and wake?

(I.ii.9)

Here again, in the contrast between himself and 'honest madam's issue', Edmund is following Montaigne's essay 'Upon Some Verses of *Virgil*' (which fascinated Marston and Webster also).[29]

Montaigne there qualifies his intense admiration for Virgil's lines describing the coupling of Venus and Vulcan with the thought

that he depainteth her somewhat stirring for a maritall *Venus*. In this discreete match, appetites are not commonly so fondling; but drowsie and more sluggish.

(3.72)

Later, however, he notes that in Virgil, Venus 'becomes a suiter' to Vulcan 'in the behalfe of a bastard of hers', Aeneas (3.90). Through this extraordinary essay, which weaves in and out between admiration for the language of Virgil and Lucretius and many-sided comments on love, marriage and sexual mores, runs a series of contrasts between 'amorous licentiousnes' and 'languishing congression' (72–3), between 'a dull spirit' and '*a vigilant, lively and blithe agitation*' (121). When Edmund concludes his soliloquy with, 'Now, gods, stand up for bastards!', he must surely be thinking still of Montaigne and the Venus genetrix of Lucretius and Virgil.

Another passage probably contributing to Edmund's speech is that in the chapter 'Of the Caniballes' where Montaigne considers the Brazilian Indians:

I finde ... there is nothing in that nation, that is either barbarous or savage, unlesse men call that barbarisme which is not common to them. As indeed, we have no other ayme of truth and reason, than the example and *Idea* of the opinions and customes of the countrie we live in ... They are even savage, as we call those fruits wilde, which nature of her selfe ... hath produced: whereas indeed they are those which our selves have altered by our artificiall devices, and diverted from their common order, we should rather terme savage. In those are the true and most profitable vertues, and naturall properties most lively and vigorous, which in these we have bastardized, applying them to the pleasure of our corrupted taste. And ... there is no reason, art should gaine the point of honour of our great and puissant mother Nature.

(1.219)

Shakespeare certainly drew upon this and the next page for *The Winter's Tale* and *The Tempest*;[30] almost certainly he was thinking of it when writing *Lear* also – as the irony of Edmund's later words to Gloucester, 'Most savage and unnatural!' (III.iii.7), seems to confirm. In that case, Shakespeare was probably struck also by the passage at the end of the chapter describing Montaigne's talk with the Indians brought to Rouen, who had been asked what they thought of 'our pompe' and 'fashions' in France (1.228–9). Explaining that 'they have a manner of phrase whereby they call men but a moytie [a portion] one of another', Montaigne reports that

They had perceived, there were men amongst us full gorged with all sortes of commodities, and others which hunger-starved, and bare with need and povertie, begged at their gates: and found it strange, these moyties so needy could endure such an injustice . . .

This may well have suggested, as a corollary to Edmund's rise in the world, Edgar's choice of a means of escape by adopting 'the basest and most poorest shape / That ever penury, in contempt of man, / Brought near to beast' (II.iii.7). In the mere mechanics of the plot there is nothing to require Edgar to disguise himself as a naked beggar, any more than Kent.

In any case, Edgar's role as a beggar belongs to that vein of thought in the play close to the strong vein of naturalism or primitivism in Montaigne, in which he draws upon various sources in classical philosophy, Sceptical, Stoical or Epicurean, but regularly with an emphasis upon civilised 'excesse'. The word *gorged* in his report from the Indians strikes a characteristic note. In a lengthy passage in the 'Apologie', for example (2.146 ff.), he rounds upon 'the daily plaints' against man's natural condition, 'which I often heare men make'

exclaiming that man is the onely forsaken and outcast creature, naked on the bare earth, having nothing to cover and arme himselfe withall but the spoile of others; whereas Nature hath clad and mantled all other creatures, some with shels, . . . with haire, with wooll, . . . and with silke . . . And hath moreover instructed them in every thing fit and requisite for them . . . where as man only (Oh silly wretched man) can neither goe, nor speake, nor shift, nor feed himselfe, unlesse it be to whine and weepe onely, except he be taught . . .

To which Montaigne replies forcibly, 'Such complaints are false.' Man's skin can resist the weather as well as any other animal's – 'Witnesse divers Nations, which yet never knew the use of clothes'; and even among Europeans, the stomach, the part of the body which ought most to be protected against cold, has often been left uncovered:

Our forefathers used to have it bare, and our Ladies (as dainty-nice as they be) are many times seene to goe open-breasted, as low as their navill.

Reverting to 'the nations, that have lately bin discovered', Montaigne repeats that their life shows that nature can provide 'whatsoever should be needfull' to man, 'without toyling' and without 'art' (148–9). But later, he appears to extend the charge of 'excesse' beyond Europeans to mankind in general, by comparison with beasts (2.165):

> Lustfull desires are either naturall, and necessary, as eating and drinking; or else naturall and not necessary, as the acquaintance of males and females: or else neither necessary nor naturall: Of this last kinde are almost all mens: For, they are all superfluous and artificiall. It is wonderfull to see with how little nature will be satisfied, and how little she hath left for us to be desired. The preparations in our kitchins, doe nothing at all concerne her lawes ...

He adds that 'Brute beasts are much more regulare than we; and with more moderation containe themselves within the compasse, which nature hath prescribed them: yet' – with a characteristic swerve in his exposition – 'not so exactly, but that they have some coherency with our riotous licentiousnesse.' Comparisons with animals figure as prominently in this section of the 'Apologie' as in *King Lear*, though from differing points of view. Montaigne strains his ingenuity (or Pliny's, or Plutarch's) to demonstrate the rationality of animals, whereas the creatures in *Lear* are more akin to those in medieval bestiaries or express the unleashing of a predatory libido. In both, however, the comparisons are used to diminish human pride, whether intellectual or moral.

The King takes up the themes of Montaigne's 'Apologie' at the climax of his confrontation with Regan and Goneril. Hitherto, apart from brief exchanges, virtually asides, when in the company of the Fool, Lear's speeches have consisted almost entirely of affirmations of his authority – assertions, demands, imperatives, sarcasms, curses. Now, for the first time, in the course of the dispute over his retinue, as he is driven into a corner, the old man contains his will and passion for a few lines and steps far enough aside from the immediate dispute to resort to reasoning from principles:

> O! reason not the need; our basest beggars
> Are in the poorest things superfluous:
> Allow not nature more than nature needs,
> Man's life is cheap as beast's. Thou art a lady;
> If only to go warm were gorgeous,
> Why, nature needs not what thou gorgeous wear'st,
> Which scarcely keeps thee warm. But, for true need, –
> You Heavens, give me that patience, patience I need! –
>
> (II.iv.262)

Already by this point Lear becomes choked with emotion, and his repetition of 'patience' shows the opposite at work in him. What 'true need' is, he cannot or will not say. But meanwhile he has, in effect, turned to Montaigne to supply him with themes, terms and a telling illustration, in his effort to shift the quarrel to the ground of first principles. As against the stoicism in the 'Apologie', Lear maintains that man *needs* some excess or superfluity; in other words, man needs more than he needs. He cannot articulate this seeming paradox further, and breaks away from the argument. But he has begun to look from the outside at his own position, his assumptions about 'nature', for the first time in the play.

In the storm scene, just before he meets Poor Tom, Lear's prayer on behalf of 'Poor naked wretches' shows that he has travelled further along this line:

> O! I have ta'en
> Too little care of this. Take physic, Pomp,
> Expose thyself to feel what wretches feel,
> That thou mayst shake the superflux to them,
> And show the Heavens more just.
>
> (III.iv.32)

And Gloucester later – though less rhetorically or imperatively[31] – repeats the substance of the King's prayer as, after he has been blinded, he gives Poor Tom his purse in order to guide him to Dover:

> that I am wretched
> Makes thee the happier: Heavens, deal so still!
> Let the superfluous and lust-dieted man,
> That slaves your ordinance, that will not see
> Because he does not feel, feel your power quickly;
> So distribution should undo excess,
> And each man have enough.
>
> (IV.i.64)

No doubt both of these speeches stem from a broad homiletic tradition; but they have a particular thread of connection with the *Essays* in their emphasis upon inequality and superfluity, and especially in Gloucester's striking epithet, *lust-dieted*, which concentrates Montaigne's argument about man's 'lustfull desires' (as shown by 'the preparations in our kitchins'),[32] with a sharp recall of the speaker's personal history.

These speeches branch out from the main action in the play, or mark a change of direction. We can imagine that Gloucester and, even more, Lear, has not felt deeply before about social inequality;

and we can see that Lear's prayer revises what he had said about beggars in his speech to Goneril and Regan. But nothing has suggested that the faults in the two old men at the beginning have sprung directly from callousness towards the poor – just as nothing suggests subsequently that Lear will take charity as a guiding motive in what remains of his life. Nevertheless, his rejection of Cordelia (and of Kent) has come from his quality as a king, as well as a father, while Gloucester's credulity over his sons has shown a similar blindness in a man with authority. Before Lear meets Cordelia again he will have dismantled his whole conception of kingship, and his prayer in the storm is a step in that direction. It gives a new dimension to the play. For Lear himself, that new dimension is confined to ideas and those ideas are to be intensified but also distorted by the onset of his madness. But in the middle scenes, what goes on in Lear's mind is crucial to the play.

What breaks his sanity down is meeting a 'poor naked wretch' face to face in the person of Poor Tom. For a moment, he tries to identify himself with beggary, to act out the abject state he had only begun to imagine before. Here, at what is virtually the mid-point and the turning-point in the tragedy, the nadir of his royalty, the King again borrows themes and language from Montaigne;[33] but with a variation that suggests the deliberateness and the subtlety of Shakespeare's use of the *Essays*. One of the main passages Shakespeare recalls here is that in the chapter 'Of Phisiognomy' (III, xii; Florio, 3.304–6), where Montaigne criticises the teachings of philosophers on preparation for death (developing his reflections in the earlier chapter (I, xix), 'That to Philosophize, is to Learne how to Dye'). Montaigne has been describing an epidemic of plague in his district, the digging of 'graves' and the exemplary 'resolution' of the country people; and then he turns towards men of 'learning' for a disadvantageous comparison:

Wee have forsaken nature, and yet wee will teach her her lesson . . . learning is compelled to goe daily a borrowing, thereby to make her disciples a patterne of constancy, of innocency and of tranquilitie. It is a goodly matter to see how these men full of so great knowledge, must imitate this foolish simplicitie . . . [and] that our wisedome should learne of beasts . . . [how] we should live and die, husband our goods, love and bring up our children, and entertaine justice. A singular testimonie of mans infirmitie: and that this reason we so manage at our pleasure, ever finding some diversitie and noveltie, leaveth unto us no maner of apparant tracke of nature. Wherewith men have done, as perfumers do with oyle, they have adulterated her, with so many argumentations, and sofisticated her with so diverse farre-fetcht discourses, that she is become variable and peculiar to every man, and hath lost her proper, constant and universall visage: whereof we must seeke for a testimony of beasts, not subject to favor or corruption, nor to diversity of opinions.

The 'borrowing' and the sophisticating here spring from the intellect, not from the human condition as such. Montaigne continues by illustrating (from Seneca) philosophy's advice to meditate *'Banishments, torments'* and the like as an armour against *'misadventure'*; and he demands, 'What availeth this curiosity unto us...?':

surely it is a kind of fever, now to cause your selfe to be whipped, because fortune may one day chance to make you endure it: and at Mid-Sommer to put-on your furr'd Gowne, because you shall neede it at Christmas? ... It is certaine, that preparation unto death, hath caused more torment unto most, than the very sufferance.

Lear, of course, is genuinely in torment of mind, in a state verging on banishment, but he reacts to the sight of the outcast with a self-mortifying gesture directly contrary to Montaigne's counsel, while shifting the reproach of being 'sophisticated' (Shakespeare's only use of this word) from philosophy to the normal – though admittedly, as Montaigne has noted elsewhere, not universal – protection of dress:

Thou wert better in a grave than to answer with thy uncover'd body this extremity of the skies. Is man no more than this? Consider him well. Thou ow'st the worm no silk, the beast no hide, the sheep no wool, the cat no perfume. Ha! here's three on's are sophisticated; thou art the thing itself; unaccommodated man is no more but such a poor, bare, forked animal as thou art. Off, off, you lendings! Come; unbutton here.

(III.iv.99)

Shakespeare seems to be balanced between challenge and agreement in his attitude towards his source. His characters are in a condition of 'extremity', as if to test the strain of complacency within Montaigne; and the King cannot be equated with the 'rusticall troupe of unpolished men' the essayist has justifiably admired. Yet the Fool comments in Montaigne's spirit with, 'Prithee, Nuncle, be contented; 'tis a naughty night to swim in.' Just possibly, Lear has intended to share his clothes with the beggar, but the main drive behind his gesture of undressing is his wish to treat his own case as exemplary, to force its exemplariness to the uttermost. He is placing himself outside of the human condition by the very gesture of trying to identify himself with it completely. Shakespeare is surely indebted to Montaigne for the terms in which he poses Lear's problem at this crucial place in the play.

In his madness Lear touches extremes of humility and arrogance. During the storm scenes, he sees himself as at once a helpless scapegoat and a merciless judge. In the later scene where he meets Gloucester near Dover he is prophet and despot, disabused but irresponsible, all-accusing and all-permitting. But there is lucidity as well as derangement in his harangues to Gloucester on adultery and then authority – 'matter and impertinency mix'd', as Edgar says of the latter speech; 'Reason in madness' (IV.vi.172). And here once again, Montaigne has furnished Lear with the 'matter' for his exposure of contradictions at the basis of social life. In the first of these two speeches (IV.vi.107–31), when the King proclaims

> die for adultery! No:
> The wren goes to't, and the small gilded fly
> Does lecher in my sight,

and again when he denounces the 'riotous appetite' in women, he is extracting ideas from Montaigne, principally from the essay 'Upon Some Verses of *Virgil*'[34] (though he ignores what Montaigne has to say against the double standard in sexual morals). And when he denounces 'yond simp'ring dame, / Whose face between her forks presages snow; / That minces virtue, and does shake the head / To hear of pleasure's name', Lear seems to be thinking of another essay in Montaigne, 'Of Vanitie' (III, ix; 3.237):

To what purpose are these heaven-looking and nice points of Philosophie, on which no humane being can establish and ground it selfe? . . . I often see, that there are certaine Idaeas or formes of life proposed unto us, which neither the proposer nor the Auditors have any hope at all to follow; and which is worse, no desire to attaine. *Of the same paper, whereon a Judge writ but even now the condemnation against an adulterer, hee will teare a scantlin, thereon to write some love-lines to his fellow-judges wife. The same woman from whom you came lately, and with whom you have committed that unlawfull-pleasing sport, will soone after even in your presence, raile and scold more bitterly against the same fault in her neighbour, than ever Portia or Lucrece could. And some condemne men to die for crimes, that themselves esteeme no faults.*

There is a violent reversal in the midst of Lear's speech on adultery, as his mind swings from his false belief in the 'kindness' of 'Gloucester's bastard son' to his obsession with his own progeny; but the thread of association follows the lines of Montaigne's exposure of hypocrisy.

This thread reaches into Lear's more coherent harangue on 'authority' (IV.vi.148–71). Montaigne's attacks on the law are frequent, ranging from his contrast between positive and natural laws in the 'Apologie' to more biting criticism in his third Book, such as the passage I have just quoted, or his earlier comment – 'The Schoolemaster whippeth his scholler for his docility, and the guide striketh the blinde man he leadeth. A horrible image of justice' (III, i; 3.20) – and to the radical attacks in his final chapter: 'How many condemnations have I seene more criminall, than the crime it selfe?'; and, 'Lawes are now maintained in credit, not because they are essentially just, but because they are lawes. It is the mysticall foundation of their authority; they have none other: which availes them much' (III, xiii; 3.329, 331).[35] These passages provide the 'matter' for Lear's

> great image of Authority:
> A dog's obeyed in office.
> Thou rascal beadle, hold thy bloody hand!
> Why dost thou lash that whore? Strip thine own back;
> Thou hotly lusts to use her in that kind
> For which thou whipp'st her. The usurer hangs the cozener.

Lear's mind soon wavers to 'None does offend, none, I say, none; I'll able 'em'; but not before he has denounced the 'mysticall foundation' his own authority had rested on.

With this speech, the borrowings from Montaigne in *King Lear* come very nearly to an end;[36] there is nothing evidently from Montaigne, for instance, in the great scenes of reconciliation between the King and Cordelia. Moreover, Lear's speeches on adultery and authority correspond to some of the central preoccupations in Shakespeare's work; they form a kind of weird reprise on the themes of *Measure for Measure*, with Lear in effect revoking the edict behind the plot of the Viennese play and meditating afresh on the absurdity of 'proud man, / Dress'd in a little brief authority'. Nevertheless, as Muir says, 'it would be unreasonable to deny that Montaigne had a substantial influence on the thought of *King Lear*' – especially in those speeches reflecting critically on the King's initial assumptions about Nature. What is striking is how selectively and consistently Shakespeare has applied his extensive borrowings from the *Essays*.

In a sense, it can even be felt that Montaigne had too much influence on *King Lear*. The thoughts prompted or supported by him vastly extend the scope of the legend. The passages where his influence can be traced are among the most memorable in the play. They are like *Essays* in miniature, speculative and sententious. But, setting aside their contribution to the planning of the opening scenes, for the most part Shakespeare's borrowings from Montaigne remain relatively theoretical. To exaggerate a little, they are felt as marginal commentaries rather than essential to the action. And it is just the quality that makes them memorable that makes them seem relatively detached.

Moreover, the Montaigne passages in the play are critical in tendency rather than constructive; they teach what Lear has to unlearn in the course of his suffering, rather than what he has positively to learn. In H. A. Mason's study of the play, where he opposes the tendency common among critics to interpret it along the lines of moral allegory, the writer remarks about the two prayers uttered by Lear and Gloucester and the run of scenes connecting them that

so many of the speeches are put in not to make us aware of how one man responds to a situation but to suggest how mankind is placed generally.

By the fourth act, he complains, it is difficult to 'resist ... the invitation to generalise everything and to suspend our normal expectations of probability'. And, in order to explain this flaw – as he sees it – he puts forward, at least as 'a hypothesis to be tested', the consideration that

from now on the play wants, and suffers from the want of, an element to control the other elements. This special want is created by the madness of Lear, which in this context means his failure to make sense of what is happening.

No other character can be allowed to overshadow Lear; 'but we must have lights on the experiences that are now beyond Lear to interpret'; in other words, 'a few dramatic ultimates, things which cannot in the context of the fiction be questioned or made to look subordinate to anything else'.[37] As against this, one may well feel that in order for the recognition scene with Cordelia to reach its full dramatic effect it has been necessary during the middle scenes to keep Lear's mind – in a double sense – *distracted*; tormentedly questioning his own world and status but yet unable to see, or even think about, his feelings and motives clearly. That Shakespeare had something like this in view seems evident from the way he altered the incidents from the chronicles and the old play by cancelling Lear's wish to leave Britain with the express object of meeting Cordelia again. Shakespeare's Lear in the middle scenes has almost forgotten Cordelia; there is a dramatic gap, which his madness triumphantly fills. In those scenes Lear attains at times the stature of 'a prophet' (as Mason says) 'for whom madness had been a revelation of painful general truths'; truths which may appear to be no more than 'partial' but which 'make what was merely fantastical in the storm scenes a grim reality'.[38] For those 'general truths' Shakespeare owed much to Montaigne; but only at a price; the price of turning attention to some extent aside from the central emotional current in the play.

There were limits to what Shakespeare could utilise from Montaigne. An essential theme in *King Lear*, a vital part in the tragedy's power, is the presentation of evil, and of a human response to evil. Goneril and Regan do not seek to explain themselves, still less to exult in villainy, like Shakespeare's earlier villains; they are what they are. They are too sure of themselves to need self-justification, even primly satisfied: 'Prescribe not us our duty.' Nor do they need to invoke demonic powers, like Lady Macbeth; in a way they are too natural, and that is partly what makes them horrifying. But Montaigne, it seems, could offer little to Shakespeare imaginatively here, any more than he could suggest the quality of Edmund in action, as distinct from the rationalisations Edmund uses against his father and brother. Montaigne has fine and deeply felt things to say about cruelty, from his reading about the conquest of the New World and his experience of the civil war. But he remains too firmly rational, too civilised – in spite of his primitivist sympathies – to submit to the imaginative pull of evil subjectively (as in his curt, decisive but dismissive comment on the imprisoned witches he had talked to: 'in my conscience, I should rather have appointed them Helleborum, than Hemlocke').[39]

In *Macbeth*, Shakespeare himself enters the mind of evil imaginatively, involves his audience in a kind of sympathy with it. In *Lear* his approach is more external, and until we are forced to watch the blinding of Gloucester (a scene of raw cruelty which has no counterpart in *Macbeth*) our principal response to it follows its effects on others, mainly through the moral shock of bewilderment in the King: 'is there any cause in nature that make these hard hearts?' But this response is deeply intensified in the middle scenes, partly through the nervous shock of the storm, but chiefly through the ravings of Edgar in his role as Poor Tom and through their consequences for Lear's mind as well. Here Shakespeare makes use of another literary source, as remote as Montaigne from the narrative starting-points for the tragedy. He had drawn upon Montaigne's essay about fathers and children to bring out the lines of potential conflict between reason and emotion in his opening scenes. But as the play travels from irrational impulses towards mental breakdown, he takes material from a source of a very different stamp, Harsnett's exposure of alleged demonic possession.

The indisputable borrowings from Harsnett are confined to Poor Tom's part in the storm scenes and some passages connected with it psychologically. Since Shakespeare was adding Edgar's disguise as Tom to the sub-plot scheme he had taken over from Sidney, it again seems clear that he was turning to an extra-narrational source for specific dramatic purposes. Before meeting Tom, the King has feared he may go mad, and his prayer in the storm on behalf of 'Poor naked wretches' seems to show that he feels he has reached the limits of self-criticism compatible with his self-command. Tom is the living embodiment of his prayer and, worse, it seems, a raving madman. In sympathy with him, Lear's sanity breaks. Tom's essential dramatic function, then, is to precipitate Lear's collapse, the transformation of his kingliness. For this, Shakespeare drew liberally, though not exclusively, on Harsnett – not as to Tom's nakedness (there are no beggars in Harsnett) but as to his pretended hallucinations. Evidently these were considered a major attraction in the play, since the title-page of the 1608 Quarto featured Edgar's life-history 'with his sullen and assumed humor of Tom of Bedlam'. Madness scenes had of course been popular on the stage, in *The Spanish Tragedy* for instance and in *Hamlet*. But in this case Shakespeare was taking on exceptional theatrical risks.

When, in phrases provided or suggested by Harsnett, Edgar describes his sufferings and names his devils, he pretends to be genuinely tormented (for which he has cause) and genuinely crazy. In type, his alleged symptoms were certainly common among Jacobean mentally disturbed patients.[40] But the specific manifestations Edgar has adopted had been set down by Harsnett as palpable, sinister and ridiculous impostures. Harsnett's officially sponsored *Declaration* attacks a team of Jesuit missionaries who had brainwashed and exploited some maidservants and young men in order to win converts by exhibiting exorcisms. So that when Edgar cries out how 'the foul fiend' has placed 'knives under his pillow', 'halters in his pew' and 'ratsbane by his porridge' (III.iv.50–4) he is citing what, on Harsnett's showing, had been merely clumsy tricks.[41] And

Harsnett has had great fun, in the style of Marprelate or Nashe, with 'these new strange names' of devils that Edgar is to reproduce, comparing them with gypsies' 'gibridge', calling on 'Trismegistus' and 'the old Platonicall sect' to explain them if possible, and printing the subsequent deposition of one of the pretended demoniacs, Sara Williams, who relates how she had denominated one of her devils from memories of 'a merry tale of *Hobberdidaunce*' and many of the rest from graffiti (some 'very strange names' written on a wall); her reason had simply been to give in to the priests (Harsnett, pp. 45–50, 180–1). Now, Edgar needs strange, not well known, devils' names, if only in order not to clash with the pagan setting of the play. But he does not need to remind those who have read, or heard about, the *Declaration* that they are trumpery inventions. Yet, in one of his last speeches as Tom, he even takes the risk of drawing attention to his source:

> Poor Tom hath been scar'd out of his good wits: ... Five fiends have been in poor Tom at once; as ... Hoberdidance, prince of dumbness; ... Flibbertigibbet, of mopping and mowing; who since possesses chambermaids and waiting-women...
>
> (IV.i.55–62)

Flibbertigibbet was surely incongruous enough, without the pointed topical allusion.

There is a wide difference between assuming madness for self-protection – Edgar's motive – and faking madness for profit. Shakespeare courts the risk that his public's response to one kind of deception will block their feeling for the other. In the storm scenes he treads a knife-edge between pandemonium and absurdity. He makes Edgar's 'counterfeiting' seem real enough to provoke Lear's emotions, but contrived enough to reveal the strain of pretending, while leaving the main emphasis on the force of delusion in the mind of the King.

A hint as to his methods lies in Edgar's first speech as Poor Tom, 'Through the sharp hawthorn blow the cold winds. Humh! go to thy bed and warm thee.' This picks up words from the Induction to *The Taming of the Shrew*: 'Go by, Jeronimy! go to thy cold bed, and warm thee';[42] the nobleman turned beggar recalls the tinker turning nobleman. Edgar says nothing about Hieronymo. But the scene he is introducing is to resemble that in *The Spanish Tragedy* (III.xiii) where Hieronymo, the grief-crazed judge, meets the petitioner, Don Bazulto, and confounds Bazulto's case with his own. Shakespeare places his borrowings from Harsnett within the frame of this (already complex) theatrical model.

'This cold night', says the Fool, 'will turn us all to fools and madmen' (III.iv.77). Although he is terrified by Tom at first, the Fool remains detached from him and from his effect upon Lear; beside them both, he stands for the hold of sanity, however perverse, paradoxical or fantastic in its expression. But he has already driven home his commonsense criticisms of Lear's conduct; and to leave him alone as Lear's chief companion in the storm would leave the dialogue between them merely static. Tom forces Lear, and our imagination, further. At the same time, Lear in his mental breakdown cannot be left for long to mere incoherency (in the manner of Othello's momentary fit), nor, evidently, does Shakespeare mean to keep him at the pitch of frenzied rage, the pitch of Seneca's Oedipus. Edgar forces him to contemplate the image of an outcast harried by guilt and, beyond that, the image of an exposure to nature, even identification with nature, more extreme and revolting than anything he has imagined:

Poor Tom; that eats the swimming frog, the toad, the todpole, the wallnewt, and the water; that in the fury of his heart, when the foul fiend rages, eats cow-dung for sallets; swallows the old rat and the ditch-dog; drinks the green mantle of the standing pool; who is whipp'd from tithing to tithing, and stock-punish'd, and imprison'd . . .

(III.iv.126)

This nightmare imagery is independent of Lear. It seems to Lear a reality (in his next speech, he calls Tom 'this philosopher'). It projects the forces of evil that Edmund – and the other main characters – have unleashed. Nevertheless, it is a piece of acting, just as Lear's response, beginning with the tearing off of his clothes, is an imitation of Edgar, a piece of acting. This play-acting within the play can reveal psychological possibilities or tendencies beyond the scope of the characters' sincere, consciously willed, reactions. But, by being presented as play-acting, it is kept distinct from the sense of an ultimate reality.

Tom's horrible diet has not been borrowed from Harsnett, but it is in keeping with the demonic fantasies Harsnett reports, and Shakespeare picks up material from the *Declaration* again in Tom's following lines, with 'Smulkin' and, 'The Prince of Darkness is a gentleman; Modo, he's called, and Mahu.' At one level, Shakespeare's reaction is very unusual for him, in that he cuts out the comic – sadistically comic – vigour from his source.[43] But at another level, it seems that Harsnett set Shakespeare thinking about episodes of sadism and moral perversion, taken from recent experience but not to be met with in any versions of the Lear story; they are documented instances of evil assuming the form of the grotesque. The principal torture Harsnett describes consists of tying the victim-accomplice to a chair, pouring a noxious mixture down his or her throat, and then holding the victim's face over burning brimstone or feathers, as an infallible means of inducing symptoms of possession:

Now I present to your imaginations, *Sara Williams* sitting bound in a chayre (as poor wench she often did) with a pinte of this *holy potion* in her stomacke, working up into her head, and out at her mouth, and her eyes, nose, mouth, and head, stuffed full with the smoake of holy perfume, her face being held down over the fume, till it was all over, as black as a stocke, and think if you see not in your minde, the lively *Idaea* of a poore devil-distressed woman in deede ... There is neither Horse, nor Asse, nor Dogge, nor Ape, if he had been used, as these poore seely creatures were, but would have been much more devillishly affected than they.

(Harsnett, 40–1)

As a clever propagandist, Harsnett makes a great deal of the priests' hot hands traversing the girls' bodies in search of devils; and he relates how they bully-ragged the young people into thinking that their illnesses were not natural, but diabolic, that Sara's menstruation was devil-caused, and that she would be unable to have children (which proved false (Harsnett, pp. 62–3, 84, 191, 201, 270)). The whole business was 'against nature' (as Sara said of the procedure of thrusting a holy relic, one of Edmund Campion's bones, into her mouth (p. 186)).

Images of malevolence, torment and degradation, apparently suggested by Harsnett, stretch across Shakespeare's play, still mainly connected with Edgar's story, but hence also with Lear's madness. The first echoes from the pamphlet come in I.ii, with Gloucester's word *machinations* (*l.* 109; compare V.i.46, but not used elsewhere by Shakespeare; Harsnett applies the term to Jesuit plots (Sig. A 3^v)) and with Edmund's strange aside about his 'cue' for 'villainous melancholy, with a sigh like Tom o' Bedlam', as he prepares to deal with Edgar's first arrival on the stage. As Muir has pointed out, Harsnett has a running fire of theatrical metaphors:[44] he emphasises melancholy as a cause of belief in witchcraft (pp. 131–2, 137): and Shakespeare's conspirator and forger probably owes his very name to the Jesuit Father Edmunds, the '*rector chori*' in Harsnett's 'holy Comedie' (p. 1) – the 'devil Edmunds' who stages dialogues composed by himself, being 'alone the Author, Actor, and penner of this play' (p. 86). Next from Harsnett (at II.iii.15) comes Edgar's mental picture of the mutilations of Bedlam beggars; and then – though still before Poor Tom emerges – comes the Fool's reaction to the sight of Kent in the stocks (*nether-stockes* being also one of Harsnett's words):[45]

Ha, ha! he wears cruel garters. Horses are tied by the heads, dogs and bears by th'neck, monkeys by th'loins, and men by th'legs: when a man's over-lusty at legs then he wears wooden nether-stocks.

(II.iv.7)

Shakespeare constantly imagines the human body in movement; images of constriction, deformation of the body seem to be some of the main things that struck him in Harsnett. In the same scene, the King's symptom, '*Hysterica passio*' (II.iv.55), is a complaint mentioned and discussed more than once in the pamphlet (pp. 25, 257, 263). And, after the storm scenes, Cornwall's torture of Gloucester – 'Bind fast his corky arms' (III.vii.29) – picks up from Harsnett (p. 23) an adjective Shakespeare uses only this once; it goes with the action of tying a victim to a chair.

Edgar's trick to exorcise his father's despair seems to follow the same line of thought set going by Harsnett, even though no verbal echoes from Harsnett have been traced in the Dover Cliff scene. If so, the stage action as a whole of Edmund's conspiracy and its consequences owes more to Harsnett than to Sidney.

At times, Shakespeare uses material from Harsnett and from Montaigne in close proximity. While Tom's lurid vision of his animal-form demons comes largely from Harsnett, Lear's response about the 'sophistication' of mankind is taken from Montaigne. Harsnett has contributed something to the physical horror of the scene of the blinding of Gloucester, while the sequel to it in Gloucester's development conforms with Montaigne's aphorisms to the effect that we must lose our sight to become wise.[46] Conversely, the *Declaration* may have led Shakespeare to think of the structural motif of mock exorcism in the Dover Cliff episode (IV.vi), but Montaigne has supplied something of the psychological insight into sense-deception and, more materially, of the physical imagery that supports it. But later in the same scene Lear's half-mad harangue about adultery swerves from the moral paradoxes adapted from Montaigne into the hysterical climactic images about 'the sulphurous pit' in women, strongly coloured by Harsnett. Broadly, then, while much of the considered reasoning by the characters, at least as far as the end of the fourth act, comes from the *Essays*, many of the images of physical immediacy, grotesque or horrifying, have been suggested by the *Declaration*.

Shakespeare took profit where he found it. In contrast to the anodyne previous versions of Lear's story and Sidney's coolly decorous episode of romance, Harsnett gave Shakespeare keys to a direct rendering of the experience of evil, in a little world of Bosch-like images, diminished but also rendered more perplexing and sinister by the writer's insistence that its offences 'against nature' have been factitiously contrived. On the other hand, Shakespeare keeps this material subordinate to the sustained questioning of man's place in nature borrowed very largely from his reading in Montaigne; and even that, on the whole, is kept within dramatic bounds. Probably Montaigne stimulated Shakespeare to the most searching questions in the play; but the thoughts borrowed or converted from the *Essays* are those of the characters, Edmund's or Lear's thoughts for instance, not the play's ultimate statements. These borrowings indicate Shakespeare's recognition of the most fruitful thinker of his time. But the way he places his borrowings also confirms his economy as a dramatist, his highly selective artistry.

8. 'Wit' in Jacobean comedy

Go, write it in a martial hand, be curst and brief. It is no matter how witty, so it be eloquent and full of invention.

Twelfth Night

The change in Elizabethan comedy, from the romantic settings and lyrical tone of Shakespeare's early years to the urban settings and anti-romantic tone preferred by his younger contemporaries, has attracted considerable interest from literary historians. Most of the current discussion stems from *Drama and Society in the Age of Jonson* (1937), where L. C. Knights argues for the basic seriousness of late-Elizabethan and Jacobean comedy; in his view, it expressed the reaction of a traditional social ethic to the first onset of speculative capitalism in England. Subsequent writers have learned from, but tended to modify, Knights's thesis. Brian Gibbons, for example, has maintained that the Jacobeans created a new dramatic genre, City Comedy, on the basis of formal literary satire.[1] Others have laid more stress on, or have re-examined, the specifically comic features of these plays. M. C. Bradbrook says, for example, that City comedy is 'neither didactic nor antididactic, but a finely balanced mixture of farce and realism, or Aristophanic and Terentian elements'.[2] This seems a truer critical reading than an interpretation conceived narrowly in terms of satire. Following this train of thought, I want to suggest that the idea of *wit* brings out the main common threads running through Jacobean comedies, particularly those with a London setting.

In Renaissance literature, as H. A. Mason has pointed out, it was More and Erasmus who first demonstrated what wit could mean, as a free play of the mind, combining seriousness with levity; in the long run, they showed others, including Shakespeare and Jonson and Molière, 'how to make a comprehensive criticism of society ... by blending the wisdom of classical comedy and satire with the common sense ... of the spokesman of the people, the popular jester'.[3] In ordinary English usage, however, it was some time before such a sense of the word *wit* could be clearly identified. Down to the later sixteenth century it still denoted simply mind, or mental capability. Since the eighteenth century, it has denoted chiefly a brilliant and amusing quality in speech or writing. But in the interval it passed through a fruitful metamorphosis. On one hand, it came to signify high, inventive talent (*ingenium*), especially in literature. On the other, it was attached to mere displays of verbal ingenuity, with an intonation of jesting, scoring off someone else, or, in modern slang, one-upmanship.[4] Both new branches of meaning in the word emerged in the metropolitan milieu of the Inns of Court and professional men of letters,[5] keenly aware of personal competition, and of intellectual accomplishment as a means to social advancement. If a particular date can be assigned to the literary recognition of novel and divergent meanings in the word, it is 1578, the year of Lyly's *Euphues, The Anatomy of Wit*, which gave a fresh twist to the discussion of *wits* (meaning simply capacities of mind) in Ascham's *The Schoolmaster*. And, for a time, Lyly provided a new model of witty style, in *Euphues* and his comedies.[6]

Shakespeare calls old poets 'the wits of former days' in Sonnet 59; Jonson uses the word *wit* to hail what we should call the innate genius in Shakespeare; Carew praises Donne, in his *Elegy* of 1633, as ruler of 'The universal monarchy of wit', thus paying tribute to the rapturous 'fire' in Donne's preaching as well as to his 'imperious' originality as a poet. From Shakespeare's time to Pope's, *wit* became the leading word to point out the natural gifts needed for the writing of good poetry.

At the same time, this was intertwined with the competing sense of mere verbal display, which, if revealing originality, often gave rein to mere wilfulness or the desire to excel at any cost. In practice, the two senses of the word came very close together. This was Lyly's point when he described Euphues (whose name signified nothing else than a highly educable wit, according to Ascham) as a 'younge gallant, of more wit then ... wisdome', addicted, for more than his own good, to 'those things commonly which are incident to these sharp wits' – namely, 'fine phrases, smoth quipping, merry taunting, using jesting without meane, and abusing mirth without measure'.[7] This brought out very clearly the dubious side of the term for the Elizabethans, when it was used in the new way, to denote skill with words. Harington indicates the same bias when he refers to Sir Thomas More, 'a man of great wisdom and learning', as nevertheless 'a little enclined ... to scoffing', '(as good wits are many times)'.[8] And

Gabriel Harvey fairly bristles over the question when he attacks Thomas Nashe for his 'mad-brained, or ridiculous . . . or monstrous' style as a popular pamphleteer, by contrast with the 'right artificiality' of Sidney and Spenser and 'the excellentest wittes of Greece'. He sarcastically awards his opponent 'the bell of singularity [for] humorous [= capricious] witt, and the garland of victory [for] *dominiering Eloquence*'; and he recommends those who 'intende to be fine companionable gentlemen, smirking wittes, and whipsters in the world' to study 'a smart Pamflet of knavery' by Nashe, so as to 'seeke out the Archmistery of the busiest Modernistes'. These sarcasms foreshadow the neo-classical distinction between genuine and trivial wit in writing that was to be laboured by critics in the age of Dryden.[9] On the plane of personal relations, there is a little of the same sting in the ladies' doubts about the lords in *Love's Labour's Lost*, as when Maria says that her only possible cause for not admiring Longaville 'Is a sharp wit match'd with too blunt a will' (II.i.49). Wit had become a fascinating quality, to be emulated but nevertheless questioned.

Love's Labour's Lost (c. 1595) was the first comedy with courtly wits for heroes. The novelty in Ben Jonson's early comedies was to bring the serious playfulness possible for wit in the spirit of Erasmus into engagement with the current new uses of the word, placing both in the context of contemporary London society. Pretension to wit, in the new style, is the principal target for his ridicule, as opposed to the true inventiveness of a poet or the discernment of an ideal gentleman-scholar. It argues lack of wit, in the old sense, and even more, a potentially destructive self-centredness. Jonson was always to be concerned with the moral or social and the literary ramifications of this theme together. 'There cannot be one colour of the mind', he writes in *Discoveries*, 'an other of the wit . . . Wheresoever manners, and fashions are corrupted, Language is.'[10] His great achievement as a comic playwright was to capture the effects of verve, acuteness and surprise striven after by practisers of conversational wit within a strictly controlled and ironic, yet abundantly imaginative, dialogue. But this meant that his own wit was embedded within his dialogue, not concentrated on the surface in a sparkling exchange of epigrams, as later in Restoration comedy; such a firework display would have been alien to his purpose:[11]

I doe heare them say often: Some men are not witty: because they are not every where witty; then which nothing is more foolish . . . But now nothing is good that is naturall: Right and naturall language seems to have least of the

wit in it: that which is writh'd and tortur'd, is counted the more exquisite ...
Nothing is fashionable, till it be deformed: and this is to write like a
Gentleman. All must bee as affected, and preposterous as our Gallants'
cloathes, sweet bags, and night-dressings: in which you would thinke our
men lay in, like *Ladies*: it is so curious.

Here Jonson seems to be aiming first at foppery in the choice of
words (like Fastidious Brisk's use of 'arrides' instead of 'pleases' in
Every Man out of his Humour (II.i.80–6)); but of course his
comment is applied to the whole cast of a speaker's or writer's style.

Typically, in this passage Jonson employs images of extravagant
finery and of sexual deviance to press home an argument on literary
criticism. His sense of the natural in language ran deep, and with it
his hostility towards part at least of the fashionable world, in which
he considered nevertheless that he held a right of entry and even the
privilege of instruction. A corresponding problem faced him with
regard to the stage itself, as essentially a place for show (bedevilled,
moreover, by both authoritarian interference and the ignorance of
popular taste). This tension may account for the sense of strain in
some of his comedies and for his alternation between over-forceful
methods and methods obliquely indirect.[12] But that is only one side
of his writing.

Every Man in his Humour relates wit to sociability; it begins, as it
ends, with the prospect of an entertainment. In the manner of a
Roman comedy, it sets the young men, with the agile-minded servant, Musco (to follow the first, 1598, version of the play, set in
Florence),[13] in opposition to Lorenzo senior and the other older men
who, except for Doctor Clement, are either impervious or antagonis-
tic to poetry and high spirits; while Clement, the *lepidus senex*,
presides and reconciles at the end because he stands for conviviality
and love of letters, together with justice. The plot opens with Lorenzo senior reading the letter from Prospero inviting Lorenzo junior to
the city, and judging that 'the most precious wit' attributed to his
son's friend amounts to nothing better than 'geering *follie*, and
fantastique *humour*' (I.i.176–94); and it draws to an end with
Clement's delighted praise for the 'ingenium', or 'wit' revealed by
Musco in his mischievous intrigues (V.iii.146, 210).

Between these two groups come the impostors: the braggart soldier, Bobadilla, and the two young 'gulls', Matheo, the city poetas-
ter, and Stephano, the bumptious squire. These figures are more
elaborately drawn than any counterparts in Plautus or Terence, and
they are characterised specially by their taste in diction. For instance,

in the scene where Matheo marvels over hackneyed 'fine phrases' from *The Spanish Tragedy*, Bobadilla voices contempt for the man who, later, will terrify him with a beating:

Hang him Rooke, he? why he has no more judgement than a malt horse. By S. *George*, I hold him the most peremptorie absurd clowne (one a them) in Christendome: I protest to you (as I am a gentleman and a soldier) I ne're talk't with the like of him: he ha's not so much as a good word in his bellie, all iron, iron, a good commoditie for a smith to make hobnailes on.

(I.iii.164)

The impostors, or gulls (for they are both together), are at once vacuously gregarious and stiffly preoccupied with themselves. They talk merely to impress, and chiefly to impress themselves. Bobadilla is a fine specimen, with his self-contradictions (over soldiership and wordiness, for instance), his blustering misuse of jargon, expletives and slang, and – an admirably humanising touch – his flurry of hesitations and digressions, as if solemnly containing himself for the sake of some exact truth. But Jonson's irony affects the more solid characters as well; for instance, when Lorenzo senior, decrying the indecorum in Prospero's letter, concludes that previously his 'senses' have been 'abusde' by 'opinion', he is deluding himself again, as the plot shows, though he does not seem to be altogether wrong. Most of Jonson's characters are set rocking about some invisible, ideal point of mental equilibrium.

Every Man out of his Humour (1599) is yet more explicitly concerned with wit, but the plot works towards scenes of exposure, not conviviality. It starts with the ambitions to gentility in the rustic Sogliardo, who 'for his wealth . . . might be a Justice of Peace' – 'and a Constable for [his] wit' (I.ii.15);[14] and it reaches its climax at court, in the testing of 'that planet of wit, *Maddona Saviolina*' (II.iii.195), and her failure to see the obvious clodhopper in Sogliardo when he is presented to her as a traveller, wit and accomplished mimic (V.ii).

Although Saviolina appears only briefly on the stage, her mind is repeatedly blazoned by her courtly admirer, Fastidious Brisk. She has 'the most harmonious, and musicall straine of wit, that ever tempted a true ear'; her speech is 'such an anatomie of wit, so sinewiz'd and arteriz'd, that 'tis the goodliest modell of pleasure that ever was, to behold'; and, far excelling 'your wits of *Italia*', 'her braine's a very quiver of jests! and she do's dart them abroad with that sweete loose, and judiciall aime, that you would – here she comes sir'.[15] Musicality, sharp penetration (if that, and not some confused reference to *Euphues*, is what he intends with his 'anatomie'); prompt, unerring, graceful ridicule (though *loose* can be *random*); Brisk's encomia, tumbling into incoherence, evidently parody a critical affectation of the day, in keeping with his extravagance in dress. They give Saviolina prominence out of proportion to her active presence on the stage. But they make her a model of the wit in vogue; and from her, in a scale of the fashionably absurd, descend Brisk, with his sparkle of amiable fatuity; Fungoso, the farmer's son and law student, who apes Brisk's tailoring; his sister, the tradesman's wife, also dazzled by Brisk; her doting husband; Sogliardo, her uncle, at the centre of the whole network; and finally, Shift, with his aliases, who ekes out a dubious existence by imposing himself on gulls like Sogliardo as a disbanded soldier, or a bold highwayman, or an instructor in the modish mystery of inhaling tobacco. Beside this there is another scale, of ridicule: Carlo Buffone, the parasite and 'witty rogue' who mocks Brisk and everyone else; Macilente, the malcontent scholar, who holds Carlo's inveterate jesting to be 'the worst use a man can put his wit to' (I.ii.191); and Asper, who plays Macilente's part and is virtually a spokesman for the poet. Wit is crucial, then, to Jonson's theme when, as he claims through his choral commentators, he presents the innovation of a comedy 'thus neere, and familiarly allied to the time' (III.vi.200).

This boast was not an empty one. Macilente's humour of envy is clumsily handled as a lever within the plot, but Jonson gives his role as satiric observer some force for comments on patronage. And he treats the central action as a paradigm of contemporary society, as the characters bring their money and fantasies from the country to the heart of London (where the gull hires the impostor's services in Paul's Walk), and then on to the scenes of climax, or contrived anticlimax, at court. He clogged the play with excessive exposition, but this was partly justified, in so far as he was presenting something new: a criticism of manners, not by means of allegory and preaching, as in the old Morality plays, but in topical parody and dramatised comment. With the aid of comment or not, his characters act out and speak out their follies. The vital, though not the only, comedy is in their words; they are judged, not according to traditional moral standards, though Jonson draws on these as well, so much as by the aptness, inventiveness and energy in their speech. This use of *wit* gave a new direction to old methods of comedy, and a precise focus to Jonson's criticism of the here and now.

Among his mature comedies, *The Silent Woman* (1609) has a close relation to his experiments in the two *Humour* plays.[16] The main action forms a hilariously inverted celebration, a charivari conducted by Truewit with immense linguistic virtuosity so as to torment Morose, the domineering and anti-social elderly bridegroom. As instruments for the purpose, Truewit and his friends sweep in Morose's neighbours and antithetical equals, the incontinently sociable upstart Sir Amorous La-Foole, and his noisy, chattering connections. Sir Amorous in turn is paired off for comic discomposure with another gull, Sir John (or Jack) Daw, the would-be statesman who combines claims to gallantry and the writing of saccharine rhymes with an affectation of lofty disdain for professional poets and something of Morose's self-importance. And in company with these two knights come the lady Collegiates –

an order between courtiers and country-madams, that live from their husbands and give entertainment to all the Wits and Braveries o' the time, as they call 'em, cry down or up what they like or dislike in a brain or a fashion with most masculine or rather hermaphroditical authority, and every day gain to their college some new probationer.

(I.i.69)

The characters are grouped and located with great precision. By assembling this crowd of humorists for the amusement of Truewit and his friends, Jonson executes an intricate set of variations on the theme of pretension, in status, in sexual relations, and in judgement on matters of literature and sociable amusement. A sense of the miscellaneous unison of London is present in every scene: its topography, its noises, its personal freedom, its social confusion. And the London setting fosters the affectations in each of Morose's visitants, as in another way it brings out the full absurdity of his self-imposed isolation.

With *Every Man out of his Humour* Jonson began the series of what can accurately, I think, be described as City comedies; that is, plays taking both their comic point and their setting from contemporary London.[17] Jonson's desire to come 'neere ... to the time', and, with it, the assumption that conditions were notably changing, that the present was significantly different from the past, were evidently widely shared. Not, it might be said, by Shakespeare; otherwise, *Measure for Measure* would rank as a major essay in City comedy. But in *Measure for Measure*, London and Westminster are fictionalised as Vienna. It seems as if Shakespeare and other Jacobeans (Marston, for instance; and perhaps Jonson, in *Volpone*) chose a remote, quasi-fictional setting for comedy dealing with metropolitan life when they wanted to include questions of government or the court. An avowed London setting entailed the private concerns of city-dwellers, as in the New Comedy tradition. However this may be, it is striking that Jonson's fellow-dramatists also made the idea of wit central to their London comedies, though they approached it from different points of view. Whereas Jonson inspects the new connotations of the word for its literary and social value, the others are more apt to dwell on derivatives from the older senses of wit, as the name for mental capacity, commonsense, perception or alertness. They deal less with wit as a property of speech, and more obviously with wit as a property of action.

For example, Dekker and Webster's successful *Westward Ho* (1604) – taking hints, presumably, from *The Merry Wives of Windsor*[18] – celebrates the 'high wit' of London tradesmen's wives in taking their own way, as against jealous husbands and gallant would-be seducers. Wit here belongs to the tradition of sex-intrigues running back to Chaucer and Boccaccio. There is a comparable background in tradition to Cocledemoy, the 'wittie Citie Jester', whose 'deceits', or ruthless practical jokes, occupy the sub-plot of Marston's *Dutch Courtesan* (1604). Since he affects a free, eccentric style of speech, and since his exclusive victims, a vintner and his wife, are shown as sanctimonious swindlers, Cocledemoy's pranks may have been intended to reinforce the more intellectual wit of Crispinella in the main plot, which is aimed against hypocrisy (with some borrowings from Montaigne). But Cocledemoy is primarily a mischief-maker from popular jest-books.

A much more fruitful theme for Jacobean comedy was the notion of living by one's wits. This chimed with the journalism of writers like Nashe and Robert Greene. For example, the author of *The Defence of Cony-catching* (1592) – possibly Greene himself – professes to reproach Greene for unfairness in singling out card-sharpers and confidence tricksters for exposure in his pamphlets:[19]

For truth it is, that this is the Iron Age, wherein iniquity hath the upper hand, and all conditions and estates of men seek to live by their wits, and he is counted the wisest that hath the deepest insight into the getting of gains . . . If then wit in this age be counted a great patrimony, and subtlety is an inseparable accident to all estates, why should you be so spiteful, Master R. G., to poor cony-catchers above all the rest, sith they are the simplest souls of all in shifting to live in this over-wise world?

Knavery contains the spirit of the age in a purified state. The tone of the pamphlet, with its anecdotes illustrating deceivers in all trades, and the deceivers deceived, strikes a balance between indignation and amusement, but tips the scales towards amusement. Wit in such a context both is and is not the word in its earlier sense; it stands for practical cunning, a counter-cunning, and the harshly ironic enjoyment of a jest. Such an attitude opened a fresh path for the Erasmian tradition of levity in seriousness and seriousness in levity: in effect, the path taken by Jonson himself in *Volpone* and *The Alchemist*, and by Middleton in his London comedies.

An early success by Middleton was *A Trick to Catch the Old One*, written about 1605, either shortly before or shortly after *Volpone*. Like *Volpone*, it shows a little world of self-righteous swindlers, betrayed by their own obsession with gain, on the prompting of a hard-headed trickster.[20] The young prodigal, Witgood (whose name suggests his property as well as his mentality), has been fleeced of his estate by his uncle, the London usurer, Lucre; but he has learned that 'nothing conjures up wit sooner than poverty'. To recoup his losses, and to provide for his mistress, the Courtesan, he takes her from the country to London, passing her off as a wealthy, landed widow whom he hopes to marry. As he expects, Lucre and his other London creditors are now ready to fawn on him. And he even succeeds beyond expectation, since, on the bare strength of rumour about the widow's property, Lucre's rival in extortion, old Hoard, snatches her off and marries her surreptitiously in his haste, thus incidentally leaving the way clear for Witgood to marry genuine money in the person of Hoard's Niece.

In the two usurers and their circle, Middleton depicts a society wherein wit, meaning sharp practice, is identified with wisdom (as in *The Defence of Cony-catching*), and where the profit-motive is intertwined with Pharisaic legalism and with intensely personal animosities as well. Hoard resents it bitterly that Lucre ('like a cunning usurer') has fleeced another young prodigal, whom he had singled out for his own prey; and it is this 'flame of hate' and 'spirit of malice' against the other elder (I.iii) that rushes him into marrying the bogus widow, for the sake of a 'Happy revenge, ... extremely to cross his adversary', even more than the hope of 'build[ing his] own fortunes greater' on her estate (II.ii.40–52). Meanwhile, the dramatist matches Hoard's gleeful cunning with Lucre's unctuous humbug: as, for example, in the scene of reconciliation after Witgood's arrival in London with the pretended widow, where uncle and nephew each pursues his own secret wit. Reproaching Witgood for not having come straight to 'your uncle's house', as the natural base for matrimonial designs, Lucre takes the line of offended though forgiving dignity; while his nephew passes from deferential excuses to a tone of complicity in his uncle's unspoken thoughts:

Witgood: Else, my uncle's house, why 't'ad been the only make-match ... Push, nay, I know, uncle, you would have wrought it so by your wit you would have made her believe in time the whole house had been mine.
Lucre: Ay, and most of the goods too.
Witgood: La, you there; well, let 'em all prate what they will, there's nothing like the bringing of a widow to one's uncle's house.
Lucre: Nay, let nephews be ruled as they list, they shall find their uncle's house the most natural place when all's done.
Witgood: There they may be bold.
Lucre: Life, they may do anything there, man, and fear neither beadle nor summoner. An uncle's house! a very Cole Harbour! (II.i.225–37)

It makes a duet fit for Rossini. Middleton's prose is a cadenced colloquialism, blending tones for his speakers' voices from balanced periods and familiar elisions, ceremonious forms and vulgarisms, topical allusion and proverbial commonplace. And he interlocks the irony of his dialogue with the irony of the plot; for instance, Cole Harbour, which the worthy uncle so betrayingly adduces, was a Thames-side sanctuary for debtors and thieves, and for clandestine marriages, where later on Hoard will clinch his illusory triumph.

A cruder but still indicative play on similar lines is *Wit at Several Weapons* (c. 1609–20), attributed to Fletcher, but very possibly in large part by Middleton and Rowley as well.[21] The old London knight, Sir Perfidious Oldcraft, is 'a great admirer of Wit': 'all that I have', he tells his son, 'I ha' got by my wits' – apparently, by assiduous pimping – and, on principle, he refuses the young man an allowance unless he too can 'live by his wits' (I.i). Wittypate, the son, retorts in kind. With the help of a like-minded 'poor scholar' and 'a decaid Knight' and his wife, he cony-catches his father to the tune of £100; meanwhile, through a simulated highway robbery, he also discredits the rival to his father's favour, his cousin Credulous, a raw graduate from Cambridge. This resembles Middleton's *A Mad World, my Masters*. In the parallel plot, a fortuneless 'profess'd wit' (pointedly named Cunningham), the protégé of a wealthy simpleton, woos Oldcraft's Niece, in covert rivalry with his patron, and finally wins her, though chiefly thanks to the superior 'fine dexterity of her lady-wit'. This seems like Fletcher; an epilogue written for a Caroline revival of the play praises his inspiriting wit as a collaborator and the 'brisk', 'Mercurial' qualities of his 'Muse'.

Plays on lines like these form the main contribution of the Jacobeans to the comic stage. They owed much, no doubt, to the revival of poetic satire; but even at their weightiest or most pungent, as in *The Alchemist* or *A Chaste Maid in Cheapside*, it is not formal satire that shapes their construction, so much as the idea of living by one's wits, or rather, the novel patterns the dramatists extract from wit and its ambiguities. Typical plots like that of Middleton's *Trick* consist of modernised, cony-catching variations on the Roman comedy motif of antithesis between young spendthrifts and old skinflints. And, by the same token, the dramatists invert the Tudor Morality-play image of the young prodigal. Such paradoxes over the conflict between youth and age must have seemed specially piquant in the neighbourhood of the London theatres, particularly for the audiences of gallants and Inns of Court students in the private playhouses for which many of the new comedies were written in the years just after 1600.[22] They throw light also on changing economic conditions and changing class relationships.

At the centre of the stage is the type of the landed young gentleman newly arrived or settled in the capital, there obeying or else finding needs and requirements for which Jacobean society has no established place.[23] He is involved in financial shifts and intrigues. But the comic force within the plays does not reside in picturing a struggle over rank or wealth, although the characters frequently express themselves in those terms. Class relations in the plays are fluid, and the intrigue often takes place between members of the same family or class: the root of the conflict in *The Silent Woman*, for example, is that Morose, as an old courtier, envies his nephew's knighthood (II.v.85–113); while, in Middleton's plays, Londoners and gentry are often kinsmen and, if the former covet land, the latter aim at marrying into the City. The crucial dividing line between the characters in the plays is the distinction between money values and ambition for social status, which are supposed to be common to all ranks in present-day society, and something else, which can best be described, in modern terms, as the values of a leisure class. There was no recognised code for such a class in Jacobean society, and even the generalised concept of leisure, as a desirable attribute of social life, was not formulated until the Restoration period (while the term 'leisure class' had to wait for the Victorians);[24] nevertheless, the ingredients for such a concept were assembling in Jacobean London, more, perhaps, around the theatres themselves than in any other department of city life. And it was these, it seems to me, that the dramatists were designating and seeking to clarify by their positive uses of 'wit', as distinct from their ironic uses. This seems clear in Jonson (in *Epicoene*, for instance), where the positive sense of wit includes discriminating enjoyment, based on intellectual cultivation. It is not quite so clear in Middleton, whose witty intriguers might be classless rogues as far as their conduct goes, rather than men of breeding or education. Nevertheless, they are emancipated from the routine of a civic society which pays lip-service to the ideals of labouring in one's vocation, while betraying them in practice.

In Jacobean London, a humanist education was no longer felt to give any assurance of social advancement. So much is implied, for example, in *Wit at Several Weapons* (IV.i), where Wittypate lectures Credulous on the difference between academic learning and '*London* Philosophy'. Much of Jonson's irony turns from the opposite viewpoint, on a similar assumption. But perhaps it is most prominent in the comedies of Fletcher, who attempts to give it positive value. In *Wit without Money* (*c.* 1614), for example, Isabella falls in love with the 'poor scholar', Francisco; whereupon her elder sister, the wealthy widow Lady Heartwell, asks her scornfully:[25]

> Is virtue, in this age, a full inheritance?
> What jointure can he make you? Plutarch's Morals?
> Or so much penny-rent in the small poets?
>
> (III.i)

Francisco himself acknowledges the same deficiency (IV.iii); but conversely, Valentine, his elder brother, prides himself on his superiority in 'understanding ... manners and apt carriage' over gentlemen fresh from the universities, who would be mere gulls amid the taverns and pleasures of London without the benefit of his instruction. Valentine has ruined his estate, but impatiently rejects the help proffered, in all anxiety, by his uncle and his principal creditor; he chooses to live as a boon companion, at the expense of less sophisticated gallants, trading on his knowledge of the town. He is rescued from the logical consequence of his bravado by Lady Heartwell, who is so impressed by it that she takes the first step in their wooing. Valentine's role, therefore, is not merely a fresh paradox on the theme of the prodigal; it is also an exact reversal of Witgood's role in Middleton's *Trick*. Valentine owes his prosperity precisely to his flourish of indifference towards money.

By the next generation wit, however it might still elude definition, was established as the leading term for critical praise, as is shown, for instance, by the chorus of verses prefixed to the 1647 Folio of Beaumont and Fletcher.[26] In his preface to that volume, Shirley lauds their plays as 'the Authentick witt that made Blackfriars an Academy' for the 'wit and carriage' of 'the hopefull young Heirs', or those 'young spirits of the Time, whose Birth and Quality made them impatient of the sourer waves of education'. To some extent this looks inappropriate. There is not much epigrammatic sharpness in the dialogue of the plays, and their heroes seem unaware of the polite breeding that Shirley himself recommends in his comedies. They make a flourish of bravado, of self-assertion and high spirits, in defiance of decorum. Nevertheless, Fletcher knew how to employ effects of paradox and surprise, which give his plays a certain comic sparkle. Their wit lies in giving an unexpected theatrical turn to familiar assumptions. In this sense, they are lively, topical and inventive; they are neat in construction, and deliver a slight shock to received social ideas. Here they rejoin the functions of wit as the revelation and redisposition of incongruities, in Jonson and the other Jacobeans. If wit had stood for a more settled concept, less electric with contrary implications, it might have been less productive for the invention of comedies. And perhaps literary historians have not given enough attention to the contribution of Jacobean comic writers to the subsequent fortunes of the word.

9. Comic form in Ben Jonson: Volpone and the philosopher's stone

Oh, 'tis imposture all:
And as no chymique yet th' Elixir got,
    But glorifies his pregnant pot,
    If by the way to him befall
Some odoriferous thing, or medicinall,
    So lovers dreame a rich and long delight,
    But get a winter-seeming summers night.

                    Donne, *Love's alchymie*

Ben Jonson regularly presented an image of himself, in and beyond his comedies, as a figure of monolithic assurance, consistency and integrity; he could never publicly have agreed with Yeats that a poet makes rhetoric (merely rhetoric) out of his quarrels with others, but poetry out of his quarrels with himself. Behind this image of himself that Jonson projected there were the impulsions of an ideal – an ideal both of the Stoic sage, like his own Crites in *Cynthia's Revels* ('humble in his height' but 'fixed' and self-sufficient as 'a circle bounded in it selfe'), and of the humanistic orator-poet as moral instructor, 'the interpreter, and arbiter of nature, ... a master in manners'. Jonson could reply with some justice to his detractors that it was 'the offices, and function of a Poet' he was proclaiming, not simply his personal and private merits. But it has always been difficult to distinguish cleanly between learning and pedantry in these proclamations of his, between self-assertion and arrogance. Other motives, such as competitiveness, ambition and vanity, seem to be mixed with his affirmation of a noble ideal. Self-advertisement was a professional deformation he shared with other humanists – and charlatans as well – in the world of the Renaissance. And deeper needs to commend himself seem to have been at work. In his anger with the 'loathsome' ignorance and 'impudence' of his public, there may have been the spark of a suspicion that his own humanism was out-of-date. Worse still, it may have been prompted by the suppressed recognition that his own comedies were not, after all, consistently the best he felt himself capable of. So much, at least, was tactfully hinted by Thomas Carew, the most penetrating of Jonson's 'sons', after the older poet's explosion of 'immodest rage' over the fiasco of *The New Inn*.[1] Had Jonson's self-approval been as firm and stoical as he professed, he would not have betrayed such an 'itch of prayse'. He would have acknowledged, without flinching, that

> 'tis true
> Thy comique Muse from the exalted line
> Toucht by thy Alchymist, doth since decline
> From that her Zenith;

and he would have carried his laurels with indifference towards 'the extorted prayse / Of vulgar breath'. In the end, 'the quarrell lyes', not with the public, but 'Within thyne owne virge'.

Drummond of Hawthornden had already drawn, in harsher terms, a similar conclusion about Jonson:

He is a great lover and praiser of himself, a contemner and Scorner of others, . . . jealous of every word and action of those about him (especiallie after drink, which is one of the Elements in which he liveth), . . . a bragger of some good that he wanteth . . . He is passionately kynde and angry, careless either to gaine or keep . . .: oppressed with fantasie, which hath ever mastered his reason, a generall disease in many poets.

And, if one can attribute something here to the resentment of the provincial host who had been browbeaten by his London guest in his cups, Jonson had evidently provoked the apparently surprising remark about his own oppressive fantasy by such things as his stories of tricking a lady by dressing up as an astrologer, and 'consum[ing] a whole night' in contemplation of imaginary battles circling round his great toe. Similarly, fantasy, or poetic 'madness', is the theme of the tribute published by James Howell, addressing himself to Jonson as one of his 'sons':[2]

you were madd when you writt your *Fox*, and madder when you writt your *Alchymist*, . . . but when you writt your *Epigrammes*, and the *Magnetic Lady* you were not so madd; Insomuch that I perceave ther be degrees of madness in you; Excuse me that I am so free with you. The madnes I meane is that divine furie, . . . which *Ovid* speaks of.

Howell and Drummond both agree with each other and with Carew in this, that they see strong impulses in Jonson that are at odds with his public image of himself.

Although Jonson's impatience with 'the loathed stage' of his own day never subsided very far below the surface, his confidence in an ideal art of comedy never wavered. Nevertheless, there are differences of emphasis in some of his statements of the ideal, which partly correspond to the differences between his own view of his genius and that of his friends. In his earlier, more propagandist, statements[3] he dwells, as if in assured anticipation, on the effects of comedy, 'a thing throughout pleasant, and ridiculous, and accommodated to the correction of manners'; the poet writing comedy 'is said to be able to informe yong-men to all good disciplines, inflame growne-men to all great virtues' and even 'recover [old-men] to their first strength' – apparently by the sheer force and 'justice' of his 'doctrine'. However, to 'sport with humane follies' sounds less peremptory. And in the private notes he put together for *Discoveries*, late in his career, he shifts his attention, though still within the framework of the theory he had always held, from the remote or alleged effects of comedy to the means towards those effects, to what is directly perceived. Of all types of Poet, it is the Comic, he says there, who 'comes nearest' that established model of humanist culture, the Ciceronian Orator:

Because, in moving the minds of men, and stirring of affections (in which Oratory shewes, and especially approves her eminence) hee chiefly excells. What figure of a Body was *Lysippus* ever able to forme with his Graver, or *Apelles* to paint with his Pencill, as the Comedy to life expresseth so many, and various affections of the minde? There shall the Spectator see some, insulting with Joy; others, fretting with Melancholy; raging with Anger; mad with Love; boiling with Avarice; undone with Riot; tortur'd with expectation; consum'd with feare: no perturbation in common life, but the Orator findes an example of it in the Scene.   (lines 2532–43)

The variety and liveliness of the stage, and the 'perturbation' of characters 'oppressed with fantasie' – these are the features of comedy that stand out in Jonson's mind here, rather than the 'doctrine' or 'justice' of the satirist behind the scenes. And these, of course, are the features of his own successful comedies, as distinct from his 'dotages' and comparative failures. No doubt his finest achievements depend at every step on Jonson's rational control, his unrelaxing pursuit of measure, decorum and justice. But they depend no less on the release of energy from those sources in the poet that Drummond called fantasy and Howell, madness.

Granting the general bias of Jonson's mind, it seems likely that they depend even more, as Howell said, on the latter sources. Jonson never forgets his obligations as a rhetorician, moralist and contriver of intrigues in his comedies. But in half of them, his machinery is too ponderous for his material; he takes himself too seriously; there is no proportion between the intellectual power exerted and the triviality or the merely schematic significance of the characters. *Every Man in his Humour* is an exception, but there Jonson is altogether unusually light-hearted. We only see him at his full stretch in his comedies of sustained 'perturbation', in *Volpone, The Silent Woman, The Alchemist* and *Bartholomew Fair*. And even among those, there is surely a distinction between the two prose works and his two generally acknowledged masterpieces. *The Silent Woman* and *Bartholomew Fair* have a crowded vigour that no other English dramatist, I believe, can match, but even so, they remain top-heavy because the comic butts are too cramped, too limited to repay the full benefit of Jonson's laughter at their expense; he presents them as eccentrics rather than types. What distinguishes *Volpone* and *The Alchemist* is not simply the resonance and mock-heroic grandeur of Jonson's verse, but the generality of their comic themes. Their people can still be described as caricatures, but they are caricatures of deep-rooted human impulses, which seem universal even in the distorted form that Jonson imposes on them. Indeed, the distortion is necessary to the impression of universality, since it develops in each play from a common imaginative centre, with the result that the characters reinforce one another, with all their variations and extensions of gullibility and greed.

I want to suggest that there is essentially one theme at the centre of both plays, namely the idea of alchemy, or what Jonson found in it; to borrow the term Mr Ray Heffner has applied to *The Silent Woman* and *Bartholomew Fair*,[4] alchemy is the 'unifying symbol' in *Volpone*, where it is latent, as well as in the companion masterpiece, where it is declared. Whatever psychological causes may have favoured the choice, this theme gave Jonson the release he apparently needed for both sides of his personality at once, the rational and the fantastic, more than any other theme in his comic repertory. For one thing, the hope of converting base metals to gold epitomised the acquisitiveness that Jonson saw as both a permanent human failing and the special driving force in his own world, in an age of mercantilism, inflation and social pushing.[5] Secondly, the hope of finding in the philosopher's stone an elixir of life, a panacea for all diseases and a sort of hormone-substitute to confer prolonged vitality, represented a clinging to life even more primitive and deep-seated than the desire for easy money; it is the force of this motif that makes one of the principal differences between *Volpone* and *The Alchemist* on one side, and on the other, *The Devil is an Ass* and *The Staple of News*, where Jonson's allegory is more barely economic. And alchemy, which was particularly flourishing in the century after Paracelsus, offered not merely a fertile ground for quackery and delusion, as Chaucer and Erasmus had shown, but a satirically attractive pseudo-religion, with its overtones of occult theosophy and its carapace of jargon.[6] Because of its pretensions as a philosophy of nature and an esoteric tradition, it provided Jonson with the most general symbol he could probably have found for the self-willed shams he wanted to attack in the learning, religion and social behaviour around him – more general, certainly, in its intellectual applications, than Puritanism or the ballyhoo of the market-place or the humours of gentility. It was a supremely typical example of fantasy in thought and action. Treated as a 'unifying symbol', alchemy fitted in with Jonson's admiration for the classical satirists and for the humanism of More and Erasmus; at the same time, it enabled him to carry further his ambition to adapt some of the basic forms of Old Comedy to the Elizabethan stage. He made of it the image of a latter-day world-upside-down, a counter-Utopia.

Like other Elizabethans, Jonson learned much of his art in comedy from Plautus and Terence and their Italian followers. And he paid much more attention than his rivals to Renaissance theory, including the principle of concentration of interest implied in the unities of time and place, and the principle of calculated progress towards a climax implied in the parallel between plays and orations. His 'art', as he says, 'appears most full of lustre' when his humorists are 'laid flat' just as they have reached their 'flame and height'; he puts his comic intrigues together like the parts of a 'clock', so that all the pieces interact, but the 'catastrophe' is delayed or 'perplexed', 'till some unexpected and new encounter breake out to rectifie all, and make good the *Conclusion*'.[7] At the same time, Jonson develops his own distinctive method of construction, whereby he sets going a number of interests or intrigues that are separate at first, but are drawn together and inter-involved, like the currents in a whirlpool, at significant centres of action (such as Paul's Walk and then Saviolina's apartment at court in *Every Man out of his Humour*, or the pig-woman's booth and then the puppet-show in *Bartholomew Fair*). This is one of the main resources behind his crescendo effects.

In so far as Jonson drew his separate characters together by the allurements of a common folly or vice, he was plainly following the example of the Tudor Moralities. But the principal stimulus behind his methods of construction must have been the example of Aristophanes (in whom the art of comedy 'appeared absolute, and fully perfected', in spite of his 'scurrility').[8] Aristophanes provided Jonson not only with precedents for topical satire including instruction and horse-play and 'a mingling of fantasy and realism', but suggestive examples of 'a comic structure centred ... on the exploration of an extravagant conceit'.[9] The typical ground-plan of an Aristophanic comedy could be described as the execution of a preposterous scheme which brings characters of all sorts flocking round its originator. So, in *Plutus*, for example, the neighbours flock to Chremylus's house as soon as it is known that he is lodging the Wealth-god there after hitting on the idea of curing the god of his blindness – and not only the neighbours, but a host of strangers, a Just Man, an Informer, an Old Woman who has lost her kept lover, the Youth in question, Hermes (the jack-of-all-trades among the gods), the Priest of Zeus, and even Zeus the Preserver himself. So, similarly, people flock to a common attraction in *Volpone* and *The Alchemist*, and Volpone can boast that his reputation

> drawes new clients, daily, to my house,
> Women, and men, of every sexe, and age.
>
> (I.i.76)

And they flock for comparable reasons: Aristophanes' account of Plutus (who is not only blind at first, but does not know his own powers)[10] is the prime literary source for the god that Volpone and his 'clients' worship,

> Riches, the dumbe god, that giv'st all men tongues:
> That canst doe nought, and yet mak'st men doe all things.
>
> (I.i.22)

Both dramatists build on similar premises. It is true that Aristophanes has been given a variety of interpretations. And his comedies expound utopian schemes, patently fabulous, though allegedly beneficial; whereas the schemes Jonson invents for his tricksters are plausible, but fraudulent. The 'extravagant conceit' that Aristophanes develops in *Plutus* and his earlier plays involves the poetic fiction of restoring Athens to a golden age, whereas the talk of a golden age in *Volpone* and *The Alchemist* is an impudent cheat. Nevertheless, Jonson's debt to the Greek poet is vital, in that he constructs his plays around a fantastic project that overturns the values publicly honoured by society, a project that is alluring precisely because it is outrageous and defines the limits of nature. The sexual licence and the dream of rejuvenation or perpetual vigour that Jonson associates with the golden metal in *Volpone* and *The Alchemist* also belong to the scheme of things in Aristophanes.

Though *Plutus* has lost rank with modern students of Aristophanes, it was the favourite among his comedies with Jonson's age.[11] And, for Jonson, the critique of money it contains was reinforced by later classical satirists, particularly Lucian, whose 'mery conceytes and jestes' had already 'delyted' the wise Utopians.[12] Lucian's *Dialogues of the Dead*, some of which Erasmus had translated, are prominent among the sources commonly cited for the plot of legacy-hunting in *Volpone*.[13] Even more important in this connection, I think, was Lucian's *Timon*, which Erasmus had also translated. In this semi-dramatic dialogue, which darts across Lucian's characteristic satiric themes of mythology, superstition and philosophical imposture, the principal topic, following Aristophanes' *Plutus*, is the inequality and instability of wealth, and its moral consequences. Timon clamours to Zeus because in his poverty he is ignored by the very men he had flooded with gifts when rich; Zeus at last deigns to listen, and sends Plutus with Hermes down to him with a gift of treasure; whereupon Timon hugs his lucky gold to himself – and beats off the train of sycophants who have immediately hurried to renew his friendship. A cluster of details from the dialogue reappear in *Volpone*. For instance, Hermes points out to Zeus the advantages of shouting loudly (like Voltore) when pleading in court (*Timon*, 11); Zeus refers to the type of a miser, defrauded by 'a cursed valet or a shackle-burnishing steward', like Mosca (*aut scleratissimus famulus, aut dispensator*);[14] Plutus compares some of the misusers of wealth to a man who (like Corvino) 'should take a young and beautiful woman for his lawful wife' and should then 'himself induce her to commit adultery' (16). In the manner of the *Dialogues of the Dead*, Plutus also sketches the case of legacy-hunters who find that all their 'bait', their expectant gifts, have been wasted when the will is published, while the estate may pass to some 'toady or lewd slave' (like Mosca, again) who promptly gives himself airs, changes his name, and 'insults gentlemen', before squandering his gains on flatterers in his turn (22–3). Those who 'gape' after money are not necessarily blind, Plutus explains, but have their vision darkened by 'Ignorance and

Deceit, who now hold sway everywhere' (27). They are repeatedly compared to birds and beasts; for instance, Hermes calls Timon's hangers-on during his first prosperity so many 'ravens and wolves' and 'birds of prey' (*corvi, lupi, vultures*).[15] Here Jonson could have found the principal suggestion for his animal fable and the names of his Venetians.

Moreover, Timon's reaction when he strikes treasure with his pick foreshadows the ethic that Volpone is to live by:

> O Hermes, god of gain! Where did all this gold come from? Is this a dream? I am afraid I may wake up and find nothing but ashes. No, ... it is coined gold ...
>
>   'O gold, thou fairest gift that comes to man!'
> In very truth you stand out like blazing fire, not only by night but by day ... Now I am convinced that Zeus once turned into gold, for what maid would not open her bosom and receive so beautiful a lover ...?
>
> (41)

He resolves to build a tower for himself alone over the treasure, where he intends to be buried; and he promulgates for himself a law of egoism:

> 'Be it resolved and enacted into law, ... that I shall associate with no one, recognise no one and scorn everyone. Friends, guests, comrades and Altars of Mercy shall be matters for boundless mockery. To pity one who weeps, to help one who is in need shall be a misdemeanour and an infringement of the constitution [*morum subversio*]. My life shall be solitary, like that of wolves; Timon shall be my only friend, and all others shall be enemies and conspirators ... Tribe, clan, deme and native land itself shall be inane and useless names, and objects of the zeal of fools. Timon shall keep his wealth to himself, scorn everyone and live in luxury all by himself, remote from flattery and tiresome praise ... Be it once for all resolved that he shall give himself the farewell handclasp when he comes to die, and shall set the funeral wreath on his own brow ...'
>
> (42–4)

Volpone's tactics, of course, are to be directly opposite; he is to be a fox, not a wolf. But his egoism is a variant of Timon's misanthropy. When he opens his 'shrine' in the first scene, he too hails his gold 'like a flame, by night; or like the day / Strooke out of *chaos*'; he too adorns it with poetic fables, as 'the best of things: and far transcending / All stile' – 'inane and useless names' – 'of joy in children, parents, friends'. For him, as for Timon, the very idea of commiseration for others becomes a subject for scorn, as in the flattery he laps up from Mosca –

> You lothe, the widdowes, or the orphans teares
> Should wash your pavements; or their pittious cryes
> Ring in your roofes.

His basic motive for alluring clients instead of beating them off is the same as Timon's:

> What should I doe,
> But cocker up my *genius*, and live free
> To all delights, my fortune calls me to?
> I have no wife, no parent, child, allie,
> To give my substance to; but whom I make
> Must be my heire: and this makes men observe me.

And even his final and fatal trick of tormenting his dupes by spreading in person the rumour of his own death keeps in line with Timon's earnest wish to be chief if not sole mourner at his own funeral. In short, it appears as if Jonson, while inverting the circumstances, has taken over the moral scheme of Lucian's satire. Conceivably – to go a step further – it was Jonson who aroused Shakespeare's interest in *Timon*.[16]

His debt to Lucian did not end with the legacy-hunting plot. The grotesque interlude Mosca has devised for Volpone's private delectation is taken (with reinforcements out of *The Praise of Folly*) from Lucian's dialogue of *The Dream, or The Cock*, which again combines economic and philosophical satire, this time emphasising the Pythagorean doctrine of the transmigration of souls. And, as Harry Levin has claimed, the notion of metempsychosis goes 'to the core' of *Volpone* and of much in Jonson's later writing.[17] It stands for much more than a philosophical fantasy. On one side, Jonson makes it analogous to the transformation of substances in alchemy. On the other side, he relates the notion of shifting and transformed identities to the theatrical business of disguise or deception, to the principle of acting a part.

When Marlowe makes Barabas boast of his enormous profits, 'Infinite riches in a little roome,' his language is arrogant and highly coloured, but there is nothing bizarre or mysterious about it; the merchant is simply a sharp operator exploiting favourable conditions. Volpone's attitude towards his gold is decidedly more complex. He too is clearly intended to dominate the world of the play in and by fulfilling that 'desire of gold'[18] whose compulsion most of those around him are too hypocritical to acknowledge. But it is also clear from the outset that neither Volpone nor his creator is to be satisfied with that dramatic function alone. From Volpone's first lines to his hoard, 'my *saint*', 'the worlds soule, and mine', it becomes clear that he is not content merely with beating the rest of the world at their own game, but sees himself as the discoverer of a truly human destiny, which other men in their vanity have been simply blind to; he is full of scorn at their expense, but he does not adopt the pose of a disillusioned cynic. On the contrary, he sounds more like a man with a revelation, an enthusiast. According to C. H. Herford, his opening speech is a 'hymn' which 'transfigures avarice with the glamour of religion and idealism'.[19] To this comment, L. C. Knights has objected that it omits the essential, Jonson's irony; the speech 'brings the popular and religious tradition into play, but that is a different matter; religion and the riches of the teeming earth are there for the purpose of ironic contrast'.[20] But this, in turn, understates Jonson's scope and resourcefulness in his rhetoric.

No doubt Volpone brands himself with egregious folly when he speaks of his gold 'darkening' the sun and 'far transcending' love or companionship; with perversity, when he exclaims,

> Well did wise Poets, by thy glorious name,
> Title that age, which they would have the best;

and with grovelling superstition, when he repeats the word, 'saint', and offers to

> kisse
> With adoration, thee, and every relique
> Of sacred treasure, in this blessed roome.

Nevertheless, 'popular and religious tradition' would hardly dispose of him automatically for a Jacobean (not to speak of a modern) audience. When, for instance, in line 3 he hails gold as the world's 'soule', is he a sophist – or perhaps a mystic? There is awe, as well as impish belittlement, in his image of 'the teeming earth' beholding 'the long'd-for sunne /Peepe through the hornes of the celestial *ram*'; and his awe takes on a Biblical splendour when (in the image probably suggested by Lucian's Timon) he compares his gold not only to 'a flame, by night' but to

> the day
> Strooke out of *chaos*, when all darknesse fled
> Unto the center.

For his next epithet, 'O, thou son of SOL', Volpone borrows the language of alchemy; and even though Jonson diverts the effect at once towards anticlimax – with '(But brighter then thy father)' – some hint remains of a mystical faith or system at work behind the speaker's rhapsody. While an audience can be sure that Volpone's mythology is false, they are not likely to be supplied with a prompt retort from tradition; surely 'wise Poets', purveyors of secrets as they were, must have had some arcane reason for giving the 'glorious name' of golden to the 'best' of ages? There is a similar hint of clairvoyance within his impudence when Volpone makes gold 'far transcend' human love – the vain 'stile' of it – 'Or any other waking dreame on earth'. As he works towards a climax, our confident suspicion that nevertheless he has merely been juggling with paradox is brought crashing against the gross facts of common experience (or common opinion) about the power of money –

> That canst doe nought, and yet mak'st men doe all things;
> The price of soules; even hell, with thee to boot,
> Is made worth heaven! Thou art vertue, fame,
> Honour, and all things else!

And even though Mosca is allowed to deflate his patron by means of an equivocal assent –

> Riches are in fortune
> A greater good, then wisedome is in nature –

Volpone has still a higher card in his hand:

> Yet, I glory
> More in the cunning purchase of my wealth,
> Then in the glad possession; since I gaine
> No common way . . .

He is not, like Barabas, simply first among equals, but belongs to a different order of being; beside his cult of gain, the usual avenues to profit are destructive as well as trivial, so that 'nature' appears to be on his side, in addition to 'fortune':

> I use no trade, no venter;
> I wound no earth with plow-shares; fat no beasts
> To feede the shambles; have no mills for yron,
> Oyle, corne, or men, to grinde 'hem into poulder;
> I blow no subtill glasse; expose no ships
> To threatenings of the furrow-faced sea;
> I turne no moneys, in the publike banke;
> Nor usure private –

On returning from Utopia, Raphael Hythlodaye had perceived in the so-called 'commen wealth' at home nothing better than 'a certein conspiracy of riche men', stained with 'fraud, theft, ravine' and yet undermined with 'feare, griefe, care, laboures and watchinges';[21] Volpone has blandly appropriated some of this stern radicalism, combining it with a solicitous concern for Nature. And though we may feel positive already that he is practising some confidence trick, we have not been told yet what his 'cunning purchase' is. Our first general impression of him includes an uneasy perception that he is something more esoteric than a superlative swindler. Mystification is part of his character.

Volpone speaks like a virtuoso or an artist, in the special Renaissance sense of one initiated into Nature's secrets. He does not practise alchemy (he need not take the trouble), but he both nourishes and feeds upon the same extravagant hopes. According, for example, to Cornelius Agrippa – writing for the time being as an authoritative critic, with inside knowledge – it is doubtful whether alchemy should really 'be termed an Arte, or a counterfaite colouring, or a pursuite of nature', but in any case it is certainly 'a notable and a suffered deceipte'[22] –

the vanity whereof is easily perceyved in this, that it promiseth the thinges whiche nature in no wise can abide, whereas no Arte can surmounte nature, but doth imitate, and folowe it aloofe of[f], and the force of nature is farre stronger than of Arte ... Whilst that they go about to alter the kinds of thinges, and suppose to forge (as they say) a certaine blissed stone of Philosophers, with the which like *Midas*, all bodies touched become golde and silver: moreover they endeavoure to make a certaine *Quint essence* to come down from the high and inaccessible heaven, by the means whereof they promise us not onely more riches than *Croesus* had, but also expelling olde age, do promise us youth and continuall health, and almost immortalitie togither with great substance ...

Such fallacies are smiled at in Volpone's Venice, as when Mosca greets Corbaccio, carrying his 'bag of bright *cecchines*' (I.iv.69):

> This is true physick, this your sacred medicine,
> No talke of *opiates*, to this great *elixir*.

But Corbaccio is goaded by precisely the delusions that alchemy fosters, as Volpone proclaims, the moment his doddering visitant has left:

> So many cares, so many maladies,
> So many feares attending on old age,
> Yea, death so often call'd on, as no wish
> Can be more frequent with 'hem, their limbs faint,
> Their senses dull, their seeing, hearing, going,

All dead before them; yea, their very teeth,
Their instruments of eating, fayling them:
Yet this is reckon'd life! Nay, here was one,
Is now gone home, that wishes to live longer!
Feeles not his gout, nor palsie, faines himselfe
Yonger, by scores of yeeres, flatters his age,
With confident belying it, hopes he may
With charmes, like AESON, have his youth restor'd:
And with these thoughts so battens, as if fate
Would be as easily cheated on, as he,
And all turnes aire!

(I.iv.144)

Volpone mocks Corbaccio as if the old man believed literally in the myths of rejuvenation from Aristophanes, and he draws a conclusion exactly parallel to the fate in store for Subtle and his companions: 'Selling of flyes, flat bawdry, with the *stone*: / Till it, and they, and all in *fume* are gone'. Volpone speaks with a crushing sense of physical reality, with the weight of a long-tested moral tradition behind his words.

But the very tautness of Volpone's irony here demonstrates the pull of the opposing illusion. And Volpone himself is a kind of quintessence extracted from the vices of his clients – greed, double-dealing, loquacity and perversion. When he diagnoses Corbaccio's folly, he has already been heard responding to a piece of flattery from Mosca that could have been taken from the *Dialogues of the Dead*:[23]

M: when I am lost in blended dust,
    And hundred such, as I am, in succession –
V: Nay, that were too much, MOSCA.   M: You shall live,
    Still, to delude these *harpyies*.   V: Loving MOSCA ...

(I.ii.119)

And the whole of his 'cunning purchase' depends, of course, on shamming the condition of men like Corbaccio, with

my fain'd cough, my phthisick, and my gout,
My apoplexie, palsie, and catarrhes.

(I.ii.124)

So that when he jumps from his pretended sick-bed to ridicule Corbaccio, Volpone is tacitly acting for his own benefit the illusion he professes to pierce in others.

The sense that Volpone pursues an elixir, or believes he already possesses an equally magical secret, is all the more potent in the play because his obsession is not directly named. Not to say what he is after is part of his mystification; and, if anything, he thinks of himself as a Machiavellian, rather than a vulgar adept (part of the effect of Sir Pol's role in the comedy is to throw light on this kind of self-deception among the Venetians). But Volpone is an adept in spite of himself. As soon as his imagination has been inflamed by the mere description of Celia, the course he takes to see her is to disguise himself as a mountebank, with a 'precious liquor' for sale:

O, health! health! the blessing of the rich! the riches of the poore! who can buy thee at too deare a rate, since there is no enjoying this world, without thee? Be not then so sparing of your purses, honorable gentlemen, as to abridge the naturall course of life ... For, when a humide fluxe, or catarrhe, by the mutability of aire, falls from your head, into an arme, or shoulder, or any other part; take you a duckat, or your *cecchine* of gold, and apply to the place affected: see, what good effect it can worke. No, no, 'tis this blessed *unguento*, this rare extraction, that hath only power to disperse all malignant humours ...

(II.ii.84)

And, once he has caught Celia's attention from her window, he tries to hold it with praise of an even rarer secret, his powder –

of which, if I should speake to the worth, nine thousand volumes were but as one page, that page as a line, that line as a word: so short is this pilgrimage of man (which some call life) to the expressing of it ... It is the poulder, that made VENUS a goddesse (given her by APOLLO) that kept her perpetually young, clear'd her wrincles, firm'd her gummes, fill'd her skin, colour'd her hair; ... where ever it but touches, in youth it perpetually preserves, in age restores the complexion; seat's your teeth, did they dance like virginall jacks, firme as a wall ...

(II.ii.228)

Volpone here is acting, but acting with conviction; he is not trying simply to deceive the ignorant crowd, but to make an impression on the woman he intends to seduce. His rhapsody of perpetual 'life' is an ironic sequel to his diagnosis of Corbaccio.

Similarly, when he tries to seduce Celia, it is the dream of sexual vigour perpetually renewed that animates him, as he throws off his disguise of decrepit age:

> I am, now, as fresh,
> As hot, as high, and in as jovial plight,
> As when (in that so celebrated *scene*,
> At recitation of our *comœdie*,
> For entertainment of the great VALOYS)
> I acted yong ANTINOUS.

(III.vii.157)

A Jacobean spectator, struck by that precise reference, could have reflected that the role had been hardly flattering to the actor's virility, and that the famous 'entertainement' was some thirty years back. In any case, the present Volpone must be old enough for the rumour of his physical decay to be believed. Yet what riles him, when Celia holds him off, is the horror reflected in his own lucrative pretence:

> Thinke me cold,
> Frosen, and impotent, and so report me?
> That I had NESTOR's *hernia*, thou wouldst thinke.
>
> (III.vii.260)

It is significant that the turning-point of the play should come here, in a scene of attempted rape, and not in an episode of fraud. References to health, medicine, disease, images connected with the life-force, are even more insistent than thoughts and images connected with money. And with an exact sense of the appropriate, Jonson has Volpone sentenced at the end, not for obtaining money under false pretences, but for simulating disease:

> our judgement on thee
> Is, that thy substance all be straight confiscate
> To the hospitall, of the *Incurabili*:
> And, since the most was gotten by imposture,
> By faining lame, gout, palsey, and such diseases,
> Thou art to lie in prison, crampt with irons,
> Till thou bee'st sicke, and lame indeed.
>
> (V.xii.118)

Volpone has been 'by bloud, and ranke a gentleman', stooping to a beggar's cony-catching tricks. But his essential crime has been an offence against Nature.

When Shakespeare discusses drama, in *Hamlet*, for instance, his mind is chiefly on the actor; when Jonson discusses it, in his many prologues and inter-scenes, he is concerned with the poet. In Shakespeare's comedies, disguise, or play-acting within the play, usually creates a beneficial illusion; in Jonson, it usually expresses imposture, and the removal of a disguise is the exposure of a sham. He is altogether more aloof towards the players than his rival. Nevertheless, he must have observed the technique of acting very closely, and the thought of acting stood for something influential in his general view of life. 'I have considered', he was to write in *Discoveries* (1093–9), our whole life is like a *Play*: wherein every man, forgetfull of himselfe, is in travaile with expression of another. Nay, wee so insist in imitating others, as wee cannot (when it is necessary) returne to our selves: like Children, that imitate the vices of *Stammerers* so long, till at last they become such; and make the habit to another nature, as it is never forgotten.

The comparison of life to a play was of course a Renaissance commonplace, but Jonson's particular application of it here was unusual, if not unique. It contrasts sharply with his public image of himself. It suggests that there were motives arising from self-inspection and self-protection behind his repeated attacks on 'humours', charlatanism and social apery.

Volpone expresses this side of Jonson's vision of life more completely than any other of his characters. Materially speaking, the magnifico does not need to go in for fraud. He does it for his private 'glory', to 'cocker up [his] *genius*'; he feels a compulsion towards play-acting, preferably with a strain of the abnormal or the exotic. He needs spectators, but secret spectators whom he governs, including 'the curious' and 'the envious', whom he imagines spying on his love-making with Celia (III.vii.236–9). Above all, he needs to act a part, to the accompaniment of his own applause. A man of mature age, he feigns senility. As a would-be love-adventurer, he mimics a charlatan. Having recalled, to impress Celia, an image of himself as a youthful actor, he tries to dazzle her, beyond the pitch of '*vertigo*', with the prospect of making love 'in changed shapes', copied from Ovid's *Metamorphoses* and then furnished from a collector's wardrobe of exotic 'moderne formes' (III.vii.219, 221–55). Finally, escaping, thanks to Mosca, from the fear of exposure, his immediate recoil is to look for 'Any device, now, of rare, ingenious knavery, / That would possesse me with a violent laughter' (V.i.14), so that he brings retribution down on himself by way of his superfluous disguise as an officer of the law. Jonson has calculated Volpone's assumed roles so as to reflect back on his real personality; or rather, to reflect back on a being with a compulsive ego but no firm identity, a man perpetually 'forgetfull of himselfe' and 'in travaile with expression of another'.

In this respect, Volpone is by no means alone in the play. Except for Celia and Bonario, who are necessary symbols rather than characters, all the people of the play, English as well as Venetian, are engaged in pretences, stratagems real or imaginary, or sudden and opportunist changes of front. Even the court of law, at the end, is not exempt. Indeed, the theme of systematic insincerity is first put clearly

into words with regard to the lawyer, Voltore, when Mosca flatters
his hopes of inheriting Volpone's fortune:

> He ever lik'd your course, sir, that first tooke him.
> I, oft, have heard him say, how he admir'd
> Men of your large profession, that could speake
> To every cause, and that mere contraries,
> Till they were hoarse againe, yet all be law ...
>
> (I.iii.51)

The ironies of the word 'profession' are carried over from *The Jew of
Malta*, but Mosca develops them with a zest of his own –

> That, with most quick agilitie, could turne,
> And re-turne; make knots, and undoe them;
> Give forked counsell; take provoking gold
> On either hand, and put it up: these men,
> He knew, would thrive, with their humilitie.

And it is fitting that this cinematograph of the hypocrite in motion
should come from Mosca, the Fly, the mobile demon of
equivocation. When (developing a theme possibly suggested by one
of the dialogues under Lucian's name) Mosca dilates on the praise of
his own life-style, it is the physical, existential qualities of the affair
that receive his fondest attention:

> I feare, I shall begin to grow in love
> With my dear selfe, and my most prosp'rous parts,
> They doe so spring, and burgeon; I can feele
> A whimsey i' my bloud: (I know not how)
> Successe hath made me wanton.
>
> (III.i.1)

He feels a biological transformation –

> I could skip
> Out of my skin, now, like a subtill snake,
> I am so limber ...

And, for Mosca, it is precisely versatility, changefulness, that
distinguishes 'your Parasite' in the scale of creation:

> All the wise world is little else, in nature,
> But Parasites, or Sub-parasites.

The parasite's 'mystery' is 'a most precious thing, dropt from above';
by rights, a liberal 'science':

> And, yet,
> I meane not those, that have your bare towne-arte,
> To know, who's fit to feede 'hem;

nor does he mean those with a merely animal flexibility –

> With their court-dog-tricks, that can fawne, and fleere,
> Make their revenue out of legs, and faces,
> Eccho my-Lord, and lick away a moath.

No, Mosca's true-born parasite is a 'sparke' so volatile that he has no position in space or discernible identity at all:

> your fine, elegant rascall, that can rise,
> And stoope (almost together) like an arrow;
> Shoot through the aire, as nimbly as a starre;
> Turne short, as doth a swallow; and be here,
> And there, and here, and yonder, all at once;
> Present to any humour, all occasion;
> And change a visor, swifter, then a thought!

Puck or Ariel could not do better. Poetically, Mosca deserves to out-manoeuvre his patron; he does not act metamorphoses, metamorphoses are the element he lives in.

Jonson restates the principles Mosca stands for in *The Alchemist*, with fresh embellishments of burlesque: for instance, in the scene (II.v) where Subtle calls on the well-schooled Face to recite 'the vexations, and the martyrizations / Of metalls, in the worke', and to 'answere' Ananias, 'i'the language':

> S: Your *magisterium*, now?
> What's that?   F: Shifting, sir, your elements,
> Drie into cold, cold into moist, moist in-
> to hot, hot into drie.   S: This's *heathen Greeke* to you, still?
> Your *lapis philosophicus*?   F: 'Tis a stone, and not
> A *stone*; a *spirit*, a *soule*, and a *body*:
> Which, if you doe *dissolve*, it is *dissolv'd*,
> If you *coagulate*, it is coagulated,
> If you make it to *flye*, it *flyeth*.

> (36–44)

In this brilliant parody, which reproduces the technicalities of the Hermetic art with a minimum of distortion,[24] Jonson incidentally defines the speaker's role as well. Face is like the claims for the philosopher's stone because he can be almost anything or everything at once – which means that (until he declines again to Jeremy, the butler) he is really nothing at all, or an actor's mask. He embodies

Mosca's philosophy of metempsychosis, of the being that is a non-being because it is incessantly something else; and for this dramatic purpose, his connection with alchemy supplies no more than a habitation and a name. But the dramatist had already seized on the connection in *Volpone*, and had sketched it in with reference to Mosca himself. When Mosca and Volpone are gloating over their successful imposture at the first trial, and are planning already to 'vexe' the dupes further with Volpone's new – and reckless – 'device', Mosca introduces the metaphor of alchemy, with his customary ironic reservations, and Volpone, self-blinded, carries the metaphor on:

> M: ... My Lady too, that came into the court,
>   To bear false witnesse, for your worship –   V: Yes,
>   And kist mee 'fore the fathers; when my face
>   Flow'd all with oyles.   M: And sweate, sir. Why, your gold
>   Is such another med'cine, it dries up
>   All those offensive savors! It transformes
>   The most deformed, and restores 'hem lovely,
>   As 'twere the strange poeticall girdle. JOVE
>   Could not invent, t'himselfe, a shroud more subtile,
>   To passe ACRISIUS guardes. It is the thing
>   Makes all the world her grace, her youth, her beauty ...
> V: – I'le to my place,
>   Thou, to thy posture.   M: I am set.   V: But, MOSCA,
>   Play the artificer now, torture 'hem, rarely.
>
> (V.ii.95–111)

Already, by metaphor, Jonson has given Mosca the tasks of 'vexing' and 'torturing' metals that he was later to assign to Face. And the qualities Jonson finds in Mosca's metaphor are the essential poetic characteristics of the play as a whole – animal, mineral and vegetable properties 'transformed' into one another, emotional and moral values rendered 'false' in the utterance, poetic hyperbole gilding deceit.

In a world where hardly anyone follows fixed principles, nearly anything can happen, as the rogues in *Volpone* find to their cost: Corvino rushes his wife into the trap 'too soone' for Mosca's plans (III.vii.1), Mosca snatches too eagerly at Volpone's last deception. Jonson constructs his play by making the compulsive fantasies in his characters collide with one another in a 'vertigo', in a dizzying spiral. He repeats this method, with even greater virtuosity, in the action of *The Alchemist*. The rogues there manipulate their dupes as before,

Sir Epicure's dream of endless vigour in an age of gold is much the same as Volpone's, the intrigue shifts, as before, from money to sex. The dupes in *The Alchemist* are more numerous and varied. And, with 'the language' to support him, Jonson deploys his rhetoric in a bacchic extravaganza of impostures of speech – technical jargon, varieties of London slang, Spanish, fairy vocables, Puritan cant, theosophical clap-trap – until meaning itself (in Dol's assumed frenzy) threatens to disintegrate, like the materials submitted to Subtle's furnace, into

> *the antient us'd communion*
> *Of vowells, and consonants – ...*
> *A wisedome, which* PYTHAGORAS *held most high ...*
>
> (IV.v.19)

But although *The Alchemist* gives a further range to Jonson's command of rhetoric, he had already prepared for it in *Volpone*. He had already discovered there the poetic value for him of the idea of alchemy, as a latent symbol unifying mystification and power-fantasies with images of 'Pythagorean' transformation and comic myths adapted from Aristophanes and Lucian. In several of his masques he returns to the same complex of themes – the revival of Nature, 'that impostor Plutus' impersonating Cupid, and alchemy as the rival of genuine art and learning.[25]

Though alchemy was a controversial subject when Jonson was writing, the theory enjoyed exceptional prestige, even (or especially) among scientists. Jonson must have owed the spirit, though not the details, of his own critique largely to Bacon, whom he praises, in *Discoveries*, more unreservedly than any other contemporary. And it also seems possible that he owed the crystallising touch in *Volpone* to *The Advancement of Learning*, which he could have read in 1605, just before the rapid composition of the play. Years later, in *Discoveries*, Jonson summarised a section of the *Advancement*,[26] following Bacon's words closely, in the course of a discussion (lines 2031–124) of a question vital to the poet, speech as an image of the mind:

It was well noted by the late L. St *Alban*, that the study of words is the first distemper of Learning: Vaine matter the second: And a third distemper is deceit, or the likenesse of truth; Imposture held up by credulity.

(lines 2090–3)

In Bacon's words, deceit is the 'foulest' disease of learning, as that which doth destroy the essential form of knowledge, which is nothing but a representation of truth: for the truth of being and the truth of knowing are one, differing no more than the direct beam and the beam reflected.

This conjunction of knowledge and reality, and hence of learning and life, evidently impressed the dramatist deeply; and Bacon continues by defining, in effect, the psychological laws of Volpone's world – even providing a theoretical justification for the introduction of the prattling Sir Pol and Lady Would-be, to mimic the Venetians:

This vice therefore brancheth itself into two sorts; delight in deceiving, and aptness to be deceived; imposture and credulity; which, although they appear to be of a diverse nature, the one seeming to proceed of cunning, and the other of simplicity, yet certainly they do for the most part concur: for as ... an inquisitive man is a prattler, so upon the like reason a credulous man is a deceiver ...

And finally, Bacon lists alchemy among the 'arts' or 'sciences' most productive of deceit 'for the facility of credit which is yielded' to them:

The sciences themselves which have had better intelligence and confederacy with the imagination of man than with his reason, are three in number; Astrology, Natural Magic, and Alchemy; of which sciences nevertheless the ends or pretences are noble. For ... alchemy pretendeth to make separation of all the unlike parts of bodies which in mixtures of nature are incorporate. But the derivations and prosecutions to these ends, both in the theories and . in the practices, are full of error and vanity; which the great professors themselves have sought to veil over and conceal by enigmatical writings, and referring themselves to auricular traditions, and such other devices to save the credit of impostures.

In this section, which Jonson summarised as a whole, Bacon was not dealing with any picturesque illustration for argument's sake, or any freakish sideline, but with a major entanglement of contemporary thought. For Bacon, the section contained the germs of his subsequent aphorisms on the Idols of the Mind. For Jonson, it seems hardly too much to say, it contained the germs of both *Volpone* and *The Alchemist*.

Bacon has reservations, particularly in favour of alchemy. He does not reject the claims for it outright, and there was no sufficient reason in the science of the period why he should. Nor does Jonson show that he rejects them completely. On the contrary, he makes Subtle draw more varied customers, and arouse more varied feelings, than the cheats and visionaries satirised by Chaucer or Erasmus; and he could hardly have thrown so much force of mind into the play if he had assumed that Subtle's art stood for no more than a transparent fraud or a hopelessly discredited fallacy. Bacon had said that 'confederacy with the imagination' was the source of deceit in alchemy, not ignorance or blatant falsehood; and Jonson's attitude towards the theory of the subject seems like an unwilling suspension of disbelief. He could not have brought so much life into the organisation of *The Alchemist*, or of *Volpone*, if his attitude towards the idea at the centre of both plays had been remote, and single-minded.

10. Farce and fashion in *The Silent Woman*

What's sixe kicks to a man, that reads Seneca?

The Silent Woman can be a little puzzling to Ben Jonson's admirers. The detailed 'examen' in *An Essay of Dramatic Poesy*, virtually the first exercise of its kind in English, not only dwells on the excellence of the plot but claims that Jonson 'has here described the conversation of gentlemen ... with more gaiety, air, and freedom, than in the rest of his comedies'; by singling it out in this way, Dryden treats the play in effect as the model and forerunner of Restoration comedy. At another extreme, L. C. Knights, in his book on Jonson as a critic of society, merely alludes to it in passing as a piece of 'pure entertainment'. And more recently, Jonas A. Barish has noted how critics seem unable to agree whether its tone is 'gay' or 'bitter'.[1] Together with Edmund Wilson, Barish himself opts for the second choice. According to him, Jonson sets out to entertain (as the Prologue declares), that is, to appeal to a courtly public and to repudiate his own previous intolerance, now embodied in Morose; but in spite of the poet's desire to please, philosophy will keep breaking through. Approaching the play along this line, Barish effectively brings out many of the coruscations and arabesques of style in the dialogue. Yet Barish's summing-up ('the stern figure of the moralizing satirist glaring through the elegant and polished surface'; 'a series of brilliant discords') not only appears to interpret the whole piece too solemnly but attributes too large a dosage of personal temperament to a comedy that has strong affinities to the old and impersonal tradition of farce. On the other hand, modern critics have possibly underrated the originality, the novelty in Jonson's farcical scheme, which explains, if it does not justify, the preference expressed by Dryden.

Jonson himself, of course, encourages some uncertainty about his intentions, as part of the game of bluff, or sleight-of-hand, that he plays with his audience as well as his characters. Although he probably borrowed from Aretino's *Marescalco* the device of delayed disclosure of the sex of the pretended bride,[2] Jonson was the first playwright in England – or at most the second, if priority of date be assumed for *Philaster* – to spring a surprise like this on his audience, preparing them for it with no more than the hint (a fairly broad one, however) contained in the first of the play's two titles. But this *coup de théâtre* is simply the climax to a series of unexpected reversals whereby the characters appear to overshoot themselves wildly, only to land exactly where the plot requires them. No sooner have we been told (in II.iv) that the 'ignorantly officious' Truewit has simply wrecked Dauphine's plans by his impulsive and flamboyant visit to Morose than the news comes that Morose in rage and spite has jumped into the trap his nephew had been laying for him, and Truewit can crow a second time, over a triumph unearned; so that the audience has been prepared for, but can hardly consciously expect, a repetition of the same movement at the end of the play, when, after it has been shown again and again that Truewit is the brilliant improviser who can turn every occasion to his own prestige and his friend's advantage, the last trick discloses that Dauphine, after all, is the deeper schemer of the two. Morose too, of course, overreaches himself in action, and not only in action but in speech as well, so that when he lets fly against the barber (III.v) he has the chagrin of finding himself cursing in chorus with his principal tormentor – 'Now, no more, sir ... Good sir, no more. I forgot my selfe ... I will forgive him, rather than heare any more. I beseech you, sir.' Daw and La-Foole are first egged on to outface fictitious slights from each other (over the invitation to dinner) and then, when the same trick has been played again on a grander scale over the mock duel, are tripped on the rebound into boasting their pretended conquests over the bride's virtue – a confession which *seems* to offer Morose his last chance of a divorce, only to drive him into Dauphine's hands when this *seems* to be snatched away from him. At one sweep Dauphine's gesture in removing Epicoene's peruke confirms his victory over his uncle, 'lurches' Truewit of 'the better half of the garland', demonstrates the two knights' fatuity and springs the trap of immodest embarrassment that the Collegiate Ladies have assiduously prepared for themselves. It completes the improvised plan of the wedding-party, by means of which each of the gulls in the play, thinking to discomfit someone else, brings about his own humiliation instead. Surely Dryden was justified in praising the sheer 'contrivance of the plot' and the chess-master's skill with which Jonson manages his 'under-plots, as diversions to the main design, lest it should grow tedious, though they are still naturally joined with it, and somewhere or other subservient to it'.

At first sight, there seems to be an exception to Dryden's statement in the scene (IV.ii) – otherwise typical of the play – where Captain Otter in his cups vents his feelings about his wife, where he is surprised and beaten by his 'deare Princesse', and she in turn is surprised and terrified by Morose. This scene adds to the noise and confusion, but it hardly advances the intrigue, and, as for the Captain, the audience may well agree with Truewit when the latter says that 'his humour is as tedious at last, as it was ridiculous at first'. Truewit's comment, which brings this episode to an end, appears to dismiss it as a mere digression from the main intrigue. But this effect also is part of Jonson's bluff. If, as Dryden says, 'the action of the play is entirely one; the end or aim of which is the settling Morose's estate on Dauphine', then the comic business between the Otters is, strictly speaking, superfluous. It is true that Morose, who had earlier called Mrs Otter 'that *Gorgon*, that *Medusa*' (III.vii.21), is impelled further by the sight of her husband-beating in IV.ii towards the desire to escape from marriage; 'I have perceiv'd the effect of it', he admits in his next scene (IV.iv), 'too late, in Madame Otter.' Nevertheless, this impulsion is unnecessary to the intrigue, in that Morose had already repented of his marriage as quickly as he had contracted it, and has cursed the barber for his interference, immediately on discovering that Epicoene 'can talke' (III.iv–v) and before his unbidden guests have brought their noise on to the stage. And yet, in another direction, the superfluous Otters are not superfluous at all. Mrs Otter, the shrew, the 'Gorgon', 'Medusa', the 'Empresse, Empresse' of Morose's sarcasm (IV.iv.32), is the confirmation of his alarm when he finds that his submissive bride 'can talke': 'She is my Regent already! I have married a Penthesilea, a Semiramis, sold my liberty to a distaffe!' (III.iv.56). And the arrogant recluse, who had disdained a dowry (II.v.89), finds himself, it seems, in exactly the same boat as the spineless roysterer who has married for 'halfe-crowne a day' and the rest of his derisory 'exhibition' (III.i). Possibly Mrs Otter's name was suggested by Falstaff on Mistress Quickly ('setting [her] womanhood aside', 'she's neither fish nor flesh, a man knows not where to have her').[3] In any case, both Mrs Otter, with her husband under her thumb, and her admired Ladies Collegiate, Haughty and Centaure, 'that live from their husbands', are variations on the same theme of noisy, unnatural and domineering femininity. Their appropriate companions are the two effeminate knights. And they are the only genuine women we see on the stage. So that Dauphine's triumphant *coup* at the end has the paradoxical effect of a double bluff. It suggests that his uncle was justified in his horror of human companionship, at least of companionship in the form of marriage. Somewhat as the Snark is shown to be a Boojum, it is proved here that the only possible Silent Woman is an Epicoene.

With this sort of theatrical logic we are plainly in the realm of farce. Medieval farce is not 'terribly serious, even savage', as Eliot once described it, but it is un- or anti-sentimental, un- or anti-idealistic, the counterpart and opposite in several ways to medieval romance. It takes a low view of human motives; the only real aims for farcical characters are food, sex, money and winning the last laugh. Life is represented as a constant battle, a battle of wits if not of fisticuffs – a battle between peasants and *bourgeois*, between trades and professions, between twisters and simpletons, as in *Maistre Pathelin*; a battle between clergy and laity; above all, a battle between husbands and wives. By convention, the bliss of the married state is a mockery; the Fool in *La Farce du povre Jouhan* sums up the tradition, as it applies to husbands, with his refrain – 'Vela tout: qui femme a noise a.'[4] John Heywood's *Foure P's* (c. 1520) illustrates the tradition of pure farce (which seems to have left fewer examples in England than on the Continent, however) from two points of view: it is a contest for 'mastrye' in lying between the Palmer, the Pardoner and the Potycary; and the winning lie is the Palmer's simple statement that in all his travels he never met 'Any one woman out of paciens'. The Pedlar, who is umpire, appeals to the audience themselves to award this fiction the prize. Heywood's *Mery Play between Johan Johan the Husbande, Tyb his Wyfe, and Syr Johan the Preest* (c. 1520) belongs to the same tradition; so does the interlude of *Tom Tyler and his Wife* (c. 1560)[5] and, of course, the main plot of *The Taming of the Shrew*.

Farcical humour often consists of bragging or deliberate absurdity, simulated madness or the spouting of Latin or foreign jargon which is sometimes gibberish and sometimes sense; or, as in some French farcical sketches, there may be a kind of pun between the action of the piece and its title or refrain.[6] All of these lines of humour are congenial to the author of *The Silent Woman*. And Jonson is also fond of the favourite device of farcical plots (as in *Pathelin*, again), the situation of the biter bit.

The more sophisticated comedy of the Renaissance extends the machinery of farce into elaborate practical jokes, which may be built up as ends in themselves, unlike the stratagems in Roman comedy (*Miles Gloriosus* or *Casina*, for instance) which they partly resemble. The whole scheme of Aretino's *Marescalco* – the pretence by the Duke of Mantua that he is forcing his reluctant farrier into wedlock – is a practical joke of this type, a joke without ulterior motive, much appreciated by all the courtiers in the play. *Il Marescalco* has been compared to a Carnival entertainment; like other Carnival jests in the sixteenth century, it subjects a sexual nonconformist or delinquent to the mocking laughter of a whole community.[7] In much the same way, the comic business of the wedding feast in *The Silent Woman* and the subsequent practical jokes reach well beyond the logical requirements of the plot (as Dryden, with classical precedents in view, describes it); only, the jokes in *The Silent Woman* cut in several directions.

One plausible definition of the aims of comedy (a formula that has been put forward as a conjecture about the missing chapters of the *Poetics*) is the purgation of such feelings as envy and malice, or malignant pleasure in the discomfiture of others; through laughter, we get rid of our self-regarding and aggressive impulses, and arrive at a just mean.[8] Whatever its merits as a reconstruction of Aristotle's thought, this definition can be applied to much of classical comedy and, to judge from the ending of *Every Man out of his Humour*, it might well have attracted Ben Jonson. It has the further merit that it carries a distinction between farce and comedy of manners or farce and satire, since the latter include some critique of character or some pointer to an ethical standard, whereas farce, although it may ridicule social abuses, leaves the possibility of moral improvement out of account. It confines itself, with wry amusement, to a tough-minded realism. This may mean simply that farce is undeveloped comedy, a titillation for the groundlings, the provocation of aimless laughter. But on the other hand it has compensatory qualities, not directly recognised in the formula of purgation of envy and malice. Medieval farce emphasises the survival-value of quick wits, of resourcefulness in action as well as speech; and, going beyond this, it seems to aim at laughter which is free from responsibility (rather than merely aimless), laughter in which there is conscious play with the brute facts of life. A psychologist might reply that the motives of envy and malice are still at work, uncontrolled, in the mental knockabout; but if so, they are not always dominant, or even apparent.

The Silent Woman will not fit neatly into any category, farce or comedy of manners or satire, but of the three it comes nearest in style as in substance to farce. Truewit is the principal spokesman of the play, and Truewit is *farceur* rather than satirist. His allocution to Morose against wiving is a characteristic display of his wit:

Mary, your friends doe wonder, sir, the Thames being so neere, wherein you may drowne so handsomely; or London-bridge, at a low fall, with a fine leape, to hurry you down the streame; or, such a delicate steeple, i' the towne, as Bow, to vault from; or, a braver height, as Pauls; or, if you affected to doe it nearer home, and a shorter way, an excellent garret windore, into the street; or, a beame, in the said garret, with this halter; [*He shewes him a halter*] which they have sent, and desire, that you will sooner commit your grave head to this knot, then to the wed-lock nooze; or, take a little sublimate, and goe out of the world, like a rat; or a flie (as one said) with a straw i' your arse: any way, rather then to follow this goblin *matrimony . . .*
(II.ii.20)

This exordium could modestly be called an expansion of the five lines in Juvenal (VI, 28–32), where the Roman poet proposes, as alternatives to marriage, suicide by hanging or by a leap from a high window or the Aemilian bridge. The original sarcasm fizzles out in Truewit's enjoyment of his own performance. He wants to torment Morose, who had aroused his curiosity as a crank, a 'stiffe peece of formalitie', before he had heard of the old man's projected marriage (I.i.143); so he takes the line that what Morose really wants is publicity and dwells at first on the modes of suicide that confer the greatest *éclat*. At the same time, and almost in spite of himself, he adopts the tone of a tourists' guide to the sights of London or a salesman of curiosities. If he intends, as Dauphine's friend, to dissuade Morose from marrying, he only succeeds in irritating Morose's self-will; this, of course, is the function of his speech in the plot.

As Barish well says about Truewit, 'unlike other Jonsonian characters of comparable linguistic talent who improvise with equal zest, [he] does so disinterestedly, unmotivated by the itch for gain or by moral fervor'.[9] But the critic is not content with this; through Truewit, Barish argues, Jonson is attempting to align himself with Ovid against Juvenal, to lay the spirit of satire in him – and in the long run failing, because indignation is more congenial to him than elegance. Thus, where Truewit continues his speech by converting Juvenal's reference to the chastity of the golden age into a fantastic contrast between past and present, Barish comments that his words

are a 'controlled parody', that the speaker is even more severe than
his model, and that 'Jonson satirizes the satirist without losing the
satirist's insight.'[10] This sounds a very complicated box of tricks. It is
hard to find in what follows that *an attack on Juvenal* is the
underlying meaning:

Alas, sir, [Truewit goes on] doe you ever think to find a chaste wife, in these
times? now? when there are so many masques, plaies, puritane preachings,
mad-folkes, and other strange sights to be seene daily, private and publique?
if you had liv'd in king Ethelred's time, sir, or Edward the Confessors, you
might, perhaps, have found in some cold countrey-hamlet, then, a dull
frostie wench, would have been contented with one man: now, they will as
soone be pleas'd with one leg, or one eye. I'll tell you, sir, the monstrous
hazards you shall runne with a wife . . .

Admittedly, this has a parodistic effect; Truewit harps on the itch for
novelty in modern London because he wants to play on Morose's
kink, his agoraphobia. But surely Jonson's dramatic intention here
is to make Truewit overdo it, so that Morose will only notice the
mockery behind his brilliant nonsense, and react accordingly. The
speech has Jonson's characteristic technique of ironic hyperbole and
self-contradiction, but the characteristic drive of his satire is absent.

There is a similar technique in Truewit's subsequent lecture on
women (his third), where, in Ovidian manner this time, he gives
Dauphine what purports to be friendly advice on the art of
seduction:

You must approach them i' their owne height, their owne line . . . if shee love
wit, give verses, though you borrow 'hem of a friend, or buy 'hem, to have
good . . . If she love good clothes or dressing, have your learned counsell
about you every morning, your French taylor, barber, linnener, &c. Let your
poulder, your glasse, and your combe, be your dearest acquaintance . . .

Barish, pointing out that this passage (IV.97–108) interrupts what
otherwise is a paraphrase from Ovid, complains that Truewit
degrades the Latin poet's picture of love, and convicts Jonson of
unwitting Juvenalianism: 'Truewit, ostensibly a defender of courtly
folly, becomes in this way its most insidious enemy.'[11] But the point
of Truewit's dissertation is, first, that it makes the gallant look even
more absurd than his mistress and, second, that in the upshot
Truewit himself will turn out to be not quite as clever as he thinks.

Whereas Dryden had noted that 'Truewit was a scholar-like kind
of man, a gentleman with an alloy of pedantry', Barish objects that
he is neither 'the Stoic moralizer' nor 'the fashionable gallant' nor
'the dupe of fashion'.[12] On his first entry, Truewit upbraids

Clerimont with waste of time – 'with what justice can wee complaine, that great men will not looke upon us, nor be at leisure to give our affaires such dispatch, as wee expect, when wee will never doe it our selves'; then, upon Clerimont's humorous protest, he agrees to 'leave this Stoicitie alone', and to talk about 'pinnes, and feathers, and ladies, and rushes, and such things', conceding, with dramatic irony, tht he will 'doe good to no man against his will' (I.i.57–69). This is not consistent, certainly. But this opening dialogue provides a framework to the farce by touching on seriousness. It picks out the officious strain in Truewit's character (need we take his name entirely at face value?). And it is consistent enough with the social position of the wits in the play – men like Donne and others in Jonson's circle of friends, enjoying a sophisticated idleness somewhere between the Court and the City while they wait for the property that will establish them or the patronage that will direct their abilities or scholarship into a purposeful career. Barish makes Truewit out to be dramatically inconsistent only because he tries to force the play into a mould of his own. The premise of his argument, partly shared with Edmund Wilson, is that 'the victory of Truewit over Morose represents Jonson's attempt to assert the values of the world and the flesh over the consolations of philosophy'.[13] If Jonson thought Morose was a kind of Aunt Sally representing philosophy, somewhat like Socrates in *The Clouds*, it is no wonder that his aim was poor.

While plumbing for depths that Jonson's play does not offer, critics have neglected what is really there. Morose is no hermit. Still less is he, as Edmund Wilson perversely announces, a harmless invalid whom Jonson lampoons, having met him somewhere 'on a visit to the country'.[14] Morose is a petty tyrant. He is an ex-courtier, who considers himself a man of the old school and keenly resents his nephew's title; a martinet, who expects and fears contradiction; a self-tormentor who, hating noise and recoiling from personal contacts, elects to live in a double-walled room in a narrow lane near, of all places, the heart of fashionable London. All this may not add up to an Alceste or a Coriolanus.[15] But Jonson gives him human qualities that are consistent, strongly rooted and recognisably common, however unpleasing. They are qualities appropriate to comedy of manners rather than farce. In part he resembles the sour old men of classical comedy. However, Jonson, unlike Plautus and Terence, does not set out to cure Morose (he punishes him, of course) or to explain him, even though – or should it be, because? – he may have seen some likeness between Morose's temper and his own. Nor does Morose acquire the symbolic magnitude of Volpone, though he takes over Volpone's position at the centre of the play. On the other hand, as with Volpone, Jonson matches Morose exactly to his stage surroundings. The Londoners who invade him make a varied pattern of frivolity corresponding to his own harshness. The comic effect of their visitation is double-edged.

We first hear of Morose in opposition to the cries of London – the fishwives and orange-women, a pewterer's prentice, the city waits and the bell-man, a bearward, a professional fencer drumming for spectators (I.i). Truewit torments him with a vision of endless jostling crowds (II.ii), and the penance he imagines for himself, in lieu of marriage, would be to join the crowd, in Westminster Hall, Paris Garden, or even at a play (IV.i); but when he ventures out to consult the lawyers he is driven back by such clamour that the bedlam at his wedding seems a 'silence too't! a kind of calme mid-night!' (IV.vii). And the other men in the play represent Morose's world, whether he likes it or not, the post-Elizabethan London of 'the Wits, and Braveries o' the time, as they call 'hem', who are near the Court but not of it, who lodge in the City but do not belong to it, who are beginning to form a separate, gossip-filled milieu of their own, the future 'town'. The genuine wits are, for the time being at least, not courtiers like the wits in Shakespeare, but men-about-town who set out to make the most of their condition of irresponsibility; they could be taken from those frequenters of the Mermaid whose company Francis Beaumont regrets in his verse-letter to Jonson, written from 'banishment' in the country. Sir Jack Daw, 'the onely talking sir i' th' towne', 'being a Bravery, and a Wit too' as Truewit says (I.ii.66, II.iv.120), is ridiculed not only as an example of modern pretentiousness and ignorance in letters but as a would-be councillor of state, who in this respect parallels Morose; Clerimont twits him with political ambition (II.iii) and his spontaneous asseveration is, 'As I hope to finish Tacitus' (IV.v.50). Sir Amorous La-Foole, on the other side, is 'one of the Braveries, though he be none o' the Wits'. He is the exact antithesis to Morose, coming up, not down, the ladder of rank, and obsessively sociable:

He will salute a Judge upon the bench, and a Bishop in the pulpit, a Lawyer when he is pleading at the barre, and a Lady when shee is dauncing in a masque, and put her out. He do's give playes, and suppers, and invite his

guests to 'hem, aloud, out of his windore, as they ride by in coaches. He has a
lodging in the Strand for the purpose. Or to watch when ladies are gone to
the China houses, or to the Exchange, that hee may meet 'hem by chance,
and give 'hem presents, some two or three hundred pounds-worth of toyes,
to be laught at. He is never without a spare banquet, or sweet-meats in his
chamber, for their women to alight at, and come up to, for a bait.

(I.iii)

It is appropriate that Morose's wedding-guests should consist of
La-Foole's party, including Captain Otter, who has joined the
company of Wits and Braveries from the bear-pit, through the back-
door of marriage.

Jonson pin-points the time and place of his action precisely.
Epicoene was the first of his plays to be printed with the direction,
The Scene LONDON.[16] He alludes (I.i.122) to the new statues at
Aldgate which were unveiled in 1609, a few months before his play
was acted; and the perpetual bell-ringing 'by reason of the sicknesse',
that drives Morose to double-line his walls and ceilings (I.i.183),
must refer to the visitations of the same year and the previous year,
which had forced the theatres to close.[17] Above all, the essential
datum of Jonson's plot is topical: Morose's agoraphobia, like the
sinister plague, is a sympton of the overcrowding in London, which
had 'so much encreased in people, and building' within fifty years
(according to the chronicler, Edmund Howes, in 1615) 'as no
knowne Cittie of the Universe, may compare with it'.[18] Dekker
describes the medley of ranks and occupations to be seen in Paul's
Walk about 1608:

What swearing is there, what facing and out-facing? What shuffling, what
shouldering, what jostling, what jeering, what biting of thumbs to beget
quarrels ... what casting open of cloaks to publish new clothes, what
muffling in cloaks to hide broken elbows ... foot by foot and elbow by
elbow shall you see walking the knight, the gull, the gallant, the upstart, the
gentleman, the clown, the captain, the apple-squire, the lawyer, the usurer,
the citizen, the bankrupt, the scholar, the beggar, the doctor, the idiot, the
ruffian, the cheater, the Puritan, the cut-throat.[19]

Since 1580 the government had taken alarm at the growth of London
and had tried ineffectively to stop it. One of James I's earliest
proclamations, in September 1603, was directed against 'Inmates,
multitudes of dwellers in straight roomes, and places, in and about
the Citie of London ...: but', adds the chronicler, 'nothing was done
touching that matter'; and, by the time *The Silent Woman* was
written, this proclamation had been followed by others in 1605,

1607 and 1608. In 1613, referring to the district of Lincoln's Inn Fields, the Privy Council observed, 'there is nothing more frequent in the skirts and confines of the Citty than new created buildings'.[20]

The unhappy Marescalco in Aretino's play wonders why he ever accepted employment at a court. If noise and crowds are what Morose wants to escape from, he has chosen a strange time and a stranger place. Amid the general influx to London, a specially important social element consisted of the 'gentlemen of all shires' who, in the words of an Elizabethan writer, 'do fly and flock to this city', either 'to see and show vanity' or 'to save the cost and charge of hospitality' in the country;[21] such permanent or seasonal immigrants were apt to be denounced, as in a sermon of 1613, as 'the wealthy Gentlemen that turne townes into sheep-walkes' and 'contrive hospitality into the narrow roome of a poore lodging taken up in the Citie'.[22] Sir Amorous La-Foole is directly typical in this respect: almost as soon as 'it pleas'd [his] elder brother to die', he 'went downe to [his] tenants, in the countrey, and survai'd [his] lands, let new leases, tooke their money' (I.iv.61) – and hastened to occupy his 'lodging in the Strand'. Sir Walter Whorehound, in *A Chaste Maid in Cheapside* (1611?), and Lady Honour, in Nathan Field's *Amends for Ladies* (1611?), who lodges with a glover, are other stage representatives of the same social class. During the early years of James I, while more and more of the gentry travelled to London, not only for business but for education, pleasure or social convenience, the 'season' of London fashion seems to have taken shape, as if to keep pace with the renewed increase in luxury trades since the peace treaty with Spain in 1604.[23] John Wynn, a gentleman living as far away as North Wales, wrote in 1605, 'I am resolved to spend the greatest part of my lyf for the wynter and springe quarter about london'; and Chamberlain's letters over the next few years are scattered with references to such visitors (including, for instance, the mention, in December 1608, of Sir Henry Cary bringing his wife 'to towne ... in great pompe accompanied with five coaches besides many horsemen and herself in a litter because she is with child').[24] About 1605, according to Howes, 'began the ordinary use of Caroaches'; by 1619 they were common enough to cause traffic-jams around the Blackfriars.[25] The coaches mentioned in *The Silent Woman* were thus another sign of the times, particularly the coach that the Collegiate Ladies want for Epicoene so that she can accompany them 'to Bed'lem, to the China houses, and to the

Exchange' (IV.iii).[26] And the great ladies' association with Mrs Otter is a sign of the times as well. Sir Amorous's cousin is 'the rich China-woman, that the courtiers visited so often, that gave the rare entertainment' (I.iv.27). The entertainment in question may have been the banquet given in 1609 by the East India Company at the launching of the *Trade's Increase*, where the King, Prince Henry and all the other guests were presented with 'fine China Dishes',[27] or it may refer to the occasion, in April of the same year, when James opened the newly built Exchange in the Strand, naming it Britain's Burse, 'many of the upper shoppes' in the building being 'richly furnished with Wares', while the King and the royal family, 'with many great Lords, and chiefe Ladies', were 'there entertained with pleasant speeches, giftes, and ingenious devices'. The latter ceremony meant that the emergent West End now boasted a shopping centre under royal patronage. At this period, we are told, the Strand, where Sir Amorous lodges so conspicuously, and Drury Lane were 'the places where most of the *Gentry* lived'.[28] There is a special force, therefore, in the tight construction of Jonson's play, which makes it clear that Clerimont, Daw and Mrs Otter all live near Sir Amorous. And it is in this quarter that Morose has fixed his retreat. From Mrs Otter's house ''tis but over the way, hard by' (III.iii.69); Mrs Otter is his 'neighbour' (III.vii.19).

Jonson's point, however, about Morose, as about Volpone, is that he is partly justified; if Morose deserves some of his neighbours, they also deserve him. Jonson does not set up a standard of the just mean in sociability or conviviality in the play, as he does in poems like 'Inviting a friend to supper'. But among the many Jacobean comedies touching on the subject, only *The Silent Woman* breaks through generalities to a sharp, animated, farcical portrayal of the discomforts and vexations of metropolitan life.

Jonson even gives a fresh and expressive twist to the traditional burlesque of marriage. Mrs Otter, the 'Gorgon', who affects a horror of even dreaming about the City (III.ii), is described as a monstrous compound from the City's shops: 'All her teeth were made i' the Blacke-friars', says her amiable husband, 'both her eye-browes i' the Strand, and her haire in Silver-street. Every part o' the towne ownes a peece of her' (IV.ii). The Collegiate Ladies seem almost indistinguishable from each other; but it is their role in the play to have no separate identities, to represent a collective scurrying after novelty: 'Why, all their actions are governed by crude opinion, without reason or cause; they know not why they doe any thing'

(IV.vi). At the same time, their assumed independence was a product of the day. They embody the danger with which Truewit tries to alarm Morose: 'This too, with whom you are to marry, may have made a convayance of her virginity beforehand, as your wise widdowes doe of their states, before they marry ...' (II.ii.140). Such 'wise widows', it seems, were no invention: in 1618, Chamberlain relates how his brother's widow, 'that bragges she had the refusall of a whitestaffe', has 'made her capitulations with Sir R. Wainman' (the husband of her second choice) 'to live in London all the winter, not to be troubled with his children, to reserve 400^{li} a yeare for her own maintenance, leaving him 800^{li} a yeare to dispose of, besides 2000^{li} ready monie and other ymplements that she brings with her'.[29] By 1618, also, Sir John Wynn of Gwydir, who had previously been set upon a life in London, was warning his eldest son against marriage with 'sootherne weomen, & those that bee bredd aboute London (in that abominable libertie there used)'; women accustomed to the extraordinary 'libertie used abowte London' are 'able to overthrow anie man's estate what soe he bee, both in minde (which is most) & in his fortunes'.[30] The marital bugbears that frighten Morose come from the same source as the noise and the overcrowding around him.

The special freedom of social life in Jacobean London led to a renewal of the old controversy about women in popular literature[31] and on the stage. Here *The Silent Woman* seems to have had an immediate effect. In 1609–11 Nathan Field brought out *A Woman is a Weathercock*, promptly followed by *Amends for Ladies*; both plays are set in Jonson's London, and in the second Field borrows from *The Silent Woman*, in which he had acted. Beaumont and Fletcher, who made the battle of the sexes their central comic theme, also began to produce their series of comedies with London settings about 1609. In Fletcher's *Woman's Prize, or, The Tamer Tamed* (1611?), a comedy intended as a sequel and riposte to *The Taming of the Shrew*, the setting is transferred to London (and one of the characters is named Moroso). In this play, Petruchio's second wife strikes successfully for the kind of freedom ridiculed by Jonson:

> Liberty and clothes,
> When, and in what way she will; continual moneys,
> Company, and all the house at her dispose;
> No tongue to say, *why is this?* or, *whither will it?*
> New Coaches, and some buildings, she appoints here;
> Hangings, and Hunting-horses ...

(II.vi)

This foreshadows the proviso scenes of Etherege and Congreve; Jonson and his contemporaries have sketched out the territory of Restoration comedy.

The battle of the sexes as such is hardly a subject where Jonson is at his best. But he has a sharp eye for the social conditions in which it flourishes. There can be few plays so thoroughly topical as *The Silent Woman*. What makes it something more than a historical document or a passing joke is Jonson's intense response to the conditions of living in the present, his ability to 'sport with human follies' engendered in the everyday frictions of a metropolitan society.

11. Crowd and public in *Bartholomew Fair*

Now, good people, pay attention, if you really like plain speaking. For now the poet feels impelled to reproach the spectators.

The Wasps

Probably no English dramatist has created the impression of a crowd upon the stage as vividly as Ben Jonson in *Bartholomew Fair*. There is a score of speaking parts, besides supers, calling for the audience's attention, in the midst of noise, smell, brawling, and confusion; and in contrast to his previous comedies, Jonson has not provided a master intrigue or a pair of master manipulators to impose an evident cohesion on the plot. Instead, we are to be shown at least half-a-dozen different characters or groups of characters – Littlewit and his party, Cokes and his party, Winwife and Quarlous, Overdo, the people of the Fair, Troubleall, the Watch – each of them pursuing their separate aims or interests at the Fair, and pursuing them, what is more, without any drive or consistency. It is true that Littlewit's desire to have his puppet play shown and his manoeuvring to witness it form a constant factor in the total action; but this wish is not announced until the end of Act I, and does not govern the general action of the play until Act V. Similarly, Cokes is constant in his desire to see the sights; but then Cokes is a scatterbrain, the quintessential sucker, incapable of resisting each successive distraction, still less of planning realistically to influence anybody else. The denizens of the Fair – Ursla, Knockem and Edgworth, and their associates, and Leatherhead and Joan Trash – are also consistent in their desire to exploit their visitors, but they are opportunists by nature, and their professional purpose breaks up, in dramatic terms, into separate cony-catching tricks and combinations, similar but not cumulative; they have tactics, as it were, but no dramatic strategy. As against them, Overdo and Busy wish persistently to expose the Fair or denounce it, but the targets of their officiousness are chosen at random; while Quarlous, the gentleman-gamester, the only character whose role approaches that of the skilful intriguers in Jonson's earlier plays, also changes his objectives, and only emerges as an active intriguer in the second half of the play. No one, in effect, pursues the same specific goal for long, or continuously shares a goal with any other character.

Moreover, as Richard Levin points out in his lucid and influential analysis, a central motif in the action is the way the little parties of visitors to the Fair disintegrate when they get there and then reassemble in unexpected groupings – Grace, for example, escaping from Coke's party to marry Winwife, Littlewit's widowed mother-in-law falling to Quarlous, and Littlewit's wife and Cokes's married sister fluttering together into Knockem's care as potential 'birds o' the game'. The general effect of organised confusion, or 'controlled complexity' as Richard Levin calls it,[1] resembles a kermess by Bruegel; with the difference that in a Bruegel painting there may be a common activity, a dance or a wedding feast, to consolidate the composition, whereas Jonson, until the end, eschews any such focus. Toward the end of each act, he clusters a number of his actors together: for Overdo's oration at the close of Act II, for Nightingale's ballad and then Busy's assault on the gingerbread basket in Act III, in Act IV for the game of 'vapours' and then for the scuffle at the stocks, and in the last act for the puppet play. But the cast is not the same from one such episode to another, the participants in each are at cross-purposes, whether as doers or observers; and until the puppet play, which is no more, after all, than a sideshow, brings nearly all of the actors to the same part of the Fair, these gathering-points of the action are more like happenings than revels. In the play as a whole, the characters converge and affect each other because of an annual commercial attraction, the Fair; but they affect one another chiefly by contiguity, covertly or haphazardly, without any mark of collective order. Although it is a holiday occasion, they are not a community but a crowd.

The play would require an amazingly retentive spectator to summarise the plot. In performance, however, the confusion is not merely appropriate to the fairground setting but a source, as Jonson twice promises, of 'delight'.[2] It is orchestrated; it has a rhythm and pattern, in the use of different areas of the stage, in the introduction of alternating character groups and alternating types of motive, and in the sequences of the action. Beneath the surface disorder, there is an ebb and flow.

In attempting to describe this process in more detail, it will be helpful to take advantage of Professor R. B. Parker's likely conjectures about the staging of the first production of the play, at the Hope.[3] Briefly, he envisages two tents or booths, stage right and stage left, and the stocks mid-way between them, probably front-stage. If that was the arrangement, the tent at stage right could have been used, he points out, as the setting for Littlewit's house and later for the puppet show, the product of Littlewit's brain; stage left, in the traditional location for Hell-mouth, would be Ursla's pig booth; and the open central area of the stage could be used for the pitch of the toyman and the gingerbread woman, and the miscellaneous comings and goings of the Fair. If so, there would be a spatial rhythm in the action. Act I concentrates on the 'house' at stage right; the middle acts divide attention between the central stage and stage left, with a strong emphasis on Ursla's booth in Act II, more fluid movement in Act III, and staccato interchange in Act IV between the unlocalised mid-stage, the booth and the stocks; while Act V swivels attention toward stage right again.

Such an arrangement would make for an orderly, quasi-cinematic pattern. But Jonson both reinforces and complicates the pattern by the way he handles his characters. The Stage-keeper who comes on first in the Induction prepares the audience right away for 'he that should begin the play, Master Littlewit, the Proctor'; so that, although Littlewit does not follow 'instantly', as promised, there is no surprise when he enters in soliloquy at the start of Act I. But each act thereafter begins with a speaker new, or virtually new, to the play: Justice Overdo, then Captain Whit, Troubleall, and finally Leatherhead, 'translated' from toyman to puppeteer. None of them offers the audience a clear expository statement to begin with, but each of them launches into an exclamation or the like, with a promise of significant incoherence. 'A pretty conceit, and worth the finding!' says Littlewit; 'I ha' such luck to spinne out these fine things still, and like a Silke-worme, out of my selfe': words arousing curiosity instead of providing information, but already hinting at qualities to be important in the play, the speaker's self-centredness and naïve self-satisfaction. Overdo soliloquises in a similar manner, dramatising himself for an audience of one:

Well, in Justice name, and the Kings; and for the commonwealth! defie all the world, *Adam Overdo*, for a disguise.

This is not the first time the main audience have heard of this speaker, but the first time that they realise that he has a striking part in the play. The third act opens with a minor character, but a new topic – the speaker upbraiding the Watch – and a fresh accent, Captain Whit's stage Irish:

Nay, tish all gone now! dish tish phen tou vilt not be phitin call, Master Offisher!

Then Jonson reverses his procedure for an act opening, by reintroducing the Watch, but this time with a new and weird-looking interlocutor, Troubleall, whose first words are arresting, not for their content, but for their manner of enunciation: 'My Masters, I doe make no doubt, but you are officers.' And the last act begins with a recall of Littlewit's opening speech, together with a promise of fresh noise:

Well, Lucke and Saint *Bartholomew*; out with the signe of our inuention, in the name of *Wit*, and do you beat the Drum, the while.

$$(\text{V.i.1–3})$$

Each of these opening lines discloses a separate humour or seems to impart a new direction to the plot. And yet each of them harks back to the idea of 'judgement', which had been the key word in the Induction – either judgement in 'conceit' or judgement by law. This procedure sketches out the general movement of the plot, which appears to advance in zigzags, only to return, by a roundabout route, towards the point of departure.

According to Richard Levin, the key to the pattern in the plot is the deferred meeting and simultaneous 'rearrangement' of the two parties accompanying Cokes and Littlewit to the Fair, together with the discomfiture of their respective censors, Wasp and Busy, and the more formidable general censor, Overdo. Winwife and Quarlous stand apart as wits, 'understanding and judging', rather than tricking, the gulls. The motive forces at work are 'Luck and Saint Bartholomew'. And the people of the Fair, who remain unchanged at the end, are only incidental to the plot. While this analysis goes a long way, it is open to several objections, the chief of which is that it does not point to any reason within the play itself why the reshuffling of the two parties of visitors should be so important. Though each of these visitors carries his or her special interest, not one of them is given enough prominence by the dramatist to make his fortunes seem to the audience a primary concern. Nor does Levin's analysis explain why the outstanding funny scenes should be devoted to the enemies of the Fair, or why Justice Overdo (who has no family connection with the Littlewits) should take the dominant part among them.

Again, while Luck, or Fortune, is a regular agent in Elizabethan comedies, there are different ways of representing its workings, and Jonson hints in the Induction that his way will not include marvellous coincidences such as those in *The Tempest* and *The Winter's Tale*. The luck of the Fair is partly gambler's luck (Quarlous is a 'gamester'), but chiefly the natural- or mechanical-seeming result of collisions among the members of a crowd; except that these collisions, in turn, resolve themselves into a pattern of human appetites and errors.

Besides the grouping of the characters within the Littlewit and Cokes parties, three other groupings among the characters and their motives seem significant to the plot. Previously, Jonson had grouped his comic figures chiefly as cheats or gulls, or as humorists or wits. Here, the division between cheats and gulls corresponds to that between the people of the Fair and most of their customers or visitors (including their self-appointed inspector, the Justice in disguise). It is true that the people of the Fair have no egregious master-plan like Subtle and Face, and that they remain unpunished and apparently unchanged at the end; nevertheless, they have a vested interest in catering, or seeming to cater, for their customers' pleasure, and this vested interest is essential, not incidental, to the play. Secondly, in this play Jonson's usual distinction between humorists and wits follows a particular line, that of attitudes towards the pleasures of the Fair, ranging from the enthusiasm of Cokes and Littlewit at one extreme to the intolerance of Wasp, Busy and Overdo at the other, Grace and the two gentleman-wits standing somewhere between. The initial movement of the plot takes rise from this matching of attitudes between Littlewit and Cokes. And thirdly, there is a distinction between the characters as actors, creatures of impulse, and the characters as observers.

This third distinction is not entirely new in Jonson's comedy, of course, nor is it a rigid one, but in this play it takes on a special importance, because the visitors go to the Fair in the capacity of spectators even more than customers: Cokes at first says he wants 'to shew Mistris *Grace* my Fayre' (I.v.65) and Littlewit proposes that Win should 'long' to eat pig as a ruse to enable them to 'see' the 'sights' in the Fair, particularly his own puppet play (I.v.148; III.vi.4). All the visitors, and the Fair people themselves, are alternately observers of a sort and impulsive actors, and sometimes both together. While Quarlous, for example, is first mainly an observer of others and then mainly an impulsive plotter on his own account, the special humour of Littlewit and of Overdo is to imagine that they are 'apprehending' conceits or 'detecting' 'enormities'; and the closing scenes, concerning the puppet show, indicate that witnessing can be also a mode of acting, an expression of character. By this time it is clear that the assembly of people at the Fair constitute not only a crowd but a public. This links the actors on the stage with the real spectators in the Hope, who had found themselves the principal subjects, if not exactly the heroes, of Jonson's Induction. As the plot unfolds, the motive forces behind it are first the opposition between admirers and opponents of the Fair and the clash between the people of the Fair and their visitors, and finally, the transition from observing to acting. All three themes are intertwined, however, and the last is present from the outset.

The first phase of the play, to the end of Act II, Scene iv, is relatively static and expository, showing the intending visitors to the Fair and the sources of friction between them, and then Ursla and her confederates under the squint-eyed watch of Overdo. The second phase begins, and the action starts to quicken, with the entry of Winwife and Quarlous, who are at once engaged in a squabble with Knockem and Ursla, with the result that the termagant scalds herself with her own pan. Ursla in this scene has been described as the emblematised spirit of Discord in the play,[4] but the first concern she voices is not fighting but custom, and it is clearly the gentlemen who begin the verbal aggression; at this point they consider themselves in the Fair but not of it (II.v.25 ff.). And their initiative is followed by Overdo's oration on 'the fruits of bottle-ale and tobacco', an oration designed, with the Justice's crazy logic, to protect the 'lamb' he has singled out, Edgworth the 'civil' cutpurse – who takes the occasion of the small crowd that gathers to rob Cokes, the orator's natural protégé, while, in reward for his interference, it is Overdo who gets beaten. After the scenes introducing the Watch, who missed the rumpus, and showing Littlewit's party pushing into the pig booth, this phase of the action is brought to a close in Overdo's part-overheard soliloquy (III.iii) in which he professes to examine the lessons of his experience and cheerfully adjures himself to persist in his chosen course:

To see what bad euents may peepe out o' the taile of good purposes! the care I had of that ciuil yong man, I tooke fancy to this morning (and haue not left it yet) drew me to that exhortation, which drew the company, indeede, which drew the cutpurse; which drew the money; which drew my brother *Cokes* his losse; which drew on *Wasp's* anger; which drew on my beating; a

pretty gradation! And they shall ha' it i' their dish, i' faith, at night for fruit: I
loue to be merry at my table.

(III.iii.13–21)

This part of the soliloquy illustrates the Justice's Littlewit-like (or
Polonius-like) complacency with his own figures of speech, but it
also illuminates, by caricature, the play's indecorous and arsy-versy
logic of 'events', which Overdo both sees and does not see; and it
points forward to the supper promised at the end. Altogether, the
soliloquy marks a resting-point in the action, a partial gathering of
the threads; Winwife and Quarlous, who are also present on the
stage, cap it with a brief interchange in the choric manner of Mitis
and Cordatus, in *Every Man out of his Humour*:

> – What does he talke to himselfe, and act so seriously? poor foole!
> – No matter what. Here's fresher argument, intend that.

(III.iii.42–5)

This 'fresher argument' is the re-entry of Cokes and his party and
Bartholomew's enthusiastic purchases, which lead to a new phase in
the action, virtually a counter-offensive by the people of the Fair.
Now that Cokes is back on stage, Nightingale has the audience he
wants for one of his ballads. And in one way the ballad scene (III.v)
follows exactly the pattern that Overdo has just sagaciously
discerned: in effect, the ballad, *A Caveat against Cutpurses*, follows
the line of his own declamation against ale and tobacco; Edgworth
picks Cokes's purse again; and again it is Overdo who gets the
blame. But this time the incident has been planned by Edgworth and
Nightingale, as a professional manoeuvre (and also in response to
Cokes's challenge to the unknown cutpurse). And after a counter-
sortie in the next scene (Busy's attack on the toys and gingerbread),
the people of the Fair resume their offensive in Act IV (against Wasp,
Win and Mrs Overdo).

The ballad episode marks a decisive turn. It prompts Wasp to
snatch back the box holding the marriage licence from his charge,
and it causes Wasp, Cokes and Mrs Overdo to hustle Adam Overdo
away towards the stocks – thus beginning the break-up of Cokes's
party by leaving Grace on the stage with Winwife and Quarlous.
Above all, it converts Quarlous from an observer into an intriguer,
since, having seen Edgworth cut the purse, he decides to enlist him
against Wasp; and although at first he seems to intend no more than
a biting practical joke, the humiliation of a 'serious ass' (III.v.265),
his plans gather momentum as he goes along.

The climax of confusion is reached in Act IV. Through most of Acts II and III the presence of Leatherhead and Trash on the stage has provided a sort of continuity to the scene, but by the end of Act III they have decamped, and in the course of Act IV the stage is several times left empty, as if to emphasise the even more jerky movement of the plot, to and fro between mid-stage, pig booth and stocks. To add to the confusion, Overdo's forgotten victim, Troubleall, appears as a zany *persona ex machina*. But on the other hand, Quarlous's inventiveness begins to work towards a settlement. By using Edgworth and his partners, who trap Wasp into the game of 'vapours', he causes 'the date' of Wasp's 'authority' to end, as well as gaining possession of the licence; by disguising himself as Troubleall, he is enabled to cheat Overdo out of his control over Grace; and by attracting Mrs Purecraft, in his character of madman, he frustrates Busy's matrimonial hopes. It is true that he too is made to look foolish at the end of the 'vapours' game, that he loses Grace to Winwife, and that in the end he silently swallows his initial diatribe against widow-hunting. Nevertheless, his 'madcap' opportunism rounds off the pattern of events constituted by petty roguery, officious misjudgement and luck, and he stands out as the most authoritative opponent of the opponents of the Fair and the most successful 'discoverer' in the cast.

This does not mean, on the other hand, that Quarlous becomes Jonson's spokesman, or sums up the themes and ideas latent in the play. When he tells the magistrate, 'remember you are but *Adam*, Flesh and blood! you haue your frailty, forget your other name of Overdoo' (V.vi.96–8), he delivers a satisfying reproof, but leaves untouched the questions raised about the values of the Fair as such. In the 'disputation' over the puppet show, for example, the decisive point had been precisely that the puppets were not flesh and blood. In any case, Quarlous had been off-stage during the puppet show and the 'disputation'.

The argument of the play, considered as thematic idea, is not exactly the same as its 'argument', considered as a pattern of events. As a spectacle, *Bartholomew Fair* exhibits Londoners in a crowd and glances at topical abuses. Many of the abuses were well-known targets for satire or complaint – false measures, the wiles of the 'civil cutpurse *searchant*', tobacco, drunkenness and the proliferation of tippling-houses (a particular concern of the mid-Jacobean years),[5] prostitution, the offence of 'swaggering' or 'roaring', the defects of

Justices of the Peace and of the watch, wardship, the miseducation of young heirs, superstitious recourse to fortune-tellers,[6] and 'the petulant ways' of 'your land's Faction', which Jonson singles out in his Prologue addressed to the King; and in addition, there is noise, a symptom of metropolitan overcrowding to which the poet was specially sensitive. But his tone here is ironic gaiety rather than an earnest spirit of satiric correction. The very miscellaneity of these abuses is appropriate to the spectacle of the Fair, but no one of them carries dramatic weight enough to give coherence to the whole. It has been maintained that the governing idea of the play is the ridicule of false authority, or else the lapse of authority in social life,[7] or else (with the Court performance in mind) that the very 'absence' of order within the play is meant to point towards an ideal order embodied in the audience, James and his Court.[8] But the Court, *ex hypothesi*, were absent from the Hope; and, while it is clear that pretensions to authority form an important component theme, they do not account (as Richard Levin's article brings out) for the meanders of the plot. Nor does Jonson suggest what established authority, legal, religious or scholastic, could or should do to correct the follies on display; *Bartholomew Fair* is a comedy, not a Morality.

Another significant but still marginal theme, related to the confusion over sources of authority indicated in the play, is the commercialisation of social life, including the commercialisation of values for the landed gentry increasingly settling in the capital. This was indeed a focal subject for Jacobean comedy, especially as it concerned the educated gentry, often magistrates or potential magistrates, and the Inns of Court men, who formed the nucleus of 'the judicious' in the playhouses, or what Jonson in the Induction calls 'the Commission of Wit'.[9] Like his earlier comedies, *Bartholomew Fair* illustrates the disorderly mixture of social standards in London, and the pretensions and aggressive self-assertion that go with it; 'vapours' here are in large part the same as the 'gentleman-like monster' of 'humours' in his previous plays. And 'wit' was crucial, on the Jacobean stage, to the portrayal of the gentleman in London, expressing his response, in words and action, to a world where his inherited standards were slipping away. From this point of view, Winwife and Quarlous share a good deal with such resourceful gentlemen of leisure as Witgood in *A Trick to Catch the Old One*, or the heroes of Fletcher's *Wit without Money*. In spite of this, however, it cannot be said that their wit shows to the same advantage, or governs the plot to the same extent, as that of Truewit and his friends in *The Silent Woman*.[10] And, conversely, it cannot be said that the economic aspect of the Fair takes up Jonson's interest to the same extent as the business transactions in *The Devil is an Ass*. It is noticeable, for instance, that he virtually ignores the cloth trading and the sale of horses that were still important at Smithfield,[11] except for the drunken northern clothier who figures briefly in the 'vapours' game, and the veterinary blarney of the horse courser, Knockem, which is merely a colouring for his dramatic role as roarer and pimp.

The Fair Jonson presents on the stage is a place of commercial entertainment; his comedy is the spectacle of a spectacle, with a dominant interest in those who go to see the sights. The Induction dwells on the relations between author and spectators; the cast is distributed between those who profit from, those who are lured by, those who can tolerate, and those who denounce extravagantly the pleasures of the Fair; and the action is introduced by a disquisition on poetic wit, turns on a street ballad, and culminates in a puppet show. In short, the underlying theme is London society considered as a literary or theatrical public. The expression 'the public', in its literary sense, meaning society at large conceived of as the market for books and plays, was not formulated until the generation after Jonson.[12] But *Bartholomew Fair* hinges upon an effort to assemble and clarify the materials for such a concept, undertaken by the most wholeheartedly professional of Jacobean writers.

Jonson belonged to a generation of dramatists, humanists by formation, who were obliged to adapt themselves to the novel but already changing conditions of a commercial theatre. To write English poetry in conformity with Renaissance principles was a comparatively untried ambition; to acquire fame, or even part of a living, by writing for the plaudits of chance assemblies in playhouses was more unfamiliar still. 'Shame', wrote the university satirist at the very beginning of Jonson's career.

> that the Muses should be bought and sold,
> For every peasants Brasse, on each scaffold.[13]

In those conditions, who was qualified to write, and what was his proper scope? Who was qualified to judge him, and how should he be judged? Even, who were his ultimate paymasters, and what did they really want? Ever since Marlowe's haughty dismissal of 'such conceits as clownage keeps in pay' and Greene's unhappy protest against exploitation by the players, these and similar questions must have pressed hard upon the eager or reluctant recruits to the new profession of writing for the stage.

Consciously or not, the Elizabethans reverted to the Aristophanic practice of discussing or alluding to their profession in the course of their plays. In the public theatres, Shakespeare was the first to do so. He was specially concerned with the rapport between actors and audience, ideally a national audience with courtly patrons at their head – though he makes Hamlet wryly note that the latter might well include a Polonius, expecting 'a jig or a tale of bawdry, or he sleeps'. Shakespeare's younger contemporaries, Jonson among them, were relatively more dependent on London and more affected by the changing atmosphere of the turn of the century: satire and censorship, personal rivalries, vocal if not published criticism. They used inductions or prologues, and even prefaces added to the printed texts of their plays, in order to educate, repress, conciliate or, at the least, describe the unpredictable responses of their mixed auditories. Marston, for instance, told the audience of the Blackfriars, about 1604:

> the highest grace we pray
> Is, you'll not tax until you judge our play.
> Think, and then speak: 'tis rashness, and not wit,
> To speak what is in passion, and not judgment, fit.
>
> (*The Dutch Courtesan*)

In the Induction to *The Malcontent* at the Globe, Webster makes Burbage ask, speaking in his own person, 'Why should not we enjoy the ancient freedom of poesy? No, sir, such vices as stand not accountable to law, should be cured as men heal tetters, by casting ink upon them.' These statements sound like replies to possibly influential, as well as captious, patrons; other playwrights emphasise the levelling-down effect of the playhouse, where (as Dekker explains to his Gull, or initiate in London gallantry)

your Stinkard has the selfe same libertie to be there in his Tobacco-Fumes, which your sweet Courtier hath: and . . . your Car-man and Tinker claime as strong a voice in their suffrage, and sit to give judgment on the plaies life and death, as well as the prowdest *Momus* among the tribe of *Critick*.

The theatre, in short, is the 'Royal Exchange' for poets, where their 'Muses' have become 'Merchants'.[14] And some of the consequences of this state of affairs are described by Dekker and Middleton in the epilogue to their *Roaring Girl* (at the Fortune, *c.* 1608), where they compare their task to that of the painter who ruined his portrait by altering it, feature by feature, in the vain hope of satisfying every prospective buyer:

> And thus,
> If we to every brain that's humorous
> Should fashion scenes, we, with the painter, shall,
> In striving to please all, please none at all.

Like Marston, they assume that every individual criticism is likely to be 'humorous', capricious, ungrounded on common principles. With the benefit of historical hindsight, we may congratulate Shakespeare's contemporaries on the golden opportunity they enjoyed in writing at the same time for the groundlings and the judicious; but the challenge must have seemed as much daunting as invigorating to the men on the job.

Jonson was more engaged than any other in critical exhortation and reproof, from his pioneering *Every Man out of his Humour* onward; and his view of the writer's condition was more fully articulated and complex than that of anyone else. At first he mainly emphasises the principles on which he claims appreciation; but then increasingly he examines those factors in the reception of his work that affect or hinder appreciation. Briefly, they are competition, patronage, censorship or interference, and popular taste; and his achievement as a critic or theorist of drama was partly to draw these together into something like a coherent system. In the 1607 preface to *Volpone*, addressed to the two Universities, he refers to attacks or dangers from several sides at once. In order to reassert 'the dignity of poet', he hits out both at the 'licence' of vulgarians who degrade 'stage-poetry' and at the malice – which he had good reason to fear – of 'invading interpreters' with access to highly placed patrons. But at the same time he concedes some reason to 'those severe and wise patriots' who would like to turn the clock back or retrench the liberty of the stage, and he points out that he has met their case in part by so arranging the 'catastrophe' of the play as 'to put the snaffle in their mouths, that cry out, We never punish vice in our interludes' – though this means incurring 'censure' from academic purists. Between poetasters, informers, statesmen, classicists, and Puritans, the dramatist has a difficult course to steer, precisely because the would-be censors of the stage have some legitimate cause for complaint. In the preface 'To the Reader', attached to the 1612 edition of *The Alchemist*, Jonson goes to the root of the problem as he sees it: the alliance between bad writing and popular taste. The uninstructed reader is bound to be 'cozened' by plays, because now, the concupiscence of jigs, and dances so reigneth, as to run away from nature, and be afraid of her, is the only point of art that tickles the spectators;

and the source of the cheat is to be found in 'the multitude, through their excellent [*supreme*] vice of judgement':

For they commend writers, as they do fencers or wrestlers; who if they come in robustuously, and put for it with a great deal of violence, are received for the braver fellows . . . For it is only the disease of the unskilful, to think rude things greater than polished; or scattered more numerous than composed.

Sensationalism and aimless bustle, then, are the typical vices of mind displayed on the popular stage. And in turn they constitute, in effect, the basic motivation of the characters in *Bartholomew Fair*.

In opposition to such vices, the Induction to the *Fair* urges settled individual judgements. Confronting a typical audience in a public playhouse, Jonson now surveys their inclinations more comprehensively (but also more genially) than before. He takes account of their variety, 'the favouring and judicious' as well as 'the curious and envious'; and he touches on what he sees as ignorant approval as well as wrongheaded opposition to the stage – the 'concupiscence of jigs and dances' (again) as well as prudish suspicion of 'profaneness'; the stock responses of those stick-in-the-mud stage fans who have not changed since 'Master Tarlton's time' or the days of '*Jeronimo* or *Andronicus*' as well as the industrious perversity of any lurking 'state-decipherer, or politic picklock of the scene'. His method is an ironic conflation of opposites. The Stage-keeper says the 'master-poet' has been too obstinate; the Book-holder, too indulgent. The groundlings in the Hope become 'the grounded judgements here', and the hidebound admirer of *The Spanish Tragedy* 'shall pass unexcepted at here as a man whose judgement shews it . . . hath stood still', since, 'next to truth, a confirmed error does well'. And, in the pose of an honest tradesman, the author concedes to every paying spectator his 'free-will of censure', exactly 'to the value of his place – provided always his place get not above his wit'. The further conditions of the bargain are 'that every man here exercise his own judgement, and not censure by contagion, or upon trust, . . . as also that he be fixed and settled in his censure' (Induc. 100–1); above all, that he should show sufficient self-respect to measure trifles at their right proportion –

else you will make him [the author] justly suspect that he that is so loth to look on a baby or an hobby-horse here, would be glad to take up a commodity of them, at any laughter or loss, in another place.

(Induction, 162–5)

The stage is precisely the place where trivialities can (ideally) be exhibited for what they are, without arousing either 'concupiscence' or indignation. Failure to perceive this is, at bottom, failure in self-respect. Or, as the Court Prologue states it, the play is presented

> for your sport, without particular wrong,
> Or just complaint of any private man
> Who of himself or shall think well or can.

(lines 8–10)

There is still a hint of irony here, a challenge to the spectator to think well of himself – if he can; but the main statement is close to Jonson's statement of his fundamental moral viewpoint in *Discoveries*: 'I know no disease of the *Soul*, but *Ignorance*; not of the Arts, and Sciences, but of itself.'[15] What the Prologue and Induction to *Bartholomew Fair* propose as the solid ground for 'censure' of the play, favourable or not, is personal 'judgement' stemming from and confirming self-knowledge. And it is not accidental that references to censorious objectors and such phrases as 'the Commission of Wit' in the Induction suggest judgement of a legal kind as well as the expression of taste; as Jonson saw it, the institutional status of the theatre and its literary quality were interdependent. Would-be censors and confirmed spectators formed a continuous public.

The Induction is a miniature play, in the style of prologues to the *commedia erudita*, bridging the gap, or blurring the distinction, between the reality of the spectators and the fiction of the stage. 'The poet' and 'his man, Master Brome, behind the arras' stand on the same plane as the legendary Kindheart and Master Tarlton and the pretended Stage-keeper and Book-holder of the company and 'Master Littlewit', who is said to be mending his stocking – an actor described by the name of his part. The pretended 'argument' of the Induction-as-play is the question of what the audience are to expect or not expect – predictably, a factor in the performance itself. There is a similar sleight-of-hand with reality and fiction in the scenes leading to the puppet show, as when Littlewit explains that he has made *Hero and Leander* 'a little easy, and modern for the times'; or when Cokes, having identified one of the puppets with the leading player in the real company ('Which is your Burbage now? ... Your best actor. Your Field?'), identifies the puppet Leander in turn with one of his 'fairings', his 'fiddle-stick' (V.iii.85–137); or when Leatherhead, as puppet master, sagely counsels the poet not to 'breed too great an expectation' of the show among his friends – 'that's the onely hurter of these things' (V.iv.13–14). And these ironic variations on themes from the Induction begin to round off the play proper, which is an extension of the same group of ideas.

Littlewit and Cokes, who lead their respective parties to the Fair, are complementary to one another, as rhymester of puppet plays and archetypal 'favourer of the quality', and are likewise complementary in other ways to the Fair people who cater for them and also to minds like Busy and Overdo, as enemies of the Fair. A similar want of the 'judgement' designated in the Induction operates in or for them all. Littlewit opens the play proper with his pun about the licence: 'Bartholomew upon Bartholomew! There's the device!' – which turns out to be exact in the heraldic sense, if childish as a conceit. And his self-appreciation a moment later prepares an intellectual position for Overdo to occupy (as well as another for Mooncalf, by Ursla's fire):

When a quirk, or a *quiblin* does scape thee, and thou dost not watch, and apprehend it, and bring it afore the constable of conceit: (there now, I speak *quib* too) let 'hem carry thee out o' the Archdeacon's Court, into his Kitchin, and make a *Jack* of thee, in stead of a *John*. (There I am againe, la!)

(I.i.13–18)

Littlewit's 'apprehension' of 'quirks' prepares the way for the disguised magistrate's 'detection' of 'enormities', and similarly his account of his home-bred wit prepares the way for Busy's 'inspiration' and Knockem's 'vapours':

A poxe o' these pretenders to wit! your *Three Cranes, Miter,* and *Mermaid* men! . . . But gi' mee the man, can start up a *Justice of Wit* out of six-shillings beare, and give the law to all the Poets and Poet-suckers i' towne.

(I.i.33–40)

Though he is an amiable ass, his 'ambitious wit' (as Quarlous calls it) is essential to the satiric scheme of the plot. And his 'apprehension' shows its true colours at the Fair. Not only does he lose his wife, but he lends Cokes the money to watch his own puppet play, and then fails to see it himself.

If Littlewit and Cokes together represent the upholders of the shows at the Fair, Busy and Overdo are their complementary opposites. The puppet show and the like are indeed 'enormities', but they are incapable of seeing why. Busy's marvellously self-hypnotic verbiage is a magnified version of his intended son-in-law's 'quibs'; 'Good Banbury-vapours', in Knockem's condescending appraisal. But (as C. H. Herford remarked),[16] he is no Tartuffe; and his final 'confutation' by the puppets is no head-on satiric retort to the Puritan case against the stage. It merely shows that he cannot observe what is in front of him, or tell the difference between puppets and players. It is consistent that in the end he should 'become a beholder' with the rest (V.v.116); in part, the implication is that his noisy and irrelevant objections merely serve to sustain the real abuses in plays.

Overdo is both a more complex and, within his limits, a more formidable figure. Unlike Busy, he has genuine authority, as far as it goes; and in part he is the contemporary type of an upstart and irresponsible Justice of the Peace.[17] But in his language, with its mixture of complacent pedantry and pulpit clichés, he is allied both to Littlewit and – in spite of surface opposition – to Busy.[18] And, however 'parantory', 'severe' and 'angry' he may have been on the bench (IV.i.70–8), his role on the stage is a caricature of that of the disguised Duke in *Measure for Measure* – to pretend to observe others, while forgetting to know himself. After declaring that he has come to inspect the Fair in disguise, so as to avoid having to rely upon the evidence of 'other men's ears' and 'other men's eyes' (II.i.29–30), he promptly turns to the amiable Mooncalf for information about the characters at the Fair; and when he comes to deliver his diatribe against ale and tobacco, he picks up his medical warnings from Knockem (II.iii.20; II.vi.13). He is essentially literary and dramatic 'judgement' (or misjudgement) in action, rather than a representative of the law. In spite of his professed familiarity with 'my Quintus Horace', he is a foe to poetry, in the line of old Knowell, in *Every Man in his Humour*; with a special naïvety that makes him susceptible to the crudest junk if it carries a surface message that he approves. He suspects Nightingale 'of a terrible taint, poetry' (III.v.6), but he stays to hear his ballad against cutpurses – (which must be Jonson's riposte to the Autolycus scenes in *The Winter's Tale*) – precisely because the ballad 'doth discover enormity' (III.v.112); and, because he stays to 'mark it more', he finds himself in the stocks. As the observer who wilfully fails to observe, he is both a representative of those civic magistrates who tried to restrict or suppress the acting of plays and the outstanding negative example in the comedy of the principle of exercising one's own judgement.

Wasp is related to Overdo and Busy less by any pretence of

ideology than by temperament. His name suggests a probable source of suggestions for Ben Jonson – the Aristophanic comedy about Philocleon and the other irascible jurymen who cling to the shadow of power through formal legal authority because they do not possess the substance (as a 'friend of Cleon', the old man is also at first an enemy of the poet). Like Philocleon, Jonson's Wasp has a passion to contradict; and like him, he tumbles over into riotous misbehaviour once his show of authority is taken away. As his name suggests, he exhibits in an extreme form the aimless restlessness that agitates Overdo and Busy – which is not very different from the qualities he so scornfully diagnoses in Bartholomew's mind:

> He that had the meanes to travel your head, now, should meet finer sights then any are i' the Fayre; and make a finer voyage on't; to see it all hung with cockle-shels, pebbles, fine wheat-strawes, and here and there a chicken's feather and a cobweb.
>
> (I.v.93–7)

This is perhaps the most striking statement in the play about the psychological qualities that link its humorists together; and its jerky vehemence characterises Wasp himself almost as much as Cokes. As Quarlous has said, a few minutes earlier, 'it's cross and pile' between master and man. When Jonson wants to voice a considered judgement about Bartholomew, he delivers it in a different tone:

> Talke of him to have a soule? heart, if hee have any more then a thing given him instead of salt, onely to keepe him from stinking, I'le be hang'd afore my time, presently.
>
> (IV.ii.54–6)

This more judicial observer is the 'civil cutpurse', Edgworth, who has just helped to strip Cokes of his cloak and sword. No doubt the cutpurse as such was an indispensable figure in a gallery of comic portraits representing the world of the Jacobean playhouses in general. But it is one of Jonson's sharper ironies that he is the only character on the stage self-respecting and dispassionately observant enough to ask whether the prime enthusiast for street ballads and puppet shows can have such a thing as a soul.

12. *The Revenger's Tragedy* and the Morality tradition

Tourneur's plays have too often been described as if they were texts for illustration by an Aubrey Beardsley. They have suffered as a result. Symonds read *The Revenger's Tragedy* as a melodrama with agreeable thrills and some needless moralising; and, on this reading, it was not difficult for William Archer, applying the standards of naturalism, to make the play appear ludicrous. Though Mr Eliot has supplied a corrective by pointing out that the characters are not to be taken as studies in individual iniquity, but as figures in a pattern with a poetic life of its own, his essay on Tourneur again misrepresents him. He is made 'a highly sensitive adolescent with a gift for words...'

The cynicism, the loathing and disgust of humanity, expressed consummately in *The Revenger's Tragedy*, are immature in the respect that they exceed the object. Their objective equivalents are characters practising the grossest vices; characters which seem merely to be spectres projected from the poet's inner world of nightmare, some horror beyond words. So the play is a document on humanity chiefly because it is a document on one human being, Tourneur; its motive is truly the death motive, for it is the loathing and horror of life itself.

(*Selected Essays*, p. 189)

This is the reading of the 'nineties again. Tourneur's poetry, however, unlike the Romantic poetry of decadence, has a firm grasp on the outer world. Cynicism, loathing and disgust there are in *The Revenger's Tragedy*; but if Tourneur were merely giving expression to a neurotic state of mind, he could hardly have written successful drama at all. The 'object' of his disgust is not the behaviour of his characters, singly or together, so much as the process they represent, the disintegration of a whole social order. It is this theme, particularised and brought to life by the verse, that shapes the pattern of the play; and it is developed with the coherence, the precise articulation, of a dramatist assured that his symbols are significant for his audience as much as for himself. Tourneur is writing in the contemporary Revenge convention; but behind the Revenge plays is another dramatic influence, working in harmony with Tourneur's narrowly traditionalist outlook, that of the Moralities. *The Revenger's Tragedy* is a logical development from the medieval drama.

The Moralities had been the staple of popular drama when Marlowe began writing, and their methods were absorbed into the blank verse narrative play. That they were absorbed, not abandoned, is clear from *Faustus*; and Mr Knights has pointed out that their influence on Jonson and his contemporaries was considerable and varied.[1] They offered the Elizabethans a group of stock situations, types and themes which had been utilised for the representation of social and religious problems throughout the changes of a century;[2] and the later drama could rely on their familiarity in presenting fairly complex situations simply and effectively on the stage. The Morality influence makes itself felt, under the Senecanism and the literary satire, through the conventions of the Revenge plays themselves, and in *The Revenger's Tragedy* most strongly of all. The characters in the Moralities are personified abstractions and moral or social types, representing the main forces making for or against the salvation of the individual and social stability; they have no dramatic functions outside the doctrinal scheme. The actions on the stage are symbolic, not realistic, and the incidents are related to each other logically, as parts of an allegory, or as illustrations of the argument. *The Revenger's Tragedy* is constructed on closely similar lines. Miss Bradbrook has analysed the narrative into 'a series of peripeteia', representing 'the contrasts between earthly and heavenly vengeance, and earthly and heavenly justice'[3] – linked as the parts of an allegory rather than as a natural sequence of events. The characters are exclusively the instruments of this movement, and it is from this point of view that they explain themselves to the audience; their speeches reveal their world, rather than individual minds. The Duke and his court are simply monstrous embodiments of Lust, Pride and Greed; Vendice and the other revengers, despite the intensely personal tone of their speeches, are portrayed in the same way. The characters' motives are generalised and conventional – Lussurioso, for example, is an extreme case of Pride and Lust – and many of the speeches are general satiric tirades, spoken in half-turn towards the audience. This is a narrower dramatic pattern than Marston's, and more like those of the Moralities; but Tourneur gains in dramatic coherence from the earlier examples. With Jonson, he was the last writer to apply them successfully.

'I see now', says Ambitioso in the underplot – the traditional comic underplot in which the Vices are confounded – 'there's nothing sure in mortality, but mortality.' The contrast between the skeleton and the specious overlay provided by wealth and sensuality is fundamental to Tourneur and the Morality writers alike. When Pride, in Medwall's *Nature*, leads Man to debauchery, he prepares for him 'a doublet of the new make':

> Under that a shirt as soft as silk,
> And as white as any milk
> To keep the carcase warm.

These lines might have provided Tourneur with his text. Medwall, however, writes with an equanimity, a sense of security in the values of Nature, that Tourneur has lost. His sense of decay, of the skull, is overpowering:

> Advance thee, O thou terror to fat folks,
> To have their costly three-piled flesh worn off
> As bare as this; for banquets, ease, and laughter
> Can make great men, as greatness goes by clay;
> But wise men little are more great than they.

The Stoical conclusion is feeble beside the savage intensity of the first lines. Death has triumphed, and the only course left open to Vendice is to convert a horrified recoil into a grim acceptance, turning the forces of death against themselves. Nevertheless, the fascination of physical decay has not corrupted Tourneur's satiric purpose; there is nothing mechanical in Vendice's wielding of the lash. The changes of tone in this first soliloquy with the skull imply an attitude active and controlled:

> When two heaven-pointed diamonds were set
> In those unsightly rings – then 'twas a face
> So far beyond the artificial shine
> Of any woman's bought complexion,
> That the uprightest man (if such there be
> That sin but seven times a day) broke custom,
> And made up eight with looking after her.
> O, she was able to ha' made a usurer's son
> Melt all his patrimony in a kiss;
> And what his father fifty years told,
> To have consumed, and yet his suit been cold.
> But, O accursed palace!

Thee, when thou wert apparelled in thy flesh,
The old duke poisoned . . .
O, 'ware an old man hot and vicious!
'Age, as in gold, in lust is covetous.'

(I.i)

The contrasts between life and death, between natural virtue and the
effects of lust and greed, are not merely presented – they are shown as
a unified process in Vendice's mind, a process which extends through
the whole world of the play. The imagery associated with the skull is
concrete, exact and dramatically useful; Tourneur builds up a system
of relationships between images and situations which gains in
cumulative effect – these lines, for example, have a bearing on the
ironic undertones of the scene where the Duchess tempts Spurio,
who is wearing her jewel in his ear ('had he cut thee a right diamond
. . .'), and, again, on the second appearance of the skull, poisoned
with cosmetics. The pun in the first line is flat, but not extraneous; it
emphasises the way in which the symbols are to be taken – the
physical world is treated, in a peculiarly direct and consistent
manner, as emblematic of the moral order, man in relation to the
divine will. This moral order is rigidly identified with the traditional
social hierarchy of ranks and obligations; but the narrowness of
Tourneur's outlook makes for concentration, and his poetic material
is ranged and ordered by reference to the experience of society as a
whole. In this passage, the physical contrast between the 'diamonds'
and their sockets, visible on the stage, prepares for, and supports, the
crude cynicism of the parenthesis, which marks the change of tone.
The complete degeneration of virtue is represented by placing the
'usurer's son' on the same footing of sensuality as 'the uprightest
man', the mock inflation overturning any protest from
respectability. Here, however, the tone changes again: the
'patrimony', by implication the ill-gained result of greed, is itself
'melted' away, and, though virtue cannot be reinstated, divine justice
is vindicated in the rhyme. Vendice's tone mounts again as he reverts
to the palace; but the Duke, with the 'infernal fires' burning in his
'spendthrift veins', has already been paralleled with the usurer's son
– the two types of social disintegration are juxtaposed throughout
the play – so that Vendice's exultant determination on revenge
appears as part of an inevitable cycle of feelings and events.

The trite 'sentences' at the end of Tourneur's most passionate
speeches are meant to enforce this sense of inevitability by lowering
the tension and appealing to the commonplace. Tourneur himself

calls them 'conceits', and continually draws attention, in Marston's manner, to his virtuosity in using them. The resemblance to Marston, however, is only superficial; they are more closely akin to the popular moralists and the Morality writers. Vendice's emblem is an example:

A usuring father to be boiling in hell, and his son and heir with a whore dancing over him.

Again:

> O, you must note who 'tis should die,
> The duchess' son! she'll look to be a saver:
> 'Judgement, in this age, is near kin to favour.'
>
> (I.iv)

> Could you not stick? See what confession doth!
> Who would not lie, when men are hanged for truth?
>
> (V.i)

These popular aphorisms and tags of Seneca Englished gave Marston and Tourneur a large part of the raw material from which their more ambitious speeches are developed. But while Marston works up his material as a self-conscious littérateur, Tourneur adheres to the Morality mode. The language of the latter is plain and colloquial, but adequate, as a rule, to the simple didactic purpose; a speech to the audience from Lupton's *All for Money* is typical:

> Is not my grandfather Money think ye of great power
> That could save from hanging such abominable whore,
> That against all nature her own child did kill?
> And yonder poor knave that did steal for his need
> A few sort of rags, and not all worth a crown,
> Because he lacks money shall be hanged for that deed,
> You may see my Grandsire is a man of renown:
> It were meet when I named him that you all kneeled down.
> Nay, make it not so strange, for the best of you all,
> Do love him so well, you will come at his call.

The audience is included in the framework of the play, the function of the speeches being to expound the theme to them from their own point of view. Marston's sophisticated railing has quite a different effect; it draws attention to itself:

> *Pietro:*   Tell me; indeed I heard thee rail –
> *Mendoza:* At women, true; why, what cold phlegm could choose,
>   Knowing a lord so honest, virtuous,

> So boundless loving, bounteous, fair-shaped, sweet,
> To be contemn'd, abused, defamed, made cuckold!
> Heart, I hate all women for't; sweet sheets, wax lights, antique bed-posts,
> cambric smocks, villanous curtains, arras pictures, oiled hinges, and all the
> tongue-tied lascivious witnesses of great creatures' wantonness.
>
> (*The Malcontent*, I.vii)

The lively phrasing here is at odds with the ostensible moral purpose – it is true that Mendoza is gulling Pietro, having cuckolded him himself, but his speech is in the same style as the Malcontent's own speeches; the literary exhibitionism accompanies a confusion of dramatic motives. Tourneur's railing is more surely realised; it is presented in the older and simpler dramatic mode:

> *Vendice:* Now 'tis full sea abed over the world:
> There's juggling of all sides; some that were maids
> E'en at sunset, are now perhaps i' the toll-book.
> This woman in immodest thin apparel
> Lets in her friend by water; here a dame
> Cunning nails leather hinges to a door,
> To avoid proclamation.
> Now cuckolds are coining apace, apace, apace, apace!
> And careful sisters spin that thread in the night
> That does maintain them and their bawds i' the day.
> *Hippolito:* You flow well, brother.
> *Vendice:* Pooh! I'm shallow yet;
> Too sparing and too modest; shall I tell thee?
> If every trick were told that's dealt by night,
> There are few here that would not blush outright.

The direct appeal to the audience, as Miss Bradbrook remarks, is bathetic (*Themes and Conventions*, p. 173); but it is significant of the condition of success for the first speech, Tourneur's single-minded attitude towards subject and audience together. The shaping influence is that of the Moralities, transmitted directly through Jonson.

It was this influence which enabled him to use the Revenge conventions so successfully. His main preoccupations appear in his first work, *The Transformed Metamorphosis*, clumsily set forth in the form of a vision. The institutions of church and state, and even the objects of the physical world, are perverted from their original and proper functions; Pan, for example, the church, has become a 'hellish ill o're-mask'd with holiness' – 'Pan with gold is metamorphosed.' The Prologue describes the poet's bewilderment at the Cimmerian darkness in which he finds himself:

> Are not the lights that Jupiter appointed
> To grace the heav'ns, and to direct the sight,
> Still in that function, which them first anointed,
> Is not the world directed by their light?
> And is not rest, the exercise of night?
> Why is the sky so pitchy then at noon,
> As though the day were govern'd by the Moon?

This has the naïvety, the misplacement of emotion, that finds its counterpart in the cynicism of *The Revenger's Tragedy*. The conceits are painstakingly clumsy because Tourneur is genuinely bewildered; he treats them as if they were literal statements of fact. It is evident, however, that they are not affectations of style, as with many of his contemporaries, but organic parts of his thought. The symbolism of the poem reappears in the play, in the pervasive imagery of metamorphosis, falsification and moral camouflage. It has been thoroughly assimilated to the rhythms of dramatic speech:

> Last revelling night,
> When torch-light made an artificial noon
> About the court, some courtiers in the masque,
> Putting on better faces than their own,
> Being full of fraud and flattery . . .

> (I.iv)

> Ha, what news here? is the day out o' the socket,
> That it is noon at midnight? the court up?

> (II.iv)

The details are worked out in relation to a central group of metaphors, repeated, on the level of action, in the disguises and deceptions which compose the plot. Here again, the method is derived from the Moralities.

These disguises and deceptions are symbolic, not naturalistic – an occasion is even created for making Castiza herself appear in a false character. Vendice is disguised three times – when, as Piato, he enters 'the world' and becomes 'a man o' the time', a court pander; a second time, when he appears as a fantastic 'character' of himself, a melancholy, litigious scholar; and finally, as a masquer. The disguises are distinguished from the disguiser; what Vendice does in his assumed roles affects his character as Vendice, but the relationship is circumscribed and conventional; no provision is made to render it plausible, realistically, that Vendice would or could have sustained his roles.[4] When he tempts his sister, he is not Vendice in disguise, he is Vendice-become-Piato; Piato and Vendice are sharply distinguished. Nevertheless, Vendice suffers for what Piato has to do; and the separate roles, moreover, are complementary to each other. At first, Vendice is the honest malcontent, the nobleman wronged and depressed by poverty; then he becomes a member of the society that has wronged him. He is sardonically aware of himself in his role, as if necessity, not policy, had changed him, just as it threatens to change his mother (this is the way in which Flamineo and Bosola fuse the roles of villain and critic). He is morally involved in his actions as Piato; and when he appears in the conventional fatal masque, he is justly the victim as well as the instrument of heavenly vengeance. The second disguise is a caricature of his original position. Thus the different roles are not linked together by reference to circumstantial probability, but by reference to the dramatic and social functions of the original character, as with Edgar in *Lear*. The disguisings are related symbols of a transformation within the moral and social order.

Symbolic disguising with a similar dramatic purpose was a stock convention of the Moralities; sometimes there is a change of dress, sometimes only of name. This was not merely a convention of the stage; it embodied popular beliefs about the methods of the Deceiver – 'the devil hath power / To assume a pleasing shape'. Thus, in Medwall's *Nature*, Pride and Covetise beguile Man under the names of Worship and Worldly Policy, the other Deadly Sins being disguised in the same way. Moreover, the disguisers, besides their attributes as moral types, are usually given, more specifically than any other figures in the play, the attributes of a particular social class. Man, in *Nature*, is a noble, but he is made representative of humanity in general; it is emphasised, on the other hand, that Pride is a knight, and the Deadly Sins only appear as officers of the household. In the later Moralities, social themes, as distinct from theological, become more prominent; and the moral role of the disguisers is often completely merged into their role as the agents of social change.[5] In the Marian play, *Respublica*, for example, the Reformation is engineered by the profiteer Avarice, disguised as Policy; and the characters with aliases in *The Tyde Taryeth No Man* are the broker, Hurtful Help, who operates under the deceptive title of Help, and his accomplices.

The disguisers are contrasted with the other characters in that the latter represent the permanent and unequivocal moral standards which maintain social stability. Even in the middle-class Moralities of the sixteenth century, the disguisers – and the vices in general –

frequently stand for 'usury' in its various forms;[6] the other characters, for its opponents and victims. Traditional ethics under the
Tudors subsume social and economic questions directly under moral
categories; the system rests on the belief that the social order has
been established by Nature in accordance with the divine will. This is
expounded by Nature herself at the beginning of Medwall's play:

> Th' almighty God that made each creature,
> As well in heaven as other place earthly,
> By His wise ordinance hath purveyed me, Nature,
> To be as minister, under Him immediately,
> For th' enchesoun [*the reason*] that I should, perpetually,
> His creatures in such degree maintain
> As it hath pleased His grace for them to ordain.

This is the ethic of a society predominantly agricultural, in which
'everything ... seemed to be the gift of nature, the obvious way of
life, and thus the result of the Divine ordering, whether as a good gift
or as a penalty'.[7] In order to enjoy the divine bounty, to maintain
each individual in the sufficiency appropriate to the station in which
he was born, it was necessary to observe the conditions on which it
was given; and the satisfaction of the profit-motive, of 'greed', or,
equally, the wasteful gratification of selfish pleasure, whether on the
part of knight, burgher or peasant, interfered with this primary
necessity. They were 'against nature', contrary to the obvious expression of the divine will. Opportunities for personal aggrandise-
ment, by means of capital investment, organising ability
or technical innovation, were, relatively, too few and unimportant,
before the sixteenth century, seriously to disturb this traditional
order; and it seemed evident that they could only be taken at
someone else's expense. By the end of the century, as commercial
enterprise, money power and new industrial techniques began to
dominate economic life, they seemed to involve a change in the
whole relationship between man and nature, between the individual
and his vocation.[8] To conservative minds, it meant the substitution
of appearances for realities.

Hence, while the Elizabethans applied the Morality conventions
of disguise to a variety of new purposes, the earlier associations were
not lost. The tradition of dramatic allegory, with disguising as an
essential part, was also maintained by the Court masque; and
Cynthia's Revels, in particular, with its satire on the social climbers
and rootless adventurers infesting the Court, is avowedly a
combination of masque and Morality. 'The night is come', says one

of the Children in the Induction, explaining the plot, 'and Cynthia intends to come forth ... All the courtiers must provide for revels; they conclude upon a masque, the device of which is ... that each of these Vices, being to appear before Cynthia, would seem to be other than indeed they are; and therefore assume the most neighbouring Virtues as a masquing habit.' Here Jonson turns the popular ethic against the courtly, the Morality against the masque; for it was the convention of the masques that the courtiers who came to dance as virtues or deities were in fact the incarnations of the qualities they assumed; the masque itself was a social institution, representing the Court as the magnificent embodiment of the virtues by right of which it claimed to govern. *The Malcontent*, *Women Beware Women* and *The Revenger's Tragedy* make ironic use of this function of disguisings in the masque. In Tourneur's case, especially, the masque, as a symbol of courtly riot, is treated from the point of view of the Morality. The courtiers in the masque described by Antonio are Morality Vices –

> Putting on better faces than their own
> Being full of fraud and flattery;

and, throughout the play, descriptions of revels form the nucleus of the satire, leading up to the fatal masque at the end. They are associated with the references to bastardy and prostitution, and to 'patrimonies washed a-pieces', and with the images of cosmetics and of justice 'gilt o'er' with favour. Against the 'forgetful feasts' is set the image of the skeleton. The corruption of the Court by wealth and luxury, and its violation of the moral order which justifies high rank, is set beside the effects of usury, both alike overthrowing the standards of nature. Virtue and honour, on the other hand, are identified, as in Castiza's first soliloquy, with the norms of the traditional manorial order, which Tourneur makes to stand for social norms in general. Several of his metaphors are taken from the payment of rents – vengeance, for example, is a 'quit-rent'.

Professor Wilson Knight's description of the structure of a Shakespearean play, then, is peculiarly appropriate to *The Revenger's Tragedy* also: it is 'an expanded metaphor, by means of which the original vision has been projected into forms roughly correspondent with actuality, conforming thereto ... according to the demands of its nature'.[9] The central metaphors, and the technique of presentation, are the products of medieval ways of thought, as they had taken shape on the stage in the conventions of the Moralities. With his narrow and hypersensitive mentality, his imperviousness to the psychological make-up of individuals, and his intense preoccupation with ethics, Tourneur could not have written successful drama except by means of their example.[10]

The total impression created by the development of his plot, by the figures of the lecherous old Duke and his court, by the imagery and rhythms of the verse, is that of a hectic excitement, a perverse and over-ripe vitality on the verge of decay; the themes of the *danse macabre*, suggested in *Hamlet* and *The Malcontent*, dominate *The Revenger's Tragedy*. But the satire is not hysterical; Tourneur maintains an alert sardonic irony which makes its objects grotesque as well as disgusting. The sense of proportion expressed in the style is not that of the Revenge plays; it comes from the Moralities, and from Jonson. Jonson's influence is most apparent in the scene where Vendice tempts his mother and sister; the subject is from *The Malcontent*, the style from *Volpone*:[11]

> *Vendice:* Would I be poor, dejected, scorned of greatness,
> Swept from the palace, and see other daughters
> Spring with the dew o' the court, having mine own
> So much desired and loved – by the duke's son?
> No, I would raise my state upon her breast,
> And call her eyes my tenants; I would count
> My yearly maintenance upon her cheeks,
> Take coach upon her lip, and all her parts
> Should keep men after men, and I would ride
> In pleasure upon pleasure . . .
>
> How blessed are you! you have happiness alone;
> Others must fall to thousands, you to one,
> Sufficient in himself to make your forehead
> Dazzle the world with jewels, and petitionary people
> Start at your presence . . .

These passages are not mere echoes of Jonsonian phrasing; they have the energetic hyperbole and the finely measured scorn of Jonson's best manner. The scene continues with a passage of brilliant extravaganza:

> *Vendice:* O, think upon the pleasures of the palace!
> Secured ease and state! the stirring meats,
> Ready to move out of the dishes, that e'en now
> Quicken when they are eaten!
> Banquets abroad by torchlight! music! sports!
> Bareheaded vassals, that had ne'er the fortune
> To keep on their own hats, but let horns wear 'em!
> Nine coaches waiting – hurry, hurry, hurry –

Castiza: Ay, to the devil.
Vendice: Ay, to the devil! (*Aside*) To the duke, by my faith.
Gratiana: Ay, to the duke: daughter, you'd scorn to think o' the devil, an
you were there once.

(II.i)

The excitement of these passages is hardly the product of a
nightmare vision. On the contrary, it is controlled and directed by a
sense of the crude realities underlying the court's fantastic
behaviour. The source and character of Tourneur's grotesquerie is
indicated, again, by Spurio's soliloquy:

> Faith, if the truth were known, I was begot
> After some gluttonous dinner; some stirring dish
> Was my first father, when deep healths went round,
> And ladies' cheeks were painted red with wine,
> Their tongues, as short and nimble as their heels,
> Uttering words sweet and thick; and when they rose,
> Were merrily disposed to fall again.

(I.ii)

The nervous and sinister tones of the mockery are balanced by the
'primitive' realism.

Nevertheless, Tourneur does not escape from his cycle of decay;
there is nothing in the play, in its scheme of moral and social values,
to compensate for Vendice's fall. In the process of commercial
development, which had brought new hopes and possibilities to the
middle classes, Tourneur saw only that the Court had been uprooted
from the people and the soil, while the old-fashioned gentry were left
to their honour, their poverty and their discontent. As, throughout
the sixteenth century, landlord and ploughman alike had been
submitted to a growing dependence on money, and their customary
incomes had proved inadequate to meet rising costs and a rising
standard of living, the stability of the old hierarchy had broken
down. Many of the nobility and gentry were forced to give up their
'hospitality' or to sell their estates; and their successors and
survivors, knowing, with Burghley, that 'gentility is nothing else but
ancient riches', had acted accordingly.[12] The nobility themselves had
become enclosers, joint stock-holders, company-promoters,
monopolists; the Court, at the turn of the century, was the happy
hunting-ground for adventurers and profiteers. Until the end of
Elizabeth's reign, this commercialisation of the nobility was in
harmony with the main economic and political needs of the middle

classes: but when the latter had outgrown their royal tutelage, the powers of the Court became obstructive; and when titles were sold and honours conferred on irresponsible favourites, it became clear that the system of Court privileges opened the way to the machiavellian and the sycophant. The fount of honour was poisoned at the source. While 'the disproportion between honour and means' became more glaring, large numbers of the lesser gentry, deprived of the security of the old order, found themselves landless men, dependent on an uncertain or an insufficient patronage, men without 'vocations'.[13] Tourneur's Vendice is one of the dramatic spokesmen of these malcontents. His independence belongs to the past; the present is contaminated by the values of 'gold'. On the basis of this contrast, which is extended to society as a whole, Tourneur's poetry formulates an exceptionally coherent response to the life of his time. But the business of buying and selling, the accumulation of wealth without social responsibility, which has hoisted sensuality to its evil eminence in his court, is accepted as normative and final; it becomes a process by which the values of nature and the impulses which go to maintaining a civilised life are inevitably decomposed into their opposites. This conception forms the organising principle in Vendice's second speech to the skull, where the complex themes and symbols of the whole play are concentrated into a single magnificent passage.

The irony of this speech is reinforced by the dramatic situation: 'all the betrayed women are in a sense represented by the poisoned skull of Vendice's mistress – not only she herself, but Antonio's wife, Castiza, who would have been betrayed, and the imaginary "country lady" whom the Duke thought he was about to seduce'.[14] Similarly, 'yon fellow' is the imaginary profligate turned highwayman, the approaching Duke, and the Duchess's youngest son, who has already appeared under judgement for rape, and is ironically despatched in the next scene. Thus the skull becomes the fitting symbol, as it is the final result, of the process represented by the action and the imagery, in which solid realities are exchanged for treacherous appearances. The metaphor of 'exchange' is important; Vendice's irony turns, in this speech, on the ambiguities of the word 'for', referring both to equivalence in exchange and to purpose or result. In the first lines, a complex group of relationships are associated in the image contrasting the 'labours' of the worm – physically present in 'expend' and 'undo' – with the silken bedizenment of the lady for whom they are undertaken, a contrast which appears, at the same

time, as one between the silk and the skeleton it covers; it is for the
skull that the labours are ultimately intended. The 'silkworm' is also
the worm of the grave; it suggests, too, the poor weaver, 'undone' for
the sake of the wealthy – the contrast between rich and poor is made
explicit in the next speech; and the colours of the silk and of the gold
which is paid for it are made flat and wan by the suggested
comparison with her 'yellow' face. The speech is developed round a
further series of exchanges:

> Does the silkworm expend her yellow labours
> For thee? for thee does she undo herself?
> Are lordships sold to maintain ladyships
> For the poor benefit of a bewitching minute?
> Why does yon fellow falsify highways
> And put his life between the judge's lips,
> To refine such a thing, keeps horse and men
> To beat their valours for her?
> Surely we're all mad people, and they
> Whom we think are, are not; we mistake those,
> 'Tis we are mad in sense, they but in clothes.

> (III.v)

In the third and fourth lines, the process of commercial exchange is
again ironically invoked; the social stability implied by 'lordships'
and 'maintained' is undermined in the colloquial sarcasm of
'ladyships', and the 'bewitching minute' of lust is a 'poor benefit' to
exchange for an inherited estate – 'poor', too, in the sense that
procreation is made futile. 'Bewitching' recalls the earlier scene in
which it was suggested that Gratiana's attempt to prostitute her
daughter was due to diabolic possession; it detaches Vendice from
the dissolution he contemplates and yet implies that it is inescapable.
'Yon fellow' implicates the Duke and his stepson as well as the
broken gallant, so that 'falsify' attaches to the royal justice itself
together with the royal highway. There is also a suppressed pun on
counterfeit coinage, which, with the corrosive impression of 'falsify',
is carried on in the next lines: by his emphasis on the root senses of
the verbs ('maintain', 'falsify', 'refine'), Tourneur sets up a
characteristic tension between the imagined activities and the ideal
relationships to which they ought to conform. In the old
dispensation – as in Medwall's play – Nature had appointed Reason
to govern Sensuality; here, Reason has been overturned. It takes its
revenge, against the irrationality of the 'bewitching minute', in the
contrast between the life and the moment of sentence. The
judgement is also the Last Judgement. As before, the mounting

rhythm then returns, after a pause, to the slow, heavy syllables referring to the skull, the final cause, it is suggested, as it is the final stage, of the whole movement – 'to refine such a thing'. The phrase, coming at this point, implies both that the overlay of 'refinement' on her 'ladyship' is as futile, and as deathly, as the poisoned cosmetic on the skull, and that this comparison actually clarifies a state of affairs present wherever bones are clothed with flesh. The next phrase again catches in its puns the self-destruction of a powerful stimulus; 'keeps' relates it to 'maintains', four lines above; 'beat their valours' refers primarily to the fierce courage of the highwaymen, but 'beats' also means 'abates', and 'valours' are 'values' – once again the purchase of death for life. Thus the perversion of the impulses making for life finds its culminating expression in the image of violent action, and the activity is simultaneously nullified by means of the puns. The last three lines generalise what has already been revealed to the senses. Just as the great lady of the first lines has dissolved into her 'ladyship', so all seeming realities have been reduced to the skull; so that to murder the Duke with the poisoned skull is a fully appropriate revenge.

Tourneur's symbols, then, are organised by applying to the contemporary world the standards of the medieval social tradition, as it had survived through the sixteenth century. But *The Revenger's Tragedy*, with its alternation between finely wrought passages of high mental and nervous tension and passages of clumsy sententious generalisation, represents an emotional equilibrium which Tourneur evidently could not maintain. He had profited by the example of Jonson, who had remodelled the Morality drama, with its barely delineated types and its sparse, loosely connected incidents, into something solid and closely-knit; but Jonson's mind was the more elastic, more confident of the permanent validity of his standards, more independent and detached. His dramatic structures allow of a varied interplay of motives and experiences; Tourneur's do not. In *The Revenger's Tragedy* he succeeded in directing the response to his situation by presenting Morality figures who express, or arouse, acute and powerful, but narrowly restricted emotions. When, instead of dealing with types, he tried to examine individual motives, and to argue out the reasons for his judgements, he failed. By comparison with the earlier play, *The Atheist's Tragedy* is abstract and forced. The best passages, such as the description of Charlemont's supposed death at Ostend, are set speeches, almost independent of their dramatic contexts; the symbolism is mechanical, the poetic theorising lame and unconvincing. Charlemont, who, unlike Vendice, leaves his revenge to heaven, is an uninteresting paragon; and D'Amville's villainy and Castabella's innocence are so naïvely paraded that Tourneur defeats his purpose – if Castiza's shrill chastity were emphasised in the same way, so that the puppet became a person, she would be nauseating. Charlemont and his father have some of the virtues Tourneur attributed to Vere and Salisbury; but when he comes to offer his positive values, they are formal and, dramatically, lifeless.

With Jonson and *The Revenger's Tragedy*, the influence of the medieval tradition virtually came to an end. None of the Stuart dramatists whose main work came later – with the partial exception of Massinger, in his comedies – attempted to revive it; the trend of dramatic writing was towards semi- or pseudo-naturalism. Webster fumbled with the Revenge conventions in the effort to develop something relatively new to the stage – to excite varied or conflicting sympathies for individuals at odds with their surroundings. His picture of society resembles Tourneur's; but the Morality elements, which had represented for the latter the dramatic equivalents for a central core of judgements and feelings, have disappeared; and Webster, unable to come to rest on any attitude, from which to value his people, more stable or more penetrating than a pose of stoical bravado, could not write coherent drama at all. Where they are not simply melodrama, his plays depend on exploiting immediate sensations, disjointed from their dramatic contexts; and this applies not only to his stagecraft, but to his verse, which works by analogous means, and which gains, as Tourneur's loses, from quotation in short passages. His plays, with their unrealised 'sense of tragic issues' in the individual, point towards a dramatic reorientation, a development from Shakespeare, which they do not themselves achieve. After Shakespeare, the only dramatist to achieve such a reorientation was Middleton.

13. *The Changeling* and the drama of domestic life

In one of the earliest of critical allusions to Middleton, Leigh Hunt observed that 'there is one character of his (De Flores in *The Changeling*) which, for effect at once tragical, probable, and poetical, surpasses anything I know of in the drama of domestic life'.[1] The terms of Leigh Hunt's praise were happily chosen, especially if in his brief classification he meant to distinguish *drama* from *tragedy*. For *The Changeling* is a serious, exciting play, a drama of strongly tragical cast, without quite attaining that plenary combination of emotional intensity with imaginative range for which *tragedy* would be the only appropriate description. It is a tragedy in form, of course, but not in the full possible effect. And its limitations, together with its special kind of intensity, appear to spring from its concentration upon domestic life as its subject.

Although *The Changeling* and *Women Beware Women* were by far the outstanding achievements of the London theatres in the later years of James I, and quite distinctive in their point of view, they were typical of the day in the kind of subject-matter they offered. 'Our pulpits', wrote John Chamberlain the news-reporter early in 1620, 'ring continually of the insolence and impudence of women' (he had already noted that the campaign had been orchestrated from the throne), 'and to helpe the matter forward the players have likewise taken them to taske, and so to the ballades and ballad-singers, so that they can come nowhere but theyre eares tingle.'[2] As far as plays are concerned, in one sense Chamberlain exaggerates, since they were at least as likely to defend or idealise women as to denounce them; but he hardly exaggerates the interest taken in feminine morals – an interest advertised by such titles, from the years about 1619–20, as *All's Lost by Lust*, *The Fatal Dowry*, *The Double Marriage* and *The Virgin Martyr*. All these were nominally tragedies; and most nominal tragedies of the day still kept the convention that their leading characters were of princely rank or near it. But whereas early in the reign tragic stories of domestic passion had been intermingled with 'state-affairs' (as in *Othello* or *Bussy D'Ambois*), 'state-affairs' now amounted to no more than a background or a dramatic pretext for a sexual intrigue; and *The Duchess of Malfi* (c. 1614) was the last play for many years to connect private and political morality in anything approaching an inclusive tragic vision. Meanwhile, comedy was losing satiric drive and the enjoyment of hard-headed intrigue in favour of tragi-comedy in Fletcher's manner. The contrast between Middleton's *A Trick to Catch the Old One* (c. 1605) and Massinger's *A New Way to Pay Old Debts* (c. 1625) typifies two generations; although Massinger takes over the essentials of Middleton's plot, he turns it almost into a tract. He is not more observant than Middleton about social behaviour and class distinctions, but he is much more in earnest, creating a Fletcherian melodrama rather than a comedy of intrigue. Nevertheless, Fletcher's style of playwriting was not the only style, influential as it was. A number of serious plays of the period, such as *A Fair Quarrel*, *The Witch of Edmonton* and *The English Traveller*, are neither tragedies *manqués* nor Fletcherian bravura pieces (though they are classified as 'tragi-comedy'). Nor again, though their subject-matter is domestic, are they simply didactic, like Heywood's earlier *A Woman Killed with Kindness*. At their best, these plays present, in the form of a dilemma rather than a sermon, topical problems of social life – the duelling code, the persecution of witches, incompatible marriages. They hardly constitute between them a new and distinct genre in the theatre, but they already contain some of the main ingredients of the *drame bourgeois* and the problem play of the eighteenth and nineteenth centuries. And they bring out the dominant concern of the theatres in the years round about 1620 with middle- and upper-class family life.

Two factors in particular help to account for this trend. One was the contraction of the national, miscellaneous theatre-going public of Shakespeare's day, and the consequently increased preponderance of the leisure-class audiences in the private playhouses in London. The other was the strain on the position of the gentry, made manifest by the aggressive mood of the Parliament that assembled in 1621, which brought about the downfall of Buckingham's kinsman, Mompesson, and the impeachment of Lord Chancellor Bacon.[3] Parliament was alarmed by the trading depression and the King's foreign policy, but there were also more widespread causes for disquiet. On one side, the gentry were hereditary landowners and potential servants of the Crown: 'Gentlemen are *nobiles inferiores*', as Coke reminded the Commons in 1621, 'the Lords are but *nobiles superiores*.'[4] But honours were cheapened by the sale of titles, preferment at Court was blocked by Buckingham's clan, and the King's leaning towards Spain appeared to threaten religion while denying to the aristocracy their traditional aspiration to profits and glory from war (nostalgia for military honours is a frequent theme with Fletcher's and Massinger's heroes). On the other side, the landed gentry were both rivals and allies to the merchants of the City. If they were often their debtors, they were also their business associates, eager to share in a 'free trade', and allied to them by marriage (it is significant that both in *A Trick to Catch the Old One* and in *A New Way to Pay Old Debts* the grasping City man is no stranger to the young heir, but his uncle); moreover, their whole style of living took them increasingly away from their country estates into London. For many, therefore, their actual position in society was at variance with their theoretical role. They resisted when the King tried to force them back to their duties as county magistrates at a time of economic unrest; but even a parliamentary oppositionist like Sir James Parrot could agree with the King in 1621 that one of the principal causes of 'the present decaie and weaknes of the Kingdome' was 'the prodigallitye of the Gentrie by bringing their wives soe much to London'.[5] Moral indignation over women's dress and behaviour was another aspect of the same complaint. Nevertheless, a cool observer could see that mere anti-feminism dealt at most with the symptoms of a social malaise and not its underlying causes; in the letter where Chamberlain reports the King's instructions to preachers in 1620 'to inveigh vehemently against the insolencie of our women' he adds that 'the truth is the world is very much out of order, but whether this will mende it God knowes'.[6] On the stage, what was virtually a debate over the honour of women was only part of a wider questioning or reaffirming of the general idea of honour, as the conceptual basis and justification of the social status of the gentry.

For a traditional theorist like Henry Peacham, genuine honour, as distinct from a purchased title, was 'the reward of Virtue and glorious Actions onely', but the 'Honour of blood' in a true noble or gentleman was 'innate', 'inherent and Naturall' like the lustre of a 'Diamond', infixed in 'the Frame of the whole Universe'[7] and commanding social privilege, including privileged treatment by the aw.[8] Massinger upholds a similar conception, in spite of or even because of the irrationalities it involves. For example, in *The Fatal Dowry* (written in collaboration with Nathan Field, *c.* 1619), he pits the inherited military honour of young Charalois against the mercenary and frivolous values of the City, and finally against the levelling tendencies of the law. Rewarded with the gift of a wealthy bride for the self-sacrifice he has undertaken in order to redeem his dead father's reputation, Charalois then finds his wife in adultery with the City upstart, young Novall. He kills them both, like a Spanish vindicator of the *pundonor*. His father-in-law, an upright justice, is torn between moral approval and his feelings as a father. In the closing scene, before a hostile public court, Charalois is acquitted for his integrity, 'notwithstanding you have gone beyond / The letter of the law' – though at the last moment he is murdered by a partisan of young Novall in an act of private revenge. In this way the dramatists suggest an uneasy compromise between the mystique of honour and the doctrine of retribution. But the main function of the tragic business in plays like this is to exalt the ideal of honour by submitting it to extravagant tests.

Middleton's attitude is entirely different (or the attitude he shares with Rowley in their close collaboration in *The Changeling* (1622)). The realism he is often praised for is partly a matter of creating an impression of credible surroundings from common life, and partly a matter of mental scale; he measures extravagance in his characters' thoughts by tacit comparison with the normal. This in turn has much to do with his unusual psychological penetration, his gift for exposing velleities and self-deception in his characters. Above all, Middleton's realism is a quality of moral judgement, an insistence on the unavoidable. 'Can you weep fate from its determin'd purpose?' – the terrible resonance of this line comes, not from De Flores's brutal self-assertion, and still less from any hint of an external destiny, but from the revelation of a natural force. 'Lust and forgetfulness has been amongst us', Hippolito exclaims, towards the end of *Women Beware Women*: the tragic shock for Middleton's characters is the recognition of moral facts they have always known, but have induced themselves to forget.

Middleton's realism includes social as well as psychological insight. In his best plays he sketches out a social community, however divided within itself, and the comic or tragic aberrations of his leading characters are aberrations that social intercourse permits, encourages or fosters.[9] In this respect he stands at the opposite pole to a dramatist like Massinger. Social standards in his plays are created by men, not for them; honour is not an absolute but a social convention. More than that, it can become a dangerous illusion, an instrument of self-destruction. What finally betrays Beatrice Joanna is precisely the confidence in her birth and status that she has absorbed from the society around her. And *The Changeling* is not merely a character-portrait of a perverse young woman, but a study in what can fairly be called class-consciousness.

A distinctive note in his characters is the homely way they usually express their feelings, with little of that grandeur so often assumed in earlier Jacobean tragedies. In *The Changeling*, Alsemero – the traveller, as we soon learn – thinks of marriage as his natural 'home', man's 'right home back, if he achieve it' (I.i.9); Beatrice thinks of her 'joys and comforts' (II.i.96; II.ii.32); De Flores demands to be 'eas'd' of his passion, and promises Beatrice 'peace' when she surrenders (III.iv.99, 169). Their inward goal, it seems, is commonplace tranquillity. And their language is charged with allusions to religion, in phrases like 'I keep the same church', 'I shall change my saint', 'Requests that holy prayers ascend heaven for', or 'heaven has married her to joys eternal'. These phrases come from scenes that have been attributed separately to Rowley and to Middleton,[10] and their similarity shows how closely the two writers must have worked together. But they belong in any case to the common idiom of the time. Except for Alsemero's opening soliloquy, the characters are not thinking deliberately about religion, but (with whatever unconscious irony) using religious phrases casually and unreflectingly, for the sake of affirmation. Theirs is a religion of convention, part of their feeling of security in their world.

Yet a hint of insecurity is sounded from the outset, as Alsemero questions his own impulse:

> 'Twas in the temple where I first beheld her,
> And now again the same; what omen yet
> Follows of that? None but imaginary;
> Why should my hopes or fate be timorous?
> The place is holy, so is my intent.

He voices a doubt only to suppress it, but for insufficient reason, relying illogically on the building, 'the temple'. So too Vermandero counts on the security of his castle, the principal 'place' in the drama, when he cautiously extends a welcome to Alsemero:

> I must know
> Your country; we use not to give survey

> Of our chief strengths to strangers; our citadels
> Are plac'd conspicuous to outward view,
> On promonts' tops; but within are secrets.
>
> (I.i.162)

Vermandero commands 'a most spacious and impregnable fort' (III.i.4), in which however the 'secrets' are hidden from his own knowledge, in the retired rooms which lovers but also eavesdroppers can use and in the 'narrow' stairways and dark corridors where Alonzo and then Diaphanta can be lured to their deaths. It has a moral as well as a physical existence in the play.[11] It stands for the 'labyrinth' where Beatrice loses herself (III.iv.71). And in the shock of the last scene a glimpse of this double meaning rushes into her father's unsuspecting mind: 'An host of enemies enter'd my citadel / Could not amaze like this' (V.iii.147). In military terms the 'secrets' provide the 'strengths' of the fortress, but in moral terms it is the apparent 'strengths' that make possible the 'secrets'.

Both Alsemero and Beatrice lay great store by rational 'judgement' (again, in speeches probably written by each of the dramatists).[12] But like the citadel, 'judgement' gives a false sense of security, hiding and sanctioning irrational desires. Again and again in the early scenes the characters show themselves headstrong or petulant, or attribute to others disturbed feelings that evidently belong to themselves. Alsemero, the reasoner, is the first in the play to 'change' (I.i.34), but when Jasperino asks him 'What might be the cause?', his retort seems more a reflex of his own mood than of anything in his friend's question: 'Lord, how violent / Thou art!' (I.i.40). There is no apparent provocation for Beatrice's rage against De Flores, and Alsemero can only explain it away as 'a frequent frailty in our nature' – without considering how far, in the end, his explanation may stretch (I.i.93–128). Jasperino calls himself a 'mad wag' in his flirtation with Diaphanta, giving occasion for the first mention of the madhouse in the sub-plot. In one of the many asides of the play, emphasising the contrast between professed and intimate feelings, Beatrice admits to herself 'a giddy turning' in her affections (I.i.56); and when Vermandero announces that Alonzo is 'hot preparing' for the wedding, she accuses her father of being 'violent', much as Alsemero had accused Jasperino (I.i.189–91). This leads on to a three-part refrain about 'will': 'I'll want / My will else', says Vermandero about the marriage he has planned; Beatrice rejoins in an aside, 'I shall want mine if you do it'; and after the short though significant incident with her gloves, De Flores, alone, brings the scene to an end with

> No matter, if but to vex her, I'll haunt her still;
> Though I get nothing else, I'll have my will.

By this point the word 'will' has clearly taken on its secondary meaning of sexual desire,[13] but the more general sense is still predominant. Vermandero is the brusque, affable commandant, fond of his only daughter but remote from her (as Brabantio had been remote from Desdemona). He is a man of duty, but, as he shows later, when Tomazo comes to claim justice from him (IV.ii), his self-regarding 'honour', with its strain of authoritative bluster, comes first. In the opening scene, he overbears Alsemero, good-naturedly enough but obstinately, when the latter – for the second time in the play – changes his mind: 'How, sir? By no means; / ... You must see my castle, / ... I shall think myself unkindly us'd else' (I.i.200–3). And in the same strain he goes on to boast of the match he has arranged: 'I tell you, sir, the gentleman's complete, / ... I would not change him for a son-in-law / For any he in Spain ...' – and so on, with a sting of sarcasm when Alsemero can only offer him a minimally polite congratulation:

> Als.:   He's much
>   Bound to you, sir.
> Ver.:   He shall be bound to me,
>   As fast as this tie [Beatrice] can hold him; I'll want
>   My will else.
>
>   (I.i.212–19)

Both of the men are embarrassed, for reasons that have nothing to do with the overt course of their conversation; what troubles Vermandero is any challenge to his authority, particularly from his own daughter. The context, then, of the word 'will' here is a struggle within the family, and this gives the plain sense that Beatrice intends in her aside. Even when De Flores repeats the word with a perceptible sexual overtone, his chief meaning is not that he expects to 'have [his] will' of Beatrice in the sense of raping her, but that he is determined to 'haunt her still', 'if but' (no more than) 'to vex her'; he 'cannot choose but love her', but he refuses to be humiliated by her contempt. The guiding thread throughout the long opening scene is wilfulness, self-assertion as opposed to 'judgement'. Similarly, Alonzo will brush aside his brother's warning that Beatrice's 'dulness' towards him bodes ill for his 'peace' if he persists in marrying her. 'Why, here is love's tame madness' is Tomazo's comment; and, echoing the word De Flores had applied to Beatrice, 'thus a man / Quickly steals into his vexation' (II.i.124–55). The point is not that Alonzo is exceptionally passionate, but that he has disregarded the plain evidence in front of him, rather than admit that he has made a mistake.

Beatrice is the second character in the play to change. No sooner has she delivered her sage if coquettish admonition to her fresh suitor about 'judgement' and 'rashness' than she wishes, in her first aside,

> For five days past
> To be recall'd! Sure, mine eyes were mistaken . . .
>
> (I.i.84)

She can lie to herself as well as to others, and her revulsion from De Flores – who believes that 'she knows no cause for't but a peevish will' (I.i.107) – represses a kind of fascination. So much is apparent when, at the end of the opening scene, she furiously throws down her glove as if to challenge or provoke him. In their second meeting on the stage, 'This ominous ill-fac'd fellow more disturbs me / Than all my other passions' (II.i.53) – before there has been any question of a murder.

There is a conflict, then, between the outward 'strength' of Beatrice's social position and the wishes and fears that possess her in secret. But she is presented as her father's daughter, sharing the imperiousness of the men who are her social equals, and accepting without question their system of ideas. And as Middleton unfolds her character in the scenes leading to the play's crisis, the masterstroke of his portrayal is the way the accepted ideas of her society become the excuse and even the prompting for her crime. In the source-story by Reynolds, the 'first plot and designe' of the murder comes from some 'darke and ambiguous speeches' that she 'lets fall' to Alsemero.[14] In the play, she utters no more than an indirect half-wish, and it is Alsemero who translates it into the thought of a killing, offering her the 'good service' of a challenge to his rival, as 'The honourablest piece 'bout man, valour' (II.ii.18–28). Even so, she fails to understand him for a moment, and then forbids the duel, not because she still hopes to win her father round, as in the source-story, but out of womanly fear and prudence:

> How? Call you that extinguishing of fear,
> When 'tis the only way to keep it flaming? . . .

Beatrice is placed in a similar position to Lady Ager in *A Fair Quarrel*, who tells her son a lie about her own chastity in order to prevent him from fighting a duel. But this time the woman's arguments have an entirely natural ring:

>   Pray, no more, sir.
> Say you prevail'd, y'are danger's and not mine then;
> The law would claim you from me, or obscurity
> Be made the grave to bury you alive . . .

This is the tenderest speech in the play, the moment where Beatrice is most appealingly feminine, and comes closest in sympathy to another human being:

> I'm glad these thoughts come forth; oh keep not one
> Of this condition, sir; here was a course
> Found to bring sorrow on her way to death:
> The tears would ne'er ha' dried, till dust had chok'd 'em . . .

But, with a fine subtlety of portrayal, Middleton makes her hide her thoughts at the very moment when she is claiming intimacy, and he makes the turning-point in her speech precisely her womanly sense of the fitness of things:

> Blood-guiltiness becomes a fouler visage,
> [*Aside*] – And now I think on one: I was to blame,
> I ha' marr'd so good a market with my scorn;
> 'T had been done questionless; the ugliest creature
> Creation fram'd for some use, yet to see
> I could not mark so much where it should be!
> Als.: Lady –
> Bea.: [*aside*] Why, men of art make much of poison,
> Keep one to expel another; where was my art?

Her thoughts conducing to murder are associated with 'law', housewifely thrift (the 'market'), the pride of a Jacobean gentlewoman in her knowledge of cures and simples ('my art') and, above all, religion and the social order; the fleeting image of a murderer wandering like Cain melts into the notion of decorum ('becomes') and hardens into the orthodox belief that 'the ugliest creature / Creation fram'd for some use'. Beatrice justifies her intended use of De Flores to herself exactly as a contemporary like Henry Peacham justifies the privileges of honour, as resulting from 'the Frame of the whole Universe'. In her own eyes, she is hiding her thoughts from her lover in the spirit of a mother deciding what is best for her child. But the dramatic paradox in her asides is that she borrows and identifies herself with Alsemero's proposal of 'valour' and 'service' in the very act of condemning it. The moral contradictions behind the duelling code, already criticised by Middleton and Rowley in *A Fair Quarrel*, here become part and parcel of the heroine's mind.

She has also borrowed from Alsemero the device of removing 'two fears' by a single stroke – in her view, De Flores as well as Alonzo. De Flores alarms her sexually, though she will not admit as much. His 'ugliness' is a brilliant invention by the dramatists – in the original story he had been simply 'a Gallant young Gentleman', 'a fit instrument to execute her will'[15] – since by an implicit black-and-white symbolism (not unlike that used later in *A Game at Chess*) it suggests the perverse fascination he holds for her as well as provoking her hyper-refined recoil. When she thinks of him to replace Alsemero as Alonzo's killer, she designates him, in spite of herself, as her champion, her man. Critics have debated whether her blindness to the price De Flores will demand can be psychologically convincing.[16] But here again Beatrice's social assumptions are important. There is a kind of tidiness, to her mind, in finding a 'use' for him. And, repellent though he is, he fits her purpose because he is a soldier and a 'gentleman'.[17] He can be trusted to combine violence with discretion. At the same time, she cannot imagine that a man so far beneath her in rank, disgraced by his deformity, could dream of touching the lady of the castle, the sought-after bride of some of the 'proudest' gallants in Spain, any more than she can perceive herself as contaminated by the murder she commissions from him. And this assumption would not have seemed astonishing to Jacobean spectators. For example, six years before *The Changeling* was written, after the *cause célèbre* of the Overbury murder – a parallel in some respects to Beatrice's crime – the King had commuted the death sentence on the Countess of Somerset, in view of 'the great and long service of her father, family, and friends', and with the excuse that 'she was not principal but accessory before the fact, and drawn to it by the instigation of base persons'. 'The common people take not this for good payment', Chamberlain had recorded at the time; and Chamberlain had been shocked that Somerset was to be seen in the Tower flaunting 'his garter and George about his neck' – 'a man lawfully and publicly convicted of so foul a fact ... But this age affords things as strange and incompatible.'[18] Beatrice's state of mind was no more 'incompatible' with the age. Her compact with De Flores provides a grim comment on contemporary 'honour' and chivalry.

'Payment' and 'service' are key terms in *The Changeling*. In the scenes leading to and following the murder, 'service' is spoken of again and again. Now, it has been pointed out, by Christopher Ricks, that *service* could have a sexual meaning (like a number of other words important in the play); and Ricks has argued that the essential drama turns on these ambiguities. Beatrice fails to see that she cannot have one kind of *service* from De Flores without the other; 'her failure is an egoistic single-mindedness, a tragic failure to see puns'.[19] This may be so, but it is much less than the play conveys. The dramatists are hardly suggesting that had Beatrice only been nimbler-witted, she could have got away with murder. *Service* is ambiguous socially as well as sexually; it can be privileged or lowborn, chivalric or mercenary, rewarded with love or honour or else paid for in cash. And this is the ambiguity that Beatrice plays upon (she is not 'single-minded' here) when she flatters De Flores with

> Hardness becomes the visage of a man well,
> It argues service, resolution, manhood,
> If cause were of employment...
>
> (II.ii.92)

deceiving him into responding (with a bad faith of his own) by begging for 'the honour of a service', in a gesture of chivalric devotion: 'It's a service that I kneel for to you' (II.ii.96, 117). Each tries to exploit the social duality of the idea, exchanging 'reverence' for a 'precious' 'reward' (II.ii.123, 130).

In the great central scene, the idea of payment is driven home, shattering Beatrice's illusions. In earlier plays, such as *A Chaste Maid in Cheapside* and *A Fair Quarrel*, Middleton had already used commercial metaphors to define ethical values, seriously or ironically. In the latter play, for example, Captain Ager withholds from his duel on the ground that

> he that makes his last peace with his Maker
> In anger, anger is his peace eternally:
> He must expect the same return again
> Whose venture is deceitful;

and the Physician blackmailing Jane after he has sheltered her from disgrace urges her with

> I will tell you, lady, a full quittance,
> And how you may become my creditress...
> Not in coin, mistress; for silver, though white,

> Yet it draws black lines; it shall not rule my palm
> There to mark forth his base corruption:
> Pay me again in the same quality
> That I to you tendered, – that is, love for love.[20]

De Flores retraces such arguments with a horrifying intensity when
Beatrice expects to satisfy him with money:

> Do you place me in the rank of verminous fellows,
> To destroy things for wages? Offer gold?
> The life blood of man! Is anything
> Valued too precious for my recompense?
>
> (III.iv.64)

There is devastating irony in his own choice of metaphor:

> I could ha' hir'd
> A journeyman in murder at this rate,
> And mine own conscience might have slept at ease
> And have had the work brought home.

For all the word-play of chivalry between them earlier, this
represents precisely what Beatrice had wanted to do. It is she who has
been 'forgetful', he says (94, 96); and in his passionate plea, 'Justice
invites your blood to understand me' (100), besides the sexual
vehemence there is the shock of an unmanageable truth. It is as if
indeed her virginity was the only possible 'recompense' for 'the life
blood of man'. Their dialogue pursues relentlessly the logic involved
in this primitive equation:

> Bea.: Think but upon the distance that creation
>   Set 'twixt thy blood and mine, and keep thee there.
> De F.: Look but into your conscience, read me there,
>   'Tis a true book, you'll find me there your equal . . .
>
> (III.iv.130)

For the moment, he speaks as a radical Puritan, and his 'true book' is
surely a book of accounts. His metaphors from the 'market' sweep
aside her supposed absolutes of 'blood', 'birth' and 'parentage'.

Every word in this dialogue sparkles with irony. Beatrice has
'chang'd', as he reminds her (143). As Antonio's role in the sub-plot
brings out, a *changeling* was a fool or half-wit. But it also meant a
turncoat, a renegade to nobility. In *The Nobles* (1563), for example,
Laurence Humphrey writes that 'Commonly the childe expresseth
his sire, and posterity (if not chaungeling) covets to tread the steps of
their auncestours', and that noblemen, 'if not chaungelynges,
encrease the praises of their auncestours with theyr owne prowesse';

and Shakespeare uses the word similarly when he makes Henry IV describe the Percys' followers as 'fickle changelings', or makes Aufidius declare that Coriolanus is 'no changeling' in pride, even though he has deserted from Rome to the Volscians.[21] It is a changeling status, in both senses, that De Flores fastens on Beatrice:

> Y'are the deed's creature; by that name
> You lost your first condition, and I challenge you,
> As peace and innocency has turn'd you out,
> And made you one with me.
>
> (III.iv.137)

'I challenge': he lays claim to her[22] – as someone might claim the legal guardianship of a changeling, or fool. At the same time, his lines recall her own latently Biblical image when she feared to think of Alsemero as a homeless outlaw. From this point forward, the whole movement of the play shows Beatrice's myth of 'creation' recoiling upon herself.

Apart from *Women Beware Women* (which may however have been the later of Middleton's two masterpieces), there is nothing else in Jacobean drama to compare with *The Changeling* for its penetrating analysis of a social myth. Clearly, Beatrice might have been, but is not, presented as an example of the 'insolencie' of women. Nor is she, essentially, the victim of contemporary marriage arrangements, though Isabella's role in the sub-plot helps to give a certain force to this consideration in the play. Beatrice makes her own hell; but she does so with the unconscious complicity of the men of her own rank around her, by blindly trusting in their prejudices and beliefs. Her mind is a mirror of social certitudes. Webster's Duchess of Malfi, whose tragedy Middleton and Rowley copied from and admired, had chosen a husband of lower rank virtuously or at least pardonably, but with the clear knowledge that she was defying the world. Beatrice plunges into the crime that makes her De Flores's partner in an unquestioning confidence that her world must be on her side.

At the same time, the thoroughness with which Beatrice's mind is dissected limits the total impact of the play; not that the playwrights are detached, but that they are too sternly engaged. Her fate, pathetic as it is, comes across in the end rather as a terrible demonstration of moral law than as an emotionally painful if unavoidable loss. And none of the other characters counteract this effect, or broaden its imaginative range. De Flores is as probable and poetical as Leigh Hunt declared, a cynical underdog obsessed by an impossible desire;

but though he recalls philosophising malcontents in the tradition of Iago or Bosola, the dramatists resolutely confine his role. The sub-plot is widely defended today as an extension of the main themes in the play, and by no means an excrescence. But no one could claim that it has much interest in itself, and it seems only too plainly inserted for the sake of thematic counterpoint. Tomazo's part can also be defended, since it is used to show that Beatrice and De Flores are destroyed by their own actions and not by a conventional revenger. The last speeches in the play dwell on justice and reconciliation. But dramatically they are too humane, since Alsemero becomes a dispassionate judge instead of an anguished husband. And his role after the first scenes has been restrained and unemotional, apparently with this object in view. The dramatists, in short, are more concerned by the end with justice than with tragedy. This comes near to what one critic means by accusing them of a 'failure of nerve'; yet it is unfair on that account to charge them with making deliberate 'concessions to the taste of the time'.[23] On the contrary, they seem too thoroughly committed to criticism. In the late-Jacobean theatres, only a Shakespeare perhaps could have transcended such a purpose and found subject for tragic celebration in his characters while at the same time dissecting their social morality so searchingly.

14. *Don Quixote* as a prose epic

The novel emerges in the eighteenth century as a new type of fiction, distinguished from earlier types by claiming to reflect ordinary experience instead of dwelling upon the heroic, the ideal or the marvellous. It is a commonplace of literary history that *Don Quixote* played a major part in inspiring the new literary form. But the evolution of later novels from the promptings expressed or latent in *Don Quixote* has been a many-sided affair; and several important aspects of it, connected with the idea of the prose epic, seem to have received comparatively little attention from critics.

I want to argue that in composing *Don Quixote* Cervantes applied the idea of the prose epic in highly original and fruitful ways, which helped him to give shape to his close, varied observation of men and books. Towards 1600, the idea was still new enough, and large and vague enough, to challenge an ambitious author without trammelling him. It seems to have entered critical discussion in the late sixteenth century, in an attempt to assimilate modern works such as *Amadis of Gaul* and works modern by adoption, such as the *Ethiopian History*, to the categories of Aristotelian theory. Thus, Scaliger declared that the *Ethiopian History* could be 'a most excellent example' of construction for an epic poet; Sidney quoted it to prove that 'it is not rhyming and versing that maketh a poet', and he compared *Amadis* to the *Aeneid* in respect of their heroic effect upon the reader; and Tasso cited Heliodorus and Achilles Tatius, together with the writers of chivalric romances, to show that 'a heroic poem can be formed with an amorous subject'.[1] In his admirable study of *Cervantes's Theory of the Novel*, Mr E. C. Riley has recently pointed out that these theoretical ideas – which Cervantes could possibly have met as early as his Italian travels – found expression in Spanish criticism shortly before the writing of *Don Quixote*; for example, he quotes López Pinciano, one of the first Spaniards to discuss the *Poetics* (in *Filosofia antigua poética*

(Madrid, 1596)): 'I have come to realize that the *Ethiopic History* is a much praised poem, but a poem in prose'; and further:

> the loves of Theagenes and Chariclea, by Heliodorus, and those of Leucippe and Clitophon, by Achilles Tatius, are as epic as the *Iliad* and the *Aeneid*; and all those books of chivalry, like the four poems mentioned above, have, I say, no essential difference that distinguishes them, nor do the individual conditions of one differ essentially from those of another.

Mr Riley compares these statements with the programme for a reformed version of chivalric romances outlined in some detail by Cervantes's Canon of Toledo in Part I (Chapter 47) of *Don Quixote* (1605).[2] The Canon argues that a romance of chivalry on rational lines would give its author scope to discourse on astronomy, cosmography or affairs of state, typical examples of the learning required for epic, 'and sometimes he will have a chance of coming forward as a magician if he likes'. Such an author could depict 'the craftiness of Ulysses, the piety of Aeneas, ... and in short all the faculties that serve to make an illustrious man perfect'; he could find 'unrestricted range' to display his mastery of all the traditional modes of poetry, including epic – 'for the epic may be written in prose just as well as in verse'.[3]

This late-sixteenth-century conception of the prose epic appears to rest upon the assumption that the fundamental property of poetry is 'invention' rather than verse. It need connote nothing more precise than a large-scale narrative with some resemblance to classical verse epics but also incorporating features of the prose romances and emphasising the heroic virtues of ideal lovers. Sidney's *Arcadia* and Cervantes's *Persiles and Sigismunda*, composed at the very end of his career, after the completion of *Don Quixote*, are notable examples of 'the prose epic' in this sense. Both of them are far removed from common realities.

The development in fiction which led towards the realistic novel was therefore quite distinct from this conception of the prose epic. On the other hand, it owed a great deal to the example of *Don Quixote*. The debt can be traced, at least by inference, through the statements of intention by story-tellers belonging to the early phase of the English novel such as Congreve and Horace Walpole, while it is plainly evident in *Joseph Andrews*, which Fielding advertised as 'Written in imitation of the manner of Cervantes, author of *Don Quixote*'. In the Preface to his Italianate short story, *Incognita* (1692), Congreve distinguishes between 'Romances' and 'Novels':

Romances are generally composed of the Constant Loves and invincible Courages of Hero's, Heroins, Kings and Queens, Mortals of the first Rank, and so forth; where lofty Language, miraculous Contingencies and impossible Performances, elevate and surprize the Reader into a giddy Delight, which leaves him flat upon the Ground whenever he gives of[f], and vexes him to think how he had suffer'd himself to be pleased and transported, concern'd and afflicted at the several Passages which he has Read, viz. these Knights Success to their Damosels Misfortunes, and such like, when he is forced to be very well convinced that 'tis all a lye. Novels are of a more familiar Nature; Come near us, and represent to us Intrigues in practice, delight us with Accidents and odd events, but not such as are wholly unusual or unpresidented, such which not being so distant from our Belief bring also the pleasure nearer us. Romances give more of Wonder, Novels more Delight.

By 'Novels', of course, Congreve here means *novelle*; but in this passage one can see the modern English sense of the term struggling to be born. And most of the passage would have been acceptable to Cervantes's Curate and Canon, if it was not indeed taken from them. By 1764, when Horace Walpole published *The Castle of Otranto*, realistic criteria of fiction were so well confirmed that he resorted to the medieval and Cervantine device of appealing to a long-lost chronicle to 'authorise' his romance. 'Even as such', he adds in the Preface to his first edition, 'some apology for it is necessary. Miracles, visions, necromancies, dreams, and other preternatural events, are exploded now even from romance. That was not the case when our author wrote; much less when the story itself is supposed to have happened.' In the Preface to the second edition, Walpole, writing in his own name, explains his intentions in composition more fully:

It was an attempt to blend the two kinds of romance: the ancient and the modern. In the former, all was imagination and improbability; in the latter, nature is always intended to be, and sometimes has been, copied with success. Invention has not been wanting; but the great resources of fancy have been dammed up, by a strict adherence to common life. But if in the latter species nature has cramped imagination, she did but take her revenge, having been totally excluded from old romances ... The author of the following pages thought it possible to reconcile the two kinds ...

Between Congreve's story and Walpole's came the works of Fielding, who connected realism with the idea of the prose epic, at the same time drawing heavily from Cervantes, especially in *Joseph Andrews*, with its anti-romantic satire directed against Richardson and its idealistic, impractical bookworm in Parson Adams. According to Fielding, in the Preface to *Joseph Andrews* (1742), his 'comic romance' (for he does not call it 'a novel') 'is a comic epic poem in prose'. A work of this type should be based upon 'the Ridiculous', in other words, upon social affectation truthfully recorded:

And perhaps there is one reason why a comic writer should of all others be the least excused for deviating from nature, since it may not be always so easy for a serious poet to meet with the great and admirable; but life everywhere furnishes an accurate observer with the ridiculous.

Nevertheless, in diction as distinct from 'sentiments', a comic epic poem in prose could be free to depart from nature into literary burlesque, parodying the high style of epic poetry:

In the diction, I think, burlesque itself may be sometimes admitted; of which many instances will occur in this work, as in the description of the battles, and some other places, not necessary to be pointed out to the classical reader, for whose entertainment those parodies or burlesque imitations are chiefly calculated.

Under the heading of burlesque, then, Fielding retains something of the original idea of the prose epic, alongside the more modern conception of a large-scale narrative essentially true to life; and he returns to this dual-purpose formula in *Tom Jones*. (On the other hand, Fielding did not consider that there was any vestige of 'Epic Regularity' in *Don Quixote*'s 'loose unconnected Adventures...: of which you may transverse the Order as you please, without any Injury to the whole'.)[4]

Fielding's formula of the 'comic romance' or 'comic epic poem in prose' shows how the eighteenth century interpreted Cervantes. It also shows how difficult it was for an author, at least before the nineteenth century, to devise a long story based entirely on sober observation of behaviour, without distortion towards parody or farce (and even towards the end of the nineteenth century, Gissing noted how rare were the examples of consistent naturalism). No doubt it would have been at least as difficult for Cervantes himself to conceive of a thoroughly realistic long story, in spite of his frequent references, facetious or otherwise, to the 'truth' of his remarkable 'history'. Certainly, he was even less free than Fielding after him to propose writing a long realistic narrative without support from the literary conventions of epic or romance. Yet in composing *Don Quixote* he provided a fund of suggestions to later novelists whose interest in bringing the feel of actuality into their fiction was to be deeper and wider than anything Fielding could envisage. It seems plausible to argue that the idea of the prose epic, or rather, the thought of making experiments with this idea, was a decisive factor in Cervantes's achievement; and secondly, that his experiments in construction led him from Heliodorus towards Virgil and Homer.

Both Parts of *Don Quixote* contain imitations or parodies or discussions of a wide variety of narrative forms – not only of the chivalric romances which furnish the writer's avowed target, but of ballads, epic poetry, Hellenistic and Renaissance pastoral romances, picaresque biographies, Italian *novelle*, and stage plays. Cervantes has learned much from *Celestina* and *Orlando Furioso*. In one way or another, he recalls what is virtually the whole range of fiction available in his time.[5] In addition, the many serious and comic conversations about literature, constructive digressions from the main narrative, recall another form cultivated in Renaissance letters, the critical treatise or dialogue.

Such a miscellany of narrative modes may indicate that to some extent the artist was unsure of himself, especially in Part I; it lends some support to the traditional view of Cervantes as an 'untutored genius' and to neo-classical criticism of the structure of his work, such as Fielding's. Much the same criticism reappears in, for example, the comments of Fitzmaurice-Kelly, who describes Part I, in effect, as a brilliant *trouvaille* padded out with more or less irrelevant additions. After stating that 'the essence of the story' is 'the contrast between the Knight and the Squire (each, in his own way, the victim of imagination)' and 'their encounters with the hard, real world', Fitzmaurice-Kelly goes on to argue that the inspiration flags in the second half of Part I:[6]

Cervantes felt ... that this was insufficient, and that not even his powers could concentrate the entire interest on two characters. Hence the incessant digressions, the constant introduction of picturesque types, the insertion of supplementary stories ... It is true, as Lessing pointed out, that these interpolated tales do not quite reach Cervantes's highest level of achievement, and it is likely enough that they were used, in part, because they were already written; but at any rate they serve as a relief from the perils of monotony.

This represents the opinion of many readers.

Probably a number of critics today, however, would reject this estimate of the quality of the interpolated tales together with the allied criticism of the construction of Part I.[7] Cervantes's pride in his inventive powers, and the evidence of his interest in critical theory (which Mr Riley's book illustrates at length), tell against the supposition of mere padding. And, more important, the supplementary stories in Part I are related by theme, as recent critics have suggested, to the main story of the knight and his squire. If they still seem out of proportion, unduly extended, this is probably not because Cervantes began to feel that his main idea was 'insufficient', but because the radical originality of this idea led him to experiment in order to find a narrative form to embody it adequately. He had no pattern to work by.

For (whether or not he began to write simply with the intention of producing a parody of ballads and romances on the small scale of a *novella*) the governing scheme that soon emerges in Part I is that of moulding a large-scale narrative upon the nature of a single hero, a narrative that will reveal the hero's mentality in breadth and depth, using the other figures (Sancho included) primarily as his foils. And this scheme appears to come without a precedent in fiction. Previous fiction had relied much more upon a given plot or situation. The heroes of epic and romance, much discussed by theorists, had revealed their characters by engaging upon adventures imposed by Fate or Fortune; they had either met the demands of an ideal code applauded by their society or had tried to prove to themselves that they were equal to such an ideal. No one in Don Quixote's world seriously wants the Don, or anyone else, to prove himself as a knight-errant, however; quite the contrary.[8] Again, the character of a Lazarillo de Tormes had been formed by his employers and the hard knocks of poverty as much as by anything in himself. But Don Quixote embarks on uncalled-for adventures simply because of his own state of mind. Although the *novelle* could have given Cervantes hints for comic and realistic character-drawing, they were essentially little more than anecdotes, emphasising what an Italian contemporary called 'the new and the notable' in the circumstances of the action[9] – in Congreve's phrase, 'Accidents and odd events'. In his own *novelas* Cervantes is distinctly more interested in psychology than his Italian predecessors.

In contemporary Elizabethan drama, which Cervantes, of course, could not have known, there are closer analogues to his idea. As a literary conception, the knight has some resemblance to Shakespeare's Timon and to several of Ben Jonson's 'humorists'; even in details, one is reminded of Don Quixote, for instance, by Puntarvolo's fad of saluting his wife and servants as if they were strangers in a castle in a chivalric romance, or by Sir Politic Would-be's childish pretence that he is a deep machiavellian. It is not surprising that the Spanish hero was welcomed promptly in London. And the action of a Jonsonian comedy consists of the working-out of the consequences of the characters' humours, much as in Cervantes. But while Jonson divides his interest between several cognate follies, satirises them all together, and erects a barrier to each of them in the shape of the dramatic intrigue, Cervantes, concentrating on his main figure with a deeper and more sympathetic interest, sets him free for a long time to act out his part, the part that he has made his own by an unconstrained choice expressing his whole personality. As Quixote truly says at the end, he has been 'the maker of his own Fortune' (II, 66).

Although the various qualities in his character cannot be separated from one another, there are two main constituents in Don Quixote's 'humour' – his imagination and his theory of knighthood. Renaissance writers on psychology were apt to mistrust the imagination, to which they attributed considerable occult powers, treating it as a prime source of delusion and of emotional derangement; they dwelt on its suggestibility, its 'contrariety to the understanding', its kinship with 'frenzy, peevishness and melancholy'.[10] An unbridled imagination reduced 'the lover and the poet' to the same footing as 'the lunatic'; and the story of Señor Alonso Quixano (or Quixada, or Quesada – whichever his proper surname had been) is a signal, an 'exemplary' case-history of imagination in most of its vagaries. But secondly, Don Quixote (to restore his assumed style) has a reasoned if utopian theory of knight-errantry as the means of preserving the virtues of the golden age, a theory which is coherent, logical and even noble, though it happens to be at variance with the facts of life. In Part I, broadly speaking, Cervantes associates each of these constituents of Don Quixote's humour with a different narrative method.

On the whole, the episodes in Part I where imagination predominates are the farcical, knockabout episodes (like much of the action in Jonson's comedies). They follow each other in the manner of a biographical jest-book or a picaresque tale, the main link between them, besides temporal succession, being the workings of Don Quixote's mind. The chief sequence of this type consists of the episodes of the carriers, the night at the inn of Maritornes which ends in Sancho's blanket-tossing, the adventures of the fulling mill and of Mambrino's helmet, and the release of the gang of convicts (I, 15–22). Here Don Quixote is the victim of sensory delusions – though they are partly wilful delusions, too – in all the adventures except the first (where it is Rocinante's senses that are at fault) and the last. The knight's imagination follows a manic rhythm of elation and depression, each success and each misfortune goading him anew to prove his invincibility and impose his fantasy on common sense. When at length he gains an easy triumph in the adventure of the basin or headpiece, thus remedying a defect in his knightly equipment which had troubled him from the start, he is so far carried away by elation that in the next encounter he coolly liberates the convicts, contradicting his earlier boast that he would clear the mountains of robbers (I, 14), without being subject to any hallucination at all. At this moment, his utopianism comes into play: he argues, correctly, that the prisoners are being marched to the galleys against their will; he announces that he has taken a vow 'to give aid to those in need and under the oppression of the strong'; and, as 'a mark of prudence', he requests the guards, very politely, to unlock their prisoners since it is 'a hard case to make slaves of those whom God and nature have made free' (I, 22). He is still open to 'prudence' when, after this adventure miscarries, he listens to Sancho and withdraws to the Sierra Morena (I, 23); yet soon after his fears of the law have died down, he reanimates his self-esteem by planning a superlative, though private and unopposed, demonstration of knight-errantry, outvying the love-melancholy of Amadis and Orlando for no apparent reason at all ('no thanks to a knight-errant for going mad when he has cause; the thing is to turn crazy without any provocation'). This quirk looks entirely bookish and gratuitous. But in the interval between his flight to the mountain and his decision to emulate the 'penance' of Amadis (I, 25), he has met Cardenio, who is genuinely mad from unhappiness in love and who has said of himself, as the goatherd has told Don Quixote, that he is 'working out a penance which for his many sins had been imposed upon him' (I, 23). Evidently Don Quixote's 'penance' has been suggested subconsciously by Cardenio; the meeting between the two madmen, with the quarrel springing from the latter's reference to Amadis of Gaul, forms the mid-point and the turning-point of Part I.

In those episodes where Don Quixote is not subject to delusions but where his considered theory of knight-errantry is uppermost, the narrative method is less farcical or picaresque. Here Cervantes's object seems to be to show a series of examples of Don Quixote's theory in action and to depict a series of characters in parallel or in contrast with various aspects of the hero himself. Thus, the meetings with Andres (I, 4, 31) show up Don Quixote's judgement, not his imagination; while Gines de Pasamonte resembles the knight-errant in his aliases, his obstinacy and his passion for fame (I, 22). In the sequence of chapters where Don Quixote first expounds his creed at length, he is more a commentator and a spectator of events than a direct actor in the story; these are the chapters (I, 11–14) where he meets the first group of goatherds, hears of Chrysostom, and witnesses Marcela's declaration of independence. The mood is harmonious; there are no clashes here between Don Quixote and the other characters; he admires the goatherds, sympathises with Chrysostom and applauds Marcela. These characters illuminate different sides of the pastoral convention, a literary convention resembling Quixote's romances of chivalry, but in some respects closer to actuality.

Cervantes applies similar principles of construction in the main series of 'supplementary stories' and 'interpolated tales', as Fitzmaurice-Kelly calls them, which follow Don Quixote's penance and Sancho's departure to inform Dulcinea of her true knight's frenzy. Through most of these chapters (I, 26–46) Don Quixote is inactive; he is either absent from the scene of the story, or asleep, or a passive listener (though his delusions return in sleep, leading to his onslaught on the wine-skins (I, 35); he discourses learnedly on arms and arts (I, 37–8); and he brings chaos to the inn by his second, legalistic contest with the barber over Mambrino's helmet (I, 44–5)). Meanwhile, however, the characters who occupy most of our attention reflect back on Don Quixote by likeness and contrast. In the first group of stories, involving Cardenio, Luscinda, Dorothea and Don Fernando, Cardenio is placed in antithesis to Don Quixote, since he is genuinely mad for love, his unhappiness is due to error, and his errors are due to a kind of inferiority complex, an irrational fear of asserting himself; while the courageous and resourceful Dorothea stands out in contrast to Cardenio and Don Quixote alike.

The inset *novella* of the 'Curious Impertinent' (I, 33–4) is completely detached from the rest of the plot but is closely related to the other stories in content. Anselmo, the husband, the Curious Impertinent, suffers from neurotic jealousy. He is both causelessly mistrustful and mistakenly trusting, like Cardenio; and like Don Quixote, he seeks to impose his fantasy on real life, but seeks to do so by a calculated and unwarrantable experiment on other human beings, with tragic results. Without this 'interpolated tale', the portrait of Don Quixote himself would lose some vital touches of contrast and high relief.

The linked stories of the returned Captive and his family also throw light on Don Quixote's position. The main themes here are soldiering, with its unavoidable rashness of self-exposure and its hardships, and freedom, dear alike to Don Quixote, Marcela and Gines de Pasamonte. The secondary themes are the prosperity of the Captive's brother, the Judge, and the daring of true lovers. The Captive's story (I, 39), following Don Quixote's sane but entirely academic harangue on the superiority of arms over arts in general and jurisprudence in particular, brings home the difference between supposition and experience.

The contrast brought out by the placing of the Captive's tale spreads through all the narrative digressions. Unlike Don Quixote, the Captive, who has fought at Lepanto, is a real soldier and, in a sense, a true heir to the paladins of Charlemagne. Again, Don Fernando is a genuine oppressor of damsels – who repents thanks to Fortune, persuasion and Dorothea's constancy, without any intervention from Don Quixote, without Don Quixote's even being aware of what is going on.

The only inset tale in the second half of Part I to involve the hero directly is the burlesque of romance invented by the Curate and Dorothea, in which Dorothea acts the part of the Princess Micomicona, 'queen of the great kingdom of Micomicon of Ethiopia' (I, 29). This tale is exactly calculated to suit Don Quixote's fancy and lands him (literally) in the cart. But the other digressive tales and episodes in Part I are neither imitations nor parodies of chivalric romance. In varying degrees, they combine the narrative styles of the *novella*, the Renaissance pastoral and the *Ethiopian History*; and, so far as they are linked together by plot, the later episodes, affecting Cardenio and Dorothea, the Captive and his brother, are linked in the manner of the *Ethiopian History*, with its adventures revealing constant love under trial, its supposed deaths, its disguises, its wanderings and fortunate or providential encounters involving peripeteia and recognition, and its parenthetic flash-back narrations. These conventions look artifical now, but readers in Cervantes's day were prepared to treat them seriously; if not exactly realistic, they stood for a heightened but essentially credible reality, in opposition to the wholly incredible deeds of Don Quixote's favourite heroes. (It is noticeable that the tales of the Curious Impertinent and of Marcela were translated separately into French, in 1608 and 1609 respectively, some years before the complete French translation of Part I came out in 1614; and that in the early seventeenth century both French and English playwrights took up the story of Cardenio.)[11] Together, these inset stories constitute what the Canon of Toledo calls 'a web of bright and varied threads', a possible illustration of the theory of the prose epic.

There is more than this in the Canon's discourse, however. His talk with the Curate is the third of the long conversations about literature which fill significant pauses in Don Quixote's adventures in Part I and develop a literary programme as an alternative to the popular romances. In the first of these conversations, the Curate and the Barber condemn most of Don Quixote's library while the knight sleeps, exhausted, after his first riding-out (I, 6). In the second (I, 32), while Don Quixote sleeps at the inn after his penance on the mountain, the Curate tells the inn-keeper that he should prefer 'a true history' of a hero like the Great Captain, Gonzalo de Cordova, to an absurd 'fabrication' such as that of Don Cirongilio of Thrace (the tale of the Curious Impertinent, which follows this conversation, is not exactly what the good Curate means; nor, perhaps, is the Captive's story, though nearer the mark). The Canon's talk with the Curate (I, 47) takes place after the main group of narrative digressions, while Don Quixote is being carried homewards in his cage. To some extent, it justifies the miscellaneity of the preceding episodes. But the Canon is thinking of converting romances of chivalry into something like the *Odyssey* or the *Aeneid*, rather than something like the story of Theagenes and Chariclea; he is thinking of what Fielding calls 'Epic Regularity'. He begins by requiring that a story should show 'proportion of the parts to the whole', and he goes on to specify the criteria, taken from Aristotle, of probable impossibilities and an organic plot – 'a connected plot complete in all its [members], so that the middle agrees with the beginning, and the end with the beginning and middle'. Finally, he lists some of the characteristics of epic available to a modern writer in prose. The Aristotelian thread in his discussion extends to the next chapter, to his criticism of Lope de Vega and the modern stage.

With all its effect of variety and freedom – a great part of the pleasure in reading *Don Quixote* – Part I has the marks of a guiding literary purpose, not of padding or aimless improvisation. Nevertheless, a critic like Fitzmaurice-Kelly could reply that there is still some dispersal of interest in the second half, as if Cervantes were more interested in working out a theory of wide-ranging prose epic than in developing his hero's character directly. The Canon's discourse could logically imply some dissatisfaction with the way Part I shifts from one character to another, like the critics' objections against

Orlando Furioso. And despite the great and immediate popularity of his book, Cervantes must have considered such criticisms, whether actual or possible, for in Part II he makes Samson Carrasco repeat the comment that the tale of the Curious Impertinent is an intrusion (II, 3), and later he makes the learned Cid Hamet complain of the 'intolerable drudgery' of limiting himself to one story, with few or no digressions, pleading 'that credit be given him, not for what he writes, but for what he has refrained from writing' (II, 44).[12]

Part I could have been left to stand on its own. In the period of nearly ten years between the publication of Part I and the writing of Part II, Cervantes has in effect made a fresh start, evidently the outcome of further critical thinking. Part II is more thoroughly unified: the interest is bound up more tightly with the development of Don Quixote's character – with which the development of Sancho's character, more striking and unexpected in itself, is inseparably connected. And the relations between the two men turn upon a central plot or intrigue, the pretended enchantment of Dulcinea. Towards the end of Part II, where Cervantes seems to be writing in a hurry, he repeats the structural effect of the digressions at the end of Part I (in the episodes of Ricote and his daughter, of Roque Guinart and Claudia Jeronima (II, 54, 60, 63)). But the digressions in Part II are brief; Don Quixote and Sancho are talking or acting almost continuously; and most of the action refers not merely to Don Quixote's general desire for fame but to his particular desire – carried over from the 'penance' – to meet Dulcinea and be acknowledged as her adorer. The disenchantment of Dulcinea thus becomes the central concern, the goal, of her knight's new adventures. Besides this, Cervantes supplies a framing action for the main narrative, in the two sorties of Samson Carrasco to bring Quixote home again and cure him of his madness.

Don Quixote's striving to meet Dulcinea and to free her from enchantment belongs to the scheme of chivalric romances. But at the same time, as Cervantes treats it, it recalls epic; not, this time, the multiple plot of a recognised prose 'epic' like the *Ethiopian History*, but the more unified plot of the *Aeneid* or the *Odyssey*. Cervantes had already referred to verse epics in several chapters of Part I (6, 25, 47); in Part II, such references colour the whole story. His comic irony is no less active than before, but now he brings in less horseplay, and his surface tone is loftier and more serious, especially in the consideration of epic themes such as war, justice and government. There are hints, though ironic, of an epic subject on classical lines in the first chapter, where the Curate and the Barber mention the Turkish wars to Don Quixote, and the Barber tells his anecdote of the madmen who believed that they were Jupiter and Neptune, controlling sky and sea. And when Samson Carrasco tells Don Quixote about the fame he has won from the publication of Part I, their talk (II, 3) fastens upon the central critical topics of the presentation of an epic hero and the contrast between poetry and history:

'There are those' [says Samson] 'who have read the history who say they would have been glad if the author had left out some of the countless cudgellings that were inflicted on Señor Don Quixote in various encounters.'
'That's where the truth of the history comes in', said Sancho.
'At the same time they might fairly have passed them over in silence', observed Don Quixote; 'for there is no need of recording events which do not change or affect the truth of a history, if they tend to bring the hero of it into contempt. Aeneas was not in truth and earnest so pious as Virgil represents him, nor Ulysses so wise as Homer describes him.'
'That is true', said Samson; 'but it is one thing to write as a poet, another to write as a historian; the poet may describe or sing things, not as they were, but as they ought to have been; but the historian has to write them down, not as they ought to have been, but as they were, without adding anything to the truth or taking anything from it.'

The sly contrast here between the historian's truth and the ideal truth of the poet (or critic) helps, of course, to keep up the pretence that Cervantes, transcribing the almost omniscient Cid Hamet, is a 'veracious historian'; but the conversation also helps to suggest that he is the historian of a hero worthy of epic, already legendary and 'illustrious'. If the hero reveals flaws in his greatness, so, after all, would Aeneas and Ulysses, were they to be examined closely. And the main series of adventures in Part II sustains this ironic suggestion of resemblance between Don Quixote and these two typical epic heroes, particularly Ulysses. The knight now travels further afield than in Part I. His grotesque but unimpeachably 'heroic' encounter with the lions (II, 17) is sandwiched between serious conversations about wise moderation in living and about poetry, with Diego de Miranda and his son. He is a guest at a wedding feast and witnesses quasi-epic games and contests. Because of his fame, he is no longer reduced to miserable inns, but is entertained royally by the Duke and again in Barcelona. The scope of his journeys, both real and imaginary, the respect with which he is greeted, and the wisdom intermixed with folly in his own speeches confer the status of a modern Ulysses upon the knight. Moreover, his situation recalls the *Odyssey* as well. Dulcinea is his Penelope (though it is characteristic of the complexity of motifs in Part II that his relation with her is simultaneously epic, romantic, platonic and fictitious). Supernatural powers seem to oppose his efforts to reach her, and he is delayed by friendly or amorous hosts. Altisidora corresponds to Calypso and possibly, in her mock funeral, to Dido. Carrasco's excursion recalls Telemachus; and the end of the whole adventure is that Don Quixote, like Ulysses, returns to his home.

These epic overtones in the story are particularly striking in his visit to the cave of Montesinos (II, 23). His account of his vision in the cave is partly a fulfilment in fantasy of the desire implied in his speech to the Canon of Toledo (I, 50) to emulate the knights of romance who had plunged into terrifying lakes and had found magic castles under the water. And Montesinos and Durandarte come from ballads. But, beyond all this, Don Quixote follows the tradition of the epic hero's descent to the underworld. He finds himself in the realm of the famous dead. He is welcomed by Montesinos, who has become a venerable sage-interpreter among the phantoms and who hails him as 'that great knight of whom the sage Merlin has prophesied such great things'. This resounding prophecy is connected with a mysterious task of deliverance, the appeasing of Durandarte, who cannot rest, although, as the ballads tell, Montesinos has indeed obeyed his dying instructions and cut out his heart. In keeping with tradition, the mortal visitor to the underworld refrains from eating there. And in keeping with epic tradition again, he is urgently solicited by phantoms from his own life on earth, when Dulcinea appears and sends her companion to Don Quixote to borrow six *reals* on the pledge of a petticoat. The weird absurdity of this encounter, its 'enigmatic inconsequence',[13] depends on associations more remote and lofty than a ballad alone could have provided.

This episode is the most remarkable expression of Don Quixote's imagination in Part II, but it is firmly connected with the central plot. In position, it duplicates the 'penance' of Part I. It discloses Don Quixote's rising struggle with his own sanity, with the nagging doubts of common sense about his vocation in general (it was not until later, when he was welcomed by the Duke (II, 31), that 'he thoroughly felt and believed himself to be a knight-errant in reality and not merely in fancy'; he was 'greatly astonished' to feel like this at the castle, 'and this was the first time'). And in particular, the fantasy in the cave reveals Don Quixote's anxieties about Dulcinea, which Sancho has helped to cause, and which react upon the further relations between knight and squire.

Cervantes could have taken many hints from Ariosto in his ironic use of reference to heroic poetry. But the episode in the cave also illustrates his masterly control of the texture and tempo of a narrative in prose. Poetry could hardly match the startling and yet subtle combinations and transitions of tone he achieves here, just as poetry could hardly match the sustained, varied, racy naturalism of his dialogue.

The vision in the cave makes a wonderful blending of disparate tones, exotic, pathetic, matter-of-fact and absurd. But Cervantes anchors it on commonsense observation. For example, Don Quixote's laboured, irrelevant account of the mythological origin of the lakes and the river connected with Montesinos's cave is an echo, in solemn tones, as befits the speaker, from the gossip of the guide in the previous chapter, the young scholar who is preparing a burlesque volume of topographical legends to be entitled 'Metamorphoses, or the Spanish Ovid'. And, like the notion of his penance following upon his meeting with Cardenio, the very notion of a grand display of love and heroism in fantasy seems to have been planted this time in Don Quixote's mind by his meeting shortly before with Basilio and by his praise of Basilio for winning his bride by the theatrical trick of pretending to kill himself (' "that", said Don Quixote, "is not and ought not to be called deception which aims at virtuous ends" ' (II, 22)). On the other hand, Don Quixote's self-criticism, more insistent now than at the time of the penance, results in a strange, abrupt distortion of the image of his own glory. The long-dead Durandarte refuses to be consoled when Montesinos presents Don Quixote to him as his deliverer:

'And if that may not be', said the wretched Durandarte in a low and feeble voice, 'if that may not be, then, O my cousin, I say "patience and shuffle" '; and turning over on his side, he relapsed into his former silence without uttering another word.

From the weirdness of such a cryptic, invertedly oracular pronouncement, Cervantes descends to the level of mock commentary in Sancho's interruptions, with his query as to who could have been the maker of the poniard that cut Durandarte's heart out, and his growing, and justified, scepticism as to Dulcinea's share in the business. Hence a double irony attaches to Cid Hamet's straight-faced discussion in the next chapter of Don Quixote's truthfulness and sincerity. This irony re-echoes much later, when, at the end of the expedition of the wooden horse (II, 41), Don Quixote reproves Sancho for venturing into an Ariostesque fantasy on his own account:

'Sancho, as you would have us believe what you saw in heaven, I require you to believe me as to what I saw in the cave of Montesinos; I say no more.'

Cervantes could hardly have achieved the dry subtlety of effects like this except in prose. But the total effect is far richer than anything Fielding's formula of 'the comic epic poem in prose' can suggest. It has more imaginative grandeur as well as more psychological depth. On one side, Cervantes can use minute and often trivial details, in the tones of everyday speech, to represent the interplay in his characters' minds between illusion and reality; on the other side, he can gain a variety of surprising, suggestive effects by transposing the material associated with poetry into the medium of prose. Hence, long after Fielding's day, he could help to inspire the technique of novels as original, and as different from each other, as *Madame Bovary*, along one line of development, and, on another line, *Dead Souls* and Joyce's *Ulysses*. Joyce follows Cervantes's example, not only in his use of epic allusions in a naturalistic setting, but in his central character-relationship, as of a new Sancho Panza in search of Don Quixote.

The rich achievement of Part II of *Don Quixote* still seems to be affected on every side by Cervantes's application of the idea of a prose epic. By suggesting analogies with classical verse epic, he has both carried the notion of an 'illustrious' hero further than in Part I and solved one of the major problems of Renaissance critical theory, the reconciliation of unity and variety. By the same stroke, moreover, he has solved another major problem of Renaissance poetics, the reconciliation of 'the marvellous' with 'the true'.

The importance and the difficulty of this problem are conveyed in a letter of Tasso, which Toffanin quotes in his study of Renaissance Aristotelian theory:[14]

These two things, . . . the marvellous and the probable [*il meraviglioso e il verisimile*], are very different by nature, so different that they are almost contraries. Nevertheless, both are necessary to the [heroic] poem. To excel in the art of poetry, you must couple them together: but, though many have achieved this hitherto, there is no-one (as far as I know) who can teach you how to do it.

In Part I of *Don Quixote* Cervantes had coupled the probable with the marvellous, but only by situating the latter in his hero's fantasy. In Part II he couples them more extensively and more ingeniously, even endowing the marvellous with objective existence, by making it the product of many characters' minds, deliberate and not merely fantastic. If not 'the marvellous' as such, then the desire for it becomes a part of the truth, of common reality.

We see more of conscious make-belief in Part II than in Part I. It furnishes the enveloping plot of Samson's disguises and the central plot of Sancho's pretence that Dulcinea must be enchanted. The episodes at the castle and on Sancho's 'island' (corresponding to those in Part I on the mountain and at the inn) consist chiefly of marvels staged by the Duke and Duchess for the deception of Quixote and Sancho (II, 30–57); and the bronze head at Barcelona (II, 62) is a marvel of the same kind. Since all these marvels are intended for Don Quixote, they can be regarded as cases of infection from his fantasy (after the last prank of the Duke and Duchess, Cid Hamet remarks that they must have been as crazy as their victims 'when they took such pains to make game of a pair of fools' (II, 70)). But there are other instances of play-acting or the like which are not meant specially for Don Quixote: for example, the actors, the masque at Camacho's wedding feast and Basilio's feigned suicide there, the performing ape and the puppet show, and the ladies and gentlemen playing Arcadians (II, 11, 20–1, 25–6, 58). Don Quixote now moves in a world of play-acting, where the marvellous is at home; a world, moreover, wherein pretence and earnest can change places unexpectedly. He understands quite well that the actors with their splendid costumes are nothing more than purveyors of 'fictions and semblances', 'placing before us at every step a mirror in which we may see vividly displayed what goes on in human life', but he soon forgets this consideration when he meets Samson dressed up as another knight-errant, in 'a surcoat ... bespangled with glittering mirrors' (II, 12, 14). He can be deluded by a puppet-show castle but surprised when he enters a real one. Conversely, Sancho, the governor in jest, proves himself a governor indeed; while at the castle, Doña Rodriguez, who ought to know better, begs Don Quixote in all seriousness to champion her cause (II, 45–52).

In many ways this world of illusions resembles Erasmus's empire of Folly. But Cervantes bases much of it on a particular reality. He takes advantage of the circumstance of the success of Part I to reach a unique solution of the problem of reconciling the marvellous and the true. For Don Quixote's fame is no longer, as in Part I, a joke kept up by the other characters in order to humour him, or even a poetic probability, but a current historical fact. This real fame provokes his development in Part II, for he now wishes to justify and strengthen it. Hence Sancho must concoct new yarns about Dulcinea so as to hide his old ones, while on the other hand, Sancho's fantasy of a governorship acquires a solid shape, thanks to his share in his master's renown. And the principal episodes of mystification, Samson's disguises, the Duke's prolonged play-making, and the welcome at Barcelona, all spring from the same source. By the time Cervantes comes to deal with the publication of Avellaneda's rival 'Part II' (which he mentions for the first time in Chapter 59), he can subdue it to his own devices, as little more than a fresh instance of the theme which runs through the whole book, the interpenetration of fact and fiction.

By now Cervantes has come much further than satirising the contents of Don Quixote's library. By incorporating the history of his own Part I in the composition of the sequel, he can give the reader a strong though purposely ambiguous impression of reality within the romance. And on the basis of this particular example of the marvellous which happens also to be true, he can reach a general solution to the problem of constructing a form of narrative in prose with the range and dignity of traditional epic.

Notes

1. Shakespeare and the Italian concept of 'Art'

This paper was prepared for a conference on 'Echoes and Variations: English Arts and the Italian Renaissance' at the School of Renaissance Studies in the University of Warwick, May 1984. It was given in an earlier version at the Centre for Renaissance Studies at the ETH, Zurich.

1 Paul Oskar Kristeller, 'The modern system of the arts' (1951), in *Renaissance Thought*, II (New York, 1965), 196–202, 213–21.

2 *O.E.D.*, *art*, I.6.

3 R. G. Collingwood, *The Principles of Art* (Oxford, 1938), pp. 5–7; J. J. Pollitt, *The Ancient View of Greek Art: Criticism, History and Terminology* (New Haven and London, 1974), pp. 32–7.

4 Quoted, Robert Ashton, *The City and the Court 1603–1643* (Cambridge, 1979), p. 54.

5 E. R. Curtius, *European Literature and the Latin Middle Ages* (1948), trans. Willard R. Trask (New York, 1953), pp. 36–61; see also pp. 559–70.

6 Erna Auerbach, *Nicholas Hilliard* (1961), pp. 198–9; compare R[ichard] H[aydock] trans., Paolo Giovanni Lomazzo, *A Tracte Containing the Artes of Curious Paintinge Carvinge & Building* (1598) (Amsterdam and New York, 1969), 'To the Reader', p. vj^r.

7 John Dee, *Mathematicall Preface* to *The Elements of . . . Euclid*, trans. H. Billingsley (1570), p. a.iij^r.

8 [George Puttenham], *The Arte of English Poesie* (1589), ed. Gladys Willcock and Alice Walker (Cambridge, 1936), p. 5.

9 Compare *ars*, in Thomas Cooper, *Thesaurus Linguae Romanae & Brittanicae* (1573).

10 Montaigne, *Essays*, trans. Florio (ed. L. C. Harmer, Everyman's Library, 1965), I, 219.

11 Tasso, *Gerusalemme Liberata*, XVI, 9–10 (trans. Edward Fairfax (1600), ed. Henry Morley, 1890); Spenser, *Faerie Queene*, II, xii, 58–9; compare Nashe, *The Unfortunate Traveller* (1594), ch. vii. See John Shearman, *Mannerism* (Harmondsworth, 1967), pp. 123–33; Roy Strong, *The Renaissance Garden in England* (1979).

12 See H. W. Janson, *Apes and Ape Lore in the Middle Ages and the Renaissance* (*Studies of the Warburg Institute* 20, 1952), pp. 287 ff.;

Edward William Tayler, *Nature and Art in Renaissance Literature* (New York, 1964).

13 Anthony Blunt, *Artistic Theory in Italy 1450–1600* (Oxford, 1940).

14 E. H. Gombrich, *Norm and Form: Studies in the Art of the Renaissance* (1966), pp. 1–10, 107–21; Shearman, *Mannerism*, pp. 44–8, 162–5.

15 Giorgio Vasari, *Lives of the Artists* (1568), selection, trans. George Bull (Harmondsworth, 1965), p. 85.

16 Rensselaer W. Lee, 'Ut pictura poesis: the humanistic theory of painting', *Art Bulletin*, XXII (1940), 197–269; Michael Levey, *High Renaissance* (Harmondsworth, 1975), pp. 82–6.

17 Antonio Minturno, *L'Arte poetica* (1564), trans. Allan H. Gilbert, in *Literary Criticism, Plato to Dryden* (1940; Detroit, 1962), p. 286.

18 Sidney, *Apologie for Poetrie* (1595), ed. G. Gregory Smith, in *Elizabethan Critical Essays*, I (Oxford, 1904), 197.

19 Vasari, *Preface* to Part II and *Lives* e.g. of Uccello, Ghiberti, Masaccio, Brunelleschi, Mantegna (trans. Bull, pp. 96, 107, 125, 136–7, 245).

20 *Preface* to Part III (trans. Bull, p. 249).

21 *Preface to the Lives* (trans. Bull, p. 25); compare Erwin Panofsky, *Idea, a Concept in Art Theory* (1924, 1960), trans. J. J. S. Peake (New York, 1968), pp. 60–3.

22 Vasari, 'Titian' (trans. Bull, p. 455).

23 See *Lives* (trans. Bull), pp. 112, 128, 178, 188–9, 304; on Vasari and Giulio Romano's reputation, see Marie-Madeleine Martinet, 'The Winter's Tale et "Julio Romano"', *Etudes Anglaises*, XXVIII (1975), 257–68.

24 Vasari (trans. Bull), pp. 88, 222, 323, 369; Ortelius (1574), quoted, Walter S. Gibson, *Bruegel* (1977), p. 198; see Levey, *High Renaissance*, pp. 259–89.

25 Levey, *High Renaissance*, pp. 87, 93, 96, 261, 281; see Arthur H. R. Fairchild, *Shakespeare and the Arts of Design* (University of Missouri Studies, XII (1937)); William S. Heckscher, 'Shakespeare in his relationship to the visual arts: a study in paradox', in *Research Opportunities in Renaissance Drama*, XIII–XIV (Evanston, Illinois, 1972), 5–71; David Rosand, ' "Troyes painted woes": Shakespeare and the pictorial imagination', in *The Hebrew University Studies in Literature*, 8 (1980), 77–97.

26 Compare Fairchild, *Shakespeare and the Arts of Design*, p. 132; the Stratford Last Judgement is reproduced in Kenneth Muir and Stanley Wells (eds.), *Aspects of 'King Lear'* (Cambridge, 1982), pl. 3. (However, Professor Bradbrook has reminded me that the frescoes in the Stratford Guild Chapel were whitewashed over in 1563; see Samuel Schoenbaum, *William Shakespeare: A Compact Documentary Life* (Oxford, 1977), pp. 53–4.) In a discussion, Professor Bradbrook has also commented that the association of painted images with idolatry was typical of the provincial Protestantism of the time of Shakespeare's boyhood.

27 Compare Fairchild, *Shakespeare and the Arts of Design*, pp. 65–6.

28 Compare Rosalie L. Colie, *Shakespeare's 'Living Art'* (Princeton, 1974).

29 Fairchild, *Shakespeare and the Arts of Design*, pp. 139–47; Heckscher, 'Visual arts', pp. 25–35; Rosand, ' "Troyes painted woes" '.

30 John Harris, in *The King's Arcadia: Inigo Jones and the Stuart Court* (Catalogue by John Harris, Stephen Orgel and Roy Strong, Arts Council of Great Britain, 1973), p. 28 (quoting Edmund Bolton, 1606).

31 Compare Rosand ' "Troyes painted woes" ', pp. 85–6 (quoting from Alberti, *On Painting* (1435), the advice to include a figure ' "who admonishes and indicates to us what is happening . . . or beckons us with his hand to see" ').

32 See M. R. Ridley (ed.), *Antony and Cleopatra* (Arden edn, 1954), pp. 63, 262.

33 See *ibid.*, pp. 184–5; Enid Welsford, *The Court Masque* (1927), p. 342; Roy Strong, in *The King's Arcadia*, p. 39.

34 *O.E.D.*, *touch*, II.6. On this dialogue, see W. Moelwyn Merchant, *Shakespeare and the Artist* (1959), pp. 170–5; Levey, *High Renaissance*, p. 97; compare Lomazzo, *Tracte*, trans. Haydock, p. 23.

35 Heywood, *An Apology for Actors* (1612; Shakespeare Society, 1841), p. 20.

36 Compare Dee, *Mathematical Preface*, p. Aj^v (on 'Thaumaturgike'); Lomazzo, *Tracte*, Bk II, p. 2; Shearman, *Mannerism*, p. 131; Robert Lenoble, *Mersenne ou la naissance du mécanisme* (Paris, 1943), pp. 74, 144. On the statue scene in *The Winter's Tale*, see Colie, *Shakespeare's 'Living Art'*, pp. 278–83.

37 Compare Nevill Coghill, 'Six points of stage-craft in *The Winter's Tale*', in *Shakespeare Survey*, XI (Cambridge, 1958), 40. Martinet (' "Julio Romano" ') argues for stylistic and thematic reasons behind the choice of the artist's name.

38 See J. H. P. Pafford (ed.), *The Winter's Tale* (Arden edn, 1963), pp. 169–70; Puttenham, *Arte of English Poesie*, pp. 303–7.

39 I owe this observation to a surgeon interested in literature, Dr A. R. Moore, of the University of Melbourne.

2. Is *The Merchant of Venice* a problem play?

This paper was delivered to a conference at the University of Rouen, January 1985.

1 W. H. Auden, 'Brothers and others' (*The Dyer's Hand* (1963)), in Laurence Lerner (ed.), *Shakespeare's Comedies* (Harmondsworth, 1967), pp. 143–8.

2 See Michael Jamieson, 'The problem plays, 1920–1970: a retrospect' (1972), in Kenneth Muir and Stanley Wells (eds.), *Aspects of Shakespeare's 'Problem Plays'* (Cambridge, 1982), p. 127; compare Richard P. Wheeler, *Shakespeare's Development and the Problem Comedies* (Berkeley, California, 1981).

3 Harley Granville-Barker, *Prefaces to Shakespeare, Second Series* (1930), pp. 67 ff. More recent critics: see e.g. the conclusion of C. L. Barber's

chapter on *The Merchant*, in *Shakespeare's Festive Comedy* (Princeton, 1959), pp. 189–91; D. J. Palmer, in Malcolm Bradbury and David Palmer (eds.), *Shakespearian Comedy*, Stratford-upon-Avon Studies 14 (1972), 97–120; Alexander Leggatt, *Shakespeare's Comedy of Love* (1974), pp. 117–50; Ruth Nevo, *Comic Transformations in Shakespeare* (1980), pp. 115–41. John Russell Brown, in *Shakespeare and his Comedies* (1957), pp. 61–75, stands closer to Granville-Barker.

4 Rowe's preface to Shakespeare's *Works* (1709), in D. Nichol Smith (ed.), *Shakespeare Criticism*, World's Classics (Oxford, 1916), p. 31.

5 *Johnson on Shakespeare*, ed. Walter Raleigh (1908), p. 15.

6 I have discussed Shakespeare's use of *novella* plots in his comedies in *Shakespeare and the Traditions of Comedy* (Cambridge, 1974), pp. 300–21.

7 Geoffrey Bullough (ed.), *Narrative and Dramatic Sources of Shakespeare*, I (1957), 460.

8 Barber, *Shakespeare's Festive Comedy*, pp. 183–4.

9 Morris Carnovsky (1958), cited, Nevo, *Comic Transformations*, p. 118; Brown, *Shakespeare and his Comedies*, p. 70.

10 Sigurd Burckhardt discusses 'circularity' in '*The Merchant of Venice*: the gentle bond' (1962), in Lerner, *Shakespeare's Comedies*, pp. 158–9.

11 See J. R. Brown's introduction, pp. l–lii, in his edition of *The Merchant of Venice*, Arden Shakespeare (1955).

12 See Renaissance analogues in Bullough, *Sources*; and Brown, *The Merchant of Venice*, note on IV.i.180–98, and Appendixes, pp. 156–72; compare Margaret Schlauch, *Antecedents of the English Novel 1400–1600* (Warsaw and London, 1963), p. 134.

13 Trans. Brown, *Merchant of Venice*, p. 151.

14 Nevo, *Comic Transformations*, p. 123; compare Maurice Charney, 'Jessica's turquoise ring and Abigail's poisoned porridge: Shakespeare and Marlowe as rivals and imitators', in *Renaissance Drama*, N.S. X (Evanston, Illinois, 1980), 33–44; and Leggatt, *Shakespeare's Comedy of Love*, pp. 142–3.

3. Falstaff and the life of shadows

1 Henri Bergson, *Laughter* (1900), English trans. in Wylie Sypher (ed.), *Comedy* (New York, 1956), pp. 79, 97.

2 Albert Thibaudet, *Le Bergsonisme* (Paris, 1923), II, 93; compare pp. 59–60.

3 See Harry Levin, 'Falstaff uncolted' (1946), in *Shakespeare and the Revolution of the Times* (New York, 1976).

4 See A. R. Humphreys (ed.), *1 Henry IV*, Arden edn (1960), p. 71 n.

5 Thomas Nashe, *Pierce Penniless* (1592), in *Selected Works*, ed. Stanley Wells (1964), p. 55. Compare parallels with Nashe in John Dover Wilson (ed.), *1 Henry IV*, New Shakespeare (Cambridge, 1946), pp. 191–6.

6 William Empson, 'Falstaff and Mr Dover Wilson' (1953), in G. K.

Hunter (ed.), *Shakespeare, Henry I V, Parts I and I I: A Casebook* (1970), p. 145. (Referred to here as *Casebook*.)

7　See Richmond Noble, *Shakespeare's Biblical Knowledge* (1935), pp. 169–81.

8　Maurice Morgann, 'An Essay on the Dramatic Character of Sir John Falstaff' (1777), in D. Nichol Smith (ed.), *Eighteenth Century Essays on Shakespeare*, 2nd edn (Oxford, 1963), p. 230.

9　William Hazlitt, *Characters of Shakespear's Plays*, in *Liber Amoris and Dramatic Criticism*, ed. Charles Morgan (1948), p. 309.

10　A. C. Bradley, 'The rejection of Falstaff' (1902), in *Oxford Lectures on Poetry*, 2nd edn (1909), pp. 261, 269.

11　W. H. Auden, 'The Prince's Dog' (1959), in *Casebook*, p. 188.

12　Compare *1 Henry I V*, I.ii.81–7, II.ii.10–20, II.iv.329–33, III.iii.164–8, and so on.

13　Compare *King John*, II.i.561–98; *Measure for Measure*, IV.iii.5. (Perhaps Falstaff is thinking of Proverbs, xxii.1 at this point; compare Noble, *Shakespeare's Biblical Knowledge*, p. 169.)

14　See Paul A. Jorgensen, '"Redeeming Time" in Shakespeare's *Henry I V*' (1960), in *Casebook*, pp. 231–42.

15　See Holinshed, in Geoffrey Bullough (ed.), *Narrative and Dramatic Sources of Shakespeare*, IV (1962), 276.

16　Compare the King's words about Mortimer at I.iii.85–6: 'Shall our coffers then / Be emptied to redeem a traitor home?'

17　Holinshed, in Bullough, *Sources*, IV, 191.

18　See A. R. Humphreys (ed.), *2 Henry I V*, Arden edn (1966), p. 20; Levin, 'Shakespeare's nomenclature' (1963), in *Shakespeare and the Revolution of the Times*, pp. 70, 75.

19　See Humphreys (ed.), *2 Henry I V*, introduction, p. xxvi.

20　L. C. Knights, 'Time's subjects: The Sonnets and *2 Henry I V*', in *Some Shakespearean Themes* (1959) (*Casebook*, p. 174).

4. The design of *Twelfth Night*

1　Karl F. Thompson, 'Shakespeare's romantic comedies', *P M L A*, LXVII (1952); E. C. Pettet, *Shakespeare and the Romance Tradition* (1949), pp. 122–32. 'Tempests dissolved in music' is the phrase of G. Wilson Knight, *The Shakespearian Tempest* (1953 edn), pp. 121–7.

2　This is the interpretation of John W. Draper, *The Twelfth Night of Shakespeare's Audience* (Stanford, California, 1950).

3　'Shakespearian comedy ... speculates imaginatively on modes, not of preserving a good already reached, but of enlarging and extending the possibilities of this and other kinds of good.' H. B. Charlton, *Shakespearian Comedy* (1938), pp. 277–8.

4　Enid Welsford, *The Fool* (1935), p. 251; compare E. K. Chambers, *The Mediaeval Stage* (1903), I, 403 n. Leslie Hotson gives further details connecting the play with the Feast of Misrule in *The First Night of Twelfth Night* (1954), ch. 7. To the various possible meanings of

Malvolio's yellow stockings (Hotson, *First Night*, p. 113) it is worth adding that, according to Stubbes, yellow or green 'or some other light wanton colour' was the livery of 'my Lord of Mis-rule' in the parishes (*Anatomy of Abuses* (1583), ed. Furnivall, p. 147). Stubbes is speaking of summer games, but misrule was not confined to Christmas – see *Twelfth Night*, III.iv.142: 'More matter for a May morning'.

5 P. Mueschke and J. Fleisher, 'Jonsonian elements in the comic underplot of *Twelfth Night*', *PMLA*, XLVIII (1933).

6 'Ma come si dice che egli era innamorato, subito cessa l'ammirazione, perciò che questa passione amorosa è di troppo gran potere e fa far cose assai piú meravigliose e strabocchevoli di questa. Né crediate che per altro la fabulosa Grecia finga i dèi innamorati aver fatte tante pazzie vituperose ..., se non per darci ad intendere che come l'uomo si lascia soggiogar ad amore ..., egli può dir d'aver giocata e perduta la sua libertà, e che miracolo non è se poi fa mille errori!' Bandello, *Le Novelle*, II, xxxvi (ed. G. Brognoligo (Bari, 1911), III, 252).

7 Riche's *Apolonius and Silla* (ed. Morton Luce, The Shakespeare Classics, 1912), p. 53; see p. 52: 'in all other things, wherein we show ourselves to be most drunken with this poisoned cup [of error], it is in our actions of love; for the lover is so estranged from that is right, and wandereth so wide from the bounds of reason, that he is not able to deem white from black ...; but only led by the appetite of his own affections, and grounding them on the foolishness of his own fancies, will so settle his liking on such a one, as either by desert or unworthiness will merit rather to be loathed than loved'. Contrasts between love and reason are prominent, again, in Erasmus's *In Praise of Folly* and Sidney's *Arcadia*, two likely sources of the general themes of *Twelfth Night*. Bacon's essay 'Of Love' comes nearer still to the subject-matter of Shakespeare's play, illustrating the tension of ideas there from a point of view almost directly opposite: 'The stage is more beholding to love than the life of man; for as to the stage, love is ever matter of comedies, and now and then of tragedies; but in life it doth much mischief, sometimes like a Siren, sometimes like a Fury ... Great spirits and great business do keep out this weak passion ...; for whosoever esteemeth too much of amorous affection, quitteth both riches and wisdom. This passion hath his floods in the very times of weakness, which are, great prosperity and great adversity ...; both which times kindle love, and make it more fervent, and therefore show it to be the child of folly.' This essay could almost be a commentary on Malvolio, Orsino, Viola and Sebastian.

8 The idea of representing life as a festival of misrule was already implicit, of course, in the common notion that 'all the world's a stage', and in the general Renaissance tradition of Folly, especially in Erasmus (compare Welsford, *Fool*, pp. 236–42). Robert Armin, who acted Feste, may have helped to give point to the idea; in his *Nest of Ninnies* (1600–8; ed. J. P. Collier, 1842), he represents the World, sick of a surfeit of drink and revelling, being shown a pageant of fools, who are partly endearing and partly symbols of the World's vices (compare Welsford, *Fool*, pp. 162–

5, 284). Armin does not treat of love, but John Heywood's *Play of Love* (c. 1533) is a Christmas interlude consisting of debates on the 'reasons' of love between Lover not Loved, Loved not Loving (the woman), Lover Loved, and Neither Lover nor Loved (the Vice). And much nearer to *Twelfth Night* comes Jonson's *Cynthia's Revels; or, the Fountain of Self-Love* (1600). Moreover, Shakespeare himself is very likely to have remembered the suggestive episode of 28 December 1594, when the *Comedy of Errors* was performed in the 'disordered' revels of Gray's Inn: 'So that Night was begun, and continued to the end, in nothing but Confusion and Errors; whereupon, it was ever afterwards called, *The Night of Errors* ... We preferred Judgments ... against a Sorcerer or Conjuror that was supposed to be the cause of that confused Inconvenience ... And Lastly, that he had foisted a Company of base and common Fellows, to make up our Disorders with a Play of Errors and Confusions; and that that Night had gained to us Discredit, and itself a Nickname of Errors' (*Gesta Grayorum*; E. K. Chambers, *Shakespeare* (1930), Appendix, 'Performances'). Lastly, Shakespeare uses the metaphor of life as a mask of misrule directly in *Troilus*, a play linked in several ways with *Twelfth Night*: 'Degree being vizarded, / Th' unworthiest shows as fairly in the mask' (I.iii.83).

9 This paragraph is based on Morton Luce's Arden edn of *Twelfth Night* (1906) and his edn of Riche. Luce assembles parallels between *Twelfth Night* and Riche, Bandello and *Gl'Ingannati*, from which it seems very possible, though not certain, that Shakespeare knew some or all of the latter. Luce mentions, but does not examine, Shakespeare's debt to Plautus.

10 'Due ammaestramenti sopra tutto ne cavarete: quanto possa il caso e la buona fortuna nelle cose d'amore; e quanto, in quella, vaglia una longa pazienzia accompagnata da buon consiglio' (I. Sanesi (ed.), *Commedie del Cinquecento* (Bari, 1912), I, 316).

11 'Io credo che questa sia certamente volontá di Dio che abbia avuto pietá di questa virtuosa giovane e dell'anima mia; ch'ella non vada in perdizione. E però, madonna Lelia, ... io non voglio altra moglie che voi ...' (V, iii; Sanesi, p. 393). Compare Bandello, pp. 273–5; Riche, p. 82.

12 Compare Lelia, in *Gl'Ingannati*: 'O what a fate is mine! I love him who hates me, ... I serve him who knows me not; and, worse still, I help him to love another ... only in the hope of gratifying these eyes with seeing him, one day, in my own way.' About her rival, she says: 'I pretend not to want to love her, unless she makes Flamminio withdraw from his love to her; and I have already brought the affair to a conclusion ...' (I, iii; Sanesi, pp. 322, 328). Bandello's heroine says: 'I have done so much that I want to see the end of it, come what may ... Then God will help me, who knows my heart and knows I have only taken these pains so as to have Lattanzio for a husband' (p. 262).

13 Riche, p. 64. Draper, *Audience* (ch. 6), argues that Orsino is meant as a wholly admirable or sympathetic character, and that *Twelfth Night* is 'a genial satire on the vulgar love of Malvolio and Sir Andrew in contrast to

the refined passion of Orsino, Olivia, and Viola-Sebastian' (p. 131). As regards Orsino, Riche's mildly scoffing attitude to his ducal lover hardly bears this out; nor do the quotations that Draper brings forward from the psychologists, e.g. his apt quotation from Burton: 'Love ... rageth with all sorts and conditions of men, yet is most evident among such as are young and lusty, in the flower of their years, nobly descended, high fed, such as live idly, and at ease; and for that cause (which our Divines call burning lust) ... this mad and beastly passion ... is named by our Physicians *Heroical* Love, and a more honorable title put upon it, *amor nobilis*, ... because Noble men and women make a common practice of it, and are so ordinarily affected with it' (Burton, pt. III.ii.1. 2; Draper, *Audience*, p. 122). For similar reasons, it is difficult to accept Hotson's conjecture (*First Night*, ch. 6) that Orsino is meant for the visiting Virginio Orsino, Duke of Bracciano, and Olivia for the Virgin Queen; if Shakespeare intended flattery, it seems unlikely that he would have presented both characters in an ironic light.

14 Compare Julina's speech in Riche, p. 66: 'men be of this condition, rather to desire those things which they cannot come by, than to esteem or value of that which ... liberally is offered unto them; but if the liberality of my proffer hath made to seem less the value of the thing that I meant to present, it is but in your own conceit ...' Shakespeare returns to the problems of value and the self-destruction of desire in *Hamlet* and *Troilus*. Orsino's 'shapes' and 'fancy' recall Theseus's lines in *A Midsummer Night's Dream*, V.i.4–22; and in *2 Henry IV*, Falstaff connects them with drink: 'A good sherris-sack ... ascends me into the brain ... makes it apprehensive, quick, forgetive, full of nimble, fiery and delectable shapes ...' (IV.iii.96). These are points of contact between Orsino and Sir Toby.

15 Compare Draper, *Audience*, pp. 215–19.

16 Compare *A Midsummer Night's Dream*, I.i.65–78 ('... For aye to be in shady cloister mew'd'), and Portia, in *The Merchant of Venice*, I.ii. 112–14. In *The Comedy of Errors*, Shakespeare moves the scene from the Epidamnus of *Menaechmi* to Ephesus so as to make Aemilia the priestess, or 'abbess', of Diana's temple there. Possibly he was turning to account the passage in *Miles Gloriosus*, where the courtesan pretends to give thanks to Diana of Ephesus for rescuing her from Neptune's blustering realm (Loeb edn, II.v:411 ff.; compare Aegeon's narrative of the storm in *Comedy of Errors*, I.i, which has no equivalent in *Menaechmi*). But in any case, the motif of a woman rescued from imposed celibacy after a sea-adventure is an important part of what could be called Shakespeare's mythology – Wilson Knight's 'tempest' theme; compare Portia again (*Merchant of Venice*, III.ii.53–7), and, of course, Marina, Perdita and Miranda. (There are satiric references to a convent from which the heroine runs away in Bandello and *Gl'Ingannati*.)

17 Compare II.iii. 10, III.i.58, III.iv. 124. There are other echoes, mainly comic, of the theme of Olivia–cloister–moon at: I.ii.32 (gossip);

I.iii.126–7 (Mistress Mall's curtained picture); I.v.20 ('let summer bear it out'); I.v.200 (''tis not that time of moon with me'); II.iii.58, etc. ('rouse the night-owl in a catch'); II.iv.44 ('the knitters in the sun'); II.v.160 ('Daylight and champian discovers not more'); III.i.38 ('Foolery ... does walk about the orb like the sun'); III.i.84 ('the heavens rain odours on you'); III.iv.56 ('midsummer madness'); IV.ii (Malvolio in darkness); IV.iii.1 ('that is the glorious sun'); IV.iii.28–34 ('conceal it ... heavens so shine'); V.i.153 ('To keep in darkness ...'); V.i.291–6 (Feste shouting); V.i.342 ('Kept in a dark house, visited by the priest'); and 'the wind and the rain' in Feste's epilogue.

18 Compare Orsino, I.iv.13–14. For Olivia's use of rhyme here, compare Beatrice (*Much Ado*, III.i.107), Helena (*All's Well*, I.i.216) and Cressida (*Troilus*, I.ii.282).

19 Compare I.v.52 ('... so beauty's a flower'), II.iv.38 ('For women are as roses ...'), II.iv.112 ('concealment like a worm i' th' bud ...').

20 Compare Tarquin, in *Lucrece*, 432, and the setting there. It is worth noting that Olivia's seal is a 'Lucrece' (II.v.92).

21 There is no real equivalent to this interview, or Olivia's share of it, in Shakespeare's likely sources, unless partly in Riche, p. 66 (quoted above, n. 14. But compare Pasquella, in *Gl'Ingannati*, II.iii, p. 339; and Luce, *Twelfth Night*, p. 184, cites verbal parallels from Bandello for III.i.117 and 149). As to the moral argument of the tale, both the Italians and Riche dwell on the justice and reason of exchanging love for love – e.g. *Gl'Ingannati*, I.iii (quoted above, n. 12), IV.ii (p. 349), V.ii (p. 390; the lover here decries 'ingratitude', as in *Twelfth Night*, III.iv.367), V.ii (quoted above, n. 11); Bandello, pp. 273–5. Further, Bandello's heroine tells her master that his sufferings in his second love are a just retribution for ingratitude in his first: 'you have received the return [*contracambio*] you deserved, because if you had been so much loved by a girl as beautiful as you say, you have done endlessly wrong to leave her for this one, who is avenging her without knowing it. A lover wants to be loved, not to follow someone in flight [*Egli si vuol amar chi ama e non seguir chi se ne fugge*]. Who knows if this beautiful girl is not still in love with you and living in the greatest misery for you?' (Bandello, pp. 265–6). As Luce points out (*Twelfth Night*, p. 184), this dialogue as a whole may have suggested Viola's dialogue with Orsino in II.iv.99–120; but the notion of love is still an exchange, not a gift. Similarly, Riche, p. 53, stresses 'desert', or reciprocity, as 'the ground of reasonable love', and he echoes Bandello: 'for to love them that hate us, to follow them that fly from us, ... who will not confess this to be an erroneous love, neither grounded upon wit nor reason?' Olivia's speech could almost be a reply to this.

22 See note on Shakespeare and Plautus, p. 74 above.

23 Compare Paul Reyher, *Essai sur les idées dans l'oeuvre de Shakespeare* (Paris, 1947), pp. 374–8.

24 *Twelfth Night*, I.ii.43, II.ii.40, I.v.310, II.v.146.

25 Compare the theme of 'witchcraft' (not present in *Menaechmi*) in *Com-*

edy of Errors, I.ii.100, II.ii.189, III.ii.45–52, 156, IV.iii.11, 66, and
IV.iv.147. Antonio's 'witchcraft', however, also harks back to the 'enchantment' Cesario has worked on Olivia (III.i.111).

26 Compare the sailors in the storm in *Comedy of Errors*, I.i.75–95; and
the speeches of Menaechmus of Syracuse, where, after receiving the
courtesan's gifts, he thanks the gods and hurries off 'while time and
circumstance permit' ('dum datur mi occasio / tempusque'; *Menaechmi*,
Loeb edn, III.ii:473–4, 551–3). Bandello's young man, at a similar
point in the story, also decides to 'try his luck' ('Lasciami andar a provar
la mia fortuna', p. 267), but Sebastian comes nearer to Plautus; compare
n. 23. The Italians virtually ignore the Plautine motif of resurrection,
which Shakespeare develops.

27 III.iv.223; compare Orsino's 'desires, like fell and cruel hounds' (I.i.21)
and Olivia's metaphor at III.i.118–20.

28 Compare Chambers, *Mediaeval Stage*, I, 190–8 (Christmas sword-
dances) and 206–27 (Mummers' plays); and Chambers, *The English
Folk-Play* (1933), pp. 3–9, 23–33 (the champions). Besides the rodo-
montade quoted above and the comic fighting, the following details of
contact or resemblance between the duel episode and the Mummers'
play seem worth noting: two of the main actors here are a fool and a
woman dressed as a man; there is a lady in the background, like St
George's Sabra (*Folk-Play*, pp. 25, 175), and the duel is a kind of wooing
contest (*Folk-Play*, pp. 99–104); 'cockatrices' and 'firago' suggest the
Dragon (*Folk-Play*, pp. 30, 156, 177, 204); the deliberate nonsense and
Fabian's 'bear' (III.iv.295) recall the clowning in *Mucedorus* (which has
Mummers' play associations – compare R. J. E. Tiddy, *The Mummers'
Play* (1923), pp. 84–5, 129–33); Sir Andrew's offer of a reward for
sparing his life has some resemblance to Jack of Lent's offer in the
processional game described by Machyn (Chambers, *Folk-Play*, pp.
155–6), while Antonio's entry corresponds to the entry of a Mummers'
play Doctor; and finally, like the Mummers' play combats (*Folk-Play*, p.
194), the duel is followed by a kind of resurrection – the resurrection of
one of the fighters' second self.

   On the other hand (apart from a desire to satirise the duello), there is a
possible source for this episode in the episode of feigned madness and
demonic possession in *Menaechmi*, V.ii (which Shakespeare had already
used in *The Comedy of Errors*, IV.iv). Antonio's part resembles the
sequel in *Menaechmi*, V.vii–viii, where the slave rushes in to rescue his
master's twin from a scuffle, is promised his liberty, and then loses it
again; and there, too, the episode of 'devils' leads on to a resurrection. In
addition, Antonio's part here recalls the passages in *The Comedy of
Errors* where Aegeon is arrested on a journey of love (I.i.124–39) and
where the Officer arrests Angelo for debt (IV.i); and this indirectly
strengthens the case for attributing this part of *Twelfth Night* to a
borrowing from Plautus. It is quite possible, however, that Shakespeare
noted the likeness between the resurrection motif in the folk-plays and
the resurrection motif in Plautus, and decided to exploit it.

29 Antonio's lines about 'empty trunks' hark back to Viola's speeches earlier (at I.ii.46–50 and II.ii.27–8) and to speeches in the previous comedies, e.g. Bassanio in the casket scene (*Merchant of Venice*, III.ii.73 ff.). But the tone of his 'idolatry' metaphor rather points forward to the debate between Troilus and Hector in *Troilus*, II.ii. Compare Bacon's comments on love as the worship of an 'idol', 'and how it braves the nature and value of things', in his essay 'Of Love'.

30 The first offspring of Folly, according to Erasmus, are Drunkenness, Ignorance and Self-Love.

31 Compare Morris P. Tilley, 'The organic unity of *Twelfth Night*', *PMLA*, XXIX (1914).

32 *Twelfth Night*, I.v.125–9, I.iii.84 and II.iii.145–50. There are many other instances, e.g.: I.iii.128 ('go to church in a galliard'); I.v.9–15 ('a good lenten answer ...'); I.v.28 (Maria 'as witty a piece of Eve's flesh ...'); I.v.56 ('cucullus non facit monachum'); I.v.68–70 (Olivia's brother's soul in 'hell'); II.iii.117 ('by Saint Anne'; compare Hotson, *First Night*, p. 101); II.v.41 ('Fie on him, Jezebel'); III.i.3–7 (Feste lives 'by the church'); III.ii.17 ('Noah'); III.ii.31 ('a Brownist'); III.ii.70–3 ('Malvolio is turn'd heathen, a very renegado; for there is no Christian that means to be sav'd by believing rightly can ever believe such impossible passages of grossness'); III.ii.76; III.iv.85–125 ('all the devils of hell ... The fiend is rough ... 'tis not for gravity to play at cherry-pit with Sathan ... Get him to say his prayers', etc.); III.iv.236–93 ('devil', repeated; 'souls and bodies hath he divorc'd three ... death and sepulchre ... perdition of souls'); IV.ii.1–63 (Sir Topas, 'the old hermit of Prague', 'Sathan', 'the Egyptians in their fog', Pythagoras and the soul, etc.); IV.ii.124–31 ('Like to the old Vice ... Adieu, goodman devil'); V.i.36–40 (Christmas dicing – compare Hotson, *First Night*, p. 164 – and 'the bells of Saint Bennet'); V.i.47 ('the sin of covetousness'); V.i.176–82 ('For the love of God ... the very devil incardinate'); V.i.284 ('Beelzebub'); V.i.287–96 ('gospels' – compare J. Dover Wilson (ed.), *Twelfth Night*, New Shakespeare edn, p. 168); V.i.376 (the whirligig – compare Hotson, *First Night*, p. 164). In addition, Sir Toby anticipates Sebastian's reference to astrology (I.iii.138, II.i.3). By contrast with these numerous comic references to religion, the serious actors cite mythology; and, apart from Olivia's Priest, also a little comic, they hardly refer to orthodox religion at all (unless Antonio's words at III.iv.312 and 349 contain such a reference implicitly – 'I take the fault on me', and 'Do not ... make me so unsound a man'; compare Wilson, *Twelfth Night*, p. 156). Among the sub-plot actors, however, Malvolio is notable for his references to 'Jove' (II.v.172, 178, III.iv.74–5, 82). Wilson, *Twelfth Night*, p. 97, argues that these are a sign of alterations in the text, to satisfy the statute of 1606 against blasphemy; but they seem more likely to be a comic sign that Malvolio is coming within the orbit of romance.

33 Draper, *Audience*, chs. 2–3, gives much illuminating material on the social background of Sir Toby and Sir Andrew. But he introduces the

very questionable assumption that Sir Andrew is meant to be a social climber of *nouveau riche* parentage. Draper bases his argument on Sir Andrew's 'carpet'-knighthood and his boorishness. But the son of an ambitious self-made man would have been quite likely to be sent to a university (like Yellowhammer junior in *A Chaste Maid in Cheapside*); and, on the other side, a gentleman might buy a knighthood (if that is in fact what 'carpet consideration' implies – Draper, *Audience*, p. 48). Sir Andrew's follies are simply those of a wealthy heir. He admires his horse, has no sense of humour, is quarrelsome, frowns or capers without reason, has no languages, dresses absurdly, and gets drunk – and this is the catalogue of follies in Portia's noble suitors in *The Merchant of Venice*, I.ii. He is thin, vain and insignificant, like Justice Shallow in his youth, and has grown up a similar ignoramus (2 *Henry IV*, III.ii, V.i.62–77); precisely as Orlando, too, fears to grow up if he, a 'gentleman' by birth, is kept 'rustically at home' for his education (*As You Like It*, I.i). Some of Shakespeare's contemporaries comment scornfully on the English custom of keeping a wealthy heir 'like a mome' on his estate, while his younger brother must fend for himself (T. Wilson, *The State of England*, (1600), ed. F. J. Fisher, pp. 23–4; compare *Cyvile and Uncyvile Life* (1579), Roxburghe Library edn, p. 24; Fynes Moryson, *Itinerary* (1617; ed. MacLehose, IV, 61)). Sir Andrew, with his self-esteem, seems just such an heir, now converting himself into an Improvident Gallant. In short (apart from his ambitions on Olivia, which are really very faint), the point of the satire is not that Sir Andrew is trying to climb above his class, but that he is a gentleman born, adjusting himself foolishly to changing manners and conditions. The same could be said of the comparable characters in Ben Jonson, e.g. Master Stephen or Kastril, the angry boy.

34 E.g. O. J. Campbell, *Shakespeare's Satire* (New York, 1943), pp. 84–8; Draper, *Audience*, ch. 5. The Countess's Steward in *All's Well* is apparently a gentleman by rank; Antonio in *The Duchess of Malfi* is certainly one; and the historical characters who have been suggested as possible originals for Malvolio have been of the rank of knights or above (compare Luce, *Apolonius and Silla*, p. 95; Draper, *Audience*, pp. 110–11; Hotson, *First Night*, ch. 5). The argument that Malvolio must be plebeian because he is presumptuous seems to rest on a false assumption about Elizabethan satire.

5. Shakespeare and the ventriloquists

1 John Weever, *Epigrammes in the Oldest Cut and Newest Fashion* (1599; Stratford-upon-Avon, 1922), p. 75.

2 Hazlitt, *Characters of Shakespeare's Plays* (1817), ed. Catherine Macdonald Maclean, Everyman's Library (1964), pp. 228, 233.

3 Coleridge, Lecture VII (1818), in *Miscellaneous Criticism*, ed. T. M. Raysor (1936), pp. 43–4.

4 *Miscellaneous Criticism*, pp. 54, 90; see M. M. Badawi, *Coleridge: Critic of Shakespeare* (Cambridge, 1973), pp. 58, 103–8.

5 Coventry *Slaughter of the Innocents*, ll. 487, 500–3, ed. J. Q. Adams in *Chief Pre-Shakespearean Dramas* (Cambridge, Mass., 1924).
6 F. R. Leavis, 'Tragedy and the "medium"', in *The Common Pursuit* (1952; Harmondsworth, 1962), p. 130.
7 Coleridge, *Shakespearean Criticism*, ed. T. M. Raysor (2 vols., Everyman's Library, 1960), I, 34, II, 85; compare *Miscellaneous Criticism*, pp. 43–4.
8 Peter Ure, 'Character and role from Richard III to Hamlet', in John Russell Brown and Bernard Harris (eds.), *Hamlet*, Stratford-upon-Avon Studies 5 (1963), 10.
9 'Thine evermore, most dear lady, whilst this machine is to him' (II.ii.123). Had Giordano Bruno, *De gli eroici furori* (1585), found its way into Hamlet's reading? Arguing that the soul should not repudiate the things of the senses, Bruno writes: 'Soccorrasi al corpo con la materia e soggetto corporeo, e l'intelletto con gli suoi oggetti s'appaghe; a fin che conste questa composizione, non si dissolva questa machina, dove per mezzo del spirito l'anima è unita al corpo' (*Opere italiane*, ed. Giovanni Gentile (Bari, 1927), II, 386 ['Let the body help itself with matter and bodily subject, and the intellect be content with its own objects; in order that this combination should hold firm, that this machine wherein soul is united to body by means of the spirit should not be dispersed']). In classical usage a *machine* was always a material construction (I owe this point to a letter from Professor W. S. Allen), and *O.E.D.* cites this passage from *Hamlet* as the first English example of a figurative use, 'Applied to the human and animal frame as a combination of several parts' (the only other possibly, though not certainly, Shakespearean instance of the noun comes in 'this machine, or this frame', meaning the device of the morris-dance, in *Two Noble Kinsmen*, III.v.113). In his next paragraph, Bruno continues (the Soul is addressing its own thoughts): 'Ondi vi è nato questo malencolico e perverso umore di rompere le certe e naturali legge de la vera vita che sta nelle vostri mani, per una incerta e che non è se non in ombra oltre gli limiti del fantastico pensiero?' ['Whence springs this melancholy and perverse humour of breaking the certain and natural laws of the true life dwelling within your grasp, for the sake of one uncertain and non-existent unless in the shadow beyond the limits of fantastic thought?']. This passage also invites comparison with Hamlet. In his letter to Ophelia, Hamlet, like Bruno, is commenting on a poem he has just written, in extravagantly worded prose; and finally, the poem itself contains a faintly Brunoesque speculation about the stars. All in all, it seems very possible that Bruno suggested Hamlet's unique use of the word *machine*.
10 II.ii.303–7, 551–7; III.ii.5–7, 16–19, 63–74; III.iv.55–62; IV.iv.33–9, 53–6.
11 Compare Maurice Charney, *Style in 'Hamlet'* (Princeton, 1969); R. A. Foakes, 'Character and speech in *Hamlet*', in Brown and Harris, *Hamlet*; J. M. Newton, '*Hamlet* and Shakespeare's disposition for comedy', *The Cambridge Quarterly*, IX (1979).
12 V.i.117, 137–41, 254–7, 283–5; V.ii.112–94.

6. Romance in *King Lear*

This article is a revision of lectures delivered to university audiences at Northwestern, in France and at Leicester.

1 Compare Hardin Craig, 'The shackling of accidents: a study of Elizabethan Tragedy' (1940), in Ralph J. Kaufmann (ed.), *Elizabethan Drama* (New York, 1961), p. 31.

2 S. L. Wolfe, *The Greek Romances in Elizabethan Prose Fiction* (New York, 1912), pp. 312, 366 ('th' Egyptian thief' of *Twelfth Night*, V.i.118 was Thyamis, one of the brothers in Heliodorus's *Ethiopica*).

3 Kenneth Muir (ed.), *King Lear* (1952), p. xxii.

4 Compare G. K. Hunter, 'The last tragic heroes', in John Russell Brown and Bernard Harris (eds.), *Later Shakespeare*, Stratford-upon-Avon Studies 8 (1966); Hallett Smith, *Shakespeare's Romances* (San Marino, 1972).

5 Maynard Mack, *King Lear in Our Time* (Berkeley and Los Angeles, 1965), pp. 45–51.

6 Laura A. Hibbard, *Medieval Romance in England* (New York, 1924), pp. 58–64.

7 Mack, *Lear in Our Time*, pp. 56–63; compare chapter 11, pp. 213–14 above.

8 Mack, *Lear in Our Time*, pp. 63–6.

9 Richard Harvey, *Philadelphus, or, A Defence of Brutus, and the Brutans History* (1593), quoted by Wilfrid Perrett, *The Story of King Lear from Geoffrey of Monmouth to Shakespeare* (Berlin, 1904), p. 93.

10 *Leir*, ed. Geoffrey Bullough, in *Narrative and Dramatic Sources of Shakespeare*, VII (1973).

11 William R. Elton, *King Lear and the Gods* (San Marino, 1966).

12 F. D. Hoeniger, 'The artist exploring the primitive', in Rosalie L. Colie and F. T. Flahiff (eds.), *Some Facets of 'King Lear'* (Toronto, 1974).

13 Bullough, *Sources*, VII, 317.

14 *Cymbeline*, V.iv.28; compare V.v.402, and *King John*, III.iv.70, 74.

15 *Troilus and Cressida*, V.ii.154, 156.

16 *Twelfth Night*, III.i.21 (see the Arden edn, ed. J. M. Lothian and T. W. Craik (1975), p. 75).

17 *Thebais*, translated by Thomas Newton, ed. T. S. Eliot, in *Seneca*, Tudor Translations (1927), I, 117–18 (compare Seneca, *Phoenissae*, lines 340–7, 354–7).

18 *A Knack to Know a Knave*, ed. G. R. Proudfoot, Malone Society (1964).

19 F. T. Flahiff, 'Edgar; once and future king', in Colie and Flahiff, *Facets of 'King Lear'*.

7. *King Lear*, Montaigne and Harsnett

This chapter is a revision and expansion of a paper originally submitted to a seminar on Shakespeare's use of his sources at the International Shakespeare Association Congress at Stratford-upon-Avon, in August 1981.

1 Quotations from *King Lear* in this chapter are keyed to Kenneth Muir (ed.), *King Lear*, Arden edn (1952; rev. edn 1972). Other Shakespeare quotations conform to the *Riverside* text.

2 Muir, *King Lear*, pp. 235–9. Compare Muir, *Shakespeare's Sources*, I (1957), 161–2. Muir incorporates, with reservations, source materials collected by previous scholars, notably G. C. Taylor in *Shakespeare's Debt to Montaigne* (1925) and W. B. Drayton Henderson in 'Montaigne's *Apologie of Raymond Sebond*, and *King Lear*', *Shakespeare Association Bulletin*, 14 (1939), 209–25, and 15 (1940), 40–54.

3 'At a clap' (I.iv.292; see Muir, *King Lear*, p. 236) occurs in Harsnett's *Declaration* (1603), p. 52; 'discommend' (II.ii.106), in Harsnett, p. 38.

4 Pierre Villey, *Montaigne et François Bacon* (Paris, 1913; reprinted Geneva 1973), pp. 5, 33, 54; see William R. Elton, *'King Lear' and the Gods* (San Marino, California, 1966). The parallels between *Lear* and the political teachings of Lipsius, set out by Arthur F. Kinnery in 'Some conjectures on the composition of *King Lear*' (*Shakespeare Survey*, 33, ed. Kenneth Muir (Cambridge, 1980)), seem to me too general to amount to strong evidence about sources.

5 Samuel Daniel, 'To my deere friend M. *John Florio*', in *Montaigne's Essays*, trans. Florio (ed. L. C. Harmer, Everyman's Library, 3 vols., 1965), 1.13 (volume and page references to Florio in this chapter (e.g. 2.67) are keyed to this edition).

6 Robert Ellrodt, 'Self-consciousness in Montaigne and Shakespeare', in *Shakespeare Survey*, 28, ed. Kenneth Muir (Cambridge, 1975), p. 49.

7 J. F. Danby, *Shakespeare's Doctrine of Nature* (1949); Rosalie L. Colie, 'Reason and need: *King Lear* and the 'crisis' of the aristocracy', in R. L. Colie and F. T. Flahiff (eds.), *Some Facets of 'King Lear'* (Toronto, 1974), pp. 185–219; compare G. R. Hibbard, *'King Lear*: a retrospect, 1939–79', in *Shakespeare Survey*, 33, pp. 3–8.

8 R. A. Sayce, *The Essays of Montaigne: A Critical Exploration* (1972), pp. 84–5, 270.

9 P. Villey, *Montaigne et Bacon*, pp. 30–7.

10 I have lightly modernised Florio's punctuation here.

11 Henderson, 'Montaigne's *Apologie* and *King Lear*', p. 47; see also Paul Reyher, *Essai sur les idées dans l'oeuvre de Shakespeare* (Paris, 1947), pp. 510–13.

12 Montaigne, 'Of Bookes' (II, x); 'Of Presumption' (II, xvii) (Florio, 2.92, 380). On Montaigne's use of his title-word, and the first reactions to it, see Alan M. Boase, *The Fortunes of Montaigne* (1935), pp. 2–3; Sayce, *Essays of Montaigne*, pp. 20–2; Ellrodt, 'Self-consciousness', p. 40.

13 Shakespeare uses the noun elsewhere only in Sonnet 110, where it means simply trials or experiments ('And worse essays prov'd thee my best of love'). In his note on Edmund's speech, Muir comments that *essay* and *taste* were synonyms, and he doubts any special link with Montaigne (Muir, *King Lear*, pp. 25, 237). However, *gustus*, 'taste', was exactly the word put forward by Lipsius as the nearest Latin equivalent for

Montaigne's title – though *conatus*, 'prentice effort', was soon preferred instead – (Boase, *Fortunes*, pp. 2–3). One or two of the *Essays* are cast in the form of letters, including 'Of the Affection of Fathers', which is addressed to Mme d'Estissac.

14 *Leir* I.i.26–31, ed. Geoffrey Bullough, in *Narrative and Dramatic Sources of Shakespeare*, VII (1973).

15 Compare Colie, 'Reason and need', pp. 197–8, 218.

16 See Bullough, *Sources*, VII, 313, 318, 326.

17 The word *depositaries* (unique in Shakespeare) is another borrowing from Florio; see Muir, *King Lear*, p. 237.

18 Henderson, 'Montaigne's *Apologie* and *King Lear*', pp. 210–11.

19 L. C. Knights, *Some Shakespearean Themes* (1959; Harmondsworth, 1966), p. 73.

20 See Boase, *Fortunes*, pp. 189, 192, discussing the criticisms of Montaigne and Charron by Pierre Chanet in *Considérations sur La Sagesse de Charron* (Paris, 1643). The seeming contraditions in Montaigne's view of Nature are discussed from another angle by A. Micha in 'Art et nature dans les "Essais" ', *Bulletin de la Société des Amis de Montaigne*, 19 (July–December 1956), pp. 50–5.

21 Henderson, 'Montaigne's *Apologie* and *King Lear*', p. 41; Muir, *King Lear*, p. 238.

22 I was first led to think about the probable interest of this essay for Shakespeare by a lecture by Emrys Jones on *The Winter's Tale*.

23 Muir, *King Lear*, pp. 48, 236. R. L. Colie emphasises Lear's concern with his issue ('Reason and need', p. 197). In another article in the same book, she points out how the close of Lear's speech – 'How sharper than a serpent's tooth it is / To have a thankless child' (I.iv.286) – gives an echo from Psalm 140, one of a series of Biblical echoes running strongly through the tragedy ('The energies of endurance; Biblical echoes in *King Lear*', p. 124). Further, there is a close linkage between Lear's speeches to Goneril in this scene and the hero's curses in *Timon of Athens*, especially at IV.iii.176–92, with the sequence there of 'nature', 'man's unkindness', 'womb', 'teems', 'arrogant man', animal images including the 'eyeless venom'd worm', 'abhorred births', 'one poor root', 'fertile', 'ingrateful man', 'dragons, wolves, and bears', 'new monsters', and finally, the 'marbled mansion' of heaven. It is of course characteristic of Shakespeare, as of other poets, to repeat themes or images from one work to another; but here the associations seem unusually close.

24 A. C. Bradley, *Shakespearean Tragedy* (1904; 1958), pp. 250–1.

25 *O.E.D., curiosity* §§ 5 and 9; compare Muir, *King Lear*, pp. 236, 237 (Muir's gloss on I.ii.4, 'squeamishness, false delicacy', seems to me to underplay the sting in Edmund's *curiosity*).

26 Again, I have lightly modernised Florio's punctuation (compare Montaigne, *Essais*, 2 vols., ed. Maurice Rat (Paris, 1962), 2.317–18). Sayce, *Essays of Montaigne* (pp. 194–7, 235–7), discusses Montaigne's critique of 'custom'.

27 Boase, *Fortunes*, pp. 26–7.

28 Tourneur borrows frequently from *Lear* in *The Atheist's Tragedy*, especially from Edmund's speeches (see Irving Ribner (ed.), *The Atheist's Tragedy*, The Revels Plays (1964), p. lxiv, and notes to I.i.45, II.iii.36, II.iv.136, III.ii.8, and IV.iii.105; there is a further echo, from Lear himself, as well as from Edmund, at V.ii.145–51). See Elton, '*Lear' and the Gods*, pp. 138–46, on the resemblance between Edmund's views and those of the *libertins*; on the latter, compare Boase, *Fortunes*, pp. 167, 172, and Henri Busson, *Le Rationalisme dans la littérature française de la Renaissance (1533–1601)* (Paris, 1957), pp. 461–8. Edmund's speech against astrology (I.ii.115–30) recalls Montaigne's criticisms, and its vocabulary draws upon Florio (Muir, *King Lear*, pp. 29–30, 236).

29 See A. José Axelrad, *Un Malcontent élizabéthain: John Marston* (Paris, 1955), pp. 98–101; Webster, *The White Devil*, ed. John Russell Brown, The Revels Plays (1960), I.i.46; I.ii.43, 198; IV.ii.91, 102.

30 J. H. P. Pafford (ed.), *The Winter's Tale*, Arden edn, (1963), p. 169; Frank Kermode (ed.), *The Tempest*, Arden edn (1954), pp. xxxiv, 145–7.

31 See H. A. Mason, *Shakespeare's Tragedies of Love* (London, 1970), p. 196.

32 Henderson, 'Montaigne's *Apologie* and *King Lear*', pp. 44–5.

33 See Muir's note on III.iv.101–7.

34 Henderson, 'Montaigne's *Apologie* and *King Lear*'; Muir, *King Lear*, notes on IV.vi.112, 120.

35 See Muir, *King Lear*, notes on IV.vi.145–76; Elton, '*Lear' and the Gods*, pp. 230–4. The section in Montaigne's 'Apology' contrasting positive and natural laws refers to cannibals eating their fathers and to Plato being offered 'a robe made after the Persian fashion' (Florio, 2.297–9) – references possibly recalled by Lear at I.i.116–17 and III.vi.77–9.

36 But see Muir's notes on IV.vi.176 ('we came crying hither') and V.ii.11 ('Ripeness is all').

37 Mason, *Shakespeare's Tragedies of Love*, pp. 208, 210.

38 *Ibid.*, p. 215.

39 'Of the Lame or Crippel' (III, xi; Florio, 3.286); see Sayce, *Essays of Montaigne*, pp. 248–50; compare Montaigne, 'Of Crueltie' (II, xi; 2.121) and 'Of Coaches' (III, vi; 3.146–8).

40 See Michael Macdonald, *Mystical Bedlam: Madness, Anxiety and Healing in Seventeenth-Century England* (Cambridge, 1981), pp. 155–6, 168–9, 198–217.

41 Samuel Harsnett, *A Declaration of Egregious Popishe Impostures* (1603), pp. 178, 180, 219, 253.

42 Muir, *King Lear*, note on III.iv.46–7 (compare Stanley Wells, 'The Taming of the Shrew and King Lear: a structural comparison', in *Shakespeare Survey*, 33 (Cambridge, 1980)).

43 On Harsnett's style and tone, see Muir, *Shakespeare's Sources*, I, 147–61, and M. C. Bradbrook, *Shakespeare, the Poet in his World* (London, 1978), pp. 193–8.

44 Muir, *Shakespeare's Sources*, I, 147–61.
45 Muir, *King Lear*, note on II.iv.7–9; quotations from Harsnett, p. 241.
46 See Muir, *King Lear*, p. 238.

8. 'Wit' in Jacobean comedy

 1 *Jacobean City Comedy* (1968, rev. edn 1980).
 2 *The Growth and Structure of Elizabethan Comedy* (2nd edn, 1973), p.
    219. Compare Ian Donaldson, *The World Upside-Down; Comedy from
    Jonson to Fielding* (Oxford, 1970); Alexander Leggatt, *Citizen Comedy
    in the Age of Shakespeare* (Toronto, 1973); George Hibbard, 'Ben Jon-
    son and human nature', in William Blissett *et al.* (eds.), *A Celebration
    of Ben Jonson* (Toronto, 1973); Malcolm Kiniry, 'Jacobean comedy and
    the acquisitive grasp', in Maurice Charney (ed.), *Comedy: New
    Perspectives* (New York, 1978). The lines of my own argument in this
    article have been strongly influenced by Jean Jacquot, 'Le répertoire des
    compagnies d'enfants à Londres (1600–1610)', in Jacquot (ed.),
    Dramaturgie et Société ... aux XVIe et XVIIe siècles (Paris, 1968).
 3 *Humanism and Poetry in the Early Tudor Period* (1959), ch. 3, 'The
    discovery of wit', p. 76. Compare Douglas Duncan, *Ben Jonson and the
    Lucianic Tradition* (Cambridge, 1979).
 4 C. S. Lewis, 'Wit (with *Ingenium*)', in *Studies in Words* (Cambridge,
    1961); compare William Empson, *The Structure of Complex Words*
    (1952), pp. 84–100.
 5 Robert Ellrodt, *Les Poètes métaphysiques anglais* (Paris, 1960), III,
    13–42, 94–192, 396–400.
 6 G. K. Hunter, *John Lyly: The Humanist as Courtier* (1962).
 7 *Euphues*, ed. R. Warwick Bond, in *Complete Works of John Lyly*
    (Oxford, 1902), I, 184.
 8 Sir John Harington, *A Brief Apology for Poetry*, ed. G. Gregory Smith,
    in *Elizabethan Critical Essays* (1904), II, 218.
 9 Gabriel Harvey, *Foure Letters* (1592) and *Pierces Supererogation*
    (1593), in *Elizabethan Critical Essays*, II, 234, 250, 254–5. Compare
    Lewis, *Studies in Words*, pp. 100–3.
10 *Discoveries*, ed. C. H. Herford and Percy and Evelyn Simpson, in *The
    Works of Ben Jonson*, VIII (Oxford, 1947), p. 592 (subsequently
    referred to as HS).
11 *Ibid.*, p. 581; compare Shadwell's praise of Jonson, in his Preface to *The
    Sullen Lovers* (1668).
12 Jonas A. Barish, 'Jonson and the loathèd stage', in Bissett, *A
    Celebration*; see also Duncan, *Jonson and the Lucianic Tradition*.
13 HS, III (Oxford, 1927).
14 *Ibid.*
15 II.iii.217; III.iii.26; III.ix.37.
16 See Edward Partridge (ed.), *Epicoene* (New Haven and London, 1971);
    Jonas A. Barish, *Ben Jonson and the Language of Prose Comedy*
    (Cambridge, Mass., 1960), pp. 145–86; Donaldson, *World Upside-*

Down, pp. 27–45; Duncan, *Jonson and the Lucianic Tradition*, pp. 165–88. I have discussed some of the London background in 'Farce and fashion in *The Silent Woman*' (*Essays and Studies 1967*), ed. Martin Holmes; see pp. 183, 184–7 above.

17 *The Shoemakers' Holiday* (1599) and Heywood's plays featuring historical London worthies are chronicle plays as much as comedies; compare Leggatt, *Citizen Comedy*, pp. 14–32; Anne Barton, 'London comedy and the ethos of the City', *The London Journal*, 4 (1978). '

18 Leggatt, *Citizen Comedy*, pp. 125–32, 146–8.

19 'Cuthbert Cunny-Catcher', ed. Gāmini Salgādo, in *Cony-Catchers and Bawdy Baskets* (Harmondsworth, 1972), p. 346.

20 G. J. Watson (ed.), *A Trick to Catch the Old One* (1969), introduction.

21 Ed. A. R. Waller, *The Works of Beaumont and Fletcher*, I X (Cambridge, 1910); for date, etc., compare Alfred Harbage, *Annals of English Drama*, revised, S. Schoenbaum (1964).

22 Jacquot, 'Répertoire', pp. 757–69; André Bry, 'Middleton et le public des "city comedies" ', in Jacquot, *Dramaturgie et Société*; G. K. Paster, 'The city in Plautus and Middleton', *Renaissance Drama*, N.S. VI (Evanston, 1973); Leggatt, *Citizen Comedy*, pp. 9, 33–53; on the generation conflict, Barton, 'London comedy', pp. 175–6; Maynard Mack, *Rescuing Shakespeare* (International Shakespeare Association, Oxford, 1979).

23 Compare F. J. Fisher, 'The development of London as a centre of conspicuous consumption in the 16th and 17th centuries', *Transactions of the Royal Historical Society*, 4th ser. xxx (1948), and 'The growth of London', in E. W. Ives (ed.), *The English Revolution, 1600–1660* (1968); Lawrence Stone, *The Crisis of the Aristocracy, 1558–1641* (Oxford, 1965), pp. 394–8.

24 See *O.E.D.*, *leisure*, §§ 3, 6.

25 I have used the text in *The Works of Beaumont and Fletcher*, I, ed. George Darley (2nd edn, 1883).

26 Michael Neill, ' "Wit's most accomplished Senate": the audience of the Caroline private theaters', *Studies in English Literature*, 18 (1978).

9. Comic form in Ben Jonson: Volpone and the philosopher's stone

1 'To Ben Johnson uppon occasion of his Ode to Himself' in *Ben Jonson*, ed. C. H. Herford and Percy and Evelyn Simpson (11 vols., Oxford, 1925–52), XI, 335. All quotations from Jonson in this chapter are taken from this edition, which is referred to in subsequent notes as HS.

2 *Epistolae Ho-Elianae* (1645), in HS, XI, 417 (but see E. B. Partridge on Jonson's thought, in *The Elizabethan Theatre*, IV, ed. G. R. Hibbard (Waterloo, Ontario, 1974)).

3 *Every Man out of his Humour*, III.vi.207; *Volpone*, Dedication to the Universities.

4 Ray L. Heffner, Jr, 'Unifying symbols in the comedy of Ben Jonson' (1955), in Jonas A. Barish (ed.), *Ben Jonson* (Englewood Cliffs, N.J., 1963).

5 Compare L. C. Knights, *Drama and Society in the Age of Jonson* (1937).

6 See HS, II, 89–93; F. H. Mares (ed.), *The Alchemist* (1967), pp. xxxi–xl; also: John Read, *The Alchemist in Life, Literature and Art* (1947); E. J. Holmyard, *Alchemy* (1957); and Lynn Thorndike, *A History of Magic and Experimental Science*, V–VI (New York, 1941) (esp. V, 532 ff., 617 ff.; VI, 238 ff.); Hiram Haydn, *The Counter-Renaissance* (New York, 1950); Marie Boas, *The Scientific Renaissance, 1450–1630* (1962).

7 *Every Man out of his Humour*, IV.viii.166–73; *The Magnetic Lady*, I.vii.5–16, IV.viii.27–31; compare Marvin T. Herrick, *Comic Theory in the Sixteenth Century* (Urbana, 1964), ch. 4.

8 *Every Man out of his Humour*, Induction, 256–9; *Discoveries*, lines 2643–53.

9 Heffner, 'Unifying symbols', p. 146.

10 *Plutus*, 123–97.

11 Compare Coburn Gum, *The Aristophanic Comedies of Ben Jonson* (The Hague and Paris, 1969).

12 *Utopia*, Temple Classics edn (1904), pp. 109–10; see Francis G. Allison, *Lucian, Satirist and Artist* (1927); H. A. Mason, *Humanism and Poetry in the Early Tudor Period* (1959), pp. 59–73.

13 HS, II, 50–3; compare Mario Praz, 'Ben Jonson's Italy', in *The Flaming Heart* (New York, 1958).

14 *Timon*, 14 (in *Lucian*, II, Loeb Library, trans. A. H. Harmon, 1915); Erasmus's trans. in *Luciani Opuscula* (Venice, 1516), fol. 65^v.

15 Erasmus, fol. 64; *Timon* 8 (also 21, 42, 45, 54); see also HS, IX, 687; Harry Levin, 'Jonson's Metempsychosis' (1943), in Jonas A. Barish (ed.), *Jonson: 'Volpone'* (1972), p. 89.

16 Compare M. C. Bradbrook, '*The Comedy of Timon*', in *Renaissance Drama*, IX (1966), 96–7.

17 See n. 15.

18 *The Jew of Malta*, III.v.4.

19 HS, II, 58.

20 *Drama and Society*, p. 202.

21 *Utopia*, Temple Classics, pp. 155–61.

22 Henry Cornelius Agrippa, *Of the Vanitie and uncertaintie of Artes and Sciences* (1531), trans. J. Sanford (1575), fol. 157; see Thorndike, *History of Magic*, v, 127–38.

23 See *Dialogues of the Dead*, V (Plutus and Hermes).

24 See HS, X, 87–9; Edgar Hill Duncan, 'Jonson's *Alchemist* and the literature of alchemy', *PMLA*, LXI (1946); compare Agrippa, *Vanitie*, pp. 158–9.

25 E.g. *Love Restored* (1612); *The Golden Age Restored* (1615); *Mercury Vindicated from the Alchemists at Court* (1616).

26 Bacon, *Works* (ed. Spedding, Ellis and Heath), III, 284–90; see HS, XI, 273–4.

10. Farce and fashion in *The Silent Woman*

1 Jonas A. Barish, 'Ovid, Juvenal and *The Silent Woman*', *PMLA*, LXXI (1956), 213; see also Barish, *Ben Jonson and the Language of Prose Comedy* (Cambridge, Mass., 1960), pp. 145–86.
2 Oscar James Campbell, 'The relation of *Epicoene* to Aretino's *Il Marescalco*', *PMLA*, XLVI (1931).
3 *1 Henry IV*, III.iii.122–8. Edward B. Partridge places rather heavy emphasis on the sexual freakishness of the characters in *Epicoene*, in *The Broken Compass* (1958), pp. 161–77.
4 A. Pauphilet (ed.), *Jeux et sapience du moyen âge* (Paris, 1951), p. 370.
5 In Fletcher's *Woman's Prize* (see p. 187 above), one of the women refers pointedly to Tom Tyler (II.vi; *The Works of Beaumont and Fletcher*, ed. A. R. Waller (Cambridge, 1910), VIII, 37). The interlude does not appear to have been printed before 1661.
6 Ian Maxwell, *French Farce and John Heywood* (Melbourne, 1946), pp. 39, 65.
7 Mario Apollonio, *Storia del teatro italiano* (Florence, 1940), II, 84; Enid Welsford, *The Fool* (1935; New York, 1961), pp. 206–8; see also A. D., 'The genesis of Jonson's *Epicoene*' (*Notes and Queries*, CCCIII (1948), 55–6).
8 M. Tierney, 'Aristotle and Menander', *Proceedings of the Royal Irish Academy*, XLIII (Dublin, 1936), 253.
9 Barish, *Jonson and the Language of Prose Comedy*, p. 156.
10 Barish, 'Ovid, Juvenal and *The Silent Woman*', p. 221.
11 *Ibid.*, p. 218.
12 Dryden, 'Dramatic Poetry of the Last Age' (1673), in *Essays* (Everyman edn.), p. 104; Barish, 'Ovid, Juvenal and *The Silent Woman*', p. 219; compare *Jonson and the Language of Prose Comedy*, p. 148.
13 Barish, 'Ovid, Juvenal and *The Silent Woman*', p. 213.
14 Edmund Wilson, 'Morose Ben Jonson', in *The Triple Thinkers* (1952).
15 *The Silent Woman*, V.iv.224, recalls *Coriolanus*, II.ii.98–101 ('He lurch'd all swords of the garland'). There may be deeper links between these two plays both dealing with One against the World. Jonson is likely to have listened very attentively to a Roman play by Shakespeare. It could be that his impulse to parody, or sardonic transposition, was aroused, e.g. by Coriolanus's greeting to Virgilia (II.i.175), 'My gracious silence, hail!'
16 C. H. Herford and Percy and Evelyn Simpson (eds.), *The Works of Ben Jonson*, X (Oxford, 1950). This edition is referred to in subsequent notes as HS.
17 See E. K. Chambers, *The Elizabethan Stage* (Oxford, 1923), II, 214; IV, 351.
18 Edmund Howes, Continuation of John Stow's *Annales* (1615 edn), p. 938; compare *ibid.*, p. 868.
19 Dekker, *The Dead Term* (quoted M. St Clare Byrne, *Elizabethan Life in Town and Country* (revised edn, 1961), p. 92).

20 Howes, Continuation, p. 828; Norman G. Brett-James, *The Growth of Stuart London* (1935), pp. 67, 80–8.

21 See E. G. R. Taylor, 'Camden's England', in H. C. Darby (ed.), *An Historical Geography of England* (Cambridge, 1936), p. 364.

22 John White, *Two Sermons*; see Louis B. Wright, *Middle-Class Culture in Elizabethan England* (Chapel Hill, 1935), p. 290.

23 Howes, Continuation, pp. 867–8; compare F. J. Fisher, 'The development of London as a centre of conspicuous consumption in the 16th and 17th centuries', *Transactions of the Royal Historical Society*, 4th Ser. XXX (1948), 40–3; Lawrence Stone, *The Crisis of the Aristocracy, 1558–1641* (Oxford, 1965), pp. 394–8.

24 Fisher, 'Development', p. 43; N. E. McClure (ed.), *The Letters of John Chamberlain* (Philadelphia, 1939), I, 273 (for the years 1607–9, compare *ibid.*, pp. 241, 266, 268, 272, 281, 292).

25 Howes, Continuation, p. 867; G. E. Bentley, *The Jacobean and Caroline Stage*, I (Oxford, 1941), 4.

26 *The Silent Woman* (HS, V) I.i.168, I.iii.35, II.ii.107, III.i.45, III.ii.73, IV.vi.20, V.iv.12.

27 The Simpsons cite the East India Company's banquet in their note on 'China houses' in I.iii.36 (HS, X, 11); the New Exchange is mentioned in the next phrase. For the opening of the New Exchange, see Howes, Continuation, p. '895' (for 896). Chamberlain refers to opposition to it by tradesmen from Gresham's Exchange in July 1608 (*Letters*, I, 259).

28 A. Wilson, *The History of Britain* (1653) (quoted, HS, II; note on *The Silent Woman*, I.iii.35); compare HS, X, 1.

29 Chamberlain, *Letters*, II, 181–2.

30 Quoted, Stone, *Crisis of the Aristocracy*, p. 610; compare *ibid.*, pp. 596–8, 615, 624–5, 662–71.

31 An *Apologie For Women-Kinde* came out in 1605, an *Apologie for Women* in 1609; see Wright, *Middle-Class Culture*, pp. 484–5.

11. Crowd and public in *Bartholomew Fair*

1 'The structure of *Bartholomew Fair*', *PMLA*, LXXX (1965), 172–9.

2 *Bartholomew Fair*, in *Ben Jonson*, ed. C. H. Herford and Percy and Evelyn Simpson (11 vols., Oxford, 1925–52), Prologue, 12; Induction, 83. All quotations from *Bartholomew Fair* are taken from this edition, which is hereafter cited as HS.

3 R. B. Parker, 'The themes and staging of *Bartholomew Fair*', *University of Texas Quarterly*, XXXIX (1970), 293–309.

4 See Jackson I. Cope, '*Bartholomew Fair* as blasphemy', *Renaissance Drama*, VIII (1965), 141–6.

5 On Jacobean concern over alehouses, see Joan R. Kent, 'Attitudes of Members of the House of Commons to the regulation of "personal conduct" in late Elizabethan and early Stuart England', *Bulletin of the Institute of Historical Research*, XLVI (1973), 41–71; compare W. H.

and O. C. Overall (eds.), *Analytical Index in ... Remembrancia ... of the City of London, 1579–1664* (1878), pp. 358–9, 540–5; E. A. Horsman (ed.), *Bartholomew Fair* (1960), pp. xviii–xix.

6 *Remembrancia*, p. 269 (letter from the Archbishop of Canterbury, November 1615).

7 E.g. by Jonas A. Barish, *Ben Jonson and the Language of Prose Comedy* (Cambridge, Mass., 1960), pp. 225–39; Alan C. Dessen, *Jonson's Moral Comedy* (Evanston, Illinois, 1971), pp. 148–66.

8 William Blissett, 'Your Majesty is welcome to a fair', in *The Elizabethan Theatre*, IV, ed. G. R. Hibbard (Waterloo, Ontario, 1974), p. 100.

9 Compare Jean Jacquot, 'Le répertoire des compagnies d'enfants à Londres (1600–1610)', in Jacquot (ed.), *Dramaturgie et Société ... aux XVIe et XVIIe siècles* (Paris, 1968), p. 740; Alexander Leggatt, *Citizen Comedy in the Age of Shakespeare* (Toronto, 1973), p. 13.

10 See Barish, *Jonson and the Language of Prose Comedy*, pp. 189–95.

11 Henry Morley, *Memoirs of Bartholomew Fair* (1875), pp. 150–1.

12 See Erich Auerbach, ' "La Cour et la Ville" ' (1951), in *Scenes from the Drama of European Literature* (Gloucester, Mass., 1959), pp. 133–79.

13 Joseph Hall, *Virgidemiarum*, I.iii.57–8, in A. Davenport (ed.), *The Poems of Joseph Hall* (Liverpool, 1949).

14 Dekker, *The Gull's Hornbook* (1609), ch. 6, in E. K. Chambers, *The Elizabethan Stage*, IV (Oxford, 1923), 365–6, spelling modernised.

15 HS, VIII, 588, line 801, spelling modernised.

16 HS, II, 144.

17 Compare John Bond, in the House of Commons in 1601: 'Who almost are not grieved at the luxuriant authority of Justices of Peace? ... For magistrates are men, and men have always attending on them two ministers, *libido* and *iracundia*. Men of this nature do subjugate the free subject'; quoted in Kent, 'Attitudes of Members', p. 52.

18 See Barish, *Jonson and the Language of Prose Comedy*, pp. 209–13.

12. *The Revenger's Tragedy* and the Morality tradition

1 See L. C. Knights, *Drama and Society in the Age of Jonson* (1937), p. 188; and compare M. C. Bradbrook, *Themes and Conventions of Elizabethan Tragedy* (Cambridge, 1935), p. 70.

2 The Moralities afforded a vehicle for moral and social criticism to Catholic humanists like Medwall, writing at the end of the fifteenth century, and to Protestant reformers like Lupton, writing in the middle of Elizabeth's reign. They themselves drew on the earlier medieval drama. The later Moralities have been unduly neglected; there is an excellent account of them by Louis B. Wright, 'Social aspects of some belated Moralities', *Anglia*, LIV (1930). Some have been republished in Hazlitt's Dodsley; two of the best, G. Wapull's *The Tyde Taryeth No Man* (printed 1576), and T. Lupton's *All for Money* (printed 1578), have been republished in the *Shakespeare Jahrbuch*, XLIII (1907) and XL (1904) respectively. [Both plays are now available also in Edgar T. Schell

and J. D. Shuchter (eds.), *English Morality Plays and Moral Interludes* (New York, 1969).]

3 Bradbrook, *Themes and Conventions*, ch. 7.

4 Compare Bradbrook, *Themes and Conventions*, pp. 66–72, 166–7. The speech in which he describes his motives (at the end of I.iv) makes it clear that they belong to the situation, not his character. Similarly, his behaviour in his second disguise would be ridiculous if it were really addressed to Lussurioso; but it is addressed primarily to the audience, on the assumption that every stage disguise is successful.

5 Occasionally, change of dress has a different significance, as when Everyman puts on the robe of Contrition. There is an interesting variation in *Impatient Poverty*, a late Protestant Morality ('newly imprinted' in 1560 – see J. S. Farmer, *'Lost' Tudor Plays* (1907)). The moral is that 'by peace men grow to great richesse'. Envy masquerades as Charity, and Misrule as Mirth, in the usual way; but in the case of Impatient Poverty himself, change of dress is made to imply a change of station: 'Hold this vesture and put it on thee; From henceforth thou shalt be called Prosperity' (Farmer, p. 320). He then boasts that he is 'a gentlemen bore', and wastes his substance in riot, reappearing as Poverty in consequence. Finally, he is reconciled to Peace again, and reassumes the vesture of Prosperity. On these disguisings, see W. R. Mackenzie, *The English Moralities from the Point of View of Allegory* (Boston, 1914), p. 9: in the Moralities which deal with the struggle between Vices and Virtues for the soul of Man, Man 'is regarded as inclining to good rather than to evil; consequently, in nearly every case, the Vices have to resort to subterfuge in order to win his temporary companionship ... Almost invariably ... [they] introduce themselves by assumed names as Virtues ...' Compare *ibid.*, pp. 31, 42, 47, 113, etc.; and the role of Deceit in Middleton's *World Tost at Tennis* (*Works*, VII, ed. A. H. Bullen (1886)). On the middle-class outlook of the later Moralities, see Wright, 'Social aspects', *Anglia* (1930).

6 On the hostility of early Puritanism towards 'usury', and the relation between this and the economic position of the yeomanry and the small traders, see R. H. Tawney, *Religion and the Rise of Capitalism* (1926), p. 159 and *passim*, and the introduction to his edition (1925) of Thomas Wilson, *A Discourse upon Usury* (1572), especially pp. 24 and 30.

7 E. Troeltsch, *The Social Teaching of the Christian Churches* (Tübingen, 1912; trans. 1931), I, 249. Compare Knights, *Drama and Society*, and the works of Dr Tawney. For the quotation from *Nature*, see Farmer, *'Lost' Tudor Plays*, p. 43; and compare, e.g., Lever's sermons and Sir Thomas Elyot's *Governour*. The ordinances of Nature were to be apprehended and enforced by Reason – see King Edward VI's *Remains*, quoted in Tawney's introduction to Wilson, p. 15 – but, by the end of the sixteenth century, it was felt that social changes and scientific thought had together altered the standards of Nature for human conduct – in Ralegh's words, 'there [was] a confused controversy about the very essence of nature' (*The Sceptic*, in *Works* (1827), VIII, 556; compare

Ralegh, *The History of the World*, Book I, *Works*, II). In an article on the unpublished plays of the Royalist Earl of Westmoreland, A. Harbage quotes a significant passage from the synopsis of his *Virtue's Triumph* (1644): 'Lo: Earth puts Reason to be governor or tutor to Nature; but hee growne to manhood, and frustratted by his inseparable companion Custome, together with the help of his ruffianlyke servant Will, to know his owne strength too soone rejects and casts of Reason ...' ('An unnoted Caroline dramatist', *Studies in Philology*, XXXI (1934), 33).

8 See Troeltsch, *Social Teaching of the Christian Churches*, I, 249. The capitalist economic system, he points out, is 'based on money': it 'depersonalizes values, makes property abstract and individualistic ... raises men above natural conditions of life ... replaces the idea of providence and the spirit of mutual help ... by products which are at all times ready for use ... It is the cause of the development of formal abstract law, of an abstract, impersonal way of thinking, of rationalism and relativism. *As a result, it leads to a restless and changing social differentiation which is based not upon the unchanging land, but upon accidental accumulations of money which can change anything into anything else*' (my italics). Tudor England was perplexed by the change: 'If we truly examine the difference of both conditions; to wit, of the rich and mighty, whom we call fortunate; and of the poor and oppressed, whom we account wretched; we shall find the happiness of the one, and the miserable estate of the other, so tied by God to the very instant, and both so subject to interchange (witness the sudden downfall of the greatest Princes, and the speedy uprising of the meanest persons) as the one hath nothing so certain whereof to boast; nor the other so uncertain, whereof to bewail itself' (Ralegh, *Works*, II, xl; and compare his *Instructions to His Son*, *Works*, VIII, 565–6).

9 G. Wilson Knight, 'On the principles of Shakespeare interpretation', in *The Wheel of Fire* (1930), p. 16.

10 See the *Funeral Poem* on Sir Francis Vere, and the *Character of Robert Earl of Salisbury*. The approach in each case is ethical and formal; Tourneur has none of the psychological insight, or even the curiosity, displayed by his contemporaries. *Laugh and Lie Down*, if it is his, shows another side to his temperament, but no further interest in character. At the same time, he shows a firm enough grasp of those aspects of character relevant to his dramatic purpose in *The Revenger's Tragedy*.

11 Compare the wooing of Celia in *Volpone*; and compare Knights, *Drama and Society*, pp. 185–8. *Volpone* was produced in 1606, *The Revenger's Tragedy* published in 1607. For Morality prototypes to these speeches, see *Nature* ('For my love let us some night be there, [i.e., at the stews] / At a banket or a rare supper; / And get us some wanton meat / So we may have some dainty thing – / Yet I would spend twenty shilling / Wheresoever I it get' (Farmer, '*Lost*' *Tudor Plays*, p. 95); or the scenes in *All for Money* where Money is supposed to vomit forth Pleasure, and Pleasure, Sin, on the stage.

12 The ideal ruling class, for early Tudor theorists, was a static, if not an exclusive aristocracy, combining the privileges of birth and wealth, and justifying them by means of its services to the state and the community. Sir Thomas Elyot is representative: 'It is of good congruence that they, which be superior in condition or behaviour, should have also pre-eminence in administration, if they be not inferior to other in virtue. Also they *having of their own revenues certain* whereby they have competent substance to live without taking rewards: it is likely that they will not be so desirous of lucre (whereof may be engendred corruption), as they which have very little or nothing so certain ... Also such men, *having substance in goods by certain and stable* possessions ... may ... cause [their children] to be so instructed and furnished towards the adminis-tration of a public weal, that a poor man's son ... never or seldom may attain to the semblable. Toward the which instruction I have prepared this work' (*The Governour* (1531), Bk I, ch. III; my italics). By the end of the century, the basis for this ideal harmony between birth, wealth and public service was crumbling – the oppressive system of monopolies, for example, was in large part due to the efforts of an unpaid noble bureaucracy to recoup themselves at the public expense. A member of the Parliament of 1601 complained that there were two undesirable types among the Justices of the Peace: those who 'from base stock and lineage by [their] wealth [are] gotten to be within the commission', and 'gentleman born', who were too poor for their position and were conse-quently bribable (E. P. Cheyney, *A History of England from the Defeat of the Armada to the Death of Elizabeth* (1926), II, 319–20). Another side to the change is revealed by the younger Thomas Wilson, who refers to an inventory of noble fortunes, and notes 'great alterations almost every year, so mutable are worldly things and worldly men's affairs' (*The State of England, Anno Dom. 1600*, ed. F. J. Fisher (*Camden Miscellany*, XVI, 3rd ser., LII (1936)). He remarks that the gentry are 'generally inclined to great and vain expense' (p. 38), but records with pleasure that the yeomanry are decayed because 'the gentlemen, which were wont to addict themselves to the wars, are now for the most part grown to become good husbands, and know as well how to improve their lands to the uttermost as the farmer or countryman, so that they take their farms into their hands as leases expire ...' (p. 18; compare F. J. Fisher's Introduction). For Burghley's opportunist attitude towards this state of affairs, and Henry Percy's pessimism, see G. B. Harrison's edition of Percy's *Advice to His Son* (1930); and compare Ralegh's *Instructions to His Son* and Bacon, 'Of Expense'. With Burghley's maxim on riches and gentility, compare Ralegh, *Works*, II, xxxii. etc. Neither Bacon nor Ralegh considered the hereditary nobility as a stable social force, providing the natural leadership of society; see Bacon, 'Of Nobility' ('A numerous nobility causeth poverty and inconvenience in a state, for it is a surcharge of expense; and besides, *it being of necessity that many of the nobility fall in time to be weak in fortune*, it maketh a kind of disproportion between honour and means' – my italics), and

Ralegh's *Maxims of State* (*Works*, VIII). On the changes in the position of the gentry, and on the significance of 'hospitality', see Tawney, *Rise of Capitalism*, also Knights, *Drama and Society* and Cheyney, *History*, I, 95, 108; II, 13. For a good account of the relation of the gentry to the professions and of the modifications in the theory of gentility, see R. Kelso, *The Doctrine of the English Gentleman in the Sixteenth Century* (Urbana, Ill., 1929).

13 L. C. Knights has shown how widespread was unemployment or misemployment among men of this class about the turn of the century, and how closely this was connected with the literary fashion of melancholy (*Drama and Society*, Appendix B). The second Thomas Wilson's bitter account of the position of a younger brother in a gentle family (*The State of England, Anno Dom. 1600*) gives further evidence; compare the account of Wilson's career in Fisher's Introduction to his edition of *The State of England* (*Camden Miscellany*, XVI) and see Earle's 'Character of a Younger Brother' in *Microcosmography* (1628), ed. H. Osborne (1933). Tourneur himself probably came from a gentle family (see Professor Nicoll's introduction to the *Works* (1929), pp. 2–5), and became a protégé of Sir Edward Cecil, Viscount Wimbledon (pp. 29–32). One of the few extant documents concerning him is a letter from his widow to Wimbledon, complaining that her husband had left an assured – though poorly paid – employment with the States of Holland to become Secretary to the Council of War and Secretary to the Marshal's Court in the Cadiz expedition of 1625; and that, as he had been ousted from the former, more lucrative Secretaryship, he had left her destitute.

14 I have again made use of Miss Bradbrook's analysis (*Themes and Conventions*, pp. 169–72).

13. *The Changeling* and the drama of domestic life

1 Leigh Hunt, *Imagination and Fancy* (1844), quoted, N. W. Bawcutt (ed.), *The Changeling* (1958), p. xlv (quotations from the play are taken from this edition).

2 John Chamberlain, Letters of 25 January and 12 February, 1620, quoted, Louis B. Wright, *Middle-Class Culture in Elizabethan England* (Chapel Hill, 1935), p. 493.

3 Compare Robert Zaller, *The Parliament of 1621* (Berkeley, California, 1971).

4 W. Notestein, F. H. Rolf and H. Simpson (eds.), *Commons Debates, 1621* (New Haven and London, 1935), III, 21.

5 *Commons Debates*, IV, 436–7.

6 Wright, *Middle-Class Culture*, p. 493.

7 *The Compleat Gentleman* (1622; ed. G. S. Gordon, 1906), pp. 1–3.

8 *Ibid.*, p. 13.

9 Compare Inga-Stina Ewbank, 'Realism and morality in *Women Beware Women*', *Essays and Studies 1969*. (I have gained much from the discus-

sion of Middleton's social and political connections in the draft of a forthcoming book by Margot Heinemann [*Puritanism and Theatre*, Cambridge, 1980].)

10 I.i.35, 155 (attributed to Rowley); II.ii.9, III.iv.5. See Bawcutt, *Changeling*, p. xxxix.

11 T. B. Tomlinson, *A Study of Elizabethan and Jacobean Tragedy* (Cambridge and Melbourne, 1964), pp. 204–5.

12 E.g. I.i.16, 72–9; and II.i.7, 13.

13 Christopher Ricks, 'The moral and poetic structure of *The Changeling*', *Essays in Criticism*, 10 (1960), 294.

14 See Bawcutt, *Changeling*, pp. 120–1.

15 *Ibid.*, pp. 122–3.

16 See Ricks, 'Moral and poetic structure', p. 302.

17 I.i.134; II.i.48.

18 Chamberlain to Carleton, 20 July 1616 (in T. Birch (ed.), *The Court and Times of James I* (1848), I, 419–20); compare S. R. Gardiner, *History of England, 1603–1642* (1895 edn), II, 361.

19 Ricks, 'Moral and poetic structure', pp. 296, 302.

20 III.i (ed. Havelock Ellis, Mermaid edn, II, 240), III.ii (*ibid.*, p. 247).

21 *The Nobles* (1563), c. i^v, k. i. 4^v; *1 Henry IV*, V.i.76, and *Coriolanus*, IV.vii.11. (For a similar use much later, see the farmer's letter in Godwin's *Caleb Williams*, II, ch. 2 (1794; ed. Herbert van Thal, 1966, p. 124): 'if we little folks had but the wit to do for ourselves, the great folks would not be such maggotty changelings as they are'.)

22 Compare *The Witch of Edmonton*, I.ii.209 (ed. R. G. Lawrence, in *Jacobean and Caroline Comedies* (1973)).

23 G. R. Hibbard, 'The tragedies of Thomas Middleton and the decadence of the drama', *Renaissance and Modern Studies*, I (University of Nottingham, 1957).

14. *Don Quixote* as a prose epic

This article has grown out of two papers and discussions connected with them; the papers were read on a course held by the Cambridge University Board of Extra-Mural Studies at Madingley Hall and at a meeting of the Cambridge Modern Language Society. I am very grateful for the help I received in advice and comments from the late Professor E. M. Wilson, from the late Mr J. T. Boorman and from Mr (now Professor) D. H. Green.

1 Compare Allan H. Gilbert, *Literary Criticism, Plato to Dryden* (1940; Detroit, 1962), pp. 416, 428, 487, 581.

2 E. C. Riley, *Cervantes's Theory of the Novel* (Oxford, 1962), pp. 3, 49–57.

3 *Don Quixote*, trans. John Ormsby, ed. James Fitzmaurice-Kelly, 4 vols. (Glasgow, 1901).

4 *Covent Garden Journal*, No. 24 (1752), quoted by A. A. Parker, 'Fielding and the structure of *Don Quixote*', *Bulletin of Hispanic Studies*, XXXIII (1956), 3. Professor Parker refutes Fielding's criticism of *Don*

Quixote (without, however, taking up the question of its relation to epic).

5 Mr D. H. Green has pointed out to me, in a private note, that there is a striking parallel between Cervantes's procedure at the end of the history of chivalric romances and the procedure of those who inaugurated the form. With reference to Chrétien de Troyes and the earliest German chivalric romance-writers, Mr Green says: 'They similarly ransack already existing narrative forms and make their motifs and techniques subordinate to their own (novel) purpose. The forms they ransack include therefore: the heroic epic, the classical epic (especially the *Aeneid*), the Celtic fairy-tale (already largely present in the *matière de Bretagne*), the Christian legend, etc.'

6 Fitzmaurice-Kelly, I, xxiv.

7 Compare S. de Madariaga, *Don Quixote* (1934); A. A. Parker, 'Fielding and *Don Quixote*'; Knud Togeby, *La Composition du roman 'Don Quijote'* (*Orbis Litterarum*, Supplement, Copenhagen, 1957).

8 Mr Green points out that the contrast I have drawn between Don Quixote and the heroes of chivalric romances was only relative. The latter, he explains, 'are sometimes guided to adventures by a metaphysical power, but even so the purpose is generally so that they may then fulfil themselves morally or have revealed to them some essential truth of their own personality, so that there is a strong subjective or personal element. There are also many adventures undertaken by the chivalric hero for purely personal reasons (renown, self-rehabilitation, penance or simply high spirits), without any hint of Fate or Fortune.' Mr Green would agree, however, 'that Cervantes was the first to inform the *whole* of his work with this attitude'.

9 G. Bargagli (1572), quoted, T. Gwynfor Griffith, *Bandello's Fiction* (Oxford, 1955), p. 51.

10 Phrases of Juan Huarte (who also finds constructive tasks for the imagination, however), *The Examination of Men's Wits* (1575, trans. Richard Carew, 1594, ed. Carmen Rogers, Gainesville, Florida, 1959), pp. 63–4; compare Montaigne, 'Of the Force of Imagination'. Burton repeats the common Renaissance views about imagination in *The Anatomy of Melancholy*, §§ I, 1, ii, 7 and I, 2, iii, 8 (ed. Shilleto (1923), I, 182, 291–7).

11 Compare Fitzmaurice-Kelly, I, xxvi, xxxiv[n]; Paul Hazard, *'Don Quichotte' de Cervantes* (Paris, 1949), pp. 315–22. For evidence bearing on Shakespeare and Fletcher's lost *Cardenio* (1613), see Kenneth Muir, *Shakespeare as Collaborator* (1960), pp. 148–60. H. C. Lancaster describes the plays about Cardenio by Pichou (*c.* 1628) and de Bouscal (1638) in *A History of French Dramatic Literature ... Part I* (Baltimore, 1929), 287–90, and *Part II* (1932), 274 n.

12 Compare Riley, *Cervantes's Theory of the Novel*, pp. 116–31; Gilbert, *Plato to Dryden*, pp. 264, 278–82, 499; Bernard Weinberg, *A History of Literary Criticism in the Italian Renaissance* (2 vols., Chicago, 1961), chs. 19–20.

13 Compare Gerald Brenan, *The Literature of the Spanish People* (2nd edn, Cambridge, 1953), pp. 185–90. In drawing attention to the classical elements in the vision of the cave, I do not of course wish to ignore the romance elements there too. Mr Brenan describes the vision as a transformed 'chapter from a Grail-legend story'. Mr Green has commented to me that the theme of the hero's underworld descent goes back to Celtic mythology, but was assimilated by the authors of romances to the Harrowing of Hell; the hero 'performs a Christ-like deed by liberating those in slavery'. Hence, he adds, the hero 'is greeted in almost messianic terms, as one whose coming has been eagerly expected since the beginning of time'. Mr Green continues: 'that this tradition (as well as the purely epic one) is present in Cervantes's scene is shown, I think, by the explicit reference to Merlin, acting as a kind of "secular prophet" to the "messianic hero"'. These comments tend to confirm one's impression of the rich imaginative texture of the whole episode.

14 G. Toffanin, *La fine dell' Umanesimo* (Turin, 1920), p. 204; compare Aubrey F. G. Bell, *Cervantes* (University of Oklahoma, 1947), pp. 78–97; Riley, *Cervantes's Theory of the Novel*, pp. 179–99.

Bibliographical note

1 'Shakespeare and the Italian concept of "art" ' first appeared in *Renaissance Drama Newsletter, Supplement 3*, University of Warwick, Spring 1984

2 'Is *The Merchant of Venice* a problem play?' appeared in *'Le marchand de Venise' et 'Le Juif de Malte' (texte et représentations): Actes du colloque 25–26 janvier 1985*, ed. Michèle Willems *et al.* (Publications de l'Université de Rouen, no. 100, 1985)

3 'Falstaff and the life of shadows' appeared in *Shakespearian Comedy*, ed. Maurice Charney (New York Literary Forum, New York, 1980)

4 'The design of *Twelfth Night*' appeared in *Shakespeare Quarterly*, IX (1958) (Shakespeare Association of America)

5 'Shakespeare and the ventriloquists' appeared in *Shakespeare Survey*, 34, ed. Stanley Wells (Cambridge, 1981)

6 'Romance in *King Lear*' first appeared in *English*, Spring 1978

7 '*King Lear*, Montaigne and Harsnett' appeared in *Anglo-American Studies* (Salamanca), III, no. 2 (November 1983), and in *The Aligarh Journal of English Studies*, VIII, no. 2 (1983)

8 ' "Wit" in Jacobean comedy' appeared in *Arts du spectacle et histoire des idées. Ecrits offerts en hommage à Jean Jacquot*, ed. Elie Konigson *et al.* (Tours, 1984)

9 'Comic form in Ben Jonson: Volpone and the philosopher's stone' appeared in *English Drama: Forms and Development; Essays in Honour of Muriel Clara Bradbrook*, ed. Marie Axton and Raymond Williams (Cambridge, 1977)

10 'Farce and fashion in *The Silent Woman*' appeared in *Essays and Studies 1967*, ed. Martin Holmes (John Murray, for the English Association)

11 'Crowd and public in *Bartholomew Fair*' appeared in *Renaissance Drama*, N.S. X (1979), ed. Leonard Barkan (Northwestern University Press, Evanston, Illinois)

12 '*The Revenger's Tragedy* and the Morality tradition' appeared in *Scrutiny* VI (1938)

13 '*The Changeling* and the drama of domestic life' appeared in *Essays and Studies 1979*, ed. Dieter Mehl (John Murray, for the English Association)

14 '*Don Quixote* as a prose epic' appeared in *Forum for Modern Language Studies*, 2 (1966)

Index